# Appalachian Trail Thru-Hikers' Companion

Leslie Mass
*Editor*

APPALACHIAN TRAIL
CONSERVANCY

Harpers Ferry, West Virginia

© 2008 Appalachian Long Distance Hikers Association, Inc.
All rights reserved
Printed in the United States of America on recycled paper

Fifteenth edition

Published by the Appalachian Trail Conservancy
799 Washington Street (P.O. Box 807)
Harpers Ferry, West Virginia 25425-0807

ISBN 978-1-889386-55-3

# Contents

Foreword ................................................................. iv

About the *Companion* ............................................. v

Using the *Companion* ............................................. vii

Issues on the Trail ................................................. ix


## On the Appalachian Trail

Getting to the Termini ........................................... 1

Georgia ................................................................ 9

North Carolina ...................................................... 21

Great Smoky Mountains National Park ..................... 31

North Carolina & the Tennessee Border .................. 39

Tennessee ............................................................. 53

Virginia: Part 1 (Southwest) ................................... 59

Part 2 (Central) ................................................. 73

Part 3 (Shenandoah National Park) ....................... 93

Part 4 (Northern) ............................................... 109

West Virginia ....................................................... 115

Maryland .............................................................. 121

Pennsylvania ........................................................ 127

New Jersey ........................................................... 149

New York .............................................................. 157

Connecticut .......................................................... 169

Massachusetts ...................................................... 179

Vermont ............................................................... 193

New Hampshire .................................................... 209

Maine .................................................................. 229


## Appendices

Post Offices along the Appalachian Trail ................. 257

Hostels, Camping & Showers .................................. 263

Equipment Manufacturers & Distributors ................ 267

ALDHA Membership Form ...................................... 269

# Foreword

Welcome to the fifteenth edition of the *Appalachian Trail Thru-Hikers' Companion*. Why another edition of this book? The simple answer is that the Appalachian Trail and the community that surrounds this famous footpath are continuous works in progress. Every year, businesses close or emerge, fees change, town maps need revision, shelters are built or renovated, and sections of the Trail are relocated.

Thank you for picking up this edition. The 2008 *Companion* is a carefully conceived, diligently compiled book that belongs in the possession of every Appalachian Trail hiker. Our hope is that the *Companion,* used in conjunction with Trail maps, will lead the reader into making informed decisions about towns and services for resupply options.

This book is the culmination of the volunteer efforts of more than thirty ALDHA field editors and ATC staff members who worked to make this edition as accurate as possible. To everyone who contributed in some way to the publication of this book, many thanks.

A guidebook, like the Trail, is not a static document. Each hiker may discover something previously unknown. Your contributions are vital to this process. Your comments are most welcome — and requested! We rely on hikers' feedback to help us update future editions. Please send your comments on this book to ALDHA, along with any corrections to Trail, shelter, or town descriptions.

Gotta Hike!

> Leslie Mass
> *Editor*

# About the *Companion*

The *Companion* is compiled, written, and edited by volunteers of the Appalachian Long Distance Hikers Association (ALDHA) and published by the Appalachian Trail Conservancy (ATC) as a service to those seeking to explore the Trail. It is intended for those making thru-hikes but is also valuable for those taking shorter section-hikes or overnight backpacking trips. The *Companion* provides you with details on shelters, water sources, post offices, hostels, campgrounds, lodging, groceries, restaurants, outfitters, and other related services along the Trail. In addition, the *Companion* offers information of historical significance about places you pass through while hiking the A.T. Unlike commercial guides, this book benefits from the latest information from volunteers who measure, maintain, and manage the Trail and those who hike it regularly.

*Due to publication deadlines, we cannot guarantee that the information in this book will not change by the time you arrive in an area, despite the efforts of volunteers to acquire the most up-to-date information. Businesses close or change hours, hostels change rates and policies, and the Trail itself is subject to relocation. This edition was produced in the fall of 2007.*

*As you walk, talk to other hikers, and read shelter registers. The Conservancy's Web site periodically posts updates at <www. appalachiantrail.org/companionupdates>.*

Inclusion in this book is not an endorsement by ALDHA or ATC, but rather a listing of services available. Likewise, the businesses listed in this book do not pay for "advertisements" but are listed because of their proximity to the Trail.

ALDHA members do field research for each section of the Trail and are instrumental in gathering information. Without the hard work of the following ALDHA field editors, other volunteers, and ATC staff members, this book would not have been possible: **Georgia and North Carolina**—Scott Dowling (Pilgrim), Ann W. Thomas (Timberpixie); **North Carolina and Tennessee**—Lamar Powell (Hopeful), Judy Young (Gray-Jay), Marta Clark (FiveLeafed Clover); **Southwest Virginia**—Jim Moody (Mango), Vaughn Thomas (Virginia Creeper); **Central Virginia**—Charles Davidson (Chase), J.R. Davidson III (Woodelf), Laurie Foot (Happy Feet), Leonard Adkins (Habitual Hiker); **Northern Virginia**—David Hennel (Gourmet Dave), Sue Hennel (The Real Gourmet), Gary Ticknor (Greenbriar), Jim Austin (Skyline); **West Virginia and Maryland**—Mike Wingeart (Wingheart), Tom Evans (Flatlander), ATC Information Services Manager Laurie Potteiger; **Southern Pennsylvania**—Bob and Tricia Dudley (Greyowl), ATC Mid-Atlantic Office Manager John Luthy; **Northern Pennsyl-**

vania—Mary Ann Nissley (M.A. from Pa.), Sarah Mortenson (Rainbow Brite), Arron Safford (Mountain Dew), Sarah Woodruff (Blip); **New Jersey**—John O'Mahoney (Johnny O'); **New York**—Mark Hudson (Skeeter); **Connecticut & Massachusetts**—Pete Antos-Ketcham, Laura Reed, Kevin Reardon (Slider), Hannah Reardon (Catamount); **Vermont**—Dave Hardy, Cindy Taylor-Miller (Mrs. Gorp), Smith Edwards (Old Ridgerunner); **New Hampshire**—Art Cloutman (Gabby), Jack Tarlin (Baltimore Jack), Karine Kelleher (Blister Sister); **Maine**—J.W. Gordon (Teej), Sandie Sabaka (Bluebearee), Jaime Renaud (Navigator), Steve Langley (Steve the Ferryman); **entire Trail**—Mike Wingeart (Wingheart). Foreword by Leslie Mass (Gotta Hike!). ATC Information Assistant John Fletcher also provided valuable information on town and Trail changes. Mileage figures are based on information from the 2008 edition of the *Appalachian Trail Data Book*.

Sadly, on July 20, 2006, three-year-veteran field editor and ALDHA member Cheryl Hoover (Amber) passed away.

### TRAIL-MAINTAINING CLUBS AND REGISTERS

Trail-maintaining clubs are listed throughout the book. You may use the addresses provided to contact the clubs with any comments, suggestions, or feedback. Although often a thru-hiker will leave an additional one, the official shelter registers are the property of the maintaining club and should not be removed by hikers. The register is a useful tool for information on Trail conditions and other things that are happening in its section of the A.T. It may also help locate a hiker in case of an emergency. If you wish to donate a register (assuming that one doesn't already exist), you should include a note asking the maintaining club to forward it to you when it's filled.

### GETTING TO THE TRAIL

Section-hikers looking for shuttle services should check the business and individual listings for the area in which they plan to hike. Also, check with ATC at (304) 535-6331, <info@appalachiantrail.org>, or check the ATC's A.T. shuttle and public-transportation list available at <www.appalachiantrail.org/shuttles>. (See page 1 for an important note on shuttles.) This same Web site will link to information on Trailhead parking.

# Using the *Companion*

Do not be afraid to abuse your paper *Companion*. While it has considerable information, it has been suggested that it could be made smaller. Unfortunately, no one agrees on what should be left out. So, here is an idea—do your own editing. Rip out what you don't want, use a hole-punch, a pair of scissors, or a highlighter. Send sections ahead to mail drops; mail completed sections home. Do some old-fashioned cut-and-paste. Make this book your own. Or, go to ALDHA's Web site, <www.aldha.org>, download an electronic copy of the *Companion* (in Adobe Acrobat PDF format), and print out only the pages you need.

## READING THE COMPANION

 *Road-crossings and Trailheads with significant services nearby* are indicated in south-to-north order.

*Towns and post offices* (including P.O. hours) (including P.O. hours) are printed in **bold type**. A listing of post offices can also be found on pages 255.

*East and West*—Regardless of compass direction, "**east**" or "E" and "**west**" or "W" are used as they are in the *A.T. Data Book and the series of 11 A.T. guides*: "East" is to the northbounder's right and the southbounder's left, when referring to the Trail.

*Services*—Major categories are indicated with ***bold italics***, specifically ***groceries, lodging, hostels, campgrounds, doctors or hospitals, restaurants, Internet access, laundries, veterinarians, and outfitters***.

---

*Trail-Maintaining Clubs*—Information is provided at the southern end of their sections and is offset by two rules.

---

*Abbreviations*—

    *In the body of the text:*

        M—Monday
        Tu—Tuesday
        W—Wednesday
        Th—Thursday
        F—Friday
        Sa—Saturday
        Su—Sunday
        FedEx—Federal Express
        USPS—U.S. Postal Service
        UPS—United Parcel Service

a/c—air conditioning
AYCE—all-you-can-eat
B/L/D—breakfast/lunch/dinner
CATV—cable television
EAP—each additional person
D—double
PP—per person
S—single
T—triple

*In the tables at beginning of each chapter:*

| | |
|---|---|
| C—campground, campsites | O—outfitter |
| cl—coin laundry | P.O.—post office |
| D—doctor, medical | R—road access |
| f—fuel | S—shelter |
| G—groceries, supplies | sh—shower |
| H— hostels | nw—no potable water |
| L— lodging | V—veterinarian |
| m—miles | w—water |
| M—meals; restaurants | @—Internet |

*Elevation*—The elevation column refers to the approximate elevation (in feet) of the landmark.

*Comma*—Services separated by commas are in the same location. For example, E–1.5m P.O., G means that the post office and grocery store are both located 1.5 miles east.

*Parentheses*—Services separated by parentheses are not all in the same location. For example, (E–0.2m C, S) (W–0.1m w) means that the campsite and shelter are east 0.2 mile, and the water source is west 0.1 mile from the Trailhead.

*Shelters*—May also be referred to in New England as lean-tos. Shown in **bold print**, with distance and direction off Trail, water-source location, and distance to the next shelter (in italics, both north and south). **The distance to the next north and south shelter shown in the *Companion* includes the side-trail(s) distance from one to the other.**

# Issues on the Trail

### 2,000-MILER CERTIFICATES

ATC recognizes anyone who reports completion of the entire Trail as a "2,000-Miler" with a certificate. The term "2,000-Miler" is a matter of tradition and convenience, based upon the original estimated length of the Trail. ATC policy is to operate on the honor system, assuming that those who apply for 2,000-Miler status have hiked all of the A.T. between Katahdin and Springer, not just 2,000 miles of it. In the event of an emergency, such as a flood, forest fire, or an impending storm on an exposed high-elevation stretch, blue-blazed trails or officially required roadwalks are considered viable substitutes for the white-blazed route. Issues of sequence, direction, speed, length of time, or whether one carries a pack or not are not considered. ATC assumes that those who apply have made an honest effort to walk the entire Trail.

### HUNTING SEASONS

Hunters are rarely an issue for northbounders, but southbounders need to be aware of the hunting seasons, which may begin as early as mid-Oct, as you progress south toward Springer Mountain. Hunting is legal along many parts of the Trail, and ATC's Web site lists local hunting seasons. Wearing bright ("blaze") orange is a necessity in fall, winter, and spring.

### SAFETY—OTHER HUMANS

If you tell friends you are planning a long-distance hike on the A.T., one of the first questions is likely to be, "Aren't you afraid? What will you do to protect yourself?" There are dangers in the backcountry, but, because of mass-media publicity and the popularity of backpacking, your friend was likely speaking of the dangers posed by other humans. Violent crimes have occurred on the Trail, but with a frequency rate of less than two every ten years, on a footpath that more than three million people use each year.

The difference on the A.T. and in any wilderness setting—other than people's expectations—is that you only have yourself and your instincts for protection. That means you must use common sense to avoid potential dangers.

It is best not to hike alone, but, if you choose to, a few precautions can help keep you safe:

- Don't tell strangers where you are headed or plan to camp for the night.

- If you run into a suspicious person, consider moving on to another location.

- Avoid camping or staying at shelters that are within a mile of a road crossing.

- Leave an itinerary of your trip with family or friends.

- If you use a Trail name, make sure the folks back home know what it is.

- Even with a partner, don't be lulled into a false sense of security. Two or more can also be vulnerable.

- Trust your gut. Always.

Eliminate opportunities for theft. Don't bring jewelry. Keep wallets and money on your person rather than in your pack or tent. Leaving a pack unattended at trailheads or shelters is risky, even when it is hidden, and also may attract wildlife in search of food.

ATC and most long-distance hikers strongly discourage the carrying of a gun on the Trail. Guns are not permitted on national park lands (40 percent of the route) and in many other jurisdictions through which the Trail passes. Report any crime or harassment immediately to the local police and ATC. Contact ATC at (304) 535-6331 or <incident@ appalachiantrail.org>.

## SAFETY—MOTHER NATURE

While natural dangers are inherent to backpacking, many of the dangers are misunderstood. For some, a hike in the woods conjures images of snakebites and bear attacks—both rare.

## BEARS

Black bears live along many parts of the Trail and are particularly common in Georgia, the Shenandoah and Great Smoky Mountains national parks, and north of Shenandoah on into New York. While attacks on humans are rare, a startled bear or a female with cubs may react aggressively. The best way to avoid an encounter while you are hiking is to make noise by whistling, talking, *etc.*, to give the bear a chance to move away before you get close enough to make it feel threatened. If you encounter a bear and it does not move away, you should back off, and avoid making eye contact. Do not run or "play dead," even if a bear makes a "bluff charge."

The best preventive defense against bears showing up in camp is preparing and storing food properly:

- Cook and eat meals away from your tent or shelter so food odors do not linger;

- Hang food, cookware, toothpaste, personal hygiene items, water bottles with drink mixes in a sturdy bag from a strong tree branch 10 feet off the ground, 6 feet from the tree, and away from your campsite;

- Use bear boxes, poles, or cable systems where provided;

- Never feed bears or leave food behind for them;

- A bear that enters a campsite or cooking area should be considered predatory. Yelling, making loud noises, throwing rocks may frighten it away, however you should be prepared to fight back if necessary.

- If you are attacked by a bear, fight for all you are worth with anything at hand—rocks, sticks, fists.

Less dramatic threats to safety, such as contaminated water, dehydration, and hypothermia, afflict far more hikers—particularly those who are unprepared.

If you are unfamiliar with backcountry travel, ask questions, and read and learn about backpacking safely. Learn about dehydration, heat exhaustion, and hypothermia; learn safe ways of fording rivers and purifying water; learn how to avoid lightning, rabies, and Lyme disease—the most common threats to a hiker's well-being. A good resource for learning more about these topics is the ATC publication *Step by Step: An Introduction to Walking the A.T.* Before starting an end-to-end hike, take shorter backpacking trips until you feel confident in the backcountry. Finally, information and experience are useless if you forget one thing—common sense.

### LYME DISEASE

Ticks that transmit disease may be anywhere there is vegetation. In the South, ticks can be active year-round. In the Northeast, the heightened risk for Lyme disease (LD) is Apr to Jul and Oct to Nov, which coincide with the timeframe thru-hikers pass through the states with the highest reported cases of the disease. Cases have been reported in all fourteen Trail states.

LD is a bacterial infection transmitted to humans by the bite of infected blacklegged ticks (formerly known as "deer" ticks). Hikers should watch carefully for symptoms of LD, which may include "flu-like" reactions of fever, headache, chills, and fatigue and a characteristic "bulls-eye" skin rash, called *erythema migrans,* at the site of the tick attachment. Hikers should seek immediate medical attention for treatment. If left untreated, infection can spread to joints, the heart, and the nervous system. Most cases of LD can be treated successfully with a few weeks of antibiotics.

Steps hikers can take to prevent LD include using insect repellent with Deet for exposed skin; spraying clothing items with the insecticide permethrin; removing ticks promptly; conducting a daily full-body tick check, including the head, underarms, and groin area; minimizing contact with high grass, brush, and woody shrubs; wearing long pants tucked into your socks; and wearing long sleeves, tucking your shirt into your pants to keep ticks off your torso.

### LEAVE NO TRACE

Each year, more people venture into the woods to escape the stresses of modern life. Unfortunately, this puts greater pressure on our fragile natural areas. In order to preserve and protect our wilderness, please follow guidelines developed by Leave No Trace, Inc., and endorsed by ATC and ALDHA.

- *Plan ahead and prepare.* You're more likely to damage natural areas if you haven't brought the right equipment or planned where you're going to stay and go. Know local regulations. Remember: Shelters may be full, so bring a tent or tarp.

- *Travel and camp on durable surfaces.* Stay on the Trail, and don't cut switchbacks. Keep off fragile trailside areas such as those in alpine zones. Camp in designated campsites. If you must camp elsewhere, do so out of sight of any trails, and find a spot that has not been used before, at least 200 feet from lakes and streams, being sure to leave it the way you found it. Camping in undesignated areas that show signs of use destroys ground cover and compacts soil, increasing erosion and damaging habitat.

- *Dispose of waste properly.* Pack out all trash and food waste, *including that left behind by others.* Do not bury trash or food, and do not try to burn packaging materials in camp-fires. Bury human and pet waste six inches deep in a "cathole" at least 200 feet from trail or water. All toilet paper and feminine-hygiene products should be packed out. Avoid using soap to wash yourself or your equipment. When using soap, use biodegradable soap, and dispose of the "gray water" at least 200 feet from open water.

- *Leave what you find.* Don't take flowers or other sensitive natural resources. Don't disturb historical artifacts, such as cellar holes, arrowheads, *etc.*

- *Minimize campfire impacts.* Know local regulations, which may prohibit campfires. Use a portable stove instead of a fire. If you must build a fire, make a low-impact fire, use only downed wood, use existing designated fire pits or rings, and don't add rocks to existing rings. Extinguish the fire before breaking camp. Drown out fires, and empty the fire pit. Scatter leaves and twigs to remove any signs that you have been there.

- *Respect wildlife.* Don't feed or disturb wildlife. Store food properly to avoid attracting bears and rodents. If you bring a pet, keep it leashed.

- *Be considerate of other visitors.* Limit overnight groups to 10 or fewer persons; 25 on day trips. Minimize noise and intrusive behavior. Share shelters and other facilities.

More than three million people use a portion of the Trail each year, and, unfortunately, not all of them are aware of the Leave No Trace camping ethic. Those who are less knowledgeable will observe you (respecting you as a long-distance hiker and, supposedly, an expert wilderness traveler) and your practices.

Set a good example. If you see an opportunity to teach others, do so. If Leave No Trace camping is not practiced by all, the A.T. will quickly lose its beauty.

### KENNEBEC RIVER FERRY SERVICE AND BAXTER STATE PARK

It is your responsibility to honor the established hours of operation for the free ferry service across the Kennebec River between the dates of May 16 and Oct 6, 2008; see page 241 for further details. Do not call from the Trail on your cellphone and expect "special" off-hours service or service out of the range of set dates. Due to weather concerns, hikers should do their parts and plan accordingly to reach Baxter State Park as early as possible. We suggest reaching BSP by Oct 1. After Oct 15, there is no camping inside BSP. See page 248 for posted park cut-off times and further information.

### TOWN CONDUCT

As a result of tension between hikers and some communities adjacent to the Trail, ALDHA implemented an "Endangered Services Campaign" to educate hikers to be responsible for their actions. In town, consider yourself a walking, talking billboard for all backpackers and the Trail. Your individual actions have a direct impact on the businesses that provide services for the long-distance hiking community.

*The Endangered Services Campaign*

The success of a thru-hiker's journey depends on Trail towns and the services they provide. Remember that you are a guest of the community, no matter how large or small, even though you may be pumping money into the local economy. Be courteous to those who earn their livelihood there, and remember that your conduct will have a bearing on how well—or badly—the next hiker is treated. As with so many other things in life, we are never truly alone. You are an ambassador for all those who follow you on the Trail. Nothing can turn a person or town against backpacking and the Trail quicker than an arrogant, smelly, and ill-behaved hiker.

In recent years, some business owners have reduced services or closed their doors to hikers simply because some hikers wouldn't respect their rules. Be a part of the movement that will reverse this practice and ensure that no one closes another door because of bad hiker behavior.

### DONATIONS

Many of the hostels listed in this book suggest donations for the services provided. This means that the service should not be considered a gift or that it costs the provider nothing. The honor system of the Trail requires that you leave something.

## GIVING BACK

If you would like to give back what was freely given to you by those who maintain the Trail or while you stayed in Trail towns, volunteer your time, effort, or money to the services and people who supported you. Consider contacting a Trail-maintaining club and working with them to organize or participate in a work trip, Trail-construction project, or regular maintenance. Every year, ALDHA sponsors work trips to Trail establishments. The Konnarock and other ATC crews seek volunteers during the summer, and you often will pass a Trail club working busily as you head along the path. Be sure to acknowledge their work with your thanks and respect. Giving back to the Trail and community helps keep the Trail safe and services available.

## HITCHHIKING

Hitchhiking is illegal in certain states. It is your responsibility to know the motor-vehicle law as it applies to hitchhiking for the state through which you are hiking, to avoid being fined or hitching into worse trouble. Hitchhiking poses the risk of being picked up by an unsafe driver or by someone who is personally dangerous. Hitchhiking is prohibited on interstate highways, the Blue Ridge Parkway, and Skyline Drive in Shenandoah National Park.

## HIKING WITH DOGS

If you choose to hike with your canine companion, treat your dog as another backpacker. That means bury its waste as you would your own, and carry a water bowl so your dog won't drink directly from Trailside water sources. You are responsible for your dog, and you will be held accountable if it decides to steal another hiker's food or flop its wet body on another hiker's equipment. Keep your pet under control in camp, on the Trail, and in towns. Many hostels and other accommodations don't allow dogs, and, in those that do, a dog does not belong in the communal kitchen and sleeping areas. Closely monitor your pet's feet for torn flesh, bleeding, and other sores. After the weather warms up, check for ticks. It is best to keep your dog on a leash at all times; on national-park lands (40 percent of the Trail), regulations require it. Most post offices allow only guide dogs inside. Carry current rabies-vaccine certification papers in addition to a tag on the dog's collar. Dogs are prohibited in the Great Smoky Mountains National Park, the zoo area of Bear Mountain State Park in New York, and Maine's Baxter State Park. (For information on kennels near GSMNP and BSP, see entries for those sections.)

## APPALACHIAN TRAIL MUSEUM SOCIETY

Efforts are under way to establish an Appalachian Trail museum near the geographic center of the Trail. A group has been working on this project for several years and, in 2002, formed the Appalachian Trail Museum Socicty (ATMS). The group includes representatives of ATC and ALDHA and also is working with the National Park Service. The society is collecting items for eventual display in the museum and monetary donations. They are also in need of volunteers to help in many areas. Please contact ATMS, if you'd like to help, at <www.atmuseum.org>.

## THE APPALACHIAN LONG DISTANCE HIKERS ASSOCIATION

The Appalachian Long Distance Hikers Association (ALDHA) is a nonprofit organization founded in 1983 to promote the welfare of the Appalachian Trail and the Trail community. Every year, ALDHA conducts work weekends on the Trail, speaks out on issues concerning the A.T. and its environs, and collects the information for this guidebook. In past years, the group has tackled such issues as backpacker etiquette and environmental threats. More recently, it has worked with various clubs and hostels to maintain areas widely used by hikers. ALDHA is open to anyone (even if your longest hike is a walk around the block at home); there are no membership requirements. To find out more, e-mail ALDHA at <aldha@aldha.org>, or write to 10 Benning Street, PMB 224, West Lebanon, NH 03784. Visit our Web site at <www.aldha.org>. A membership form is included at the back of this book.

## THE GATHERING

Every fall, members get together for the Gathering. Besides tending to routine business, the Gathering provides an inspirational weekend filled with fun and informative workshops and slide shows on long-distance trails, as well as panel discussions on lively topics. The 2009 Gathering, ALDHA's 27th annual get-together, will take place Columbus Day weekend, October 10–12, 2008, at Concord University in Athens, West Virginia. Camping facilities will be provided close to campus. Registration fees are $10 for individuals or $20 for couples. A calendar-year's membership in ALDHA is $10 per family *or* individual (additional to the registration fee) and includes a copy of the annual ALDHA directory and the quarterly newsletter, *The Long Distance Hiker*. To preregister before September 1, send a check with your name, address, and telephone number to ALDHA, 10 Benning Street, PMB 224, West Lebanon, NH 03784. A registration form appears on page 269.

## AN INVITATION

This is the fifteenth edition of the *A.T. Thru-Hikers' Companion,* and ALDHA will again depend on comments, suggestions, and volunteers to update it in the fall of 2008. If you see information that needs correcting or come across information that should be included, or would like to be a volunteer field editor, please contact the editor at <companion@aldha.org>. We've included a form at the back of the book that you can tear out and mail back to us as well.

# 2008 Calendar

### January

| Su | M | Tu | W | Th | F | Sa |
|----|----|----|----|----|----|----|
|  |  | 1 | 2 | 3 | 4 | 5 |
| 6 | 7 | 8 | 9 | 10 | 11 | 12 |
| 13 | 14 | 15 | 16 | 17 | 18 | 19 |
| 20 | 21 | 22 | 23 | 24 | 25 | 26 |
| 27 | 28 | 29 | 30 | 31 |  |  |

### February

| Su | M | Tu | W | Th | F | Sa |
|----|----|----|----|----|----|----|
|  |  |  |  |  | 1 | 2 |
| 3 | 4 | 5 | 6 | 7 | 8 | 9 |
| 10 | 11 | 12 | 13 | 14 | 15 | 16 |
| 17 | 18 | 19 | 20 | 21 | 22 | 23 |
| 24 | 25 | 26 | 27 | 28 | 29 |  |

### March

| Su | M | Tu | W | Th | F | Sa |
|----|----|----|----|----|----|----|
|  |  |  |  |  |  | 1 |
| 2 | 3 | 4 | 5 | 6 | 7 | 8 |
| 9 | 10 | 11 | 12 | 13 | 14 | 15 |
| 16 | 17 | 18 | 19 | 20 | 21 | 22 |
| 23 | 24 | 25 | 26 | 27 | 28 | 29 |
| 30 | 31 |  |  |  |  |  |

### April

| Su | M | Tu | W | Th | F | Sa |
|----|----|----|----|----|----|----|
|  |  | 1 | 2 | 3 | 4 | 5 |
| 6 | 7 | 9 | 9 | 10 | 11 | 12 |
| 13 | 14 | 15 | 16 | 17 | 18 | 19 |
| 20 | 21 | 22 | 23 | 24 | 25 | 26 |
| 27 | 28 | 29 | 30 |  |  |  |

### May

| Su | M | Tu | W | Th | F | Sa |
|----|----|----|----|----|----|----|
|  |  |  |  | 1 | 2 | 3 |
| 4 | 5 | 6 | 7 | 8 | 9 | 10 |
| 11 | 12 | 13 | 14 | 15 | 16 | 17 |
| 18 | 19 | 20 | 21 | 22 | 23 | 24 |
| 25 | 26 | 27 | 28 | 29 | 30 | 31 |

### June

| Su | M | Tu | W | Th | F | Sa |
|----|----|----|----|----|----|----|
| 1 | 2 | 3 | 4 | 5 | 6 | 7 |
| 8 | 9 | 10 | 11 | 12 | 13 | 14 |
| 15 | 16 | 17 | 18 | 19 | 20 | 21 |
| 22 | 23 | 24 | 25 | 26 | 27 | 28 |
| 29 | 30 |  |  |  |  |  |

### July

| Su | M | Tu | W | Th | F | Sa |
|----|----|----|----|----|----|----|
|  |  | 1 | 2 | 3 | 4 | 2 |
| 6 | 7 | 9 | 9 | 10 | 11 | 9 |
| 13 | 14 | 15 | 16 | 17 | 18 | 16 |
| 20 | 21 | 22 | 23 | 24 | 25 | 23 |
| 27 | 28 | 29 | 30 | 31 |  |  |

### August

| Su | M | Tu | W | Th | F | Sa |
|----|----|----|----|----|----|----|
|  |  |  |  |  | 1 | 2 |
| 3 | 4 | 5 | 6 | 7 | 8 | 9 |
| 10 | 11 | 12 | 13 | 14 | 15 | 16 |
| 17 | 18 | 19 | 20 | 21 | 22 | 23 |
| 24 | 25 | 26 | 27 | 28 | 29 | 30 |
| 31 |  |  |  |  |  |  |

### September

| Su | M | Tu | W | Th | F | Sa |
|----|----|----|----|----|----|----|
|  | 1 | 2 | 3 | 4 | 5 | 6 |
| 7 | 8 | 9 | 10 | 11 | 12 | 13 |
| 14 | 15 | 16 | 17 | 18 | 19 | 20 |
| 21 | 22 | 23 | 24 | 25 | 26 | 27 |
| 28 | 29 | 30 |  |  |  |  |

### October

| Su | M | Tu | W | Th | F | Sa |
|----|----|----|----|----|----|----|
|  |  |  | 1 | 2 | 3 | 4 |
| 5 | 6 | 7 | 8 | 9 | 10 | 11 |
| 12 | 13 | 14 | 15 | 16 | 17 | 18 |
| 19 | 20 | 21 | 22 | 23 | 24 | 25 |
| 26 | 27 | 28 | 29 | 30 | 31 |  |

### November

| Su | M | Tu | W | Th | F | Sa |
|----|----|----|----|----|----|----|
|  |  |  |  |  |  | 1 |
| 2 | 3 | 4 | 5 | 8 | 7 | 8 |
| 9 | 10 | 11 | 12 | 13 | 14 | 15 |
| 16 | 17 | 18 | 19 | 20 | 21 | 22 |
| 23 | 24 | 25 | 26 | 27 | 28 | 29 |
| 30 |  |  |  |  |  |  |

### December

| Su | M | Tu | W | Th | F | Sa |
|----|----|----|----|----|----|----|
|  | 1 | 2 | 3 | 4 | 5 | 6 |
| 7 | 8 | 9 | 10 | 11 | 12 | 13 |
| 14 | 15 | 16 | 17 | 18 | 19 | 20 |
| 21 | 22 | 23 | 24 | 25 | 26 | 27 |
| 28 | 29 | 30 | 31 |  |  |  |

## KEY DATES TO REMEMBER

**March 5**—25th anniversary of ALDHA's creation

**April 25–26**—Trailfest, Hot Springs, N.C.

**May 16–18**—Appalachian Trail Days, Damascus, Va.

**June 7**—National Trails Day

**Aug. 15–17**—Vermont Long Trail Festival, Rutland, Vt.

**Sept. 26–28**—ALDHA West Gathering on West Coast

**Oct. 10–12**—27th Annual Gathering, Concord University, Athens, W.Va.

# Getting to the Termini

## An important note about shuttle services

Beginning in 1995, USDA Forest Service law-enforcement rangers in the South—who report to the regional office rather than the supervisor of an individual forest—began enforcing agency regulations on "special-use permits." The regulations say anyone taking money for a service involving Forest Service lands (including roads) must obtain a permit to do so; profit is not a factor. Permit-holders must pay a fee (up to $75) and, more prohibitively, carry high-premium insurance. Some A.T. shuttlers have been fined. Responding to questions from ATC and its Park Service partners, regional officials made it clear they will continue to enforce the policy and cited directives stating that it is to be enforced consistently and nationally. The A.T. crosses six national forests in the South and two in New England. ATC will continue to provide names of shuttle services, but keep that policy in mind—**call ahead to ensure the person is still performing this service,** and be prepared to help those who helped you if a fine appears in their future.

## Getting to Amicalola Falls State Park, Georgia

No public transportation is available to or from Amicalola Falls State Park, but hikers have several options from Atlanta, Gainesville (located 40 miles southeast of the park), and the mountain town of Dahlonega (located 16 miles east of Amicalola Falls).

### LEAVING ATLANTA

If you fly into Atlanta, you can take Atlanta's rapid-transit trains (MARTA) from the airport to either the Greyhound bus station or the Amtrak station. To reach either station, take the MARTA train north from MARTA's airport station ($1.75 fare). To reach the Greyhound bus station, exit the train at Garnett Station. The bus station is located at 232 Forsyth Street, within sight of the entrance to the MARTA station. To get to the Amtrak station, continue north on the train to the Arts Center Station. From the Arts Center Station, bus No. 23 (departing the station every 10 minutes) will take you to the Amtrak station, located about 10 blocks north on Peachtree. If you wish to walk to the Amtrak station, follow Peachtree Street approximately one mile north; the station is on the left (west) at 1688 Peachtree NW. For more information, call MARTA, (404) 848-4711. Other options from the airport to the bus and train stations include taxis and the Atlanta Airport Shuttle, (404) 524-3400, a privately owned bus service. Atlanta Airport Shuttle vans leave the airport every 15 minutes, from south baggage claim, bound for the bus station and Amtrak station ($18.50 fare). In addition, AAA Airport Express, (800) 354-7874, <www.aaaairportexpress.com>, from space 10 of the pink aisle in the ground-transportation area, offers rides from the airport to Gainesville hotels, $40. The shuttle leaves the airport every two hours from 6:30 a.m. to 10:30 p.m. Reservations recommended.

## ATLANTA TO GAINESVILLE

Two buses and one Amtrak train leave daily from Atlanta for Gainesville. At publication time, Greyhound buses, (800) 229-9424, <www.greyhound.com>, departed the Atlanta station for Gainesville at 7:45 a.m. and 3:15 p.m. ($11.88 M–Th, $14 F–Su) and arrived in Gainesville at 9:20 a.m. and 4:55 p.m. Buses departed Gainesville for Atlanta at 10:25 a.m. and 6:55 p.m. However, Greyhound routinely revises its schedule; call for current information. Amtrak's train was scheduled to depart from Atlanta daily at 8:08 p.m. and arrive in Gainesville at 9:03 p.m. ($11). A train was scheduled to depart Gainesville for Atlanta daily at 7:08 a.m. Reservations are required. Call (800) 872-7245, or log on to <www.amtrak.com>.

**Gainesville**—*Lodging:* Motel 6, (770) 532-7531, $47.95S $48.59D weekdays, $45.99S $49.99D weekends, $3EAP, pet-friendly n/c; Lanier Center Best Western, (800) 782-8966, $99.95D, no dogs, hot B; Ramada Limited, (770) 287-3205, $59, B buffet, small pets $10; Hampton Inn, (770) 503-0300, $115, no pets, hot B; Best Value Inn, (770) 534-0303, $55–$65, no pets. All are within four miles of the bus and train stations.

## GAINESVILLE TO AMICALOLA FALLS STATE PARK

UNITAXI, (770) 534-5355 or (770) 297-0255, offers service to Amicalola Falls State Park ($65 fare); transports dogs and accepts only cash. Service to the Trailheads at Nimblewill Gap and USFS 42 available at an additional cost.

## GAINESVILLE TO DAHLONEGA

Some hikers choose to stay in Dahlonega rather than Gainesville. The site of the country's first gold rush, in the 1830s, Dahlonega sits 16 miles east of Amicalola Falls and offers all major services. UNITAXI (see above) offers service to Dahlonega.

**Dahlonega**—*Hostel:* A.T. Hiker Hostel run by Josh and Leigh Saint, (770) 312-7342, <www.hikerhostel.com>, <hikerhostel@yahoo.com>, by reservation; $62 thru-hiker's special includes pick-up at North Springs MARTA station in Atlanta or bus/train station in Gainesville, bunk, fuel, stop at outfitters if needed, B, and shuttle to Springer or Amicalola. Gear shipment to hostel available. Bunk & B $15, private room & B $34D. Fuel (white gas & alcohol), shuttle service, free Internet access. See Web site or contact hostel for shuttle rates. *Lodging:* Hotel rates in Dahlonega vary with the season. After May 1 and on weekends, expect listed rates to increase. Holiday Inn

Express, (706) 867-7777, $79–$99D, $5EAP, includes B, no pets;
Super 8, (706) 864-4343, $47D, includes B, $8 for dogs, WiFi;
Days Inn, (706) 864-2338, $49–$70, no pets, WiFi; Econo
Lodge, (706) 864-6191, $50–$60, $5EAP, includes B, no pets;
Smith House, (800) 852-9577, <www.smithhouse.com>,
$79–$250, includes B, no dogs. The Smith House Restaurant,
in operation since 1922, is famous for its family-style AYCE
fare: L (beginning in April) Tu–F 11–3, D Tu, Th, F 4–8, Sa,
Su 11–8. Hours are seasonal and may vary. Call ahead.

### ALTERNATIVES

Several Trail enthusiasts in the Atlanta area offer shuttles from
Atlanta to the park and Springer Mountain. The ATC is con-
tinually updating its list. Many people who offer shuttles do
so on their time off; arrangements are best made at least a
week or two in advance. You can check the ATC Web site,
<www.appalachiantrail.org/shuttles>, for a downloadable file.
Alternatively, if you'd prefer a hard copy of the list, contact
ATC (address on copyright page), ATTN: Shuttle List, and one
will be sent out *via* first-class mail.

### AMICALOLA FALLS APPROACH TRAIL

| Miles from Springer | Features | Services | Elev. | Miles from AFSP |
|---|---|---|---|---|
| 8.8 | Amicalola Falls State Park; Visitors Center; **AFSP Shelter** 0.0mS; 7.3mN | R, C, L, M, S, sh, cl, w (W–19 m O) | 1,700 | 0.0 |
| 7.6 | Amicalola Lodge Rd | R, L, M, w | 2,550 | 1.2 |
| 7.4 | +Len Foote Hike Inn Trail | E–5m L, M | 2,600 | 1.4 |
| 5.6 | High Shoals Rd | R | 2,800 | 3.2 |
| 4.0 | Frosty Mtn | C, w | 3,382 | 4.8 |
| 4.5 | +Len Foote Hike Inn | E–1m L,M | 3,310 | 5.3 |
| 3.7 | Frosty Mtn. Rd USFS 28 | R | 3,192 | 5.1 |
| 2.8 | Nimblewill Gap, USFS 28 | R | 3,100 | 6.0 |
| 1.5 | **Black Gap Shelter** 7.3mS; 1.7mN | C, S, w | 3,300 | 7.3 |
| 0.0 | Springer Mountain | | 3,782 | 8.8 |

+ Fee charged

### THE APPROACH TRAIL

**Amicalola Falls State Park**—Its facilities nestled almost nine
miles southwest of Springer Mountain, the park is the gateway
to the southern terminus of the A.T. Scales to weigh packs and
showers are located near the center entrance, as well as a restroom, pay phone, snack machines, and water fountain. The
visitors center sells guidebooks, maps, and gift items. The park

holds UPS and USPS packages sent c/o Amicalola Falls State Park, 240 Amicalola Falls State Park Rd., Dawsonville, GA 30534. Indicate on the box to hold the package at either the visitors center or the lodge. The visitors center, (706) 265-4703, is open 9–5 daily. While at the park, sign the hiker register inside the visitors center. Long-distance hikers may leave vehicles only in the parking area opposite the visitors center. A $2-per-vehicle user fee is charged to all park visitors. Dogs must be on a leash within the park. ■ *Camping:* The park also offers campsites and cabins: campsites $20 with shower, coin laundry, 1- to 3-bedroom cabins $79–$150. ■ *Lodging:* The desk at Amicalola Lodge, (706) 265-8888, (800) 573-9656, <www.gastateparks.org>, is staffed around the clock; rooms $59–$129. Reservations suggested for cabins, campsites, and the lodge. ■ *Restaurant:* The lodge houses the Maple Restaurant, daily buffets, B 7–10, L 11–4, D 5–9.

**West** 19 miles to *Outfitters:* North Georgia Mountain Outfitters, Collin and Gil Carter, (706) 698-4453, (706) 698-4454, <www.hikenorthgeorgia.com>, <info@hikenorthgeorgia.com>, 49 Oak St., East Ellijay, GA 30540, closed Tu–W; open M, Th, F 10–7; Sa 9–6; Su 12–6; full-service outfitter, Coleman and alcohol fuels by the ounce, canister fuels, short-term food resupply; will hold packages w/o fee; shuttles to Atlanta Airport, Amicalola, Springer Mountain, and Neels Gap; call for possible delivery of packages and store items. Ellijay Outfitters, W–F 11–6, Sa–Su 10–6, 10 N. Main St., Ellijay, GA 30540; (706) 698-GEAR, <www.ellijayoutfitters.com>. Mark (Trail Trucker, '01) and Anne Micallef can shuttle as time allows.

**Amicalola Falls State Park Shelter** (1993)—Located 50 yards behind the visitors center, sleeps 12, and available to thru-hikers at no charge. Built by a group of Trail backpacking enthusiasts from nearby Canton in memory of their friend, Max Epperson. The "A.T. Gang" spent 800 hours constructing the facility. Epperson hiked the Trail as far north as Connecticut before his health failed. Afterward, he continued to offer shuttles and support for his hiking friends. Water source and restroom 50 yards away at visitors center.

**Approach Trail to Springer Mountain**—From the park visitors center, it is an 8.8-mile trek to the first white blaze, most of it uphill. To cut off the steep, one-mile ascent of the falls, catch a ride to the top of the falls, and pick up the blue blazes there. The southern end was recently relocated just past its start at the visitor center.

**Approach Trail *via* Nimblewill Gap**—This alternative puts you 2.2 miles south of Springer Mountain on the Approach Trail but requires a bumpy, muddy drive up Forest Service roads. From the park entrance, go east 9.5 miles on Ga. 52 to abandoned Grizzles Store. Turn left on Nimblewill Road, and continue past Nimblewill Church at 6.6 miles. Just beyond the church, pass a road on the left where the pavement ends. Continue to the right on the unpaved road, and reach Nimblewill Gap at 14 miles. This is a very rough road and probably should not be attempted unless you have a vehicle with high ground clearance.

**From Amicalola Falls to Springer Mountain *via* Forest Service roads**—The easiest and quickest route takes you within one mile of the Springer summit. From the park, go west on Ga. 52 for 13.6 miles to Roy Road, at Cartecay Church and Stanley's Store. Turn right, and proceed 9.5 miles to the second stop sign. At the stop sign, bear right, and go 2.3 miles to Mt. Pleasant Church on the left. Across from the church, turn right onto unpaved Forest Service Road 42. This well-graded gravel road, suitable for all vehicles, winds 6.6 miles to the A.T. crossing at Big Stamp on the north side of the road. To reach the summit of Springer Mountain, walk 0.9 mile south. If you don't want to retrace your steps on the A.T., an alternative is to continue 1.7 miles past the A.T. crossing to USFS 42's intersection with the Benton MacKaye Trail (BMT). The BMT leads 1.5 miles up Springer and joins the A.T. just north of the southern terminus.

**Len Foote Hike Inn**—(800) 581-8032, <www.hike-inn.com>. This $1-million lodge is similar to the huts in New Hampshire's White Mountains. The 40-bed, 20-room inn is approximately 5.0 miles north of Amicalola Falls State Park facilities and 4.5 miles south of the Springer Mountain summit. The yellow-blazed Hike Inn Trail creates a loop with the blue-blazed Approach Trail that leads from Amicalola Falls State Park to Springer. Overnight stays, which include family-style B/D, are $97S, $140D, rates subject to change; no dogs allowed. Amenities include linens, hot showers, composting toilets, and electricity (outlets in bath house only). Owned by the Georgia Department of Natural Resources, the inn is operated by the Appalachian Education and Recreation Services, Inc., a non-profit corporation affiliated with the Georgia Appalachian Trail Club. Walk-ins are allowed, subject to availability. Registration is at the Amicalola Falls State Park visitor center, where you can check on room availability. Open year-round, guest rooms in the bunkhouse are heated. Sleeping bags recommended Nov–Mar.

**Black Gap Shelter** (1953/1995)—Sleeps 8. privy. Once the Springer Mountain Shelter, before being dismantled and moved to its present location in 1995. This shelter is 1.5 miles south of the summit of Springer Mountain on the Approach Trail. Water is located 300 yards downhill to the right of the shelter.

## Getting to Baxter State Park, Maine

No public transportation is available to or from Baxter State Park, but arrangements can be made to conclude or begin your journey with little difficulty. This usually means going through Boston, Portland, and/or Bangor, then to Medway, and then to Millinocket, still 20 miles southeast of the park. The nearest airport is in Bangor; the Portland airport is said to have more competitive rates, and Boston more so. For services and accommodations in Bangor, see page 255. Bus transportation is available from Portland to Medway and also from Boston to Portland.

### LEAVING BANGOR

Cyr Bus Lines of Old Town, Maine, (207) 827-2335, (207) 827-2010, or (800) 244-2335, <www.cyrbustours.com>, <info@cyrbustours.com>, serves northern Maine. A bus leaves Bangor Greyhound bus station at 6:00 p.m. and Concord–Trailways bus station at 6:30 p.m. and arrives at Medway at 7:40 p.m. A bus leaves Medway at 9:30 a.m. and arrives at Concord-Trailways station at 10:50 a.m. and at Bangor Greyhound station at 11:10 a.m. ($11.50 fare). The A.T. Lodge in Millinocket, (207) 723-4321, shuttles.

### MEDWAY TO MILLINOCKET

From Medway, you have to hitch on Maine 157 or call a taxi to go to either Millinocket, 10 miles to the west, or Baxter State Park, about 30 miles away. Town Taxi, (207) 723-2000, charges $45 to Baxter State Park gate and to Katahdin Stream Campground. For information on lodging and facilities near Baxter State Park in Medway and Millinocket, please see the entries on pages 252–254.

**Baxter State Park**—The park, (207) 723-5140, has 10 campgrounds available May 15–Oct 15 by reservation on a first-come, first-served basis, $9PP, two-person minimum ($18 per site) except at the Birches. The Birches campsite, near Katahdin Stream Campground, is intended for long-distance hikers who have hiked 100 miles or more on their current trip. Hikers staying at the Birches must sign up at the information kiosk just north of Abol Bridge. Please see the entry for Baxter on page 248 for more information and details about camping and regulations near Katahdin. Southbound hikers should reserve a regular lean-to or tentsite at Katahdin Stream or Abol campgrounds. Reservations may be made by telephone four months in advance of the date you wish to stay in the park and can be made using a credit card. More information and a chart outlining when reservations can be made is available at <www.baxterstateparkauthority.com>. Inside the park, ranger stations do NOT accept credit cards. Every hiker must register *with a ranger* upon entering Baxter. Information kiosks are located at Abol Stream and Katahdin Stream campgrounds.

*Pets*—No dogs or other pets are allowed; see Medway and Millinocket entries for kennels (pages 252-254).

*Parking*—No long-term parking is available, and parking at all trailheads and campgrounds is at a premium and controlled by permits issued at the entrance gates; when the space is gone, that specific parking lot is closed. Plan ahead!

### APPROACH TO KATAHDIN

*A note for would-be southbounders*—Katahdin is no stroll in the park. The profile and topo on the MATC's maps only give you a hint of what to expect—the single greatest sustained climb on the A.T. Get yourself physically prepared before you start at Baxter State Park (you will be on your own once you get past the ranger station). Northbounders routinely leave their full packs on the ranger's porch and hike up with daypacks provided there for that purpose. Every year, several stubborn southbounders, invariably much less-conditioned than seasoned northbounders, insist on carrying their fully loaded packs up the A.T. beyond Katahdin Stream Campground. This results in knee injuries and aborted climbs or even entire A.T. hiking plans. Take a hint from the northbound veterans: Hike Katahdin with a day pack, and pick up your full pack on your way back through the campground—you will still be a thru-hiker, and you will enjoy your day, rather than suffer the entire time and predispose yourself to any number of injuries or the need for a rescue on your first Trail day. The footpath below treeline is more rocks and roots than soil—no problem for the hikers who have been rock-hopping for 2,000 miles, but not a pleasant journey straight from the desk chair. Above treeline, you pull yourself over rocks in a few places and walk across slanted, roof-sized boulders in others. The climb is tough, even without a pack. The park recommends you bring or borrow a day pack (plenty of water, lots of snacks, sunscreen, a first-aid kit, gloves, hat, and extra layers of clothing). If you don't want to retrace your steps, you might consider going up the Abol Trail (part of which is referred to as the "Abol Slide," because of the loose rocks and steepness formed by a nineteenth-century landslide) and down the Hunt Trail (A.T.). That requires a two-mile walk or ride from Katahdin Stream along the Perimeter Road to Abol Campground before starting your hike. The Abol Trail usually opens after the Hunt Trail; until the sandy, gravelly soils dry out, the trail is slippery, and boulders can become dislodged.

"Weather permitting," you can begin a southbound hike as early as May 31. Before then, trails are so wet, even without snow and ice, that foot traffic would irreparably harm the alpine and subalpine areas. However, even for the following few weeks, the tiny, biting blackflies can drive you out of the woods in agony and frustration, leaving behind a contribution of your blood to the North Woods ecosystem. Overnight camping season in Baxter is May 15–Oct 15. Baxter State Park posts daily weather reports at the Trailheads at 7 a.m. during the hiking season. Categories tell you what is to be expected for the day:

- *Class I*—Recommended for hiking above treeline.

- *Class II*—Not recommended for hiking above treeline.

- *Class III*—Not recommended for hiking above treeline, with the following trails closed (specified trails will be listed).

- *Class IV*—All trails closed at the trailhead. A hiker who climbs Katahdin on a Class IV day is subject to a court summons, fine, seizure of equipment, and permanent revocation of park privileges.

---

### Drought Alert

At the time of publication, the southern two-thirds of the Trail was suffering from severe to extreme drought conditions. While the effect of late-fall and winter precipitation cannot be predicted, this development should be taken seriously into any thru-hiker's plans for 2008. Most of the natural water sources noted in this book are sources for "normal" years, but might be unavailable early in the year without major restorative rain and snowfall over the winter.

# Georgia

| Miles from Katahdin | Features | Services | Elev. | Miles from Springer |
|---|---|---|---|---|
| 2,176.2 | Springer Mtn | | 3,782 | 0.0 |
| 2,176.0 | **Springer Mtn Shelter** *1.9mS; 2.8mN* | E–0.2m S, C, w | 3,730 | 0.2 |
| 2,175.2 | USFS 42 | R | 3,350 | 1.0 |
| 2,173.4 | **Stover Creek Shelter** *2.8mS; 5.2mN* | S, w | 2,870 | 2.8 |
| 2,172.4 | Stover Creek | w | 2,660 | 3.8 |
| 2,171.9 | Three Forks, USFS 58 | R, C, w | 2,530 | 4.3 |
| 2,171.1 | Trail to Long Creek Falls | w | 2,800 | 5.1 |
| 2,170.2 | Logging Rd | R | 3,000 | 6.0 |
| 2,168.4 | **Hawk Mtn Shelter** *5.2mS; 7.6mN* | W–0.2m S; 0.4m w | 3,200 | 7.8 |
| 2,167.9 | Hightower Gap, USFS 42/69 | R | 2,854 | 8.3 |
| 2,166.0 | Horse Gap | R | 2,673 | 10.2 |
| 2,165.0 | Sassafras Mtn | | 3,300 | 11.2 |
| 2,164.4 | Cooper Gap, USFS 42/80 | R | 2,800 | 11.8 |
| 2,163.8 | Justus Mtn | | 3,224 | 12.4 |
| 2,162.4 | Justus Creek | C, w | 2,550 | 13.8 |
| 2,161.1 | **Gooch Mtn Shelter** *7.6mS; 12.4mN* | W–0.1m S, w | 3,000 | 15.1 |
| 2,159.7 | Gooch Gap, USFS 42 | R, w | 2,784 | 16.5 |
| 2,157.5 | Ramrock Mtn | | 3,260 | 18.7 |
| 2,156.1 | Ga. 60, Woody Gap **Suches, GA 30572** | R (W–0.1m w; 2m PO G, C, D, cl, sh, f) (E–7m H, f, @) | 3,150 | 20.1 |
| 2,155.1 | Big Cedar Mtn | | 3,737 | 21.1 |
| 2,153.8 | Dan Gap | | 3,300 | 22.4 |
| 2,151.0 | Burnett Field Mtn | | 3,480 | 25.2 |
| 2,150.5 | Jarrard Gap | W–0.3m w; 1m C, sh, w; 2m M | 3,250 | 25.7 |
| 2,149.2 | **Woods Hole Shelter** *12.4mS; 1.7mN* | W–0.4m S, w | 3,600 | 27.0 |
| 2,149.1 | Bird Gap-Freeman Trail | | 3,650 | 27.1 |
| 2,148.7 | Slaughter Creek Campsite | C, w | 3,800 | 27.5 |
| 2,147.9 | Blood Mtn, **Blood Mtn Shelter** *1.7mS; 9.8mN* | S, nw | 4,450 | 28.3 |
| 2,146.5 | Flatrock Gap, Trail to Byron Reece Memorial | W–0.2m w | 3,450 | 29.7 |

| Miles from Katahdin | Features | Services | Elev. | Miles from Springer |
|---|---|---|---|---|
| 2,145.5 | U.S. 19 & 129, Neels Gap | R, H, O, cl, sh, f, @ (E–0.3m L) (W–3m C, G, cl, sh; 3.5m C, L, cl, sh) | 3,125 | 30.7 |
| 2,144.4 | Bull Gap | C, w | 3,690 | 31.8 |
| 2,144.0 | Levelland Mtn | | 3,942 | 32.2 |
| 2,143.4 | Swaim Gap | | 3,470 | 32.8 |
| 2,142.7 | Rock Spring Top | w | 3,520 | 33.5 |
| 2,142.2 | Corbin Horse Stamp | | 3,620 | 34.0 |
| 2,142.1 | Wolf Laurel Top | | 3,766 | 34.1 |
| 2,141.3 | Baggs Creek Gap | C, w | 3,800 | 34.9 |
| 2,140.8 | Cowrock Mtn | | 3,842 | 35.4 |
| 2,140.0 | Tesnatee Gap, Ga. 348 | R | 3,138 | 36.2 |
| 2,139.5 | Wildcat Mtn | | 3,500 | 36.7 |
| 2,139.3 | **Whitley Gap Shelter** *9.8mS; 5.8mN* | E–1.2m S; 1.5m w | 3,370 | 36.9 |
| 2,139.1 | Hog Pen Gap, Ga. 348 | R, w | 3,450 | 37.1 |
| 2,138.2 | White Oak Stamp | | 3,470 | 38.0 |
| 2,137.2 | Poor Mtn | | 3,620 | 39.0 |
| 2,135.5 | Sheep Rock Top | | 3,600 | 40.7 |
| 2,134.7 | **Low Gap Shelter** *5.8mS; 7.2mN* | S, w | 3,050 | 41.5 |
| 2,133.3 | Poplar Stamp Gap | C, w | 2,990 | 42.9 |
| 2,130.9 | Cold Springs Gap | | 3,300 | 45.3 |
| 2,129.7 | Chattahoochee Gap | E–0.5m w | 3,500 | 46.5 |
| 2,129.1 | Red Clay Gap | | 3,485 | 47.1 |
| 2,128.4 | Campsite | C | 3,600 | 47.8 |
| 2,128.2 | Spring | w | 3,500 | 48.0 |
| 2,127.5 | **Blue Mtn Shelter** *7.2mS; 8.0mN* | S, w | 3,900 | 48.7 |
| 2,126.7 | Blue Mtn | | 4,025 | 49.5 |
| 2,125.3 | Ga. 75, Unicoi Gap **Helen, GA 30545** | R (E–9m PO G, M, L, cl, @) (W–3.8m C, L, G, cl, f, @) | 2,949 | 50.9 |
| 2,124.7 | Stream | w | 3,300 | 51.5 |
| 2,124.0 | Rocky Mtn | C | 4,017 | 52.2 |
| 2,122.7 | Indian Grave Gap | R | 3,113 | 53.5 |
| 2,122.0 | Tray Mtn Rd, (USFS 79) | R | 3,580 | 54.2 |
| 2,121.7 | Cheese Factory Site | C, w | 3,590 | 54.5 |
| 2,120.9 | Tray Gap, Tray Mtn Rd, (USFS 79) | R | 3,847 | 55.3 |
| 2,120.1 | Tray Mtn | | 4,430 | 56.1 |

| Miles from Katahdin | Features | Services | Elev. | Miles from Springer |
|---|---|---|---|---|
| 2,119.7 | **Tray Mtn Shelter** *8.0mS; 8.0mN* | W–0.2m S; 0.3m w | 4,200 | 56.5 |
| 2,116.1 | Blue Ridge Swag | | 3,400 | 60.1 |
| 2,114.9 | Sassafras Gap | w | 3,500 | 61.3 |
| 2,114.1 | Addis Gap | C (E–0.5m w) | 3,304 | 62.1 |
| 2,113.1 | Kelly Knob | | 4,276 | 63.1 |
| 2,112.2 | **Deep Gap Shelter** *8.0mS; 8.5mN* | E–0.3m S, w | 3,550 | 64.0 |
| 2,111.1 | McClure Gap | C | 3,650 | 65.1 |
| 2,110.9 | Powell Mtn | | 3,850 | 65.3 |
| 2,109.9 | Moreland Gap | | 3,200 | 66.3 |
| 2,109.3 | Streams | w | 2,650 | 66.9 |
| 2,108.7 | U.S. 76, Dicks Creek Gap **Hiawassee, GA 30546** | R, w (W–1.5m H, f; 3.5m H, f, cl; 11m PO, G, M, L, O, D, V, cl, sh, @) | 2,675 | 67.5 |
| 2,107.6 | Campsite | C, w | 3,150 | 68.6 |
| 2,106.9 | Cowart Gap | | 2,900 | 69.3 |
| 2,105.4 | Bull Gap | | 3,690 | 70.8 |
| 2,104.2 | **Plumorchard Gap Shelter** *8.5mS; 7.4mN* | E–0.2m S, w | 3,050 | 72.0 |
| 2,103.5 | As Knob | | 3,460 | 72.7 |
| 2,102.9 | Blue Ridge Gap | | 3,020 | 73.3 |
| 2,101.9 | Campsite | C, w | 3,500 | 74.3 |
| 2,101.7 | Rich Cove Gap | | 3,390 | 74.5 |
| 2,099.9 | Ga.–N.C. State Line | | 3,825 | 76.3 |

The Trail begins in Georgia at Springer Mountain and follows a rugged, often rocky terrain, reaching a height of more than 4,461 feet and never dipping below 2,500 feet. It passes through five major gaps and more than 25 smaller ones. Thru-hikers starting their journey in March or April will probably see snow, which can add to the difficulty. Spring melts give way to many of the wildflowers common throughout the mountains, including bloodroot, trillium, and azalea. Forests are mostly second-growth hardwoods of hickory, oak, and poplar.

**Georgia Appalachian Trail Club**—GATC maintains the 76.4 miles from Springer Mountain to Bly Gap, just over the North Carolina line. Correspondence should be sent to GATC, P.O. Box 654, Atlanta, GA 30301; (404) 634-6495; <trails_supervisor@georgia-atclub.org>.

**Chattahoochee National Forest**—The Trail in Georgia winds through the Chattahoochee National Forest, created by Congress in 1936. By that time, much of the land had been laid bare from intensive timber harvesting. Today, little virgin timber remains, but the hardwoods have reestablished themselves with the help of 69 years of management and protection. Half of the Trail lies within five designated wilderness areas in the forest.

*Bear problems*—With the loss of habitat from development in the mountains, black bears are roaming farther in search of food. To combat this problem, the GATC and the USFS are placing bear cables for hanging food at the shelters most affected. If bear cables are not available, secure food using bearproof techniques.

**Springer Mountain**—Springer has served as the A.T.'s southern terminus since 1958. Before that, Mt. Oglethorpe, to the southwest, was the southern terminus. In 1993, GATC members and the Forest Service installed a new plaque marking the Trail's southernmost blaze. The hiker register is located within the boulder on which the plaque is mounted. The origin of the mountain's name is a bit foggy. The best guess is that it was named in honor of William G. Springer, a settler who, in 1833, was appointed by the Georgia governor to implement legislation to improve conditions for North Georgia Indians. The original bronze plaque marking the southern terminus, one of three intended for road crossings, was created in 1934 by GATC member and amateur sculptor George Noble at a cost of $20—a hefty amount in those days. Warner Hall, the club's second president, served as Noble's model and coined the phrase, "A footpath for those who seek fellowship with the wilderness." That plaque was moved to the mountain in May 1959; keep an eye out for the other two plaques at road crossings along the Trail in Georgia. The overlook at the 3,782-foot summit provides views to the west—a nice sunset spot.

**Springer Mountain Shelter** (1993)—Sleeps 12. Privy. Near the summit, about 250 yards north of the bronze plaque, then east on a blue-blazed side trail about 200 yards. Use the designated tentpads in this heavily trafficked area, and use the food-hoist cables to discourage local bears. Water source is a spring located 80 yards on a blue-blazed trail in front of the shelter; spring may go dry in times of drought.

**Stover Creek Shelter** (2006)—Sleeps 16. Privy, tentpads, bear cables. The fourth incarnation, this nearby alternative to the often-crowded Springer Mountain Shelter was moved to its present location in 1984; new shelter built in 2006. Water source is the creek. No tenting near water.

**Hawk Mountain Shelter** (1993)—Sleeps 12. Privy. Army Rangers from nearby Camp Frank D. Merrill use the area for training exercises and have been spotted all times of the day and night. Food-hoist cables available; bear activity often reported. Water source is located 300 yards on a blue-blazed trail behind the shelter.

**Gooch Mountain Shelter** (2001)—Sleeps 14. Privy. Nearly 2,000 volunteer hours were spent constructing this double-decker shelter and nearby tentpads. Additional tenting space farther north at Gooch Gap, near the old shelter site. Excellent water source is 100 yards behind the shelter.

**Ga. 60/Woody Gap/Suches**—At the gap are picnic tables and a privy. A spring is on a poorly marked side trail west of the A.T. on the northern side of the gap.

**East** 7 miles to *Hostel:* A.T. Hiker Hostel run by Josh and Leigh Saint, (770) 312-7342, <www.hikerhostel.com>, <hikerhostel@yahoo.com>. Bunk & B $15, private & B $34D; 5 p.m. pick-up at Woody Gap, Feb 26–Apr 29. Fuel (white gas & alcohol), shuttle service, free Internet; see Web site or contact for shuttle rates.

**West** 2 miles to **Suches, Ga. [P.O. ZIP 30572: M–F 7:30–11:30 & 1–4:30, Sa 7:30–11:30; (706) 747-2611].** ■ *Camping:* Two Wheels Only, (706) 747-5151, tentsite $7PP, hot showers, L 11–2 Sa, Su; D 6–8:30 F, Sa; open Apr–Oct. ■ *Groceries:* Dale's General Store (short-term resupply), (706) 747-2271, Coleman fuel by the ounce, pay phone outside, BBQ 11–4 Sa–Su, holds UPS packages shipped to 12905 Wolf Pen Gap Rd., Suches, GA 30572. Open M–Sa 7–6, Su 8–6. ■ *Other services:* Don L. Pruitt, M.D., (706) 747-1421, open M–Tu Th–F 9–4, walk-ins 9–11. Jim and Ruth Ann Miner, (706) 747-5434, live in town and are available if you need help. ■ *Shuttles:* Wes Wisson, (706) 747-2671.

**Jarrard Gap**—A blue-blazed trail to the west leads 1 mile to USFS Lake Winfield Scott Recreation Area, which offers tentsites, showers, $12; dogs must be leashed. Lenny's Grill, hours F, Sa 4–9, Su 10:30–3; turn left at LWS entrance, and continue 1 mile.

**Wood's Hole Shelter** (1998)—Sleeps 7. Privy. Located 0.4 mile west on a blue-blazed side trail, this "Nantahala design" shelter is named in honor of the late Tillie and Roy Wood, operators of the Woodshole Hostel near Pearisburg, Virginia. Food-hoist cables available. Water source is an unreliable spring along the side trail to the shelter.

**Bird Gap**—From here, the Freeman Trail leads 1.7 miles around the south slope of Blood Mountain and rejoins the A.T. 1.1 miles from Neels Gap. Those who choose this blue-blazed route miss the climb to the Trail's high point in Georgia; it serves as a foul-weather route around Blood Mountain.

**Slaughter Gap**—Reached by a side trail (after a major relocation to restore this overused area), tentsites have been built near Slaughter Creek to ease the load on Blood Mountain.

**Blood Mountain**—According to tales of the Creek and Cherokee, a battle between the two nations on the slopes of the mountain left so many dead and wounded that the ground ran red with blood, which inspired the name. Blood Mountain is the most-visited spot on the A.T. south of Clingmans Dome, and the impact of more than 40,000 visitors a year has taken its toll. Vandalism in and around the shelter has been a chronic problem. In an effort to counter visitor impact, fires have been banned along a 3.3-mile section between Slaughter Gap and Neels Gap.

**Blood Mountain Shelter** (1934)—Sleeps 8. Privy. Located atop the highest peak on the A.T. in Georgia (4,461 feet), this historic two-room stone structure was last refurbished in 1981. No water or firewood available; no fires permitted. Northbounders can get water from a stream 0.3 mile north of Bird Gap or on a blue-blazed side trail at Slaughter Gap, 0.9 mile from the shelter. Southbounders can get water at Neels Gap or at a spring located on the blue-blazed trail to Byron Reece Memorial, 0.2 mile from where the trail joins the A.T., 2.4 miles south of Neels Gap. Overuse could close the shelter to hikers in the future.

**U.S. 19 & 129/Neels Gap**—Mountain Crossings at Walasi-Yi Center is a full-service *Outfitter* with all stove fuels and gift shop (short-term resupply) operated by Winton and Marjorie Porter, (706) 745-6095; open daily 8:30–6. UPS and USPS packages held, $1 donation. Ship packages to 9710 Gainesville Hwy., Blairsville, GA 30512. ■ *Hostel:* Walasi-Yi, <www.mountaincrossings.com>, open year-round, $15PP, with shower, coin laundry, possible Internet access, pay phone, nonguest shower $3.50, pets outside. Call for possible cabin rentals (available by reservation), up to 8 people (2 minimum), $30 PP.
    **East** 0.3 mile to *Lodging:* Blood Mountain Cabins, (800) 284-6866, <www.bloodmountain.com>. Cabins with showers, kitchens, and satellite TV sleep 6; thru-hiker rate $50, no pets. A trail leads from the Walasi-Yi Center to the resort office.
    **West** 3 miles to *Camping:* Vogel State Park, (800) 864-7275, <www.gastateparks.org>. Tentsites with shower $12–$22, showers only $3. Other park services include a camp

store (short-term resupply), coin laundry (detergent 75¢), and rental cabins; reservations are suggested for tentsites and cabins. Leash dogs inside the park.

**West** 3.5 miles to *Lodging:* Goose Creek Cabins, (706) 745-5111, <www.goosecreekcabins.com>. Owners Keith and Retter Bailey offer free shuttles from Neels Gap with cabin or tentsite rental. Special hiker rates for cabin begin at $25PP; dogs permitted. Tentsites with shower, $10PP. Amenities include laundry ($5/load), lodge with game room, CATV, trout-fishing, and shuttles to a nearby restaurant each evening. UPS packages can be shipped to Goose Creek Cabins, 7061 U.S. 19/129S, Blairsville, GA 30512; <goosecreek@alltel.net>.

**Whitley Gap Shelter** (1974)—Sleeps 6. Privy. This shelter is located 1.2 miles east of the A.T. down a steep side trail. Food-hoist cables available. Water source is a spring 0.3 mile behind the shelter.

**Low Gap Shelter** (1953)—Sleeps 7. Privy. Food-hoist cables available; a 2000 hiker reported waking in the shelter to a black bear straddling him. Water source is crossed at the shelter; a second source can be found 30 yards in front of the shelter.

**Chattahoochee Gap**—A blue-blazed side trail leads east to Chattahoochee Spring, source of the Chattahoochee River, which supplies drinking water to Atlanta and almost half of the state's population. Some 500 miles from this point, the river empties into the Gulf of Mexico. Springs rising on the other side of the continental divide flow to the Tennessee River and eventually to the Mississippi.

**Blue Mountain Shelter** (1988)—Sleeps 7. Privy. Located on a short side trail, this shelter is notorious for cold north winds that blow up Blue Mountain from the gap below. Food-hoist cables available. Water source is a spring on the A.T. 0.1 mile south of the shelter.

**Ga. 75/Unicoi Gap—East** 9 miles to **Helen, Ga. [P.O. ZIP 30545: M–F 8:30–5, Sa 8:30–12; (706) 878-2422]**, Georgia's "Gatlinburg." The town's year-round population of 300 can play host to as many as 30,000 people in a day, so there are many motels and restaurants from which to choose. A good place to start in town is the visitors center, found behind the post office, which has a map and free phone from which to call motels to find the best rates. Rates vary greatly according to season but are generally at their lowest Jan–Mar. Expect rates to increase after Apr 1 and on the weekends and for Oktoberfest (held early Sep–Oct). Retail shops abound as well.
■ *Lodging:* Hofbrau Riverfront Hotel, (800) 830-3977, $69D $10EAP, small dogs $10, ATM, possible shuttle to Trail, B, microwave, refrigerator; Helendorf River Inn, (800) 445-2271,

$34S $54D, $5EAP, shower only $5, coin laundry, detergent $1, dogs $5, B, heated pool; Comfort Inn, (800) 443-6488, $50–$159, $5EAP, B, no pets; Super 8 Motel, (800) 535-1251, next to laundromat, hiker rates $35S $55D exclude weekends, B, microwave, refrigerator, no pets, WiFi, heated pool; Best Western, (800) 435-3642, $35–$65, $5EAP, WiFi, B, no pets, free possible shuttles to Trail M–F; Motel 6, (706) 878-8888, $40–$80, $6EAP, pets allowed; Ramada Limited, (706) 878-1451, $50–$179D, B, no pets; Alpenhof Motel, (706) 878-2268, $25–$139D, $5EAP, excluding weekends and holidays, pets $13–$15, B; Days Inn, (706) 878-4079, $45–$149D, B, pets $10 and less than 25 lbs. in limited rooms; Chalet Kristy, (877) 464-3536, hiker rate $29–$119D, excluding weekends and holidays, $5–$17EAP, B at Alpendorf Motel, pets $15; Rodeway Inn, (706) 878-2141, $36–$200, $5EAP, pets $10 and less than 15 lbs.; Helen accommodations, <www.helenga.org>. ■ *Groceries:* Betty's Country Store (long-term resupply), open daily 7–8. ■ *Restaurants:* numerous. ■ *Internet access:* White County Library, Helen Branch. ■ *Other services:* The Soap Opera Laundromat; bicycle rentals available at Woody's Mountain Bikes, (706) 878-3715; pharmacy. ■ *Shuttles:* Mall Shuttle Transport Service, (706) 219-1653.

**East** 17 miles to *Medical:* Cleveland, Ga., Neighborhood Health Care, (706) 865-1234, M–F 8–5.

**West** 1.3 miles, then left 2.5 miles on Ga. 180 to *Lodging:* Enota Mountain Retreat, (800) 990-8869, <www.enota.com>; waterfalls, organic gardens, and an animal sanctuary; $10 membership per visit and $5 campfire fee; tentsites $20, bunkhouse $25, cabins $100–$165, dogs $5. Amenities include free long-distance phone, coin laundry with soap, B 8–10:30 with advance notice, L/D, satellite TV, video library, Internet access, Jacuzzis in some cabins, massage 1½ hours $100, possible $2/mile shuttle to Trail. General store (short-term resupply) open 9–8, including Coleman, alcohol, and canister fuels. Enota holds packages, for guests only, mailed to 1000 Hwy. 180, Hiawassee, GA 30546.

**Cheese Factory Site**—In the mid-1800s, an eccentric New Englander established a dairy near Tray Mountain, about 15 miles from the nearest farmhouse. Other Georgians, who received parcels in the mountains after a government survey of former Indian lands in the 1830s, opted to sell their land to speculators rather than attempt to tame the untamable. For several years, the man ran his dairy successfully and reportedly produced a superior cheese that won several awards at state agricultural fairs. Little evidence of the dairy remains today, although the spot is a designated campsite with a spring.

**Tray Mountain**—Spectacular views from the 4,430-foot summit and probably the southernmost breeding area in the United States for Canada warblers. These small, active songbirds may be spotted in the rhododendron thickets along the southern approach to the summit. Males are blue-gray above and yellow throughout the chest. Look for the distinctive "necklace" on both the males' and females' chests. The Canada warbler's song is an irregular burst of beautiful notes.

**Tray Mountain Shelter** (1971)—Sleeps 7. Privy. Food-hoist cables. Excellent overnight spot for taking in the sunset and sunrise from the summit or from viewpoints along the 0.2-mile trail to the shelter. Water source is a spring located 260 yards behind the shelter.

**Deep Gap Shelter** (1983)—Sleeps 12. Privy. Food-hoist cables. Shelter is designed like the Springer Mountain Shelter and located on a 0.3-mile side trail to the east. Water source is on the blue-blazed trail to the shelter.

 **U.S. 76/Dicks Creek Gap/Hiawassee**—At road are parking lot, picnic tables, and small creek.

**West** 1.5 miles to *Hostel:* Cloud9 at the Upper Hightower Trout Farm, (706) 896-8959 or (706) 896-1825, <www.upper-hightowertrout.com>, <cloud9ga@hughes.net>, look for the Trout Farm sign on left, walk down drive at mailboxes, 7120–7150 Canaan Drive, Hiawassee, GA 30546, owned by Laura and Frank; open Feb–May 25; tenting $10PP/night and tree house $20PP/night with bathroom privileges only; $25 up PP/night in Cloud9 cabin includes shower with towel, one load of laundry with detergent, fully equipped kitchen, living room, pool/ping-pong/game tables and Jacuzzi, wireless Internet access, satellite TV; dogs welcome at $10/night; free shuttle to and from Trail, 10-mile shuttle service for nominal fee; bed linens $2; will hold packages 15 days, no charge for guests, nonguests $2; will ship packages for a fee; Coleman and alcohol fuel for sale; work for stay on a limited basis; parking $5; trout-pond fishing; trout dinners for donation; major credit/debit cards accepted.

**West** 3.5 miles to *Hostel:* Blueberry Patch Hiker Hostel, a Christian ministry owned by '91 thru-hiker Gary Poteat and his wife, Lennie. Look for the Blueberry Patch sign on the left side of the highway as you descend from Dicks Creek Gap; (706) 896-4893. Evenings are the best time to reach the Poteats. If you can't reach them, keep trying; they cannot return long-distance calls. Open Feb 15–May 1. Hostel remains open by generosity of hiker donations. Includes shower, laundry service, B, and shuttle back to the Trail at 9:30 a.m. Bunks for 7 with accommodations for up to 10. Please arrive no earlier than 10 a.m. and no later than 6 p.m. Coleman fuel by the ounce. The Poteats hold UPS and USPS packages mailed to 5038 U.S. Hwy. 76, Hiawas-

"We are sincere in the belief that we have a very
desirable section of the Trail down here and dare say
that a great many ideas about Georgia will be
changed on a hike through its mountainous portion."

—CHARLIE ELLIOTT, GEORGIA A.T. CLUB, 1931

see, GA 30546. NO pets, alcohol, drugs, or tobacco products.

**West** 11 miles to **Hiawassee, Ga. [P.O. ZIP 30546: M–F 8:30–5, Sa 8:30–12; (706) 896-3632].** ■ *Lodging:* Mull's Motel, (706) 896-4195, $55 and up, holds packages for guests only, no dogs, 213 N. Main St., Hiawassee, GA 30546; Hiawassee Inn, (706) 896-4121, open Feb–Nov 15, reservations required in July, one person $45, two $25 each, three $17 each, dog $10, one evening restaurant shuttle, laundry with detergent $3.50, shower only $3, $5PP shuttle back to Trail, will pick up at Dicks Creek or Unicoi gaps with reservation, holds UPS packages, 193 East Main St., Hiawassee, GA 30546; Holiday Inn Express, <www.hiexpress.com/hiawasseega>, (706) 896-8884, special hiker rates of $99D, $6EAP, no pets, B included, coin laundry with free detergent, indoor whirlpool, free bicycle use, shuttle to Trail for a fee, WiFi, will hold UPS packages, 300 Big Sky Dr., Hiawassee, GA 30546. ■ *Groceries:* Dill's Food City, Ingles, both long-term resupply; Wealth of Health, short-term resupply. ■ *Restaurants:* Georgia Mountain Restaurant, B only on weekends, L/D; Shoney's, AYCE buffet, B/L/D (about one mile from the town center); Subway; China Grill AYCE; Dairy Queen; Monte Alban Mexican, L/D; Daniel's Steakhouse, L/D AYCE; Donna's; Huddle House; various other fast foods. ■ *Outfitter:* 4 miles west on U.S. 76 from town center, on Ga. 75, next to Fieldstone Inn, is the Upper Hi Fly, (706) 896-9075, <www.upper-hi-fly.com>, limited hiker gear, open 9–5 M–Sa, 9–2 Su, closed Tu, Su Jan–Mar. ■ *Internet access:* Towns County Public Library. ■ *Other services:* Western Union; coin laundry; Chatuge Regional Hospital, (706) 896-2222, known for treatment of blisters; Open Door Clinic on Thursdays, (706) 896-6241, 120 River St., fee based on income; pharmacy; dentist; banks with ATM; hardware store; Hiawassee Animal Hospital, (706) 896-4173. ■ *Shuttles:* To all points in the Georgia, North Carolina, and Tennessee mountains, available through Mull's Motel, (706) 896-4195, and Hiawassee Inn, (706) 896-4121.

**Plumorchard Gap Shelter** (1993)—Sleeps 14. Privy. The stump in front of the shelter has been a residence of copperhead snakes. Water source is a creek that crosses the trail to the shelter or a spring located 200 yards west of the A.T., opposite the shelter trail.

**Bly Gap**—If you are thru-hiking, it is time to celebrate your first (or last) state line. When you see the gnarled oak in a clearing, you're officially in North Carolina. The gap, with its grassy area and views to the northwest, makes a good campsite. Water can be obtained from a spring about 100 yards south on the A.T.

*View from Wayah Bald, North Carolina. Photograph by Peter McIntosh.*

# North Carolina

| Miles from Katahdin | Features | Services | Elev. | Miles from Springer |
|---|---|---|---|---|
| 2,099.9 | N.C.-Ga. State Line | | 3,825 | 76.3 |
| 2,099.8 | Bly Gap | C, w | 3,840 | 76.4 |
| 2,097.9 | Sassafras Gap | | 4,300 | 78.3 |
| 2,097.0 | **Muskrat Creek Shelter** *7.4mS; 4.9mN* | S, w | 4,600 | 79.2 |
| 2,096.3 | Whiteoak Stamp | | 4,620 | 79.9 |
| 2,096.0 | Chunky Gal Trail | | 4,700 | 80.2 |
| 2,095.1 | Wateroak Gap | | 4,490 | 81.1 |
| 2,093.0 | Deep Gap, USFS 71, Kimsey Creek Trail | R, w (W–3.7m C, G, sh) | 4,341 | 83.2 |
| 2,092.1 | **Standing Indian Shelter** *4.9mS; 7.6mN* | S, w | 4,760 | 84.1 |
| 2,090.6 | Lower Trail Ridge Trail, Standing Indian Mtn | (E–0.2m summit) (W–0.2m w) | 5,498 | 85.6 |
| 2,087.7 | Beech Gap | C, w | 4,460 | 88.5 |
| 2,084.9 | Timber Ridge Trail | | 4,700 | 91.3 |
| 2,084.5 | **Carter Gap Shelter** *7.6mS; 6.8mN* | S, w | 4,540 | 91.7 |
| 2,080.8 | Betty Creek Gap | C, w | 4,300 | 95.4 |
| 2,079.9 | Mooney Gap, USFS 83 | R | 4,460 | 96.3 |
| 2,079.7 | Spring | w | 4,500 | 96.5 |
| 2,079.6 | Bear Pen Trail, USFS 67 | R | 4,790 | 96.6 |
| 2,078.3 | Albert Mtn | | 5,250 | 97.9 |
| 2,077.7 | **Big Spring Shelter** *6.8mS; 5.3mN* | S, w | 4,940 | 98.5 |
| 2,074.9 | Glassmine Gap | | 4,160 | 101.3 |
| 2,072.4 | **Rock Gap Shelter** *5.3mS; 8mN* | S, w | 3,760 | 103.8 |
| 2,072.3 | Rock Gap; Wasilik Poplar; Standing Indian Campground | R (W–1.5m C, G, sh) | 3,750 | 103.9 |
| 2,071.7 | Wallace Gap, Old 64 | R | 3,738 | 104.5 |
| 2,068.6 | Winding Stair Gap, U.S. 64 **Franklin, NC 28734** | R, w (W–10m PO, G, M, L, O, D, V, cl, f, @) | 3,770 | 107.6 |
| 2,067.7 | Campsite | C, w | 3,970 | 108.5 |
| 2,067.5 | Swinging Lick Gap | | 4,100 | 108.7 |
| 2,066.6 | Panther Gap | | 4,480 | 109.6 |
| 2,064.9 | **Siler Bald Shelter** *7.8mS; 8mN* | E–0.5m S, w | 4,600 | 111.3 |

| Miles from Katahdin | Features | Services | Elev. | Miles from Springer |
|---|---|---|---|---|
| 2,062.7 | Wayah Gap, N.C. 1310 | R | 4,180 | 113.5 |
| 2,060.9 | USFS 69 | R, w | 4,900 | 115.3 |
| 2,060.4 | Wine Spring | C, w | 5,290 | 115.8 |
| 2,058.5 | Wayah Bald | R | 5,342 | 117.7 |
| 2,058.1 | Campsite | C, w | 5,200 | 118.1 |
| 2,057.6 | **Wayah Shelter** 7.8mS; 4.8mN | S, w | | 118.6 |
| 2,056.3 | Licklog Gap | W–0.5m w | 4,440 | 119.9 |
| 2,054.0 | Burningtown Gap, N.C. 1397 | R | 4,236 | 122.2 |
| 2,052.8 | **Cold Spring Shelter** 4.8mS; 5.8mN | C, S, w | 4,920 | 123.4 |
| 2,052.1 | Copper Ridge Bald Lookout | | 5,080 | 124.1 |
| 2,050.9 | Trail to Rocky Bald Lookout | | 5,030 | 125.3 |
| 2,050.6 | Spring | w | 4,900 | 125.6 |
| 2,049.2 | Tellico Gap, N.C. 1365 | R | 3,850 | 127.0 |
| 2,047.8 | Wesser Bald Observation Tower | | 4,627 | 128.4 |
| 2,047.1 | Spring | w | 4,100 | 129.1 |
| 2,047.0 | Wesser Creek Trail, **Wesser Bald Shelter** 5.8mS; 4.9mN | C, S, w | 4,115 | 129.2 |
| 2,045.4 | Jump-up Lookout | | 4,000 | 130.8 |
| 2,042.1 | **A. Rufus Morgan Shelter** 4.9mS; 7.7mN | S, w | 2,300 | 134.1 |
| 2,041.3 | U.S. 19, U.S. 74, Nantahala River, Nantahala Outdoor Center, Wesser, N.C. **Bryson City, NC 28713** | R, G, L, M, O, cl, sh, f (E–1m C, G, L; 13m PO, G, M, L, D, cl) (S–1m C, sh) | 1,740 | 134.9 |
| 2,039.7 | Wright Gap | R | 2,390 | 136.5 |
| 2,038.2 | Grassy Gap | | 3,050 | 138.0 |
| 2,035.3 | Swim Bald | | 4,710 | 140.9 |
| 2,034.4 | **Sassafras Gap Shelter** 7.7mS; 9.1mN | S, w | 4,330 | 141.8 |
| 2,033.2 | Cheoah Bald | | 5,062 | 143.0 |
| 2,030.8 | Locust Cove Gap | C, w | 3,690 | 145.4 |
| 2,029.8 | Simp Gap | | 3,700 | 146.4 |
| 2,027.7 | Stecoah Gap, N.C. 143 | R, w | 3,165 | 148.5 |
| 2,026.7 | Sweetwater Gap | | 3,270 | 149.5 |
| 2,025.3 | **Brown Fork Gap Shelter** 9.1mS; 6.1mN | S, w | 3,800 | 150.9 |

| Miles from Katahdin | Features | Services | Elev. | Miles from Springer |
|---|---|---|---|---|
| 2,025.1 | Brown Fork Gap | | 3,600 | 151.1 |
| 2,023.3 | Hogback Gap | | 3,540 | 152.9 |
| 2,022.5 | Cody Gap | C, w | 3,600 | 153.7 |
| 2,020.1 | Yellow Creek Gap, Yellow Crk Mtn Rd | R | 2,980 | 156.1 |
| 2,019.2 | **Cable Gap Shelter** 6.1mS; 6.6mN | S, w | 2,880 | 157.0 |
| 2,017.8 | Black Gum Gap | | 3,490 | 158.4 |
| 2,016.4 | Walker Gap, Yellow Creek Trail | W–2.5m PO, G, L, M, O, cl, f | 3,450 | 159.8 |
| 2,016.2 | Campsite | C, w | 3,200 | 160.0 |
| 2,013.7 | N.C. 28 **Fontana Dam, NC 28733** | R (E–5m G, f; 6m L, f, @) (W–2m PO, G, L, M, O, cl, f) | 1,810 | 162.5 |
| 2,012.6 | **Fontana Dam Shelter** 6.6mS; 11.3mN | R, S, w | 1,775 | 163.6 |
| 2,012.3 | Fontana Dam Visitors Ctr | R, sh, w | 1,700 | 163.9 |

At Bly Gap, northbounders enter the Nantahala National Forest with 4,000-foot gaps and 5,000-foot peaks. Nantahala is Cherokee for "land of the noonday sun." Long climbs between the Stecoah–Cheoah Mountain area and Cheoah Bald offer panoramic views of western North Carolina. Don't rush; enjoy the landscape from an observation tower or two. Take a pit stop at the NOC playground on the Nantahala River for some food and a rafting trip.

**Nantahala Hiking Club**—NHC maintains the 58.5 miles between Bly Gap and the Nantahala River. Correspondence should be sent to NHC, 173 Carl Slagle Rd., Franklin, NC 28734; <www.maconcommunity.org/nhc/>.

*No road access to the A.T. is available between Bly Gap and Rock Gap during Jan, Feb, and part of Mar. The Forest Service closes USFS 71 to all vehicular traffic until Mar 1 and USFS 67 until Mar 15. Frequently used Trailheads at Deep Gap, and others, are inaccessible.*

**Muskrat Creek Shelter** (rebuilt 1995)—Sleeps 8. Privy. Birthplace of "The Old Pros," a legendary backpacking group that included Ron Tipton (now SVP of the National Parks Conservation Association), Dave Sherman (retired from the Forest Service Washington office), and the late Ed Garvey. This shelter uses the "Nantahala design." Water source is just south and visible from the shelter.

**Deep Gap**—From here, the Kimsey Creek Trail leads 3.7 miles to the Forest Service's Standing Indian Campground (see next page).

**Standing Indian Shelter** (1996)—Sleeps 8. Privy. "Nantahala design" shelter east of the A.T. Water source is a stream opposite the side trail to the shelter. Recent bear sightings; *use bear-proofing techniques.*

**Standing Indian Mountain**—The 5,498-foot summit of the mountain 0.2 mile east is reached *via* a blue-blazed side trail. Cliff-top views to the south gave it the nickname, "Grandstand of the Southern Appalachians." According to Cherokee legend, a great winged monster once inhabited the mountain, and, during the monster's reign, warriors were posted on the mountain as lookouts. As the story goes, a tremendous bolt of lightning shattered the mountain and killed the monster. During the strike, a lone Cherokee sentinel was hit by the bolt and turned into stone, supposedly for being a poor sentry. Remnants of the stone "Standing Indian" are visible today. At the top are flat areas for camping and views south toward Blood Mountain. A spring is located 0.2 mile downhill on an unmarked trail near the A.T. junction with Lower Trail Ridge Trail. Please tread lightly if you choose to camp here; the area receives tremendous use.

**Carter Gap Shelter** (1959 old/1998 new)—Two shelters, the old and the new. Old shelter sleeps 6; new shelter sleeps 8. Privy. The new shelter uses the "Nantahala design." Water source is a spring located downhill behind the old shelter, on the west side of the Trail.

**Mooney Gap**—This gap has been identified as among the wettest places in the eastern U.S., with an estimated annual precipitation of 93.5 inches.

**Big Spring Shelter** (1959)—Sleeps 8. Privy. Food-hoist cables available. Water source is Big Spring, behind and to the left of the shelter.

**Rock Gap Shelter** (1965)—Sleeps 8. Privy. Located only 0.5 mile from the road. Older shelter with a recently added overhang for cooking. Food-hoist cables available. Water source is a spring to the left and behind the shelter.

**Rock Gap/Standing Indian Campground—West** 1.5 miles on a paved road to the Forest Service campground with tentsites $14, restroom, warm showers ($2 shower only), and pay phone; small campstore open Memorial Day–Nov 30; opens according to weather but usually weekend before Easter.

**Wasilik Poplar**—At Rock Gap, a blue-blazed side trail leads **East** 0.5 mile to the second-largest poplar tree in the United States, now dead. In 1996, the tree measured 27 feet in circumference, 8.6 feet in diameter, and 125.5 feet in height (to a broken-off top). In the early 1900s, when logging companies began cutting the timber in this area, workers cut down another poplar similar in size to the Wasilik. However, its weight so badly strained the oxen transporting the tree the lumberjacks decided against harvesting this one.

**U.S. 64/Winding Stair Gap**—**East** 10 miles to **Franklin, N.C.** **[P.O. ZIP 28734: M–F 8:30–5, Sa 9–12; (828) 524-3219].** Although a bit spread out, most major services are within walking distance along Business U.S. 441; <www.franklin-chamber.com>. ■ *Lodging:* Franklin Motel, (800) 433-5507, $30–$45, microwave, refrigerator, will hold packages for guests, 17 West Palmer St., fuel by the ounce, laundry including detergent $3, pets allowed $10, shuttle list available; Haven's Budget Inn,

**Franklin**

0      0.5 mile

N

Cody's Roadhouse

Angel Urgent Care

Ace Hardware

Franklin Motel

Motor Grill

Main St.

Banks

Haven Motel

Palmer St.

Rathskeller

Laundry.

B&D Restaurant

P.O.

Ingles Laundry

Maple St.

Depot St.

Forest Ave.

Visitor Center

Georgia Rd.

10 Miles to A.T.

U.S. 64

Bus. 441

Lowes

Outfitters

Kerr Drug

Siler Road

U.S. 23/64/441

Ingles, K-mart, Western Union, Laundry, BBQ, Kerr Drugs, Subway

UPS Store

Library

Medical Clinic, Shoe Store, Book Store

ATM

Huddle House

Dairy Queen

Arby's, Microtel Motel

Pizza Hut

Shoney's

Wendy's, The Factory

Zaxbys

(828) 349-4231, <tiamalle@aol.com>, $35S/D $5EAP, free a.m. Mar–Apr shuttle to town, outfitter, and Trail, pets welcome with $50 deposit/pet, in-room phone, free local calls, Internet access, will hold packages, 433 E. Palmer St.; Microtel Inn & Suites, (828) 349-9000, $40–$54, pets allowed, free long-distance phone (U.S.), has a local shuttle list. ■ *Groceries:* Ingles Supermarket (long-term resupply). ■ *Restaurants:* Shoney's, AYCE; Cody's Roadhouse; Huddle House; Rathskeller Snack, Lunch and Coffee Shop, Tu–Th 11–7, F–Sa 11–11; and various other restaurants. ■ *Outfitter:* Three Eagles Outfitters, (828) 524-9061, open M–Sa 10–6, Su 12–4, full-service outfitter; Coleman and alcohol fuel by the ounce, Esbit and canisters; will ship and hold packages, 78 Siler Rd., 1 Three Eagles Place. ■ *Internet access:* Macon County Library, by appointment or chance; Rathskeller. ■ *Other services:* UPS Store, (828) 524-9800, M–F 8–6, Sa 9–1; coin laundry; cobbler; hospital; Angel Urgent Care Center, (828) 369-4427, M–F 8–6, Sa–Su 10–4; pharmacy; veterinarian; banks with ATM; City Taxi, (828) 369-5042 until 6 p.m., after 6 p.m. by appointment; visitors center, (866) 372-5546, M–Sa 9–5. ■ *Shuttles:* Roadrunner Driving Services, (706) 201-7719, <where2@mac.com>.

**Siler Bald Shelter** (1959)—Sleeps 8. Privy. Located 0.5 mile on a blue-blazed loop. Food-hoist cables available. Water source is 80 yards down a blue-blazed trail from the shelter.

**Wayah Bald**—John B. Byrne Memorial Tower. The stone observation tower at the summit of Wayah Bald (5,342 ft.) was built in 1937 by the CCC and renovated in 1983. Byrne was the supervisor of the Nantahala National Forest who first proposed the route of the Appalachian Trail in this area. Wayah is Cherokee for "wolf."

**Wayah Shelter** (2007)—Nantahala-type shelter sleeps 8 with overhang for cooking shelves and seating. Privy. Five tentsites and fire ring near shelter. Water source is Little Laurel Creek, 600 feet west of A.T. on blue-blazed trail. This shelter was built by NHC in memory of Ann and Larry McDuff, thru-hikers and ALDHA members who were killed about a year apart in eerily similar accidents, hit by vehicles while riding bikes near home.

**Cold Spring Shelter** (1933)—Sleeps 6. Privy. Food-hoist cables available. Shelter built by the CCC. Tentsites are reached *via* a trail on the east side of the Trail 200 yards north on the A.T. Water source is 5 yards in front of the shelter.

**Wesser Bald**—Formerly a fire tower, the structure atop Wesser Bald is now an observation deck offering panoramic views. The Great Smoky Mountains and Fontana Lake dominate the view to the north.

**Wesser Bald Shelter** (1994)—Sleeps 8. No privy. This was the first of the "Nantahala design" shelters. Food-hoist cables available. Tentsites available in clearing where the blue-blaze heads to the shelter. Water source is a spring 0.1 mile south on the A.T., then 75 yards on a blue-blazed trail.

**Rufus Morgan Shelter** (rebuilt 1989)—Sleeps 6. No privy. Located in a small cove, this shelter is named after the Nantahala club's founder. The water source is a stream across the A.T. from the shelter.

**U.S. 19/Nantahala River/Nantahala Outdoor Center**—At U.S. 19, the A.T. passes through the Nantahala Outdoor Center (NOC), (828) 488-2175 or (800) 232-7238, <www.noc.com>, an outdoor-adventure center with many services for backpackers; call ahead for shuttles. Between the store and River's End Restaurant, the A.T. crosses a pedestrian bridge over the Nantahala River. ■ *Lodging:* NOC, office hours Sep–Apr 8–5, May–Aug 8–9; after hours, go to Base Camp (behind Relia's Garden Restaurant), a winterized hostel that may be full on weekends, $15 for bunk space; motel rooms $49–$89. NOC Nantahala Inn, $89D, satellite TV, pets in select units. ■ *Groceries:* Wesser General Store (short-term resupply), M–F 8 a.m.–10 p.m., Sa–Su 11–11. ■ *Restaurants:* River's End Restaurant (8–7) serves B/L/D; Relia's Garden and Sloe Joe's Café, L (outdoors), open seasonally. ■ *Outfitter:* NOC Outfitters (short-term resupply), 8–8, offers backpacking gear, Coleman and alcohol fuel by the ounce, Esbit and canisters, ATM, stamps, ATC publications. Pay phone, coin laundry with detergent (after-hours change and detergent not available), restroom, and shower with towel $3 (except with bunkroom) are located on the southern side of U.S. 19. NOC accepts USPS, UPS, and FedEx packages sent to 13077 Hwy. 19W, Bryson City, NC 28713. Check with the front desk; packages must be marked "Hold for A.T. Hiker." NOC can ship packages; extra charge on weekends.

   **South** 1 mile to *Camping:* Lost Mine Campground, (828) 488-6445, across from NOC on Silvermine Road, sites $15 Apr–Oct, showers, pay phone, dogs on leash.

   **East** 1 mile to *Groceries:* Nantahala Food Mart with ATM (short-term resupply), daily 7 a.m.–9 p.m. ■ *Lodging:* Carolina Outfitters Cottages, (800) 468-7238, <www.carolinaoutfitters.com>, check-in at Nantahala Food Mart, $50D, $10EAP, kitchen, no pets, shuttle to/from Trail. ■ *Camping:* Nantahala Wesser Campground, (828) 488-8708, located near Nantahala Food Market on Wesser Rd; turn right at gem-mine sign; tentsite $7PP, showers, open Apr–Oct.

   **East** 13 miles on U.S. 19 to **Bryson City, N.C. [P.O. ZIP 28713: M–F 8:30–5, Sa 10–12; (828) 488-3481].** Bryson City is a large town with many services, including Ingles Supermarket (long-term resupply), pharmacy, coin laundry, several restaurants, banks with ATM, Western Union, hospital, and several hotels.

**Whitewater Rafting**—The Nantahala marks the northbound-er's first chance at Trail-side whitewater rafting. The French Broad River in Hot Springs, N.C., and the Nolichucky River in Erwin, Tenn., are also whitewater hot-spots. Guided tours on the Nantahala are available through NOC for about $25 on nonpeak days, but you can rent a raft or "ducky" for less, with shuttles to the put-in point upstream included. Mountain biking and horseback riding also available.

**Smoky Mountains Hiking Club**—SMHC maintains the 101 miles between the Nantahala River and Davenport Gap. Correspon-dence should be sent to the SMHC, P.O. Box 1454, Knoxville, TN 37901; <www.smhclub.org>.

**Sassafras Gap Shelter** (2002)—Sleeps 14. Privy. Located in a ravine 100 yards in on a blue-blazed side trail, this wood-framed shelter features a covered porch and benches. Water source is a reliable spring in front of the shelter.

**N.C. 143/Stecoah Gap**—A good spring can be found by following the paved road west 200 feet to an over-grown logging road. Spring is located down the logging road on the left.

**Brown Fork Gap Shelter** (1996)—Sleeps 6. Privy. Constructed by the SMHC, Konnarock Crew, and the USFS. Water source is a reliable spring to the right of the shelter.

**Cable Gap Shelter** (1939/1988)—Sleeps 6. Privy. Shelter origi-nally built by the CCC. The water source is a reliable spring in front of the shelter.

**Walker Gap**—The Yellow Creek Trail leads 2.5 miles west to Fontana Village. However, it is a poorly marked, difficult short-cut to the resort.

**N.C. 28/Fontana Dam—East** 5 miles to *Groceries:* Friendly Fields General Store (short-term resupply), 7–7 year-round, phone, Coleman and alcohol fuel, snacks and baked goods, hot sandwiches.

**East** 6 miles to *Lodging:* The Hike Inn, (828) 479-3677, <www.thehikeinn.com>, <hikeinn@graham.main.nc.us>. A hikers-only inn, owned and operated by Jeff and Nancy Hoch. Open Feb 15–July 10, Sep 1–Dec 1, other dates by reservation only. For pick-up, continue north on the A.T. to the Fontana Dam Visitors Center (see below), and call from the pay phone. Thru-hikers, call from NOC or Hot Springs for reservations. Five rooms with max 2 per room. No credit cards. Thru-hik-ers (check in by 5 p.m., check-out 9 a.m. firm), $50S, $55D. Rate includes shuttle to and from dam, one load of laundry, evening shuttle to Robbinsville for dinner and supplies. Section-hikers,

$40S/D (room only). Packages accepted for guests only c/o Hike Inn, 3204 Fontana Rd., Fontana Dam, NC 28733. Shuttles, slack-pack, Coleman and alcohol fuel. Internet access available at public library.

**West** 2 miles to Fontana Village Resort. **Fontana Dam, N.C. [P.O. ZIP 28733: M–F 8:30–12 & 12:30–4:30, Sa 10–12; (828) 498-2315],** is located 2 miles from Fontana Dam within the Fontana Village Resort. *Please note: Some services may close or be under reduced hours during off-season, and supplies are limited; most services available by Apr 1.* Constructed in 1946 for TVA workers building Fontana Dam, the village is now a seasonal recreational area and resort using many of the original buildings.
■ *Lodging:* Fontana Lodge, <www.fontanavillage.com>, (800) 849-2258, $69D, EAP no charge; cabins also available.
■ *Groceries:* Fontana General Store (short-term resupply).
■ *Outfitter:* Hazel Creek Outfitter, limited hiker gear and all stove fuels. ■ *Other services:* restaurant, ATM, Internet access, coin laundry, detergent available at outfitters 50¢, ice cream/soda fountain (open in May), mountain-bike rentals, and fitness center. Shuttle to and from Fontana Marina for $2; dial 265 from the boat-dock pay phone. Backcountry permits available.

**Fontana Dam Shelter** (1982)—Sleeps 24. Restroom and water located at shelter. Known as the "Fontana Hilton," this spacious shelter is located 0.3 mile south of the dam on TVA land. Pay phone and shower facilities are located at the dam; see below.

**Fontana Dam**—At 480 feet, Fontana Dam is the highest dam in the eastern United States. This facility offers a visitors center with restrooms and shower that is normally open May–Nov, 9–7. If the national terrorism-alert level is high (red), public facilities at the dam will close, and hikers must follow a blue-blazed route over the Little Tennessee River below the dam.

*"Happiness is found along the way, not at the end of the Trail."*
—NOLAND HISEY (AT '89)

*Clingmans Dome, GSMNP. Photograph by Peter Rajaniemi.*

# Great Smoky Mountains National Park

| Miles from Katahdin | Features | Services | Elev. | Miles from Springer |
|---|---|---|---|---|
| 2,012.3 | Fontana Dam Visitors Ctr | R, sh, w | 1,700 | 163.9 |
| 2,010.9 | Little Tennessee River, Fontana Dam; southern boundary, Great Smoky Mtns. National Park | R | 1,800 | 165.3 |
| 2,007.9 | Shuckstack | | 3,800 | 168.3 |
| 2,006.7 | Birch Spring Gap | C, w | 3,680 | 169.5 |
| 2,004.4 | Doe Knob | | 4,520 | 171.8 |
| 2,003.0 | Ekaneetlee Gap | w | 3,842 | 173.2 |
| 2,001.3 | **Mollies Ridge Shelter** *11.3mS; 2.5mN* | S, w | 4,570 | 174.9 |
| 2,001.2 | Devils Tater Patch | | 4,775 | 175.0 |
| 1,999.6 | Little Abrams Gap | | 4,120 | 176.6 |
| 1,998.8 | **Russell Field Shelter** *2.5mS; 3.1mN* | S, w | 4,360 | 177.4 |
| 1,995.9 | Eagle Creek Trail to **Spence Field Shelter** *3.1mS; 6.5mN;* Bote Mtn Trail | E–0.2m S, w | 4,915 | 180.3 |
| 1,994.7 | Rocky Top | | 5,440 | 181.5 |
| 1,994.1 | Thunderhead (east peak) | | 5,527 | 182.1 |
| 1,993.8 | Beechnut Gap | w | 4,920 | 182.4 |
| 1,993.1 | Mineral Gap | | 5,030 | 183.1 |
| 1,990.7 | Sugar Tree Gap | | 4,435 | 185.5 |
| 1,989.6 | **Derrick Knob Shelter** *6.5mS; 5.5mN* | S, w | 4,880 | 186.6 |
| 1,989.4 | Sams Gap | w | 4,995 | 186.8 |
| 1,986.8 | Buckeye Gap | w | 4,817 | 189.4 |
| 1,984.1 | **Silers Bald Shelter** *5.5mS; 1.7mN* | S, w | 5,460 | 192.1 |
| 1,983.9 | Silers Bald | | 5,607 | 192.3 |
| 1,982.4 | **Double Spring Gap Shelter** *1.7mS; 6.8mN* | S, w | 5,505 | 193.8 |
| 1,979.9 | Clingmans Dome | E–0.5m R, w | 6,643 | 196.3 |
| 1,978.3 | Mt. Love | | 6,446 | 197.9 |
| 1,976.1 | **Mt. Collins Shelter** *6.8mS; 8mN* | W–0.5m S, w | 5,870 | 200.1 |
| 1,973.3 | Indian Gap | R | 5,286 | 202.9 |

| Miles from Katahdin | Features | Services | Elev. | Miles from Springer |
|---|---|---|---|---|
| 1,971.6 | U.S. 441, Newfound Gap **Gatlinburg, TN 37738** | R, w (W–15m PO, G, L, M, O, D, f) (E–18m PO, G, L, M, D, f) | 5,045 | 204.6 |
| 1,968.9 | Boulevard Trail to Mt. LeConte | W–5m L, M | 5,695 | 207.3 |
| 1,968.6 | **Icewater Spring Shelter** *8mS; 7.8mN* | S, w | 5,920 | 207.6 |
| 1,967.8 | Charlies Bunion | | 5,905 | 208.4 |
| 1,965.8 | Porters Gap, The Sawteeth | | 5,577 | 210.4 |
| 1,962.5 | Bradley's View | | 5,200 | 213.7 |
| 1,961.2 | **Peck's Corner Shelter** *7.8mS; 5.6mN* | w (E–0.4m S, w) | 5,280 | 215.0 |
| 1,958.5 | Mt. Sequoyah | | 6,069 | 217.7 |
| 1,957.0 | Mt. Chapman | | 6,417 | 219.2 |
| 1,956.0 | **Tri-Corner Knob Shelter** *5.6mS; 7.7mN* | S, w | 5,920 | 220.2 |
| 1,954.8 | Guyot Spur | | 6,360 | 221.4 |
| 1,954.2 | Guyot Spring | w | 6,150 | 222.0 |
| 1,954.1 | Mt. Guyot Side Trail | | 6,395 | 222.1 |
| 1,952.2 | Snake Den Ridge Trail | | 5,600 | 224.0 |
| 1,948.8 | Cosby Knob | | 5,150 | 227.4 |
| 1,948.3 | **Cosby Knob Shelter** *7.7mS; 7.1mN* | S, w | 4,700 | 227.9 |
| 1,945.5 | Side Trail to Mt. Cammerer Fire Tower | W–0.6m | 5,000 | 230.7 |
| 1,945.0 | Spring | w | 4,300 | 231.2 |
| 1,943.4 | Spring | w | 3,700 | 232.8 |
| 1,941.2 | **Davenport Gap Shelter** *7.1mS; 10.7mN* | S, w | 2,600 | 235.0 |
| 1,940.3 | Davenport Gap, Tenn. 32, N.C. 284; eastern boundary, Great Smoky Mtns. National Park | R (E–1.3m Ranger Station; 2.3m C) | 1,975 | 235.9 |

Established in 1934, the Smokies is the most visited of the traditional national parks; for this reason, it is especially important to practice Leave No Trace in this area. The highest elevation on the A.T. is here at Clingmans Dome at 6,643 feet. The Smokies also has the most rainfall and snowfall on the A.T. in the South, and many hikers are caught off-guard by the snow and cold temperatures that the high elevation means. On the other hand, extreme drought in 2007 left many water sources extraordinarily low or dry.

**Great Smoky Mountains National Park**—<www.nps.gov/grsm>. The Trail through the park officially begins for northbounders on the northern side of Fontana Dam; for southbounders, Davenport Gap is the beginning. In recent years, the park has hosted more than nine million visitors annually. Home to the most diverse forest in North America, the park includes more than 100 species of trees, 1,570 species of flowering plants, 60 species of mammals, more than 25 different salamanders, and 2,000 varieties of mushrooms.

*Backcountry Permits*—Backcountry permits must be obtained before entering the park. A self-registration facility is located near the pay phone at the Fontana Dam visitors center (page 29). Forms and a deposit box are also available at the "Fontana Hilton" for northbounders. Southbounders—if you do not get a permit at the USFS office in Hot Springs, you must trek 1.3 miles east on Tenn. 32 from Davenport Gap to the park's Big Creek Ranger Station. Section-hikers (considered to be anyone not beginning and ending a hike 50 miles outside the park) can make reservations by calling the GSMNP Reservations Office at (865) 436-1231. Anyone caught without a permit will be issued a $125 ticket!

*Human Waste and Privies*—In past years, the park's administration shunned privies at backcountry facilities. Instead, "toilet areas" were designated where backpackers are supposed to dig cat holes and bury their waste. In the 1990s, a privy-building campaign, underwritten by ATC and SMHC, resulted in new facilities at the more heavily used shelters. Spence Field, Double Spring Gap, Tri-Corner Knob, Pecks Corner, Mt. Collins, and Icewater Spring shelters now have moldering privies. Although privies mainly provide an aesthetically acceptable way to deal with many hikers' refusal to use proper Leave No Trace methods, they are costly to maintain and a management last resort. The best decision is to do your business away from the shelter area before you get to camp or after you leave. Pick a spot far from any trails and 200 feet or more from any water, and practice Leave No Trace methods.

*Horses*—Within the park, half of the A.T. is open to horseback riding; horse users may also share A.T. shelters. SMHC and ATC have made a concerted effort to resolve issues with the horse users, who have helped with major rehabilitation and other projects along the Trail in that half.

*Bears*—Between 400 and 600 bears reside in the park. They become more active in the early spring and remain active through the fall. Over the years, they have developed a taste for the food humans carry. Following a few simple guidelines can help keep bears and other animals away from people and safe within the park. Be sure to hang food on the provided bear-bag system, and do not feed or leave food for these wild creatures to eat. Many shelters no longer have chain-link fences to keep bears out. Whenever possible, eat away from the shelters.

*Dogs*—Dogs are not permitted on trails in the park. Hikers violating this rule will be fined up to $500. Those hiking with dogs should arrange to board their pets. Several kennels provide this service, including Loving Care Kennels, (865) 453-2028, in Pigeon Forge, Tenn., near Gatlinburg. Owner Lida O'Neill will provide shopping services, as well as accept mail drops sent to 3779 Tinker Hollow Rd., Pigeon Forge, TN 37863. She will also pick up and drop off your dog at Fontana Dam and Davenport Gap. Cost is $250 for one dog, $350 for two dogs, or $400 for 3 dogs. Rippling Water Kennels, <www.ripplingwaterkennel.com>, (828) 488-2091, will pick up, board, and deliver pets for $225, up to 7 days; $50 deposit, reservations necessary.

*Pests and Disease*—At Clingmans Dome and throughout the park, you will witness changes in the Smokies' ecosystem. The most obvious has been the death of conifers at higher elevations. Atmospheric pollution weakens the trees, which makes it easier for the balsam woolly adelgid to attack and eventually kill the park's Fraser firs. The small, waxy insects attack the firs, which then overreact to the feeding aldegids, clogging their own transport tissues. Trees die within five years of infestation. Other pests and diseases affecting the park's ecosystem include chestnut blight, southern pine beetle, hemlock woolly adelgid, and dogwood anthracnose.

*Air Pollution*—This is one of the Smokies' most conspicuous problems. Pollution can drop visibility from 93 to 22 miles on an otherwise clear day. Ironically, this effect enhances sunset colors. Along with sulfur, nitrogen provides the basis for acid deposition, which includes acid rain. Ozone can make breathing difficult and causes visible damage to black cherry, milkweed, and thirty other species of plants in the park. The park's ozone, nitrogen, and sulfur levels are among the nation's highest and often remain high longer than in nearby urban communities. Much of this pollution comes from distant cities and power plants to the west.

*Shelter Renovation/Replacement*—The SMHC and the ATC are working to rebuild or replace all the shelters in the Smokies. Double Spring Gap may be done this year; work has been completed at Mollies Ridge, Spence Field, Derrick Knob, Silers Bald, Icewater Springs, Pecks Corner, Tricorner Knob, Cosby Knob, and Davenport Gap shelters. To improve shelter sanitation, the rebuilt shelters do not have chain-link fencing separating shelter users from park wildlife. Keep a clean camp!

*Shelter Policy*—Park regulations require that you stay in a shelter. While other backpackers must make reservations to use backcountry shelters, thru-hikers are exempt from this park regulation, and from Mar 15 to Jun 15, four spaces at each A.T. shelter are reserved for thru-hikers. If the shelter is occupied by reservation and four thru-hikers, however, additional thru-hikers should tent close by and use the bear cables. Because only thru-hikers are permitted to tent-camp at the shelters, the burden is on them to make room inside shelters for other campers who have reserved space.

*Shelters South of Newfound Gap*—Seven shelters and a campsite are located between the Little Tennessee River (Fontana Dam) and Newfound Gap.

**Birch Spring Campsite**—Former shelter site with water, bear cables, and tentpads.

**Mollies Ridge Shelter** (1961/2003)—Sleeps 12. No privy. Food-hoist cables available. Legend says the area was named for a Cherokee maiden who froze to death looking for a lost hunter and that her ghost still haunts the ridge. Water source is a somewhat reliable spring 200 yards to the right of the shelter.

**Russell Field Shelter** (1961)—Sleeps 14. No privy. This section of Trail is popular with riders. Food-hoist cables available. Water source is a spring 150 yards down the Russell Field Trail toward Cades Cove. A short walk beyond the spring is an open, grassy area with views into Cades Cove; the Russell Gregory family grazed stock here in the 1800s.

**Spence Field Shelter** (1963/2005)—Sleeps 12. Privy. Shelter is located 0.2 mile east on the Eagle Creek Trail. Food-hoist cables available. This section of Trail is popular with riders and frequently is visited by bears. Spence Field, to the north of the shelter, offers azaleas, blueberries, and open views into North Carolina and Tennessee from the largest grassy bald in the Smokies. James Spence cleared 100 acres here in the 1830s for cattle grazing. Water source is a reliable spring 150 yards down the Eagle Creek Trail.

**Derrick Knob Shelter** (1961)—Sleeps 12. No privy. Food-hoist cables available. Shelter site is the former location of Crede Hall's herder cabin. Water source is a reliable spring near the shelter.

**Silers Bald Shelter** (1961/2001)—Sleeps 12. No privy. Food-hoist cables available. Named for Jesse Siler, who once grazed stock here. The increasingly overgrown bald 0.3 mile north of the shelter offers views of Clingmans Dome and sunsets over Cove Mountain. Water source is to the right of the shelter; a trail leads 75 yards to a reliable spring.

**Double Spring Gap Shelter** (1963)—Sleeps 12. Privy. Food-hoist cables available. Two unfortunate hikers were killed by lightning inside this shelter in 1980. Gap was named to indicate the existence of two springs, one on each side of the state line and both now unreliable. The better water source is on the North Carolina side, 15 yards from the crest; second source is on the Tennessee side, 35 yards from the crest.

**Clingmans Dome**—At 6,643 feet, this is the highest point on the A.T. There are no feet-on-the-ground views from the tree-clad summit, but the observation tower provides 360-degree views. The summit is usually busy; a park road leads to within 0.5 mile of the tower. Restroom and water are available near the day-hiker parking lot. From here to the northern end of the park, Fraser firs and red spruce are now dying *en masse*—a dramatic change from the southernmost 30 miles of the park.

**Mt. Collins Shelter** (1960)—Sleeps 12. Privy. Food-hoist cables available. Nestled in spruce thicket, this mountain is named for Robert Collins, who guided geographer Arnold Guyot's explorations in the Smokies in the 1850s. Water source is a small spring 200 yards beyond the shelter on the Sugarland Mountain Trail.

**U.S. 441/Newfound Gap**—The only road crossing along the Trail in the Smokies. Great Smoky Mountain National Park shuttle, (828) 497-5296, makes regularly scheduled stops at Newfound Gap, Gatlinburg, Tenn., and Cherokee, N.C. (May–Dec); hiker drop-off/pick-up at any GSMNP pullover by arrangement; $12 round-trip cash or travelers checks, $7 one-way; purchase tickets from driver or at welcome center on Tsali Blvd./U.S. 441N. A North Carolina state grant to the Cherokee makes the shuttle possible.

**East** 18 miles to **Cherokee, N.C., [P.O. ZIP 28719: M-F 9-4:30, Sa 10-11:30; (828) 497-3891]**, <www.cherokee-nc.com>, home of the Eastern Band of the Cherokee and its reservation, with more than 40 motels and most major services. Attractions include the Museum of the Cherokee Indian, Unto These Hills Mountainside Theatre, and Qualla Arts & Crafts center.

**West** 15 miles to the resort town of **Gatlinburg, Tenn. [P.O. ZIP 37738: M–F 9–5, Sa 10–12; (865) 436-3229],** <www.gatlinburg.com>, with most major services. Most current information on hiker-friendly services is available at the Happy Hiker or Smoky Mountain Outfitters. There's plenty of traffic through Newfound Gap, with its large parking lot, shuttle (see above), and scenic overlook; usually an easy hitch into Gatlinburg. Once in town, a trolley service, Nov–Mar 10–6, Apr–Oct 8–12, takes you to most services and costs a quarter. ■ *Lodging:* Nearly 100 hotels and motels are in Gatlinburg. ■ *Restaurants:* More than 70, including Shoney's, with AYCE B and soup/salad bar, and most fast-food chains. ■ *Groceries:* Battle's Food Center and Food City (both long-term resupply). ■ *Outfitters:* The Happy Hiker, (800) HIKER01 or (865) 436-6000, <www.happyhiker.com>, open 9–5 daily, fuel and denatured alcohol by the ounce, holds packages and will ship packages for you *via* UPS or other means. Send packages to the Happy Hiker, 905 River Rd., Suite 5, Gatlinburg, TN 37738. To get to the Happy Hiker, turn left at the first stop light as you enter town, then walk one block to the small shopping center. Smoky Mountain Outfitters, (865) 430-2267, 9–6 M–Sa, 9–5 Su, canister fuel, white gas, and denatured alcohol by the ounce, holds mail drops, 453 Brookside Village Way, Gatlinburg, TN 37738. Take the "blue trolley" to Winery Square. Brookside Village Way runs through the square. ■ *Other services:* Banks with ATM, and doctor. ■ *Dog shuttle/kennel:* A Walk in the Woods, <www.awalkinthewoods.com>, (865) 436-8283, dog-shuttling and boarding.

**Boulevard Trail**—This side trail, located 2.7 miles north of Newfound Gap, leads 5 miles to the summit of Mt. LeConte. A shelter and LeConte Lodge, (865) 429-5704, <www.lecontelodge.com>, are located at the top (reservations required; $93PP includes B/D). The 10-mile round-trip to this spectacular mountain may be worth it, if you have the time.

*Shelters North of Newfound Gap*—GSMNP has five shelters between Newfound Gap and Davenport Gap.

**Icewater Spring Shelter** (1963/1999)—Sleeps 12. Privy. Food-hoist cables available. Water source for this heavily used shelter is 50 yards north on the A.T.

**Charlies Bunion**—Views of Mt. LeConte to the west. It got its name on a hike in 1929, when Charlie Conner and Horace Kephart, an A.T. pioneer and famed writer/conservationist of the period, discovered this feature, created by a landslide after a disastrous rain the same year. The two decided the rocky outcropping stuck out like a bunion on Charlie's foot. The narrow path was blasted out by the National Park Service.

**Pecks Corner Shelter** (1958/2000)—Sleeps 12. Privy. Food-hoist cables available. Follow the Hughes Ridge Trail 0.4 mile to a junction with the side trail to the shelter. This shelter gets its name from a corner marker for two state land grants to the Peck family. Water source is in front of the shelter 50 yards.

**Tri-Corner Knob Shelter** (1961/2004)—Sleeps 12. Privy. Located on the North Carolina side of the A.T., this is the most remote shelter in the GSMNP. The water source for this shelter is a reliable spring 10 yards in front of the shelter. In wet weather, this shelter may be a very soggy place.

**Cosby Knob Shelter** (1959)—Sleeps 12. Privy. Shelter is located 100 yards east down a side trail. Food-hoist cables available. Water source is a reliable spring 35 yards downhill and in front of the shelter.

**Mt. Cammerer Side Trail**—This trail to the west leads 0.6 mile to the Mt. Cammerer firetower, a historic stone-and-timber structure originally built in 1939 by the CCC and rebuilt in 1994. Panoramic views from its platform.

**Davenport Gap Shelter** (1961/1998)—Sleeps 12. No privy. Named for William Davenport, who surveyed the state line in 1821. Your last, or first, GSMNP A.T. shelter, dubbed the "Smokies Sheraton." Water source is a spring to the left of the shelter.

**Tenn. 32, N.C. 284/Davenport Gap—East** 1.3 miles to Big Creek Ranger Station, (828) 486-5910, with phone and self-registration backcountry permits (southbounders—see note on page 33 about registration); 1 mile farther to the station's seasonal campsites, $12 per site, no showers. The Chestnut Branch Trail leads out from the ranger station and, in two miles, meets the A.T. one mile south of Davenport Gap Shelter.

# North Carolina & the Tennessee Border

| Miles from Katahdin | Features | Services | Elev. | Miles from Springer |
|---|---|---|---|---|
| 1,940.3 | Davenport Gap, Tenn. 32, N.C. 284; eastern boundary, Great Smoky Mtns. National Park | R (E–1.3m Ranger Station; 2.3m C) | 1,975 | 235.9 |
| 1,939.0 | State Line Branch | C, w | 1,600 | 237.2 |
| 1,938.8 | Pigeon River | R | 1,400 | 237.4 |
| 1,938.4 | I-40 | R | 1,500 | 237.8 |
| 1,937.9 | Green Corner Rd | R (W–0.1m H, G, cl, sh, f, @) | 1,800 | 238.3 |
| 1,935.6 | Painter Branch | C, w | 3,100 | 240.6 |
| 1,934.7 | Spanish Oak Gap | | 3,730 | 241.5 |
| 1,933.2 | Snowbird Mtn | | 4,263 | 243.0 |
| 1,932.7 | Campsite | C, w | 4,100 | 243.5 |
| 1,930.7 | Deep Gap, **Groundhog Creek Shelter** *10.7mS; 8.4mN* | E–0.2m S, w | 2,850 | 245.5 |
| 1,927.8 | Brown Gap | R, C, w | 3,500 | 248.4 |
| 1,925.1 | Max Patch Rd; N.C. 1182 | R | 4,380 | 251.1 |
| 1,924.3 | Max Patch Summit | | 4,629 | 251.9 |
| 1,922.5 | **Roaring Fork Shelter** *8.4mS; 4.9mN* | S, w | 3,950 | 253.7 |
| 1,918.9 | Lemon Gap, N.C. 1182, Tenn. 107 | R | 3,550 | 257.3 |
| 1,917.6 | **Walnut Mtn Shelter** *4.9mS; 9.9mN* | S, w | 4,260 | 258.6 |
| 1,915.2 | Bluff Mtn | | 4,686 | 261.0 |
| 1,913.6 | Big Rock Spring | w | 3,730 | 262.6 |
| 1,911.1 | Garenflo Gap | R | 2,500 | 265.1 |
| 1,907.7 | **Deer Park Mtn Shelter** *9.9mS; 14.2mN* | S, w | 2,330 | 268.5 |
| 1,904.5 | U.S. 25 & 70, N.C. 209 **Hot Springs, NC 28743** | R, PO, H, C, G, L, M, O, cl, sh, f, @ | 1,326 | 271.7 |
| 1,903.1 | Lovers Leap Rock | | 1,820 | 273.1 |
| 1,901.2 | Pump Gap | | 2,130 | 275.0 |
| 1,899.6 | Campsite | C, w | 2,490 | 276.6 |
| 1,898.6 | U.S. 25 & 70 overpass, Tanyard Gap | R | 2,270 | 277.6 |
| 1,896.3 | Rich Mtn Fire Tower Side Trail | C, w | 3,600 | 279.9 |
| 1,895.2 | Hurricane Gap | R | 2,900 | 281.0 |

| Miles from Katahdin | Features | Services | Elev. | Miles from Springer |
|---|---|---|---|---|
| 1,893.5 | **Spring Mtn Shelter** *14.2mS; 8.6mN* | S, w | 3,300 | 282.7 |
| 1,892.0 | Spring | w | 3,190 | 284.2 |
| 1,889.8 | Allen Gap, N.C. 208, Tenn. 70 | R, w | 2,234 | 286.4 |
| 1,888.2 | Log Cabin Drive | R (W–0.7m C, L, G, sh, f) | 2,560 | 288.0 |
| 1,884.9 | **Little Laurel Shelter** *8.6mS; 6.8mN* | S, w | 3,620 | 291.3 |
| 1,883.6 | Camp Creek Bald, side trail to Fire Tower | R | 4,750 | 292.6 |
| 1,881.9 | Spring | w | 4,390 | 294.3 |
| 1,881.6 | Blackstack Cliffs | | 4,420 | 294.6 |
| 1,880.6 | Big Firescald Knob | w | 4,360 | 295.6 |
| 1,878.1 | **Jerry Cabin Shelter** *6.8mS; 5.9mN* | S, w | 4,150 | 298.1 |
| 1,876.2 | Big Butt | C | 4,750 | 300.0 |
| 1,874.9 | Spring | w | 4,480 | 301.3 |
| 1,874.6 | Shelton Graves | | 4,490 | 301.6 |
| 1,872.2 | **Flint Mtn Shelter** *5.9mS; 8.9mN* | S, w | 3,570 | 304.0 |
| 1,871.3 | Campsite | C, w | 3,400 | 304.9 |
| 1,869.5 | Devil Fork Gap; N.C. 212 | R | 3,100 | 306.7 |
| 1,869.0 | Rector Laurel Rd | R | 2,960 | 307.2 |
| 1,866.2 | Frozen Knob | | 4,579 | 310.0 |
| 1,865.6 | Big Flat | C, w | 4,160 | 310.6 |
| 1,864.6 | Rice Gap | R | 3,800 | 311.6 |
| 1,863.4 | **Hogback Ridge Shelter** *8.9mS; 10.2mN* | E–0.1m S; 0.3m w | 4,255 | 312.8 |
| 1,862.8 | High Rock | | 4,460 | 313.4 |
| 1,861.0 | Sams Gap, U.S. 23, I-26 | R | 3,850 | 315.2 |
| 1,860.3 | Springs | w | 4,000 | 315.9 |
| 1,858.7 | Street Gap | | 4,100 | 317.5 |
| 1,857.3 | Low Gap | C, w | 4,300 | 318.9 |
| 1,855.3 | Spring | w | 4,850 | 320.9 |
| 1,854.5 | Big Bald | (C, w N on A.T. 0.2m then W 0.3m) | 5,516 | 321.7 |
| 1,854.2 | Big Stamp | W–0.3m C, w | 5,300 | 322.0 |
| 1,853.3 | **Bald Mtn Shelter** *10.2mS; 10.6mN* | S, w | 5,100 | 322.9 |
| 1,852.9 | Campsite | C, w | 4,890 | 323.3 |
| 1,851.9 | Little Bald | | 5,220 | 324.3 |

| Miles from Katahdin | Features | Services | Elev. | Miles from Springer |
|---|---|---|---|---|
| 1,849.9 | Whistling Gap | C, w | 3,650 | 326.3 |
| 1,849.6 | Trail to High Rocks | | 4,100 | 326.6 |
| 1,848.1 | Campsite | C, w | 3,490 | 328.1 |
| 1,846.6 | Spivey Gap, U.S. 19W | R | 3,200 | 329.6 |
| 1,847.0 | Ogelsby Branch | w | 3,800 | 329.2 |
| 1,842.9 | Spring | w | 3,300 | 333.3 |
| 1,842.7 | **No Business Knob Shelter** *10.6mS; 10.5mN* | S, w | 3,180 | 333.5 |
| 1,840.3 | Temple Hill Gap | | 2,850 | 335.9 |
| 1,836.4 | Chestoa Bridge, Nolichucky River **Erwin, TN 37650** | R, H, C, O, cl, f, @ (W–1.3m L, @, cl; 3.8m PO, C, H, G, M, L, D, V, cl, sh, f, @) | 1,700 | 339.8 |
| 1,835.1 | Nolichucky River Valley | R | 1,780 | 341.1 |
| 1,832.2 | **Curley Maple Gap Shelter** *10.5mS; 12.2mN* | S, w | 3,070 | 344.0 |
| 1,828.1 | Indian Grave Gap, Tenn. 395, N.C. 197 | R (W–7m Erwin, Tenn.) | 3,350 | 348.1 |
| 1,827.0 | USFS 230 | R | 3,980 | 349.2 |
| 1,825.8 | Beauty Spot | | 4,437 | 350.4 |
| 1,825.3 | Beauty Spot Gap | R, C, w | 4,120 | 350.9 |
| 1,824.3 | Deep Gap | C, w | 4,100 | 351.9 |
| 1,823.7 | USFS 230 | R | 4,660 | 352.5 |
| 1,822.7 | Unaka Mtn | | 5,180 | 353.5 |
| 1,822.4 | Spring | w | 4,750 | 353.8 |
| 1,821.0 | Low Gap | w | 3,900 | 355.2 |
| 1,820.0 | **Cherry Gap Shelter** *12.2mS; 8.9mN* | S, w | 3,900 | 356.2 |
| 1,818.5 | Little Bald Knob | | 4,459 | 357.7 |
| 1,817.3 | Iron Mtn Gap, Tenn. 107, N.C. 226 **Unicoi, TN 37692** | R (E–3m G, f) (W–4.7m G, M; 10.3m PO, G, M, D) | 3,723 | 358.9 |
| 1,816.0 | Stream | w | 3,950 | 360.2 |
| 1,813.1 | Greasy Creek Gap | R (E–0.6m H, G, C, M, sh, f, @) (W–0.2m w) | 4,034 | 363.1 |
| 1,812.3 | Campsite | C, w | 4,110 | 363.9 |
| 1,811.2 | **Clyde Smith Shelter** *8.9mS; 6.5mN* | W–0.1m S, w | 4,400 | 365.0 |
| 1,810.3 | Little Rock Knob | | 4,918 | 365.9 |
| 1,808.1 | Hughes Gap | R | 4,040 | 368.1 |
| 1,806.3 | Ash Gap | C, w | 5,350 | 369.9 |

| Miles from Katahdin | Features | Services | Elev. | Miles from Springer |
|---|---|---|---|---|
| 1,805.5 | Trail to Roan High Bluff, Rhododendron Gardens | R, w | 6,200 | 370.7 |
| 1,804.8 | **Roan High Knob Shelter** *6.5mS; 4.8mN* | S, w | 6,275 | 371.4 |
| 1,803.3 | Carvers Gap, Tenn. 143, N.C. 261 | R, w | 5,512 | 372.9 |
| 1,801.4 | Trail to Grassy Ridge | E–0.5m C, w | 5,770 | 374.8 |
| 1,800.0 | **Stan Murray Shelter** *4.8mS; 2mN* | S, w | 5,050 | 376.2 |
| 1,798.3 | Yellow Mtn Gap, **Overmountain Shelter** *2mS; 8.5mN* | C (E–0.2m w; 0.3m S) | 4,550 | 377.9 |
| 1,796.7 | Little Hump Mtn | | 5,459 | 379.5 |
| 1,795.9 | Bradley Gap | C, w | 4,950 | 380.3 |
| 1,795.0 | Hump Mtn | | 5,587 | 381.2 |
| 1,792.6 | Doll Flats, N.C.–Tenn. State Line | C, w | 4,600 | 383.6 |
| 1,790.2 | Spring | w | 3,060 | 386.0 |
| 1,790.1 | **Apple House Shelter** *8.5mS; 8.7mN* | S, w | 3,000 | 386.1 |
| 1,789.6 | U.S. 19E **Elk Park, NC 08622; Newland, NC 28657; Roan Mtn, TN 37687** | R (E–0.5m M; 2.5m PO, G, M; 9m PO, G, M, f, cl, @) (W–0.3m H, C, L, f, sh; 3.4m PO, G, M, D, V; 7.5m C) | 2,895 | 386.6 |

This section has plentiful 360-degree views and ever-changing scenery flowing from rich mountain coves, boreal forests, and heath balds. Highlights are Max Patch, Big Bald, Beauty Spot, Unaka Mountain, Roan Mountain at 6,285 feet (where an annual rhododendron festival is held), and the open, grassy bald of Hump Mountain.

**Carolina Mountain Club**—CMC maintains the 93.7 miles between Davenport Gap and Spivey Gap. Send correspondence to CMC, P.O. Box 68, Asheville, NC 28802; <www.carolinamtnclub.com>.

*Due to trailhead vandalism, the supervisor of trails for the CMC advises, "We do not recommend leaving cars at trailheads for anything more than a day trip."*

*Water sources—Several water sources are located between Davenport Gap and Deep Gap. State Line Branch may be polluted.*

**Green Corner Road—West** 0.1 mile to *Hostel:* Standing Bear Farm Hiker Hostel, (423) 487-0014, <http://standingbearfarm.tripod.com>, <cvowen@wildblue.net>; operated by Maria Guzman and Curtis Owen; $20PP cabin, $15 bunkhouse or tentsite, includes hot shower, laundry, phone, Internet $5/hour, kitchen; campstore with enough Trail foods and supplies to get you to Hot Springs or Fontana, including stove fuels by the ounce plus cook-your-own pizzas and sandwiches; dogs outside $5/night; shuttles available; parking $2 per day; debit and credit cards accepted; for all services without stay, donations accepted; whitewater rafting trips on the Pigeon River. Stop on by to say hello and fill up your water bottles. Holds packages sent to 4255 Green Corner Rd., Hartford, TN 37753. *Directions:* After walking under I-40, continue north on the A.T. 1.0 mile beyond the stone stairs to the first gravel road (Green Corner Rd.), turn left, walk 200 yards to white farmhouse.

**Groundhog Creek Shelter** (1939)—Sleeps 6. Privy. Stone shelter located 0.2 mile on a blue-blazed side trail. Water source is a reliable spring to the left of the shelter.

**Max Patch**—The site of an old homestead and logging camp, Max Patch was originally forested, but early inhabitants cleared the mountaintop to graze sheep and cattle. The summit also has been used as a landing strip for small planes. In 1982, the USFS purchased the 392-acre grassy-top mountain for the A.T. and now uses mowing and controlled burns to maintain its bald appearance. The wide summit, at 4,629 feet, offers panoramic views of the Smokies to the south and a glimpse of Mt. Mitchell (at 6,684 feet, the highest peak east of the Mississippi) to the east.

**Roaring Fork Shelter** (2005)—Sleeps 8. Privy. Two water sources, both located on the A.T., 800 ft. north and south of side trail to shelter.

**Walnut Mountain Shelter** (1938)—Sleeps 6. Privy. An old shelter, with a water source located down the blue-blazed trail to the left of Rattlesnake Trail; difficult to locate, may be seasonal.

**Deer Park Mountain Shelter** (1938)—Sleeps 5. Privy. A former farmstead; the water source is located on the trail to the shelter.

**N.C. 209/Hot Springs, N.C. [P.O. ZIP 28743: M–F 8:30–11:30 & 12:30–4, Sa 8:30–10:30; (828) 622-3242].** The A.T., now marked by special diamonds in the sidewalk, passes through the center of Hot Springs on Bridge Street, and most services are located on the Trail. ■ *Lodging:* Duckett House B&B, (828) 622-7621, <www.ducketthouseinn.com>, $45PP plus tax including B and laundry ($8.50 B for nonguests; make reservation); bunkhouse $15PP plus tax, limited to 4 people, includes shower; tenting with shower $8 one person, $12 two persons; laundry $4, includes soap; Internet access when available; work-for-stay possible; will hold UPS and FedEx packages, for reserved guests only, sent to 433 Lance Ave., Hot Springs, NC 28743. The Sunnybank Inn, (828) 622-7206, owned by Elmer Hall, located at the white Victorian house across the street from the Dollar Store; thru-hiker rates $15PP, and organic vegetarian meals, $6 B, $10 D; section-hiker rates $20; work exchange is possible; no tents allowed; holds packages mailed to 26 Walnut St., P.O. Box 233, Hot Springs, NC 28743. Bridge Street Café and Inn, (828) 622-0002, <www.bridgestreetcafe. com>, $60–89PP. Alpine Court Motel, (828) 622-3231, $44S, $66D, $62 for 4, $5EAP subject to change; credit cards not accepted; no dogs permitted in rooms. Bright Leaf Junction, (828) 622-9358, rooms $79–$129, suites $129–$169; restaurant with entreés $6.50–$15, WiFi. Creekside Inn, (800) 303-7238, cabin $59, rooms $69–$79, CATV, a/c, gas grill; if office is closed, check at Paddler's Pub next door. Hot Springs Resort and Spa, (828) 622-7267, <www.hotspringsnc.com>, short-

**Hot Springs**

0          0.3 mile

N

term resupply; thru-hiker cabin rate $50–$72, $5EAP up to 5; tentsites $5PP up to 4; shower only, $2. ■ *Groceries:* Bluff Mountain Outfitters and Hillbilly Market (both long-term resupply); L&K's Deli (short-term resupply); Hot Springs Camp Store (short-term resupply), grill with pizza, BBQ, hoagies. ■ *Restaurants:* Smoky Mountain Diner, B/L/D; Bridge Street Café and Inn, B/L/D, open Th–Su, closed in winter; and Paddler's Pub, (828) 622-0001; Sweet Imaginations, W–Su, Mar–Nov, deli and ice cream. ■ *Outfitter:* Bluff Mountain Outfitters, (828) 622-7162, <www.bluffmountain.com>; owners, Dan Gallagher and Wayne Crosby; a full-service outfitter with fax service, ATM, Internet access, shuttle; packages can be sent to 152 Bridge St., P.O. Box 114, Hot Springs, NC 28743; ships UPS and FedEx packages. ■ *Internet access:* library, outfitter, and The Yellow Teapot ($1.50/15 min.). ■ *Other services:* coin laundry (L&K's Deli); bank; Dollar General; Gentry Hardware with Coleman fuel by the ounce; The Yellow Teapot book exchange.

**Whitewater Rafting**—Rafting companies offer guided trips on the French Broad River: Huck Finn River Adventures, (877) 520-4658; Nantahala Outdoor Center, (800) 232-7238; Blue Ridge Resort, (800) 303-7238.

**Southbound permits for Smokies**—Southbounders must have a backcountry permit before entering Great Smoky Mountains National Park (see page 33 for details). A permit can be obtained M–F 8–4:30 at the U.S. Forest Service (USFS) office, (828) 622-3202, east of the A.T. on Serpentine Ave. Employees will also answer questions about the Trail in the area and services available in town. Permits can also be obtained at Bluff Mountain Outfitters, (828) 622-7162, Sa–Su 9–5.

**Hot Springs Spa**—(828) 622-7676. At the northern end of town, on the southern bank of the French Broad River, the spa offers baths and massages at the famous therapeutic mineral baths for which the town was named. The springs were purchased in 1990 by Anne and Eugene Hicks, who developed the natural resource by adding Jacuzzi baths and piping in the 105-degree water. The springs have attracted people to the area since the late 1700s. During World War I, a detention center/prison was constructed on the spot to hold German prisoners of war, and many German-American prisoners enjoyed the springs so much that they stayed in the area after the war. During the 1800s, literature promoting the springs claimed the water could "bring vigor to a wasted frame"—just the remedy for worn-out hikers.

**Spring Mountain Shelter** (1938)—Sleeps 5. Privy. The shelter is located on the west side of the Trail. Water source is 75 yards down a blue-blazed trail on the east side of the A.T.

**Allen Gap**—Reliable piped spring **East** near Trail crossing of Tenn. 70/N.C. 208. Spring's pipe is on south side of highway, 20 yards east of the now-closed State Line Gas & Café. Pipe is attached to a tree at knee height.

**Log Cabin Drive—West** 0.7 mile to *Lodging:* Hemlock Hollow Farm Shoppe and Cabins, (423) 787-0917, <www.hemlockhollow.net>, open all year. Go West for a few hundred yards on a dirt/rock road to Log Cabin Drive (gravel road). Turn left, and follow for 0.6 mile to paved Viking Mountain Rd. Shop is across the road on Chandler Circle. Heated cabin $36D with linens, refrigerator, microwave; heated bunkhouse with kitchenette $18; no linens; tentsite $12; shower & towel included with all overnight stays; shower & towel only, $2.50. Campstore (short-term resupply); good variety of hiker foods, microwavable foods, cold drinks, fresh fruit, hot soup or chili most days during spring; fuel, Esbit, alcohol, gas canisters; water-filtering supplies; shirts, socks. Hiker dogs only, $2/day. Accepts mail drops at 645 Chandler Circle, Greenville, TN 37743. Will send out packages. Shuttles available to Erwin or Hot Springs.

**Little Laurel Shelter** (1967)—Sleeps 5. Privy. Water source is 100 yards down a blue-blazed trail behind the shelter.

**Jerry Cabin Shelter** (1968)—Sleeps 6. Privy. Water source is on a small knoll, up a path found on the opposite side of the A.T. CMC member and honorary ALDHA life member Sam Waddle was the caretaker of this shelter and 2.9 miles of the Trail, from Round Knob to Big Butt, for 26 years until his death February 1, 2005. Sam had a good sense of humor and was responsible for a light bulb and telephone installed on the shelter wall. Sam's volunteer efforts transformed this shelter from "the dirtiest shelter on the entire Trail to one of the cleanest," according to Ed Garvey, by hauling out an estimated 20 bushels of litter. He was devoted to the A.T. and an inspiration to all volunteers who share the commitment it takes to make a difference. The electric outlet and telephone may be gone, but Sam's legacy will live forever.

**Shelton Graves**—North of Big Butt is the final resting place of William and David Shelton, who lived in Madison County, N.C., but enlisted in the Union army during the Civil War. While returning to a family gathering during the war, the uncle and nephew were ambushed near here and killed by Confederate troops.

**Flint Mountain Shelter** (1988)—Sleeps 8. Privy. Site of one of the more unusual animal encounters in Trail history. In 1994, a sleeping thru-hiker was bitten on the hand by a fox in the middle of the night, despite the presence of other hikers and two dogs. Water source is on the A.T. north of the shelter.

**Hogback Ridge Shelter** (1986)—Sleeps 6. Privy. Water source is a spring 0.3 mile on a side trail near the shelter.

**Big Bald**—True to its name, Big Bald offers 360-degree views at an elevation of 5,516 feet. From 1802 to 1834, the bald was inhabited by a cantankerous hermit named David Greer. Spurned by a woman, he retreated to the mountaintop where he lived in a small, cave-like structure (no longer visible). He declared himself sovereign of the mountain and eventually killed a man, only to be acquitted on grounds of insanity. The life of "Hog Greer," called so by the neighbors because he lived like one, ended when a local blacksmith shot him in the back; the blacksmith was never charged. Greer Bald eventually became known as Big Bald. A golf and ski resort, Wolf Laurel, is just out of sight on the east side of Big Bald, on the southern approach to the summit. A spring and campsite can be found by following the A.T. 0.2 mile north of the summit to a dirt road and then walking west 0.3 mile down the dirt road.

**Bald Mountain Shelter (1988)**—Sleeps 10. Privy. This shelter is one of the highest on the A.T. (5,100 feet), and the area surrounding the shelter is too fragile for tenting. Water source is a spring located on the side trail to the shelter.

---

**Tennessee Eastman Hiking Club**—TEHC maintains the 131.5 miles between Spivey Gap and Damascus. Correspondence should be sent to TEHC, P.O. Box 511, Kingsport, TN 37662; <www.tehcc.org>.

---

**No Business Knob Shelter** (1963)—Sleeps 6. No privy. Surrounded by large Fraser magnolias and mammoth hemlocks, this concrete-block shelter was built by the Forest Service. Reliable water is found 0.2 mile south of the shelter on the A.T.

**Chestoa Bridge/Erwin, Tenn. [P.O. ZIP 37650: M–F 8–5; Sa 10–12; (423) 743-9422].** *Hostel:* Nolichucky Hostel and Outfitters; owners, John and Charlotte Shores; (423) 735-0548; <www.unclejohnnys.net>; 151 River Road, Erwin, TN 37650; where A.T. crosses River Road. Hostel $15/night; private cabins $20–$25s, $30–$34D; camping $8PP; showers with towel free with stay, shower without stay $3; laundry $3 load; shuttles and bicycles available; free Internet, WiFi, and video library available. Outfitter store sells alcohol, white gas, fuel canisters, clothing, camping food. Credit cards welcome. Shipments accepted addressed to 151 River Rd, Erwin, TN 37650.

**West** 1.3 miles to *Lodging:* 0.5 mile on River Road (best hitch), then 0.8 mile on Temple Hill Road to Holiday Inn Express, (423) 743-4100, $65D, no pets, continental B, high-speed Internet in lobby, laundry, free pint of Ben & Jerry's ice cream to each room rented for each night's stay, hot tub, swimming pool, propane grills, shuttles list available, parking for section-hikers, mail drops accepted at 2002 Temple Hill Rd., Erwin, TN 37650.

**West** 3.8 miles on River Road (best hitch) to ■ *Lodging:* Clayton's Dogwood Inn, <www.claytonsdogwoodinn.com>, (423) 735-0093, $50s/D, includes hot homestyle B, mail drops accepted at 430 Ohio Ave., Erwin, TN 37650; Best Southern Motel, (423) 743-6438, $24.99PP, no pets, newly remodeled rooms, shuttles available, mail drops accepted, 1315 Jackson Love Hwy., Erwin, TN 37650; Super 8 Motel, (423) 743-0200, $45.95S, $49.95D includes B, laundry, free shuttles to or from Trail, high-speed Internet, no pets, will accept mail drops at 1101 N. Buffalo St., Erwin, TN 37650. ■ *Camping:* Cherokee Adventures, (800) 445-7238, <www.cherokeeadventures.com>, tentsite $5PP, bunkhouse $8PP (call for availability), showers only $2, 1.6 miles west on Tenn. 81. ■ *Restaurants:* River's Edge Café, L/D, W–M (summer), Th–Su (Nov–Mar), call (423) 743-3713 to check hours, live music on weekends; China Kitchen, Su buffet; Aztec Mexican Ristorante; El Corita Mexican Restaurant; Pizza Plus; Pizza Hut; Rocky's Pizza; Dairy Ace; Hardee's; Little Caesar's; Wendy's; McDonald's; Huddle House; Sonic Burger; A&W; Long John Silver's. ■ *Groceries:* Food Lion, White's (2 locations), J.D.'s Market & Deli (all long-term resupply); Dollar General (2 locations), and Family Dollar. ■ *Outfitter:* Mahoney's, (423) 282-8889, in Johnson City, 13 miles north. ■ *Internet access:* public library; Chamber of Commerce, (423) 743-3000, M–F 8–5, Sa 9–1, also has information on shuttles. ■ *Other services:* banks; ATM; barber; coin laundries; thrift stores; hardware; dentists; 24-hour emergency center; Walgreens; Wal-Mart; shoe repair; movie theater; art gallery; veterinarian; Miss Janet's shuttle, (423) 743-1932 or (423) 948-2628, or visit <www.missjanetshouse.com> to arrange.

**Whitewater Rafting**—Rafting companies offer guided trips on the scenic, free-flowing Nolichucky River: NOC, (800) 232-7238; USA Raft, (800) USA-RAFT; Cherokee Adventure, (800) 445-7238; High Mountain Expeditions, (800) 262-9036; Wahoo's Adventures, (800) 444-RAFT, which also provides rafting on Watauga River near Hampton–Elizabethton.

**Curley Maple Gap Shelter** (1961)—Sleeps 6. No privy. Concrete-block shelter built by the Forest Service. Water source is a spring south on the A.T.

to Wal-Mart

Wendy's •

White's Supermarket,
Dollar Store, ATM, Pharmacy,
Laundry, Aztec Mexican,
Subway, Rocky's Pizza

Hardee's •

Little Caesar's • • Pizza
Hut

10th St.

7 Miles to A.T.
at Indian Grave Gap

• El Corita (Mexican)
• Laundry
• China Kitchen
• Family Dollar

**Erwin**

0      0.5 mile

• Food Lion/CVS

N

U.S. 23

Hwy. 81 to Cherokee Adventures/
River's Edge Cafe

• Laundry
• Hardware, Walgreens
• Frank's Place

Super 8 •

McDonald's
Huddle House

2nd St.

• Sonic Burger

P.O. •

Clinchfield
Drug Store

• C. of Commerce

Roller Drug,
Movie Theater,
Shoe Repair

Love St.

Library •

Main St.

Elm St.

Clayton's
• Dogwod Inn

Ohio Ave.

B.P. Food Store •
Dairy Ace •

J.D Market •
Best Southern •
Pizza Plus •
Dollar Store •

• White's Supermarket

Jackson Love Hwy.

Chestoa Pike

• A&W/Long John Silver's

Holiday Inn
Express

Temple
Hill Rd.

U.S. 23

Nolichucky
Hostel and
Outfitter

**Unaka Mountain**—With a large stand of red spruce atop its 5,180-foot summit, Unaka will remind southbounders of the Maine woods. Unaka is the Cherokee word for "white." Spring on A.T. 0.3 mile north of summit.

**Cherry Gap Shelter** (1962)—Sleeps 6. No privy. Water source is a spring found 80 yards on a blue-blazed trail from the shelter.

**Tenn. 107, N.C. 226/Iron Mountain Gap**—**East** 3 miles to *Groceries:* Buladean Shell Gas & Grocery (short-term resupply), with made-to-order sandwiches, ice cream, and Coleman fuel.

**West** 4.7 miles to ■ *Restaurant:* B & M Country Café, Tu–F 11–9, Sa 3–9. ■ *Groceries:* Limestone Cove Market, M–Sa 6–9, Su 12–6 (short-term resupply).

**West** 10.3 miles to **Unicoi, Tenn. [P.O. ZIP 37692: M–F 8–11 & 12–4 Sa 8:30–10:30; (800) 275-8777],** with Clarence's Restaurant B/L/D, Maple Grove Restaurant, mini-marts, and a doctor.

**Greasy Creek Gap**—**East** 0.6 mile to *Hostel:* Greasy Creek Friendly Hostel (short-term resupply), (828) 688-9948, <atrailagc@yahoo.com>; bunkhouse $8PP, one room (indoors) $12PP, includes shower/towel/soap for guests; nonguest shower $3; kitchen privileges; camping $5PP includes shower; shuttle, laundry, meals, ice cream, fuel, Internet; no dogs. Phillip and Connie Edmondson accept mail drops sent to Greasy Creek Friendly (GCF), 1827 Greasy Creek Road, Bakerville, NC 28705. *Directions*: At sign, go downhill to the right 0.6 mile to GCF, first house on right.

**Clyde Smith Shelter** (1976)—Sleeps 10. No privy. Water source is a spring 100 yards behind the shelter on a blue-blazed trail. Renovations include new roof and porch.

**Roan Mountain**—For northbounders, this will be the last time the A.T. climbs above 6,000 feet until Mt. Washington in New Hampshire. At the top is a parking area, with restroom and running water (May–Oct). Roan Mountain is arguably the coldest spot, year-round, on the southern A.T. Upon reaching the top of the main climb (for northbounders), enter a clearing, and pass the foundation of the former Cloudland Hotel. The Tennessee–North Carolina state line ran through the center of the hotel's ballroom when Cloudland was a thriving resort during the late 1800s and early 1900s. It was demolished in 1915, after loggers completely harvested the fir and spruce on the mountaintop. Much of the Catawba rhododendron was dug up and sold to ornamental nurseries. The remaining rhododendron flourished after the logging and quickly covered the slopes of Roan, hence the famous rhododendron gardens. The peak blooming time is usually around Jun 20. The gardens can be reached by following the Forest

Service road (visible from the hotel foundation) west, uphill, along the top of the mountain, where an information station is located.

**Roan High Knob Shelter** (1980)—Sleeps 15. No privy. The highest shelter on the A.T. (6,275 feet). Originally an old firewarden's cabin, this shelter was rebuilt by Cherokee National Forest employees. The loft is known to leak. An unreliable water source can be found on a 100-yard, blue-blazed trail near the shelter. More reliable sources are south on the A.T. at the Roan Mountain restroom, when open, or a spring at Carvers Gap picnic area, 1.3 miles north.

**Gray's lily**—A protected, red, nodding lily can be found blooming on the slopes of Round Bald, Grassy Ridge, and Hump Mountain in late Jun–early Jul. The lily is named for botanist Asa Gray, who found the plant here during the 1840s. He called the Roan range, "without a doubt, the most beautiful mountain east of the Rockies."

**Roan Mountain to Hump Mountain**—Between Roan Mountain and Hump Mountain, the Trail crosses several balds. Round Bald (5,826 feet) is the site of a USFS experiment in which goats were used to keep briars and brambles from encroaching on the bald. Although the southern Appalachians do not rise above treeline, there are many balds, the origins of which remains a mystery to scientists. Some point to the harsh conditions at high elevations, while others claim Indians cleared the mountains for religious ceremonies. Many believe extensive grazing and cropping led to treeless summits, and still others say it's the work of spacemen. The 6,189-foot summit of Grassy Ridge is reached by following a side trail to the east before the A.T. begins its descent off the ridge to Stan Murray Shelter. It is the only natural 360-degree viewpoint above 6,000 feet near the Trail. (Clingmans Dome has its observation tower, and Mt. Washington's summit in New Hampshire is covered with numerous buildings.) Please do *not* camp here; past camping has significantly harmed the rare plants. For northbounders, the A.T. veers west from the North Carolina/Tennessee line into Tennessee at Doll Flats, where it remains until crossing into Virginia 3.5 miles south of Damascus.

**N.C. 261/Carvers Gap**—Picnic area and parking area with restroom. North out of Carvers Gap, the Trail has been relocated with switchbacks to control erosion and heal the vivid scar of the old treadway. Please stay on the new treadway to allow this area to recover.

**Stan Murray Shelter** (1977)—Sleeps 6. No privy. Formerly the Roan Highlands Shelter, this shelter was renamed for the former chairman of the ATC and originator of the Appalachian Greenway concept. Water source is a spring on a blue-blazed trail opposite the shelter.

**Overmountain Shelter** (1983)—Sleeps 20. Privy. A large, red, converted barn once used as a backdrop for the movie "Winter People." Fires and cooking are permitted on the ground floor only. Water source is a spring found to the left once you reach the old road before the shelter. There are two separate water sources here, depending on the dryness of the year.

**Apple House Shelter** (1984)—Sleeps 6. No privy. Located near the road. This structure was first constructed in 1952 to store explosives for a quarry in the hollow and tools for a nearby orchard, before being rebuilt by TEHC and the Forest Service. Water source is behind the shelter.

*"Spring is when you feel like whistling, even with a shoe full of slush."*
    —Doug Larson

# Tennessee

| Miles from Katahdin | Features | Services | Elev. | Miles from Springer |
|---|---|---|---|---|
| 1,789.6 | U.S. 19E **Elk Park, NC 08622; Newland, NC 28657; Roan Mtn, TN 37687** | R (E−0.5m M; 2.5m PO, G, M; 9m PO, G, M, f, cl, @) (W−0.3m H, C, L, f, sh; 3.4m PO, G, M, D, V; 7.5m C) | 2,895 | 386.6 |
| 1,789.4 | Bear Branch Rd | R | 2,900 | 386.8 |
| 1,786.4 | Buck Mtn Rd | R | 3,340 | 389.8 |
| 1,786.1 | Campbell Hollow Rd | R | 3,330 | 390.1 |
| 1,783.3 | Campsite | C, w | 3,590 | 392.9 |
| 1,780.9 | **Mountaineer Shelter** *8.7mS; 9.5mN* | S, w | 3,470 | 395.3 |
| 1,779.3 | Walnut Mtn Rd | R | 3,550 | 396.9 |
| 1,778.1 | Stream | | 3,400 | 398.1 |
| 1,777.6 | Viewpoint | W−0.2m H | | 398.6 |
| 1,777.1 | Laurel Fork | W−0.4m H, sh, @ | 3,290 | 399.1 |
| 1,773.2 | Campsite | C, w | 3,410 | 403.0 |
| 1,771.4 | **Moreland Gap Shelter** *9.5mS; 8mN* | S, w | 3,815 | 404.8 |
| 1,770.0 | White Rocks Mtn | | 4,206 | 406.2 |
| 1,767.0 | Trail to Coon Den Falls | | 2,660 | 409.2 |
| 1,765.3 | Dennis Cove; USFS 50 | R, w (E−0.3m C, G, L, cl, sh, f, @) (W−0.2m H, C, cl, sh, f) | 2,550 | 410.9 |
| 1,764.1 | Laurel Fork Falls | w | 2,120 | 412.1 |
| 1,763.4 | **Laurel Fork Shelter** *8mS; 8.8mN* | S, w | 2,450 | 412.8 |
| 1,762.6 | Side trail to U.S. 321 | w (W−0.8m PO, G, M, L, D, f, @) | 1,900 | 413.6 |
| 1,759.6 | Pond Flats | C, w | 3,780 | 416.6 |
| 1,756.4 | U.S. 321 **Hampton, TN 37658** | R (W−2m PO, G, M, L, D, f, @; 9m L, G, M, D, V, cl, @) | 1,990 | 419.8 |
| 1,755.1 | Griffith Branch | C, w | 2,100 | 421.1 |
| 1,754.6 | **Watauga Lake Shelter** *8.8mS; 6.8mN* | S, w | 2,130 | 421.6 |

| Miles from Katahdin | Features | Services | Elev. | Miles from Springer |
|---|---|---|---|---|
| 1,753.5 | Watauga Dam (north end) | | 1,915 | 422.7 |
| 1,752.2 | Watauga Dam Rd | R | 2,250 | 424.0 |
| 1,749.5 | Spring | w | 3,400 | 426.7 |
| 1,747.8 | **Vandeventer Shelter** *6.8mS; 6.8mN* | S; W–0.3m w | 3,620 | 428.4 |
| 1,744.0 | Spring | w | 3,900 | 432.2 |
| 1,742.6 | Turkeypen Gap | | 3,840 | 433.6 |
| 1,741.2 | Spring | w | 4,000 | 435.0 |
| 1,741.0 | **Iron Mtn Shelter** *6.8mS; 7.6mN* | S, nw | 4,125 | 435.2 |
| 1,739.7 | Nick Grindstaff Monument | | 4,090 | 436.5 |
| 1,736.4 | Tenn. 91 | R | 3,450 | 439.8 |
| 1,734.3 | Campsite | C, w | 3,990 | 441.9 |
| 1,733.4 | Holston Mtn Trail, **Double Springs Shelter** *7.6mS; 8.3mN* | S, w | 4,060 | 442.8 |
| 1,729.9 | U.S. 421, Low Gap **Shady Valley, TN 37688** | R, w (E–2.7m PO, C, G, M, f) | 3,384 | 446.3 |
| 1,728.0 | Double Spring Gap | w | 3,650 | 448.2 |
| 1,726.6 | McQueens Knob | | 3,900 | 449.6 |
| 1,726.2 | McQueens Gap; USFS 69 | R | 3,680 | 450.0 |
| 1,725.1 | **Abingdon Gap Shelter** *8.3mS; 19.6mN* | S (E–0.2m w) | 3,785 | 451.1 |
| 1,718.6 | Tenn.–Va. State Line | | 3,302 | 457.6 |

In this 70-mile section, you will stroll along the Elk River, pass Jones and Mountaineer falls, see the impressive 50-foot Laurel Falls in the Pond Mountain Wilderness, look over the 16-mile-long Watauga Reservoir, and climb Iron Mountain, once home to the legendary hermit Nick Grindstaff.

**U.S. 19E**—Numerous incidents of vandalism have been reported at this parking area. Park at your own risk. **East** 0.5 mile to *Restaurant:* King of the Road Restaurant and Steak House, L Su 11–3, D Th–Sa 4–9.

**East** 2.5 miles to **Elk Park, N.C. [P.O. ZIP 28622: 28622: M–F 7:30–12, 1:30–4:15, Sa 7:30–11; (828) 733-5711].** ■ *Restaurant:* Times Square Diner, B/L/D, M–F L buffet $5.79, Sa B buffet $5.99, M–Sa 6:30–8:30; Blessings Coffee Shop, Tu–F 10–5, Sa 9–5. ■ *Other services:* two small grocery stores (short-term resupply).

**East** 9 miles to **Newland, N.C. [P.O. ZIP 28657: M–F 8:30–4:30, Sa 8:30–12; (828) 733-2500].** ■ *Restaurants:* San Dee's Restaurant; Fabio's; Papa's Pizza To Go; McDonald's; Hardee's; Subway Sandwiches & Salads. ■ *Groceries:* Ingles Food Store, Lowe's Food Store (both long-term resupply). ■ *Internet access:* library. ■ *Other services:* Avery Hardware (sells fuel), coin laundry.

**West** 0.3 mile to *Lodging:* Mountain Harbour B&B and Hostel, (866) 772-9494, <www.mountainharbour.net>. Mary and Terry Hill offer a hostel in the cabin over the barn, $15PP or semiprivate king bed $30; includes shower, linens and towels, full kitchen, wood-burning stove, and video library; tenting with shower $8; shower only $3; laundry $4; fuel available by the ounce; B during peak season $6–$7; town shuttle during stay $3–$4. B&B rooms $70, $90 & $120 suite w/Jacuzzi tub; includes B. Will hold mail drops for guests, nonguests $5, 9151 Highway 19E, Roan Mountain, TN 37687. Shuttles by prior arrangement; secure parking $5/day, $2/day with shuttle service. Hostel cabin available privately off-season. Open year-round.

**West** 2.0 miles to *Restaurant:* Frank & Marty's, pizza/subs Tu W Sa 4–9, Th–F 11–9, closed Su–M; 2.4 miles, Dollar General Store.

**West** 3.4 miles to **Roan Mountain, Tenn. [P.O. ZIP 37687: M–F 8–noon & 1:00–4:00, Sa 7:30–9:30, (423) 772-3014].** ■ *Restaurants:* Mad Martha's Café, Tu–Sa 11–5; Bob's Dairyland, M–Sa 6 a.m.–8 p.m., closed Su; Snack Shack & Pizza. ■ *Other services:* several small grocery stores (long-term resupply); bank with ATM; pharmacy; medical center, open M–F; veterinarian.

**West** 7.5 miles to *Camping:* Roan Mountain State Park on Tenn. 143, (423) 772-0190; campground with showers, $11 primitive campsite, $17.50–$20.50 for campsites with water and electricity, $95–$114 for cabins; visitors center and swimming pool.

**Mountaineer Shelter** (2006)—Sleeps 14. No privy. Water source 200 feet on blue-blaze. Constructed by the 6th annual Hard Core Trail Days volunteer crew led by Trail steward Bob Peoples and the TEHCC.

**Trail to Abby's Place**—Two side trails: 2.0 miles north of gravel Walnut Mountain Road, look for bent-over tree bench under A.T. sign, follow trail downhill under utility easement about 0.25 mile; or 6 miles north of Walnut Mountain Road, just beyond Laurel Fork Creek bridge crossing, follow blue-blazed trail along creek and old road 0.4 mile to Abby's Place, (423) 772-3450, owned by Scott Vandam; $8 for space in electrified bunkhouse with shower, Internet, and satellite TV, sleeps six; $3 shower includes soap and towel; $3 laundry includes soap; $1 Internet without stay; miscellaneous hiker-food resupply; secure daily parking of vehicles, $1/night; fishing in Laurel Fork in front of house; shuttles, call for availability; free long-distance phone; no meals or deliver-ies/mail drops, please; pets allowed if leashed while on property. B & B house guestroom $20 when available. Remote location, secluded and quiet.

**Moreland Gap Shelter** (1960)—Sleeps 6. No privy. Water source is 0.2 mile down the hollow across from the shelter. Northwest exposure; tends to get wet during storms.

**Dennis Cove Road/USFS 50—East** 0.3 mile to *Lodging:* Laurel Fork Lodge, <lclodge@usit.net>, <www.laurel-forklodge.com>, short-term resupply, (423) 725-5988; self-registration day or night; tentsite $5 two tents/site, bunkhouse $6, hostel cabin $12PP up to six people, private cabin $25PP (A.T. hiker rate) up to three people; shower only without stay $2, laundry $2.50; fully equipped hiker kitchen area, frozen pizzas and burgers, cold sodas and ice cream, limited camping supplies, Coleman and denatured alcohol by the ounce, pay phone, free Internet, free coffee at 8 a.m., mail drops accepted addressed to Laurel Fork Lodge, 1511 Dennis Cove Rd., Hampton, TN 37658. No shuttles.

**West** 0.2 mile to *Hostel:* the never-closed Kincora Hiking Hostel, (423) 725-4409, with bunkroom, showers, tentsites, cooking facilities, laundry, Coleman and denatured alcohol by the ounce, phone, shuttles to Hampton (other shuttles need to be arranged), $4/night suggested donation; owners Bob and Pat Peoples hold packages for hikers mailed to 1278 Dennis Cove Rd., Hampton, TN 37658.

**Laurel Fork Shelter** (1977)—Sleeps 8. No privy. Constructed from native rocks, this shelter is located on the blue-blazed high-water route above the Laurel Fork. Water source is a stream found 50 yards behind the shelter.

**U.S. 321—West** 2 miles to **Hampton, Tenn. [P.O. ZIP 37658: M–F 7:30–11:30 & 12:30–4:30, Sa 8–10; (423) 725-2177].** ■ *Lodging:* Braemar Castle Hostel and Guest House, (423) 725-2411 or 725-2262. The Braemar Castle was constructed to house the offices and company store for the Pittsburgh Lumber Company, which operated in the Laurel Gorge area from 1909 until 1925. Sutton and Beverly Brown (Sutton's grandfather owned Braemar Castle) offer hiker space, kitchen, and showers for $15PP; private rooms, $20S $40D. Iron Mountain Inn B&B, (423) 768-2446 or (888) 781-2399, <www.ironmountaininn.com>; private room and bath $100, includes B. Lake House, <www.wataugalakecabin.com>, $100PP (hiker rate). Creekside Chalet, <www.creeksidechalet.net>, $75PP includes hot tub on deck, pet-friendly, call from Hampton for pick-up, packages held addressed c/o Woods, 138 Moreland Dr., Butler, TN 37640. ■ *Groceries:* Brown's Grocery, (423) 725-2411, long-term resupply, closed Su; check with Sutton at the grocery store for accommodations and shuttles; Coleman fuel and denatured alcohol; holds USPS and UPS packages addressed to Brown's Grocery, 613 Hwy. 321, Hampton, TN 37658. ■ *Other services:* TS Internet Café ($5 an hour, $3 half-hour), restaurants, market, convenience stores, health clinic, banks, and ATM. ■ *Shuttles:* Hampton Trails Bicycle Shop, (423) 725-5000, owner Brian White, <www.hamptontrails.com>, <hamptontrails@embarqmail.com>. *Note: The best access to Hampton from the A.T. is the 0.8-mile blue-blazed trail in Laurel Gorge, two miles downstream from Laurel Falls.*

**West** 9 miles to Elizabethton, Tenn. ■ *Lodging:* Travelers Inn, (423) 543-3344, Su–Th $54.99D, F–Sa $59.99D includes continental B; Americourt Hotel, (423) 542-4466, <americourt-hotel@yahoo.com>, located on the U.S. 19E bypass, $59 hiker rate. ■ *Groceries:* Big G Supermarket (long-term resupply). ■ *Internet access:* library. ■ *Other services:* restaurants, convenience stores, doctor, bank, veterinarian, laundry, and ATM.

**Shook Branch Recreation Area**—This developed area on Watauga Lake offers picnic tables, restroom, water that is turned on after the last freeze of spring (usually by late Apr), and a beach for swimming.

**Watauga Lake Shelter** (1980)—Sleeps 6. No privy. A wooden structure on the shore of Watauga Lake. Water source is on A.T., south of the shelter.

**Watauga Dam**—The A.T. crosses the Watauga River on this dam at Watauga Lake. A visitors center with restroom, often closed during cold-weather months, can be reached by following Watauga Dam Road 0.9 mile east. This TVA dam, completed in 1948, displaced about 700 people living along the river banks. All told, TVA dams in the South displaced nearly 75,000 people from their homes. The trade-off was flood control, electricity, jobs, and recreational opportunities.

**Vandeventer Shelter** (1961)—Sleeps 6. No privy. Water source is 0.3 mile down a steep, blue-blazed trail south of the shelter.

**Iron Mountain Shelter** (1960)—Sleeps 6. No privy. Water source is a spring 500 yards south on the A.T.

**Nick Grindstaff Monument**—Nick Grindstaff traveled west to win his fortune but was robbed of all his money during the journey. He then returned to Iron Mountain, where he lived for more than 40 years, becoming one of the region's most famous hermits. He died in 1923, and the plaque on the chimney was erected in 1925. A distant relative, Paschel Grindstaff, shepherded hikers through Damascus, Va., during his many years as postmaster there.

**Double Springs Shelter** (1960)—Sleeps 6. No privy. Water source is a spring located 100 yards in the draw beyond the shelter.

**U.S. 421/Low Gap**—A piped spring is located in the gap, on the A.T. **East** 2.7 miles to **Shady Valley, Tenn. [P.O. ZIP 37688: M–F 7:30–11:00 & 12:00–3:30, Sa 8–10; (423) 739-2173].** ■ *Groceries:* Shady Valley Country Store & Deli, (423) 739-2325, <www.shadyvalleycountrystore.com>, daily 6–9, short-term resupply, Coleman fuel, camping $10. Shady Valley General Store & Museum, (423) 739-2040, daily 6–9, short-term resupply, Coleman fuel. ■ *Restaurant:* Raceway, (423) 739-2499, B/L/D, open every day, call for hours.

**Queens Knob Shelter** (1934)—Sleeps 4. No privy. This shelter was the first on Holston Mountain on the A.T. and is one of the A.T.'s oldest shelters. Not up to current standards, it is intended *for emergency use only,* and, even then, the unchinked walls allow for the weather to easily enter. No water at this site.

**Abingdon Gap Shelter** (1959)—Sleeps 5. No privy. Water source is a spring 0.2 mile east on a steep, blue-blazed side trail, downhill behind the shelter.

**Tennessee/Virginia State Line**—Although there is no official state-line marker, you'll know you're entering or leaving Virginia when you see the Mt. Rogers National Recreation Area sign.

*"God does not subtract the days of your life that are spent on the Appalachian Trail."*
—SHOTGUN (AT '00), UPON MEETING AN 80-YEAR-OLD SECTION-HIKER.

# Virginia—Part 1(Southwest)

| Miles from Katahdin | Features | Services | Elev. | Miles from Springer |
|---|---|---|---|---|
| 1,718.6 | Va.–Tenn. State Line | | 3,302 | 457.6 |
| 1,717.0 | Spring | w | 2,600 | 459.2 |
| 1,715.1 | U.S. 58 **Damascus, VA 24236** | R, PO, H, G, L, M, O, D, cl, sh, f, @ (W–2m V; 12m G, L, M, O, V) | 1,928 | 461.1 |
| 1,714.1 | U.S. 58, Virginia Creeper Trail | R | 1,928 | 462.1 |
| 1,711.6 | Iron Mtn Trail, Feathercamp Ridge | | 2,850 | 464.6 |
| 1,709.5 | U.S. 58, Straight Branch, Feather-camp Branch | R, w | 2,250 | 466.7 |
| 1,708.2 | Stream | w | 2,490 | 468.0 |
| 1,707.5 | Taylors Valley Side Trail | | 2,850 | 468.7 |
| 1,706.0 | Straight Mtn | | 3,500 | 470.2 |
| 1,705.7 | **Saunders Shelter** *19.6mS; 6.6mN* | W–0.2m S, w | 3,310 | 470.5 |
| 1,704.6 | Stream | | 3,150 | 471.6 |
| 1,703.5 | Beartree Gap Trail | W–3m C, sh | 3,050 | 472.7 |
| 1,703.4 | Campsite | C | 3,020 | 472.8 |
| 1,701.6 | Va. 728, Creek Jct Station | R | 2,700 | 474.6 |
| 1,701.1 | Virginia Creeper Trail, Whitetop Laurel Creek | | 2,690 | 475.1 |
| 1,700.5 | Va. 859, Grassy Ridge Rd | R | 2,900 | 475.7 |
| 1,699.3 | **Lost Mtn Shelter** *6.6mS; 12.2mN* | S, w | 3,360 | 476.9 |
| 1,698.2 | U.S. 58; Summit Cut, Va. | R | 3,160 | 478.0 |
| 1,697.0 | Va. 601 (Beech Mtn Rd) | R, w | 3,600 | 479.2 |
| 1,694.5 | Buzzard Rock, Whitetop Mtn | | 5,080 | 481.7 |
| 1,694.0 | Spring | w | 5,100 | 482.2 |
| 1,693.8 | Whitetop Mtn Rd (USFS 89) | R, C, w | 5,150 | 482.4 |
| 1,691.3 | Va. 600, Elk Garden | R | 4,434 | 484.9 |
| 1,689.3 | Deep Gap | E–0.2m w | 4,900 | 486.9 |
| 1,687.5 | Susan Spillane Trail to Mt. Rogers | | 5,490 | 488.7 |
| 1,687.1 | **Thomas Knob Shelter** *12.2mS; 5.1mN* | S, w | 5,400 | 489.1 |
| 1,686.3 | Rhododendron Gap | | 5,440 | 489.9 |
| 1,685.0 | Wilburn Ridge | | 4,900 | 491.2 |

| Miles from Katahdin | Features | Services | Elev. | Miles from Springer |
|---|---|---|---|---|
| 1,684.2 | Massie Gap | E–2m C, G, sh | 4,800 | 492.0 |
| 1,682.0 | Grayson Highlands State Park, Wilson Creek Trail, **Wise Shelter** *5.1mS; 5.9mN* | S, w (E–2m C, G, sh) | 4,460 | 494.2 |
| 1,681.7 | Campsites | C, w | 4,300 | 494.5 |
| 1,680.7 | Spring | w | 4,610 | 495.5 |
| 1,679.5 | Stone Mtn | | 4,820 | 496.7 |
| 1,677.8 | Pine Mtn | | 4,960 | 498.4 |
| 1,676.1 | **Old Orchard Shelter** *5.9mS; 5.0mN* | S, w | 4,050 | 500.1 |
| 1,674.4 | Va. 603, Fox Creek | R, C, w on A.T. | 3,480 | 501.8 |
| 1,672.4 | Hurricane Mtn | | 4,320 | 503.8 |
| 1,672.1 | Iron Mtn Trail, Chestnut Flats | | 4,240 | 504.1 |
| 1,671.8 | Stream | w | 4,190 | 504.4 |
| 1,671.1 | **Hurricane Mtn Shelter** *5.0mS; 9.1mN* | S, w | 4,300 | 505.1 |
| 1,669.7 | Stream | w | 3,000 | 506.5 |
| 1,668.0 | Hurricane Campground Trail | W–0.5m C, sh | 3,090 | 508.2 |
| 1,667.1 | Comers Creek | w | 3,100 | 509.1 |
| 1,665.9 | Va. 650, Va. 16, Dickey Gap **Troutdale, VA 24378** | R (E–2.6m PO, H, G, M; 4.9m L) | 3,300 | 510.3 |
| 1,664.4 | Raccoon Branch Campground Trail | E–0.2m w; 3.2m C, w | 3,570 | 511.8 |
| 1,663.8 | High Point | | 3,700 | 512.4 |
| 1,662.0 | **Trimpi Shelter** *9.1mS; 10.6mN* | S, w | 2,900 | 514.2 |
| 1,660.5 | Va. 672 | R | 2,700 | 515.7 |
| 1,659.2 | Va. 670, South Fork Holston River | R | 2,450 | 517.0 |
| 1,655.4 | Va. 601 | R | 3,250 | 520.8 |
| 1,651.4 | **Partnership Shelter** *10.6mS; 7.1mN* | S, w, sh | 3,360 | 524.8 |
| 1,651.3 | Va. 16, Mt. Rogers NRA Headquarters **Sugar Grove, VA 24375; Marion, VA 24354** | R (E–3.2m PO, G, L, M, f) (W–6m PO, G, M, L, cl) | 3,220 | 524.9 |
| 1,650.6 | Va. 622 | R | 3,270 | 525.6 |
| 1,650.1 | Brushy Mtn | | 3,600 | 526.1 |
| 1,647.6 | Locust Mtn | | 3,900 | 528.6 |
| 1,647.2 | USFS 86 | R, C, w | 3,650 | 529.0 |
| 1,646.3 | Glade Mtn | | 3,900 | 529.9 |

| Miles from Katahdin | Features | Services | Elev. | Miles from Springer |
|---|---|---|---|---|
| 1,644.3 | **Chatfield Shelter** *7.1mS; 7.2mN* | S, w | 3,150 | 531.9 |
| 1,644.0 | USFS 644 | R | 3,100 | 532.2 |
| 1,642.5 | Va. 615, Settlers Museum | R | 2,650 | 533.7 |
| 1,642.0 | Va. 729 | R | 2,700 | 534.2 |
| 1,639.8 | Va. 683, U.S. 11, I-81 **Atkins, VA 24311; Marion, VA 24354** | R, G, M, L, sh, f, cl (W–3.2m PO, G, M, cl; 10.2m PO, G, M, L, cl) | 2,420 | 536.4 |
| 1,638.7 | Va. 617 | R | 2,580 | 537.5 |
| 1,638.0 | Spring | E–50yds w | 2,610 | 538.2 |
| 1,637.1 | **Davis Path Shelter** *7.2mS; 11.2mN* | S, C, nw | 2,840 | 539.1 |
| 1,634.6 | Gullion (Little Brushy) Mtn | | 3,300 | 541.6 |
| 1,633.5 | Crawfish Valley along Reed Creek | w on A.T. (E–0.3m C, w) | 2,600 | 542.7 |
| 1,631.8 | Tilson Gap, Big Walker Mtn | | 3,500 | 544.4 |
| 1,630.4 | Va. 610 | R | 2,700 | 545.8 |
| 1,628.0 | Va. 42 | R (E–0.2m w) | 2,650 | 548.2 |
| 1,627.2 | Brushy Mtn | | 3,200 | 549.0 |
| 1,625.9 | **Knot Maul Branch Shelter** *11.2mS; 9.1mN* | S, nw | 2,880 | 550.3 |
| 1,625.8 | Spring | w | 2,810 | 550.4 |
| 1,625.5 | Lynn Camp Creek | w | 2,400 | 550.7 |
| 1,623.9 | Lynn Camp Mtn | | 3,000 | 552.3 |
| 1,622.7 | Lick Creek | w | | 553.5 |
| 1,621.4 | USFS 222 | R | 2,380 | 554.8 |
| 1,618.6 | Spring–fed pond | w | 3,800 | 557.6 |
| 1,616.8 | **Chestnut Knob Shelter** *9.1mS; 10mN* | S, nw | 4,409 | 559.4 |
| 1,615.5 | Walker Gap | R, w | 3,520 | 560.7 |
| 1,610.6 | Va. 623, Garden Mtn | R | 3,900 | 565.6 |
| 1,609.8 | Davis Farm Campsite | W–0.5m C, w | 3,850 | 566.4 |
| 1,606.8 | **Jenkins Shelter** *10mS; 14.3mN* | S, w | 2,500 | 569.4 |
| 1,602.6 | Brushy Mtn | | 3,080 | 573.6 |
| 1,602.0 | Va. 615, Laurel Creek | R, C, w | 2,450 | 574.2 |

| Miles from Katahdin | Features | Services | Elev. | Miles from Springer |
|---|---|---|---|---|
| 1,595.1 | U.S. 21/52 **Bland, VA 24315; Bastian, VA 24314** | R (E–2.7m PO, G, L, M, D, @; 3.3m G, L, M) (W–2.5m PO; 3.5m D) | 2,900 | 581.1 |
| 1,594.9 | I-77 Crossing | R | 2,750 | 581.3 |
| 1,594.3 | Va. 612, Kimberling Creek | R, w | 2,700 | 581.9 |
| 1,592.8 | **Helveys Mill Shelter** *14.3mS; 10.1mN* | E–0.3m S, w | 3,090 | 583.4 |
| 1,586.1 | Va. 611 | R | 2,820 | 590.1 |
| 1,583.7 | Brushy Mtn | | 3,101 | 592.5 |
| 1,583.0 | **Jenny Knob Shelter** *10.1mS; 14.2mN* | S, w | 2,800 | 593.2 |
| 1,581.8 | Va. 608, Crandon | R | 2,200 | 594.4 |
| 1,578.5 | Brushy Mtn | | 2,900 | 597.7 |
| 1,576.6 | Kimberling Creek suspension bridge | | 2,090 | 599.6 |
| 1,576.5 | Va. 606 | R (W–0.5m C, G, M, sh, f) | 2,100 | 599.7 |
| 1,574.6 | Dismal Creek Falls Trail | W–0.3m to falls | 2,320 | 601.6 |
| 1,570.7 | Ribble Trail, south jct; White Pine Horse Campground | W–0.5m C, w | 2,400 | 605.5 |
| 1,570.3 | Stream | w | 2,500 | 605.9 |
| 1,568.8 | **Wapiti Shelter** *14.2mS; 8.4mN* | S, w | 2,640 | 607.4 |
| 1,564.3 | Ribble Trail, north jct | w | 3,800 | 611.9 |
| 1,564.2 | USFS 103, Big Horse Gap | R | 3,800 | 612.0 |
| 1,562.6 | Sugar Run Gap, Sugar Run Rd (Va. 663) | R (E–0.5m H) | 3,450 | 613.6 |
| 1,560.4 | **Doc's Knob Shelter** *8.4mS; 15.0mN* | S, w | 3,555 | 615.8 |
| 1,555.2 | Campsite, spring | C, w | 3,750 | 621.0 |
| 1,554.7 | Angels Rest; Pearis Mtn | | 3,550 | 621.5 |
| 1,552.7 | Va. 634 | R | 2,200 | 623.5 |

The state's highest mountain, Mt. Rogers, an area of spectacular highland meadows, routinely receives snowfall from October to May, making it considerably colder, wetter, and snowier than other areas of Virginia. Northbounders may be tempted to mail home their cold-weather gear, only to see spring flavored by winter.

**Mt. Rogers Appalachian Trail Club**—MRATC maintains the 55.9 miles between Damascus and Va. 670 at the South Fork of the Holston River. Send correspondence to MRATC, P.O. Box 789, Damascus, VA 24236-0789; <www.mratc.org>.

**U.S. 58/Damascus, Va. [P.O. ZIP 24236: M–F 8:30–1 & 2–4:30, Sa 9–11; (276) 475-3411]**—Called "the friendliest town on the Trail" and the home of Trail Days (to be held May 16–18). First held in '87 as a commemorative event for the 50th anniversary of the A.T., the festival's activities and crowds have grown each year since. Activities include a hiker reunion and talent show, hiking-related exhibits, arts-and-crafts exhibits, a trout rodeo, street dances, live music, and the popular hiker parade through downtown. If you are unable to walk into Damascus for the weekend, rides are usually easy to find from all points along the Trail. Be aware that state open-container laws that restrict drinking in public places are enforced. Hiker camping during Trail Days is at the edge of town on Shady Lane. Camping is prohibited everywhere else, except on the grounds of The Place (see below). During your stay, keep in mind that most of the campsites are in residential areas. Please keep quiet in the late evening and early morning, and, upon departure, leave your campsite clean. Leave No Trace camping principles apply in town as well as on the Trail. You'll find all major services, except veterinary, in Damascus. ■ *Hostels:* The Place, provided by the Damascus First United Methodist Church, opens in late Mar and closes when the pipes are in danger of freezing. Stays and parking are limited to two days. A large house, with bunk space, showers, a back porch, and outside picnic tables. Four-dollar-per-night donation is requested, but larger donations are appreciated, in addition to cleaning the restroom, taking out trash, washing dishes, *etc.* Smoking is not allowed on "The Place" property; absolutely no drinking is permitted on the property of the First United Methodist Church, its parking lot, and The Place. Dave's Place Hostel, run by Mt. Rogers Outfitters, 5 rooms with two bunks each, $10/person/night, shower without stay $3, ask about staying with dogs, daily parking $2/day, no alcohol on property. ■ *Lodging:* Apple Tree B&B, (276) 475-5261, across from the library; Augusta's Appalachian Inn B&B, (276) 475-3565, 125 Laurel Ave., P.O. Box 160 Damascus, VA 24236, free WiFi, long-distance phone, one load laundry/room for hikers, accepts mail drops for guests; Damascus Old Mill Inn, (276) 475-3745, 215 Imboden St.; The Hiker's Inn, (276) 475-3788, 216 East Laurel Ave.; Lazy Fox Inn, (276) 475-5838; Mountain Laurel Inn, (276) 475-5956, west of town; A Dancing Bear's Getaway, (276) 475-5900, 203 East Laurel Ave.; Montgomery Homestead B&B, (276) 475-5125 or cell (276) 492-6283, 103 Laurel Ave., mail drops accepted for guests sent to Susie Montgomery, P.O. Box 12, Damascus, VA 24236; The Victorian Inn B&B, (276) 475-5059, 203 N. Legion St.; The Rollin' Rock Inn B&B, (276) 475-6283, 761 Orchard Hill Rd. ■ *Grocer-*

# Damascus

*ies:* Food City (long-term resupply). ■ *Restaurants:* Sicily's Pizza; Dairy King; Subway; Dot's Inn; Cowboy's Deli and convenience store, with ATM; Damascus Eats, B/L/D deli; Country Corner; In the Country; Damascus Old Mill Restaurant, L/D and ice cream; Baja Café L/D; Mojoe's Trailside Coffee House, B. ■ *Outfitters:* Mt. Rogers Outfitters (MRO), (276) 475-5416, owned and operated by 1990 thru-hiker and Damascus native Dave Patrick and son Jeff, backpacking gear and supplies, stove fuel, shuttles, accepts mail drops sent to 110 Laurel Ave. (P.O. Box 546), Damascus, VA 24236, open M–Sa 9–6, Su 12–6; Adventure Damascus Outdoor Company, (276) 475-6262 or (888) 595-2453, <info@adventuredamascus. com>, 128 W. Laurel Ave. (P.O. Box 1113), Damascus, VA 24236; Sundog Outfitter, (276) 475-6252 or (866) 515-3441, 331 Douglas Dr., Damascus, VA 24236 (mail drops can be sent *via* USPS to P.O. Box 1113, Damascus, VA 24236; UPS, to 331 Douglas Dr.), Internet access, white gas, alcohol, Coleman fuel by ounce or gallon, call ahead for shuttles (fee). Flyfishing Outfitter & Espresso Bar, (276) 475-3070 or (208) 610-4969, 101 South Shady Ave., Damascus, VA 24236, <snowmaker79@ hotmail.com>. ■ *Internet access:* Damascus Public Library, WiFi, M–Th 11–7, F 11–5, Sa 9–1; and Baja Café. ■ *Other services:* free long-term parking lot for hikers; coin laundry; medical clinic; pharmacy; hardware store; Dollar Store; two banks with ATM; Bunny Medeiros (Soothing Senses) massages, (276) 475-5140. ■ *Other attractions:* The Virginia Creeper Trail (see below). The town's July 4th celebration, known as the Beaverdam Jam, features live music and a fireworks display. The Transcontinental Bicycle Trail uses U.S. 58 (which the A.T. also follows for a stretch) as its route; don't be surprised if you see some cross-country bikers at The Place. Backbone Rock, a large rock formation that Va. 716 tunnels through, is located 3.5 miles south of town.

**West** 2 miles on U.S. 58 to Fisher Hollow Veterinary Clinic, (276) 475-5397.

**West** 12 miles on U.S. 58 to Abingdon, Va., a large town near I-81 with all major services, including a veterinarian, movie theater, and Highlands Ski & Outdoor Center, (276) 628-1329, open M–F 10–7, Sa 9–7, Su 12–6. Check bulletin boards at The Place and the outfitters for shuttles to Abingdon, as well as to Bristol, a larger city straddling the Virginia–Tennessee line.

**Virginia Creeper Trail**—The Virginia Creeper stretches 33 miles along an old railroad bed from Abingdon to the Virginia–North Carolina state line. It began as a native-American footpath. Later, it was used by pioneers, including Daniel Boone, and, beginning in the early 1900s, by a quintessential mountain railroad, its namesake, with 100 trestles and bridges, as well as many steep grades and sharp curves. The A.T. shares the Creeper route north of Damascus for 300 yards and again 10 miles farther north at Creeper Junction.

**Saunders Shelter** (1987)—Sleeps 8. Privy. Shelter is located on a 0.2-mile blue-blazed trail. Water source is behind and to the right of the shelter, then down an old road to a reliable, seeping spring.

**USFS Beartree Campground**—*via* Bear Tree Gap Trail **West** 3 miles. Part of Mt. Rogers National Recreation Area, (276) 388-3642, with a lake and swimming area 1 mile from the A.T. Campground is 2 miles beyond swimming area, with tentsites $17S, $34D, and hot showers $4. Parking $3/day. Open mid-Apr–Oct.

**Lost Mountain Shelter** (1994)—Sleeps 8. Privy. Water source is on a trail to the left of the shelter.

**Whitetop Mountain**—At 5,520 feet, this is Virginia's second-highest peak, although the Trail does not go to the top. The nearby town of Whitetop is home to a ramp festival, held the weekend after Memorial Day. The celebration includes a ramp-eating contest thru-hikers have won in past years. Ramps emerge from the forest floor in early spring. The two-leafed greens sprout from an onion-like tuber that can be used to spice up Trail meals. Other plants have a similar look, but ramps are identified easily by their smell and taste, which are akin to onions and garlic. In years past, local residents held large music festivals on Whitetop Mountain. In the 1930s, they were so popular they even attracted a visit from then-First Lady Eleanor Roosevelt.

**Va. 600, Elk Garden**—Elk Garden is named after the now-extinct eastern elk that once roamed throughout this area, along with timber wolves, mountain lions, and bison. Today, none of those animals exist here, but black bear, white-tailed deer, and wild turkey are common throughout these woodlands. Neotropical nesting birds of this area include such songbirds as Vesper's sparrow, common raven, various hawks, and several species of warblers.

**Mt. Rogers**—Virginia's highest peak, at 5,729 feet; the Trail does not go to the viewless summit, but it can be reached *via* the Susan Spillane Side Trail, going west 0.5 mile. Camping is prohibited in the area from the A.T. to the summit due to fragile plant life and the endangered Wellers salamander. The Wellers, a dark blue-black salamander with gold splotches on its back, can be found only in coniferous forests above 5,000 feet. You may also see or hear northern birds, such as the hermit thrush and winter wren. Such species nest here because of the favorable altitude at the summit area.

**Thomas Knob Shelter** (1991)—Sleeps 16. Privy (moldering). This two-level shelter was built by the MRATC and Konnarock Crew. Water source is in an enclosed area in a pasture behind the shelter; lock the gate leading to the water source to keep the feral ponies in the area from polluting the water. Be aware those ponies like to chew on packs and other salty items.

**Rhododendron Gap**—Just below the highest point on the Virginia A.T. on Pine Mountain and Wilburn Ridge. In late Jun, rhododendron blooms here in full force. Panoramic views of the rhododendron thickets can be seen from a rock outcropping. Watch your step from Thomas Knob through the Grayson Highlands State Park area; cattle and feral ponies roam the area. In the spring, you will see mares tending their foals.

**Grayson Highlands State Park**—(276) 579-7092. At Massey Gap, a blue-blaze leads **East** 0.5 mile to a parking area, then 1.5 miles farther on roads to park's campground. Park is open year-round from dawn to 10 p.m. The campstore and showers are open May 1–Oct 31, closed in cold weather; Th–Su 10–5; Jul–Aug daily 10–5; may use phone at camp store with a calling card; tentsite with shower $19, shower only $5.

**Wise Shelter** (1996)—Sleeps 8. Privy. Water source is a reliable spring south of the shelter on a trail east of the A.T. No tenting around the shelter or in the state park. Tentsites are in the Mt. Rogers NRA, across Wilson Creek, 0.3 mile north. Follow the Wilson Creek Trail 2 miles east to Grayson Highlands State Park (see above).

**Old Orchard Shelter** (1970)—Sleeps 6. Privy. Water source is 100 yards on a blue-blazed trail to the right of the shelter.

**Hurricane Mountain Shelter** (2004)—Sleeps 8. Privy (moldering). Water source is a nearby stream.

**USFS Hurricane Campground**—**West** 0.5 mile *via* side trail to Hurricane Campground, (276) 783-5196, one of nine USFS campgrounds within the George Washington and Jefferson National Forests. The campground charges $14 per site; $2 shower. Open Apr 15–Oct 31, depending on weather. Restroom and shower are available May 1–Oct 31, depending on weather.

**Va. 650 & Va. 16/Dickey Gap**—**East** 2.6 miles to **Troutdale, Va. [P.O. ZIP 24378: M–F 8–12 & 1–5, Sa 8:15–11; (276) 677-3221].** ■ *Groceries:* Jerry's Kitchen & Goods, 2.0 miles east on Va. 16, (276) 677-3010, <bartley16@hotmail.com>, M–Sa 8 a.m.–9 p.m., Su 8–7, short-term resupply, fuel (white gas, alcohol, Heet, butane/propane mix), dogs allowed, free Internet, WiFi, free shuttle to Fox Creek and Dickey Gap, fee for longer distances; also houses a restaurant serving B/L/D that closes around 7:45; mail drops accepted (USPS, UPS) if sent to 10973 Troutdale Hwy., Troutdale, VA 24378. ■ *Hostel:* Troutdale Baptist Church, Pastor Ken Riggins, (276) 677-4092, located at 10148 Troutdale Hwy., offers a place to tent or use of a hiker bunkhouse (no bunks, sleep on floor, one room heated), shower; pets welcome, donations accepted.

**East** 4.9 miles to *Lodging:* Fox Hill Inn B&B, (800) 874-3313, (276) 677-3313, 8568 Troutdale Hwy, Troutdale, VA 24378, caretaker Marie Joseph. Includes B, kitchen, grill use, private bath, possible shuttle, on-site laundry (no charge); library, satellite TV; no pets allowed; pick up groceries before arriving; for hikers who have made advance reservations, mail drops accepted (reservations suggested for weekends).

USFS Raccoon Branch Campground is 3.2 miles **East** on the blue-blazed trail; tentsites $12, no showers, open Apr–Dec, no water after Oct 31.

**Trimpi Shelter** (1975)—Sleeps 8. Privy. Water source is a reliable spring in front of the shelter.

---

**Piedmont Appalachian Trail Hikers (PATH)**—PATH maintains the 64.1 miles between Va. 670, South Fork of the Holston River, and U.S. 21/52 at Bland, Va. Correspondence can be sent to PATH, P.O. Box 4423, Greensboro, NC 27404; <www.path-at.org>.

---

**Partnership Shelter** (1998)—Sleeps 16. Privy and propane-powered warm-water shower (available during warmer months). No tenting around the shelter. Water source is a faucet behind the shelter. No alcoholic beverages allowed. For a week or more after Trail Days, expect law-enforcement officers to be checking in.

**Mt. Rogers National Recreation Area Headquarters**—(276) 783-5196 or (800) 628-7202, M–F 8–4:30 year-round, Sa 10–4 May–Oct (weather permitting). Only several hundred yards north of Partnership Shelter, the headquarters houses a bookshop and interpretive center with information about plants and animals found in the area. Water is available from a spigot outside (in nonfreezing weather). Restroom and soda machine inside. From the outside phone (free local calls, calling card needed for long distance), you can order pizza from several area pizzerias, including Pizza Hut, (276) 783-3104, to be delivered to gate. Do not sleep on the headquarters' covered porch. Obtain free permit to park overnight or weekly.

**Va. 16—East** 3.2 miles to **Sugar Grove, Va. [P.O. ZIP 24375: M–F 8–12 & 1:15–4:45, Sa 8–10:30; (276) 677-3200].** The town is home to the ATC Konnarock Volunteer Crew (see below). ■ *Groceries:* Mt. View Food Mart, (276) 677-3037, M–Sa 7–9:30, Su 8–9:30 (short-term resupply), has ATM, pizza, sandwiches, hamburgers, hotdogs, Coleman fuel by the gallon. ■ *Restaurant:* Sugar Grove Diner, (276) 677-3351, B/L/D, M–W 5–8, Th–Sa 5–8:30, possible shuttle to and from Trail, lodging available, hiker discount, call for rate.

**West** 6 miles to **Marion, Va. [P.O. ZIP 24354: M–F 8:30–5 Sa 9:30–11:30; (276) 783-5051],** a larger town near I-81 with all major services, including a Food Lion supermarket (long-term resupply), several restaurants, fast-food outlets, a coin laundry, and Greyhound bus service along the I-81 corridor, (276) 783-7114 (closed Sa, Su, and holidays). ■ *Lodging:* various motels, including the Rodeway Inn, (276) 783-5112, 1419 N. Main/U.S. 11, 0.25 mile beyond Wal-mart, hiker rate $39.95s, dogs $5, includes buffet B, CATV, in-room phones, pool.

**Konnarock Crew**—Based 1 mile from Sugar Grove post office at USFS facility. If you want part of your experience to be a week on the crew that builds and rehabilitates the Trail, call the Blacksburg, Va., ATC regional office at (540) 953-3571 before your hike to make arrangements. Getting to base camp and getting back is your responsibility, but, once there, food and amenities are provided. Commitments include 5 days/4 nights along the Trail in N.C., Ga., Tenn., or Va. Be prepared to work and have a lot of fun.

**Chatfield Shelter** (1970s)—Sleeps 6. Privy. Named in honor of North Carolina conservationist and PATH founder Louise Meroney Chatfield. Water source is a creek in front.

**Va. 615, Settlers Museum**—On USFS lands adjacent to the Trail, the farmstead and visitors center include exhibits of rural life at the time the valley was settled. Admission free to hikers.

**Va. 683, U.S. 11, I-81**—At Groseclose, Va. (no post office), this is the southernmost crossing of I-81. ■ *Restaurants:* Fifty-Four Roses Restaurant, 7327 Lee Hwy, Rural Retreat, VA 24368, <karenB6978@yahoo.com>, owner Karen Zamareh; Middle Eastern food, salads, fresh fruit, home cooking, WiFi, short-term resupply, fuel by the ounce (white gas, alcohol), open 24 hours, accepts mail drops. The Barn Restaurant, B/L/D, M–Sa 6–9, Su 6–3; ask permission for long-term parking, (276) 686-6222, mail drops accepted (no fee), 7412 Lee Hwy, Rural Retreat, VA, 24368. ■ *Groceries:* 24-hour Village Truckstop (Shell), short-term resupply, deli, ATM, Coleman, canister fuel, showers $5; Exxon station & convenience store, 7327 Lee

Highway. ■ *Lodging:* The Relax Inn, 7253 Lee Hwy, Rural Retreat, VA 24368, (276) 783-5811, $40s, $45D for 2 or more, $10 per pet; long-term hiker parking $3/day, coin laundry; call for info on shuttle to Trailhead; holds USPS, UPS, FedEx packages (nonguests $5), Please provide your ETA.

**West** 3.2 miles (on U.S. 11 south) to **Atkins, Va. [P.O. ZIP 24311: M–F 8:30–12:30 & 1:30–4:30, Sa 9–11; (276) 783-5551]**, with restaurants. ■ *Groceries:* Atkins Grocery & Deli (long-term resupply), M–F 6–10, Sa 7–10, closed Su; Pizza Plus, (276) 781-2006, will deliver. ■ *Other services:* Laundromat near grocery store, at opposite end of building (no sign), M–F 7–8, Sa 7-7, closed Su.

**West** 10.2 miles (on U.S. 11 south) to **Marion, Va.** (see above), a larger town with all services.

**Davis Path Shelter** (1984)—Sleeps 8. Privy. Tentsite. Located near an eighteenth-century settlers' route through Davis Valley. Water source is a spring 0.9 mile south of the shelter. Southbounders can carry water from Crawfish Valley, 3.5 miles north.

**Knot Maul Branch Shelter** (1980s)—Sleeps 8. Privy. Named for the knotty wood settlers used as mauls for their farm work. Water source is 0.2 mile north on the A.T.

**Chestnut Knob Shelter** (renovated 1994)—Sleeps 8. Privy. A former firewarden's cabin, the shelter was once called "the cave" but now includes plexiglass windows to let in some light. No water is available at this shelter, but water is sometimes found 0.2 mile south on the A.T., then 50 yards east on an old Jeep road. Otherwise, southbounders can find water 1.3 miles north in Walker Gap, and northbounders can find water at a spring-fed pond 1.8 miles south.

**Burkes Garden**—Chestnut Knob Shelter, elevation 4,410 feet, overlooks this unusual geologic feature, which was the Vanderbilts' first choice for their Biltmore estate, later constructed near Asheville, N.C. It is a large, crater-shaped depression surrounded on all sides by a high ridge that the A.T. follows for nearly 8 miles. From Chestnut Knob, you can see how it got its nickname, "God's Thumbprint."

**Jenkins Shelter** (1960s)—Sleeps 8. Privy. Formerly the Monster Rock Shelter, built in the 1960s when the A.T. followed the ridge of Walker Mountain. Shelter was moved to its present location in the early 1980s, when the Trail was relocated. Water source is a stream 100 yards north on a blue-blazed trail.

**U.S. 52—East** 2.7 miles to **Bland, Va. [P.O. ZIP 24315: M–F 8–11:30 & 12–4:00, Sa 8–11; (276) 688-3751]**. Larger than Bastian, with more services. ■ *Restaurants*: Bland Square Grill (in Bland Square Citgo, 8870 South Scenic Hwy, first block west of Main on U.S. 52 in downtown Bland, B/L/D M–Sa 7–7, closed Su. ■ *Groceries:* Scott's IGA Supermarket (long-term resupply), M–Sa 7–9:30, Su 8–9, credit cards accepted. ■ *Internet access:* library, (276) 688-3737, MWF 9:30–4:30, Tu, Th 9:30–8, free WiFi. ■ *Other services:* hardware store; medical clinic, (276) 688-4800, MTW 9–5, Th 9–12; bank with ATM.

**East** 3.3 miles to ■ *Lodging:* Big Walker Motel, 70 Skyview Lane, Bland, VA 24315, (276) 688-3331, $57.73 1-2 persons, $62.01 3 or more, pets OK, WiFi, will hold packages only for guests. ■ *Other services:* Dairy Queen with ATM, Subway, Dollar General. There is no place to camp in Bland.

**West** 2.5 miles to **Bastian, Va. [P.O. ZIP 24314: M–F 8–12 & 12:30–4, Sa 8–10:30; (276) 688-4631].** P.O. is **West** 1.9 miles, left on Railroad Trail, right on Walnut Drive. Two miles farther down U.S. 52 to *Other services:* Round Mountain United Methodist Church, P.O. Box 203, Pastor Alan Ashworth will pick up hikers (at three Trailheads) for free AYCE B Mondays in Apr–May, shuttle back to Trail or into Bland P.O. or grocery; medical clinic, (276) 688-4331, M, W 8:30–6, Tu 9–8, Th 8:30–8, F 8:30–5; pharmacy next door, M–F 9–5, Sa 9–12; Greyhound bus service, (304) 325-9442, available for the I-77 corridor in Bluefield, W.Va., about 10 miles beyond Bastian on U.S. 52 (closed Su and holidays).

**Outdoor Club at Virginia Tech**—OCVT maintains the 9 miles between U.S. 21/52 and Va. 611 and 18.8 miles in central Virginia between U.S. 460 and Pine Swamp Branch Shelter. Correspondence should be sent to OCVT, P.O. Box 538, Blacksburg, VA 24060; <www.outdoor.org.vt.edu>.

**Helveys Mill Shelter** (1960s)—Sleeps 6. Privy. Relocated here when the A.T. was moved off Walker Mountain in the 1980s. Water source is down a switch-backed trail in front of the shelter.

**Jenny Knob Shelter** (1960s)—Sleeps 6. Privy. Relocated here when the A.T. was moved off Walker Mountain. Water source is a spring near the shelter.

**Va. 608, Va. 42—East** 0.8 mile to the community of Crandon. The small country store once located here is closed.

**Roanoke Appalachian Trail Club**—RATC maintains the 34.4 miles between Va. 611 and U.S. 460 and 87.0 miles in the next section between Pine Swamp Branch Shelter and Black Horse Gap. Correspondence should be sent to RATC, P.O. Box 12282, Roanoke, VA 24024; <www.ratc.org>.

**Va. 606—West** 0.5 mile to *Groceries:* Trent's Grocery with deli and pizza. Open daily M–Sa 7–9, Su 9–9, Coleman and denatured alcohol by the gallon, pay phone, and soda machines. Camping, shower and laundry $5, or warm shower and laundry only $3.

**Wapiti Shelter** (1980)—Sleeps 8. Privy. Water source is Dismal Creek, just south of the turn-off to the shelter.

**Sugar Run Road/Sugar Run Gap—East** 0.5 mile to *Hostel:* Check first. Woodshole Hostel, (540) 921-1655, with bunkhouse, solar shower, and privy—all free to hikers if operating as in the past. Tillie Wood of Atlanta, who died in October 2007, summered here in a log cabin built in 1880 and operated the hostel May 8–Jun 24. Relatives of Tillie have said they are considering resuming her practices. Tillie's husband, Roy, who passed away in 1987, found the old homestead while studying a herd of elk (wapiti) in the area during the 1940s. During the Carter administration, Roy served as assistant to the secretary of the interior; Tillie was very active in the "Peanut Brigade" that helped elect President Jimmy Carter.

**Doc's Knob Shelter** (1971)—Sleeps 8. Privy. Water source is a reliable spring to the left of the shelter.

*"The flowers bloom, the song birds sing, and, 'though it be sun or rain, I walk the mountain tops with spring from Georgia north to Maine."*
    —EARL SHAFFER, "CRAZY ONE" (AT '48, '65, '98)

# Virginia—Part 2 (Central)

| Miles from Katahdin | Features | Services | Elev. | Miles from Springer |
|---|---|---|---|---|
| 1,552.7 | Va. 634 | R | 2,200 | 623.5 |
| 1,552.2 | Lane Street **Pearisburg, VA 24134** | R, L, G, sh, f (E−1m PO, G, L, M, D, V, f, cl, @; 2.9m H; 20m G, L, M, O) | 1,650 | 624.0 |
| 1,551.7 | U.S. 460, Senator Shumate Bridge (east end), New River | R | 1,600 | 624.5 |
| 1,550.2 | Clendennin Rd (Va. 641) | R | 1,750 | 626.0 |
| 1,548.0 | Springs | C, w | 3,250 | 628.2 |
| 1,545.4 | **Rice Field Shelter** *15.0mS; 12.5mN* | S (E−0.3m w) | 3,375 | 630.8 |
| 1,543.8 | Campsite, water | C, w | 3,300 | 632.4 |
| 1,540.3 | Symms Gap Meadow | C, w | 3,320 | 635.9 |
| 1,539.3 | Groundhog Trail | | 3,400 | 636.9 |
| 1,537.8 | Dickinson Gap | | 3,300 | 638.4 |
| 1,537.6 | Peters Mtn | | 3,500 | 638.6 |
| 1,535.4 | Allegheny Trail | | | 640.8 |
| 1,532.9 | **Pine Swamp Branch Shelter** *12.5mS; 3.9mN* | S, w | 2,530 | 643.3 |
| 1,532.6 | Va. 635, Stony Creek Valley | R | 2,370 | 643.6 |
| 1,531.5 | Dismal Branch | w | 2,480 | 644.7 |
| 1,530.5 | Va. 635, Stony Creek | R, w | 2,450 | 645.7 |
| 1,529.2 | Spring | w | 3,490 | 647.0 |
| 1,529.0 | **Bailey Gap Shelter** *3.9mS; 8.8mN* | S, w | 3,525 | 647.2 |
| 1,525.3 | Va. 613, Salt Sulphur Tpk | R | 3,950 | 650.9 |
| 1,525.1 | Wind Rock | | 4,100 | 651.1 |
| 1,523.9 | Campsites, spring | C, w | 4,000 | 652.3 |
| 1,520.2 | **War Spur Shelter** *8.8mS; 5.8mN* | S, w | 2,340 | 656.0 |
| 1,519.4 | USFS 156, Johns Creek Valley | R, w | 2,080 | 656.8 |
| 1,518.4 | Stream | w | 2,700 | 657.8 |
| 1,517.4 | Va. 601, Rocky Gap | R | 3,250 | 658.8 |
| 1,514.4 | **Laurel Creek Shelter** *5.8mS; 6.7mN* | S, w | 2,720 | 661.8 |
| 1,513.4 | Spring | w | 2,400 | 662.8 |
| 1,512.0 | Va. 42, Sinking Creek Valley | R (E−0.5m L) | 2,200 | 664.2 |

| Miles from Katahdin | Features | Services | Elev. | Miles from Springer |
|---|---|---|---|---|
| 1,511.1 | Va. 630, Sinking Creek | R, w | 2,100 | 665.1 |
| 1,510.7 | Keffer Oak | | 2,240 | 665.5 |
| 1,508.0 | **Sarver Hollow Shelter** *6.7mS; 6.3mN* | E–0.3m S, w | 3,000 | 668.2 |
| 1,504.4 | Sinking Creek Mtn | | 3,450 | 671.8 |
| 1,502.7 | Cabin Branch | C, w | 2,490 | 673.5 |
| 1,502.0 | **Niday Shelter** *6.3mS; 10.4mN* | S, w | 1,800 | 674.2 |
| 1,500.7 | Va. 621, Craig Creek Valley | R | 1,540 | 675.5 |
| 1,496.9 | Audie Murphy Monument | | 3,100 | 679.3 |
| 1,493.1 | Va. 620, Trout Creek | R, w | 1,525 | 683.1 |
| 1,491.9 | **Pickle Branch Shelter** *10.4mS; 13.9mN* | E–0.3m S, w | 1,845 | 684.3 |
| 1,487.7 | Cove Mtn, Dragons Tooth | | 3,020 | 688.5 |
| 1,486.7 | Lost Spectacles Gap | | 2,550 | 689.5 |
| 1,486.2 | Rawies Rest | | 2,350 | 690.0 |
| 1,485.2 | Va. 624, North Mtn Trail | R (W–0.4m G, M) | 1,810 | 691.0 |
| 1,483.6 | Va. 785 | R | 1,790 | 692.6 |
| 1,479.3 | Va. 311 **Catawba, VA 24070** | R (W–1m PO, G; 1.3m M) | 1,990 | 696.9 |
| 1,478.3 | **Johns Spring Shelter** *13.9mS; 1mN* | S, w | 1,980 | 697.9 |
| 1,477.3 | **Catawba Mtn Shelter** *1mS; 2.4mN* | S, w | 2,580 | 698.9 |
| 1,475.6 | McAfee Knob | | 3,197 | 700.6 |
| 1,475.0 | Pig Farm Campsite | C, w | 3,000 | 701.2 |
| 1,474.9 | **Campbell Shelter** *2.4mS; 6mN* | S, w | 2,580 | 701.3 |
| 1,471.8 | Brickey's Gap | | 2,250 | 704.4 |
| 1,470.5 | Tinker Cliffs | | 3,000 | 705.7 |
| 1,469.5 | Scorched Earth Gap, Andy Layne Trail | | 2,600 | 706.7 |
| 1,468.9 | **Lamberts Meadow Shelter** *6mS; 14.4mN* | S, w | 2,080 | 707.3 |
| 1,468.6 | Lamberts Meadow Campsite, Sawmill Run | C, w | 2,000 | 707.6 |
| 1,464.6 | Angels Gap | | 1,800 | 711.6 |
| 1,463.5 | Hay Rock, Tinker Ridge | | 1,900 | 712.7 |
| 1,460.0 | Tinker Creek | | 1,165 | 716.2 |

| Miles from Katahdin | Features | Services | Elev. | Miles from Springer |
|---|---|---|---|---|
| 1,459.5 | U.S. 220, Va. 816 **Cloverdale, VA 24077; Daleville, VA 24083** | R; G, L, M, cl (E–0.8m G, M, L, cl, sh, @; 2.3m PO G, L, M; 12m G, M, O, D, V) (W–0.3m G, M, O, @, f; 1m PO) | 1,350 | 716.7 |
| 1,458.3 | Va. 779, I-81 | R | 1,400 | 717.9 |
| 1,458.0 | U.S. 11, Norfolk & Western Railway **Troutville, VA 24175** | R (W–1.3m PO, C, G, M) | 1,300 | 718.2 |
| 1,457.4 | Va. 652 | R | 1,450 | 718.8 |
| 1,454.5 | **Fullhardt Knob Shelter** *14.4mS; 6.2mN* | S, w | 2,670 | 721.7 |
| 1,454.1 | Spring | w | 2,550 | 722.1 |
| 1,451.7 | USFS 191, | R | 2,260 | 724.5 |
|  | Salt Pond Rd |  |  |  |
| 1,450.9 | Curry Creek | w | 1,680 | 725.3 |
| 1,449.0 | Wilson Creek | w | 1,690 | 727.2 |
| 1,448.3 | **Wilson Creek Shelter** *6.2mS; 7.5mN* | S, w | 1,830 | 727.9 |
| 1,447.9 | Spring | w | 2,050 | 728.3 |
| 1,445.9 | USFS 186; BRP mp 97.7; Old Fincastle Rd; Black Horse Gap | R | 2,402 | 730.3 |
| 1,445.1 | BRP mp 97.0; Taylors Mtn Overlook | R | 2,350 | 731.1 |
| 1,444.0 | BRP mp 95.9; Montvale Overlook | R | 2,400 | 732.2 |
| 1,443.4 | BRP mp 95.3;Harveys Knob Overlook | R | 2,550 | 732.8 |
| 1,441.0 | **Bobblets Gap Shelter** *7.5mS; 6.6mN* | W–0.2m S, w | 1,920 | 735.2 |
| 1,440.3 | BRP mp 92.5; Sharp Top Overlook | R | 2,350 | 735.9 |
| 1,439.6 | BRP mp 91.8; Mills Gap Overlook | R | 2,450 | 736.6 |
| 1,437.9 | Va. 43, Bearwallow Gap; BRP mp 90.9 **Buchanan, VA 24066** | R (E–4.4m C, L, M) (W–5m PO, G, M, @; 7m L, M) | 2,228 | 738.3 |
| 1,436.4 | Cove Mtn |  | 2,720 | 739.8 |
| 1,436.0 | Little Cove Mtn Trail |  | 2,600 | 740.2 |
| 1,434.6 | **Cove Mtn Shelter** *6.6mS; 6.9mN* | S, nw | 1,925 | 741.6 |
| 1,432.9 | Buchanan Trail |  | 1,790 | 743.3 |

| Miles from Katahdin | Features | Services | Elev. | Miles from Springer |
|---|---|---|---|---|
| 1,431.4 | Va. 614, Jennings Creek | R, C, w (E– 0.3m w; 1.4m C, G, cl, sh, f) (W–4.5m L, M) | 951 | 744.8 |
| 1,429.8 | Fork Mtn | | 2,042 | 746.4 |
| 1,427.7 | **Bryant Ridge Shelter** *6.9mS; 5mN* | S, w | 1,320 | 748.5 |
| 1,423.3 | Floyd Mtn | | 3,560 | 752.9 |
| 1,422.7 | **Cornelius Creek Shelter** *5mS; 5.3mN* | S, w | 3,145 | 753.5 |
| 1,421.8 | Black Rock | | 3,450 | 754.4 |
| 1,420.1 | Apple Orchard Falls Trail | | 3,250 | 756.1 |
| 1,420.0 | USFS 812, Parkers Gap Rd; BRP mp 78.4 | R | 3,430 | 756.2 |
| 1,418.6 | Apple Orchard Mtn | | 4,225 | 757.6 |
| 1,418.3 | The Guillotine | | 4,090 | 757.9 |
| 1,417.7 | Upper BRP mp 76.3 | R | 3,900 | 758.5 |
| 1,417.4 | **Thunder Hill Shelter** *5.3mS; 12.4mN* | S, w | 3,960 | 758.8 |
| 1,416.4 | Lower BRP mp 74.9 | R | 3,650 | 759.8 |
| 1,416.0 | Thunder Ridge Overlook; BRP mp 74.7 | R | 3,501 | 760.2 |
| 1,414.8 | Harrison Ground Spring | w | 3,200 | 761.4 |
| 1,412.7 | USFS 35, Petites Gap; BRP mp 71.0 | R | 2,369 | 763.5 |
| 1,411.5 | High Cock Knob | | 3,073 | 764.7 |
| 1,410.5 | Marble Spring | C, w | 2,290 | 765.7 |
| 1,408.7 | Sulphur Spring Trail (south crossing) | | 2,400 | 767.5 |
| 1,408.2 | Belfast Trail, Hickory Stand | | 2,650 | 768.0 |
| 1,407.7 | Sulphur Spring Trail (north crossing) | | 2,588 | 768.5 |
| 1,406.9 | Big Cove Branch | w | 1,890 | 769.3 |
| 1,405.0 | **Matts Creek Shelter** *12.4mS; 3.9mN* | S, w | 835 | 771.2 |
| 1,404.2 | Campsite | C, w | 700 | 772.0 |
| 1,403.0 | James River Foot Bridge | | 678 | 773.2 |
| 1,402.8 | U.S. 501, Va. 130, James River, **Big Island, VA 24526; Glasgow, VA 24555** | R (E–4.7m C, G, L, cl, sh; 5.1m PO, G, M, D) (W– 5.9m PO, G, L, M, cl, f, @) | 680 | 773.4 |
| 1,402.7 | Lower Rocky Row Run Bridge | w | 670 | 773.5 |

| Miles from Katahdin | Features | Services | Elev. | Miles from Springer |
|---|---|---|---|---|
| 1,402.6 | Rocky Row Run | C, w | 760 | 773.6 |
| 1,401.7 | Va. 812, USFS 36 | R | 825 | 774.5 |
| 1,401.1 | **Johns Hollow Shelter** *3.9mS; 9mN* | S, w | 1,020 | 775.1 |
| 1,399.1 | Rocky Row Trail | | 2,400 | 777.1 |
| 1,399.0 | Fullers Rocks, Little Rocky Row | | 2,472 | 777.2 |
| 1,398.0 | Big Rocky Row | | 2,992 | 778.2 |
| 1,396.5 | Saddle Gap, Saddle Gap Trail | | 2,600 | 779.7 |
| 1,395.4 | Saltlog Gap (south) | | 2,573 | 780.8 |
| 1,393.9 | Bluff Mtn | | 3,372 | 782.3 |
| 1,392.8 | Punchbowl Mtn | | 2,850 | 783.4 |
| 1,392.3 | **Punchbowl Shelter** *9mS; 9.7mN* | W−0.2m S, w | 2,500 | 783.9 |
| 1,391.9 | Punchbowl Mtn Crossing; BRP mp 51.7 | R, w | 2,170 | 784.3 |
| 1,391.6 | Va. 607, Robinson Gap Rd | R | 2,100 | 784.6 |
| 1,389.7 | Rice Mtn | | 2,228 | 786.5 |
| 1,387.8 | USFS 39, Pedlar River | R | 990 | 788.4 |
| 1,384.8 | Pedlar Lake Rd (USFS 38) | R | 1,000 | 791.4 |
| 1,382.8 | **Brown Mtn Creek Shelter** *9.7mS; 6.2mN* | S, w | 1,395 | 793.4 |
| 1,381.0 | U.S. 60 **Buena Vista, VA 24416; Lexington, VA 24450** | R (W−9.3m PO, C, G, L, M, D, V, cl, sh; 15m PO, G, L, M, D, V, O, f) | 2,065 | 795.2 |
| 1,378.2 | Bald Knob | | 4,059 | 798.0 |
| 1,377.2 | Old Hotel Trail, **Cow Camp Gap Shelter** *6.2mS; 10.8mN* | E−0.6m S, w | 3,160 | 799.0 |
| 1,376.0 | Cold Mtn | | 4,022 | 800.2 |
| 1,374.7 | USFS 48, Hog Camp Gap | R, C, w | 3,485 | 801.5 |
| 1,373.8 | Tar Jacket Ridge | | 3,847 | 802.4 |
| 1,372.5 | USFS 63, Salt Log Gap (north) | R | 3,257 | 803.7 |
| 1,371.3 | USFS 246 | R | 3,500 | 804.9 |
| 1,370.8 | Greasy Spring Rd | R | 3,600 | 805.4 |
| 1,368.9 | N Fork of Piney River | C, w | 3,500 | 807.3 |
| 1,367.7 | Elk Pond Branch | C, w | 3,750 | 808.5 |

| Miles from Katahdin | Features | Services | Elev. | Miles from Springer |
|---|---|---|---|---|
| 1,367.0 | **Seeley-Woodworth Shelter** *10.8mS; 6.9mN* | S, w | 3,770 | 809.2 |
| 1,365.9 | Porters Field | C, w | 3,650 | 810.3 |
| 1,364.7 | Fish Hatchery Rd **Montebello, VA 24464** | R (W–2.5m PO, C, G, L, cl, sh, f) | 3,454 | 811.5 |
| 1,364.2 | Spy Rock | | 3,680 | 812.0 |
| 1,363.9 | Main Top Mtn | | 4,040 | 812.3 |
| 1,363.1 | Cash Hollow Rock | | 3,550 | 813.1 |
| 1,361.8 | Cash Hollow Rd | R | 3,280 | 814.4 |
| 1,361.0 | Va. 826, Crabtree Farm Rd, Crabtree Falls Trail | W–0.5m C, sh, w | 3,350 | 815.2 |
| 1,360.1 | **The Priest Shelter** *6.9mS; 7.4mN* | S, w | 3,840 | 816.1 |
| 1,359.6 | The Priest | | 4,063 | 816.6 |
| 1,356.6 | Cripple Creek | w | 1,800 | 819.6 |
| 1,355.3 | Va. 56, Tye River | R, C, w (W–4m C, G, sh) | 970 | 820.9 |
| 1,353.6 | Mau-Har Trail | | 2,090 | 822.6 |
| 1,352.7 | **Harpers Creek Shelter** *7.4mS; 6.2mN* | S, w | 1,800 | 823.5 |
| 1,350.7 | Chimney Rocks | | 3,190 | 825.5 |
| 1,349.4 | Three Ridges | | 3,870 | 826.8 |
| 1,348.5 | Hanging Rock Vista | | 3,750 | 827.7 |
| 1,346.5 | **Maupin Field Shelter** *6.2mS; 15.8mN* | S, w (W–2m G, L) (W–2.8m H) | 2,720 | 829.7 |
| 1,344.8 | Va. 664, Reeds Gap; BRP mp 13.6 | R | 2,650 | 831.4 |
| 1,344.3 | BRP mp 13.1; Three Ridges Parking Overlook | R | 2,700 | 831.9 |
| 1,340.5 | Cedar Cliffs | | 2,800 | 835.7 |
| 1,340.0 | BRP mp 9.6; Dripping Rock Parking Area | R, w | 2,950 | 836.2 |
| 1,337.2 | Humpback Mtn; trail to Humpback Rocks | | 3,250 | 839.0 |
| 1,336.2 | Trail to Humpback Rocks | | | 840.0 |
| 1,334.7 | Bear Spring | w | 3,200 | 841.5 |
| 1,332.5 | Glass Hollow Overlook | | 2,750 | 843.7 |
| 1,332.2 | Trail to Humpback Visitors Center | W–1.3m w | 2,150 | 844.0 |
| 1,330.7 | Mill Creek, **Paul C. Wolfe Shelter** *15.8mS; 12.3mN* | S, w | 1,700 | 845.5 |

| 1,325.7 | U.S. 250, I-64, Rockfish Gap **Waynesboro, VA 22980** | R, G, L, M (W—1m L; 4.5m PO, H, C, G, L, M, O, D, V, cl, sh, f, @) | 1,902 | 850.5 |
|---|---|---|---|---|

BRP=Blue Ridge Parkway, mp=milepost

Central Virginia's treadway is well-graded and includes several 2,000- to 3,000-foot climbs. You will traverse some of the northenmost balds on the Trail. Unusual rock formations offer up views to the valley below from the peaks of Humpback Rocks, Three Ridges, The Priest, McAfee Knob, and Dragons Tooth. This section is more rugged and remote than Shenandoah to the north and parallels the Blue Ridge Parkway for 90 miles.

**U.S.460/Pearisburg, Va.** On A.T. ■ *Lodging:* Rendezvous Motel, (540) 921-2636, $41.04s, $49.68D up to 4, dogs permitted, unlimited long-distance phone, CATV, laundry, denatured alcohol, MSR compressed gas, Coleman fuel, shuttle as schedule permits, shower without stay $8, holds mail and packages for guests addressed to 795 North Main St., Pearisburg, VA 24134. If you leave on a Sunday, they will mail your packages for you. Very hiker-friendly. ■ *Groceries:* Wade's Market (long-term resupply).

**East** 1 mile to **Pearisburg, Va. [P.O. ZIP 24134: M–F 8–4, Sa 9–12: (540) 921-1100].** ■ *Lodging:* Plaza Motel, (540) 921-2591, $35s, $45D, $50T, $5EAP, laundry, no pets, will hold packages whether guest or not, 415 North Main St., e-mail available in office; Holiday Motor Lodge, (540) 921-1551, $35.95s, $42.60D, $4EAP, Internet access, swimming pool during the season, pet-friendly, restaurant closed on premises, accepts packages for guests only, 401 North Main St. ■ *Groceries:* Food Lion, Sav-a-Lot, Little Giant Grocery, and 7-Day Market (all long-term resupply). ■ *Restaurants:* Courthouse Café, 414 Wenonah Ave., one block from P.O., gourmet coffee, tea, specialty drinks, pastry, Internet access, live music Friday nights; Subway; Hardee's; Pizza Plus, buy one pizza, get one free, AYCE salad/pizza buffet, and free delivery; Dairy Queen; Papa's Pizza Inn with subs, salads; Pizza Hut with AYCE L buffet; Queens Subs; Lucky Star Chinese; Friends & Family. ■ *Internet access:* Courthouse Café, Pearisburg Public Library. ■ *Other services:* Rite Aid with one-hour photo service; automotive and hardware stores; Mutters Shoe Shop with boot repairs, open M–Tu Th–F 8–5, Sa 8–noon, closed W; hair salon and barber; Wal-Mart Superstore; coin laundry; bank with ATM; hospital; dentist; veterinarian; municipal swimming pool open to the public Memorial Day to Labor Day for small fee.

**East** 2.9 miles, follow blue-blaze to *Hostel:* Holy Family Church Hostel, located in a peaceful setting on a hill, is hidden by trees beyond the church parking lot. Members of the church dismantled an old barn and reconstructed it as a hostel expressly for backpackers. Refrigerator, stove, microwave, wood stove, shower, and loft with sleeping pads. Porch with an exquisite view. Camping permitted on lawn and in gazebo. Stays are limited to two nights. Closed Nov 1–Mar 1. Donations are appreciated, as is cleaning the hostel. Alcoholic beverages, drugs, and pets prohibited. Side trail from hostel to Wal-Mart, 0.25 mile. Mail drops are accepted, 516 Mason Court Dr., Pearisburg, VA 24134. No pay phone. Contact Bill Gautier, (540) 921-4673, 9–3 only.

**East** 20 miles *via* U.S. 460 to Blacksburg, Va., home of Virginia Tech, with all services. ***Outfitters:*** Back Country Ski & Sports, (800) 560-6401 or (540) 552-6400, open M–Sa 10–8, Su 1–5; ATC's Virginia Regional Office, (540) 953-3571, is located at 110 Southpark Dr. in a USFS facility.

**Senator Shumate (U.S. 460) Bridge**—The large manufacturing facility in Narrows seen from the bridge over the New River is the Celco (Celanese Acetate) Plant, a major employer in the area that has been working with ATC and the Forest Service to significantly relocate the Trail north of the river.

**Rice Field Shelter** (1995)—Sleeps 7. Privy. This shelter has an excellent viewing area for sunsets and clouded valleys in the morning. Water is on a steep, 0.3-mile downhill hike behind and to the left of the shelter.

**Symms Gap Meadow**—The traverse of Peters Mountain along the Virginia–West Virginia state line is a dry one. At this mountain meadow, with views into West Virginia, a small pond is located downhill from the A.T. on the West Virginia side of the ridge, with spots for camping nearby.

**Allegheny Trail**—2.5 miles south of Pine Swamp Branch Shelter is the A.T.'s junction with the southern terminus of the Allegheny Trail, which extends about 300 miles across West Virginia to the Pennsylvania border. The trail is maintained by the West Virginia Scenic Trails Association, P.O. Box 4042, Charleston, WV 25304; <www.wvnet.edu/wvsta/a-trail.html>.

**Pine Swamp Branch Shelter** (1980s)—Sleeps 8. Privy. Stone shelter. Water is from the stream 75 yards down a blue-blazed trail west of the side trail to the shelter. Privy's okay, but the shelter was damaged in 2007 by tree falling on roof; should be repaired in 2008, but closed until that's done.

**Bailey Gap Shelter** (1960s)—Sleeps 6. Privy. Water is 0.2 mile south on the A.T., then east down a blue-blazed trail.

**War Spur Shelter** (1960s)—Sleeps 6. Privy. Water source is a stream 80 yards north of the shelter on the A.T.

**Laurel Creek Shelter** (1988)—Sleeps 6. Privy. Water is west on the A.T., 45 yards south of the shelter-trail junction.

**Va. 42, Sinking Creek Valley**—**East** 0.5 mile to *Lodging:* The Huffman House B&B at Creekside Farm, <www. thehuffmanhousebandb.com>, owned by 1999 thru-hikers Ron and Carol Baker (Leafhopper & Snowy Egret), (540) 544-6942, $105–$145D, $20EAP, reservations required, will hold packages for registered guests sent to 16 Dick Huffman Store Rd., Newport, VA 24218.

**Keffer Oak**—Located about 0.2 mile north of Va. 630, this is the largest oak tree on the A.T. in the South. Last measured, the girth was 18 feet, 3 inches; it is estimated to be 300 years old. The Dover Oak along the A.T. in New York is slightly larger.

**Sarver Hollow Shelter** (2001)—Sleeps 6. Privy. Water source is a spring located on a blue-blazed trail near the shelter.

**Sinking Creek Mountain**—This is the northernmost spot on the Trail where the route crosses a significant "continental divide." Waters flowing down the western side of the ridge drain into Sinking Creek Valley and the Mississippi River to the Gulf of Mexico. Waters flowing on the eastern side empty into Craig Creek Valley, the James River, and eventually the Atlantic Ocean. Between here and mid-Pennsylvania, except for a short section near Roanoke, the Trail is in the Chesapeake Bay watershed.

**Niday Shelter** (1980)—Sleeps 6. Privy. Water source is 75 yards down a blue-blazed trail west of the A.T.

**Audie Murphy Monument**—located on a blue-blazed trail to the west on Brushy Mountain. Murphy was the most decorated American soldier of World War II, and his single-handed capture of a large number of German soldiers made him a legend. After the war, he starred in many Hollywood war and B-grade western movies. He died in a 1971 plane crash near this site. A trail leads beyond the monument to a view from a rock outcropping.

**Pickle Branch Shelter** (1980)—Sleeps 6. Privy. Water is from the stream below the shelter.

**Dragons Tooth**—Named by Tom Campbell, an early member of RATC and prime mover in the 1930s in locating the A.T. on its current route. He also named Lost Spectacles Gap, north of Dragons Tooth, after his glasses disappeared on a scouting/work hike.

*Camping Restrictions*—Between Va. 624 and U.S. 220, camping and fires are allowed only at the following designated sites of this heavily used section: Johns Spring, Catawba Mountain, Campbell, and Lamberts Meadow shelters and Pig Farm and Lamberts Meadow campsites.

**Va. 624/North Mountain Trail**—West 0.3 mile to Va. 311, then left 0.1 mile to Catawba Grocery (short-term resupply), open M–Th 5–10, F–Sa 5–11, Su 6–10. Pay phone outside. Nearby North Mountain Trail was once the A.T. route. A 30-mile loop is possible.

**Va. 311**—West 1 mile to **Catawba, Va. [P.O. ZIP 24070: M–F 7:30–12 & 1–5, Sa 8–10:30; (540) 384-6011],** and Catawba Valley General Store, M–F 6–8, Sa 7–8, Su 10–6; sandwiches and pizzas, pay phone outside.
    **West** 1.3 miles to the Homeplace Restaurant with AYCE meals $13 for two meats, $14 for three meats, less if you're a

vegetarian. Open Th–F 4–8, Sa 3–8, Su 11–6 (closed the week of Jul 4 and two weeks in late Dec); Th is Southern-barbeque night. No public restroom.

**Johns Spring Shelter** (2003)—Sleeps 6. Privy. Site of the former Boy Scout Shelter. Unreliable water in front of the shelter; follow blue-blazed trail 0.25 mile to a slightly more reliable spring.

**Catawba Mountain Shelter** (1984)—Sleeps 6. Privy. Two water sources for this shelter: One is a piped spring 50 yards south on the A.T., and the other is crossed (south) before reaching the piped spring. Tentsites available north on the A.T.

**McAfee Knob**—Considered by many to have the best view in Virginia, McAfee Knob is a tempting campsite. However, it is absolutely *verboten* to camp here; the knob already sustains tremendous impact. Campbell Shelter or Pig Farm Campsite are good alternatives if you want to climb back up to catch the sunset or sunrise from the cliff.

**Campbell Shelter** (1989)—Sleeps 6. Privy. Water can be found by following the blue-blazed trail left and behind the shelter. Follow the trail through the "electric meadow" to the spring.

**Tinker Cliffs**—A cliff-walk half a mile long, with views back to McAfee Knob. Folklore says the name comes from Revolutionary War deserters who hid near here and repaired pots and pans ("tinkers").

**Lamberts Meadow Shelter** (1974)—Sleeps 6. Privy. Tentsites are 0.3 mile farther north on the A.T. Water is 50 yards down the trail in front of the shelter; reported dry in Aug 2007.

**U.S. 220/I-81 Interchange Area**—The interchange area offers all the comforts of interstate vehicular travel, with most services near the A.T.
    **On U.S. 220.** ■ *Lodging:* Econolodge, (540) 992-3000, hiker rates subject to availability, $50S/D–$56D, $5EAP, coin laundry, pool, will hold packages sent to 446 Roanoke Rd., Daleville, VA 24083; Howard Johnson Express Inn, (540) 992-1234, hiker rate $55S/D, $5EAP, includes continental B, holds UPS and USPS packages for registered guests sent to 437 Roanoke Road, Daleville, VA 24083, microwave & refrigerator, coin laundry, dogs permitted, $15 per pet. Both motels fill up quickly, particularly on the weekends. If you wish to stay there, make reservations during an earlier town stop. ■ *Restaurants:* Pizza Hut with AYCE salad bar; Rancho Viejo Mexican. ■ *Other services:* Several convenience stores.
    **West** 0.3 mile to Botetourt Commons Shopping Plaza. ■ *Restaurants:* Mill Mountain Coffee House, 3 Little Pigs BBQ, Wendy's, Bojangles. ■ *Groceries:* Kroger Super Store,

with pharmacy (long-term resupply). ■ *Outfitter:* Outdoor Trails, (540) 992-5850, (M–F 10–8, Sa 9–6, closed Su), a full-service outfitter, sells fuel by the ounce and holds packages mailed to it at Botetourt Commons, 28 Kingston Dr., Daleville, VA 24083; make reservation for shuttle or slackpacking. ■ *Internet access:* Outdoor Trails, if computer is not needed for the business. ■ *Other services:* UPS Store, (540) 966-0220, M–F 8–6, Sa 9–5; bank with ATM.

**West** 1 mile to **Daleville, Va. [P.O. ZIP 24083: M–F 8–5, Sa 8–12 (540) 992-4422].** Convenience stores and bank are nearby.

**East** 0.8 mile to U.S. 11. ■ *Lodging:* Travelodge, (540) 992-6700, 2619 Lee Hwy., Troutville, VA 24175, $49D, $6EAP (total of 4 per room), pool, dogs $6, continental B; Comfort Inn, (540) 992-5600, ask for the "hiker-corporate" rates of $40 up to 4 people, $5EAP, includes continental B, pool, and Internet access; Day Stop Inn (Travel Centers of America), (540) 992-3100, $58S/D, $6EAP up to 4 people, no pets allowed, 24-hour restaurant, coin laundry, showers available to nonguests $9; Red Roof Inn, (540) 992-5055, $63S/D, $5EAP, limited continental B, pets permitted, pool, hot tub, exercise room; Holiday Inn Express, (540) 966-4444, $99S/D, $5EAP, weekends add $10, Jacuzzi suites higher, microwave and refrigerator in rooms, pool, continental B, holds UPS and USPS packages for registered guests mailed to 3139 Lee Hwy. South, Troutville, VA 24175. ■ *Restaurants:* Cracker Barrel; Country Cookin', with $5.59 D; Shoney's with $5.99 ($6.99 weekends and holidays) B bar; Italian Bella with AYCE L $5.49 Tu–F; Taco Bell; Waffle House; Best Wok; Subway inside Pilot Truck Stop, which also has $9 pay shower; many fast-food restaurants.

**East** 2.3 miles to **Cloverdale, Va. [P.O. ZIP 24077: M–F 8–5, Sa 9–12; (540) 992-2334]**, *via* U.S. 220 and U.S. 11 from the interchange area. ■ *Lodging:* Hollins Motel, (540) 992-2971, $35S, $40D, $45T, $48 for 4. ■ *Groceries:* Greenway Market (short-term resupply), open till 11. ■ *Restaurant:* Cloverdale Grill, M–F 8:30–3:30.

**East** 12 miles to Roanoke. ■ *Outfitters:* Nearby in Salem, Va.: Backcountry Ski and Sports, (540) 389-8602. ■ *Other services:* Medical center that fits in hikers as schedule permits; veterinarian; CVS drug store; and several convenience stores.

**U.S. 11—West** 1.3 mile (1.5 miles north of the interchange area) to **Troutville, Va. [P.O. ZIP 24175: M–F 8:30–5, Sa 8:30–11:30; (540) 992-1472]**. Town hall, (540) 992-4401, M–F 9–5, sometimes allows hikers to camp at the city park, must check with town hall or find park manager; bathrooms and water available. ■ *Groceries:* Thriftway Market (long-term resupply), M–Sa 8–8, closed Su. ■ *Other services:* banks with ATMs. ■ *Shuttles:* Del Schechterly, (540) 529-6028, <dschecht1@juno.com>, helps hikers in need and shuttles from Pearisburg to Waynesboro.

**Fullhardt Knob Shelter** (1960s)—Sleeps 6. Privy. The water source for this shelter is an elaborate cistern system of water runoff hooked to the shelter's roof. Please make sure spigot is off when you have finished getting water.

**Wilson Creek Shelter** (1986)—Sleeps 6. Privy. Water source is a reliable stream 200 yards in front of the shelter.

**Blue Ridge Parkway**—Black Horse Gap is the A.T.'s southernmost encounter with the Blue Ridge Parkway (BRP). The A.T. parallels BRP, and later Skyline Drive, for approximately 200 miles. Much of the original A.T. route along the Blue Ridge south of Roanoke was displaced by the parkway when it was built. Hitchhiking is not permitted on the BRP.

**Natural Bridge Appalachian Trail Club**—NBATC maintains the 90.6 miles between Black Horse Gap and the Tye River. Correspondence should be sent to NBATC, P.O. Box 3012, Lynchburg, VA 24503; <happifeet@msn.com>.

**Bobblets Gap Shelter** (1961)—Sleeps 6. Privy. Built by the USFS; the water source is a spring to the left of the shelter that is prone to go dry after prolonged rainless periods. Look farther downstream if the first source is dry.

**Va. 43/Bearwallow Gap—East,** then north 4.4 miles on the BRP to Peaks of Otter Area, (540) 586-1081, with lodge, restaurant, campground (no showers). Lodge rates vary, $76–$150 depending on day and time of year; reservations suggested. Restaurant serves a B buffet Sa and Su, B/L/D daily. Campsites open May–Oct, $16, (540) 586-7321.

**West** 5 miles on Va. 43 to **Buchanan, Va. [P.O. ZIP 24066: M–F 8:30–5, Sa 10-12; (540) 254-2178].** ■ *Lodging:* Wattstull Motel & Restaurant, (540) 254-1551, is 2 miles north of town on I-81, rates $50–$65. ■ *Internet access:* Buchanan Library. ■ *Other services:* grocery store, bank with ATM, restaurants.

**Cove Mountain Shelter** (1981)—Sleeps 6. Privy. No convenient water source at this shelter. A steep, unmarked trail to the left of the shelter leads 0.5 mile downhill to a stream.

**Va. 614/Jennings Creek**—Jennings Creek is a popular swimming hole for both hikers and local residents, with good tentsites in the woods beyond the bridge.

**East** 0.2 mile to Va. 618, then 0.1 mile to the USFS Middle Creek Picnic Area with covered picnic pavilions and well water; 1.1 miles farther on Va. 618 to *Camping:* Middle Creek Campground, (540) 254-2550, tentsites for 4 with shower $26; cabins sleep 4–6, $65 for 4, $75 for 6; showers $5. Campstore (short-term resupply), Coleman fuel and denatured alcohol by the ounce, Esbit, and coin laundry; accepts packages sent to 1164 Middle Creek Rd., Buchanan, VA 24066; when available, shuttle to the A.T.

**West** 4.5 miles to Wattstull Motel & Restaurant (see Buchanan entry above).

**Bryant Ridge Shelter** (1992)—Sleeps 20. Privy. This trilevel, timber-frame shelter is one of the A.T.'s largest. Water source is a stream 25 yards in front of the shelter, also crossed on the trail to the shelter.

**Cornelius Creek Shelter** (1960)—Sleeps 6. Privy. A blue-blazed trail leads to the shelter, but just north of the turn-off is a branch of Cornelius Creek where you can find water. Water can also be found on the trail to the shelter. An unmarked trail behind the shelter leads 0.1 mile to a fire road and then left 0.2 mile to the BRP, where it is then 6 miles south to the Peaks of Otter Area.

**Apple Orchard Falls Trail**—Located 2.6 miles north of Cornelius Creek Shelter. When the water is high, these falls are impressive, making the 3-mile round-trip worth the effort.

**Apple Orchard Mountain**—When you reach the top, you will be at 4,225 feet. Once an Air Force radar base, the meadows were covered with barracks and support-service buildings for 250 people. On the northern side of the mountain, the A.T. leads you under The Guillotine—an impressively large boulder stuck over the Trail between rock formations. No camping is permitted on top of the mountain, the highest point on the A.T. between Chestnut Knob and Mt. Moosilauke in New Hampshire.

**Thunder Hill Shelter** (1962)—Sleeps 6. Privy. Water source is a walled-in spring south of the shelter, prone to go dry by late summer. A larger, reliable spring can be found by going south on the A.T. to the BRP. At the BRP, turn left, walk 0.3 mile to a gated road on the left; 500 feet down the gated road, where the road turns left, angle right to a spring basin.

**Matts Creek Shelter** (1961)—Sleeps 6. Privy. Several small swimming holes are nearby. The rocks you will find in this area are 500 million years old. Tentsites can be found north 1.0 mile, where Matts Creek flows into the James River, with river views and the sound of trains across the river. Water source is Matts Creek, in front of the shelter.

**James River Foot Bridge**—This bridge, the longest foot-use-only bridge on the A.T., is dedicated to the memory of Bill Foot, a 1987 thru-hiker and ALDHA honorary life member (Trail-named "The Happy Feet" with his wife, Laurie) whose efforts in securing the existing piers, applying for grants, and gaining numerous agencies' cooperation made the bridge a reality.

**U.S. 501 & Va. 130/James River**—The two roads diverge at a fork east of the Trail crossing. On Va. 130, **East** 4.8 miles to *Camping:* Wildwood Campground, (434) 299-5228. Owners Terry and Dona Farmer provide tentsites $20 per tent, cabins $55–$75 for 4 adults, $3EAP; camp store, showers for registered guests, laundry facilities, pool, and snack bar.

On U.S. 501, **East** 5.3 miles to **Big Island, Va. [P.O. ZIP 24526: M–F 8:30–12:30 & 1:30–5, Sa 8–10; (434) 299-5072].** ■ *Groceries:* H&H Market, (434) 299-5153, open daily 5:15–9 (long-term resupply), short-order restaurant, B/L/D, and phone. *Restaurants:* Court St. Pizza Too, (434) 299-7111, M–Sa 1:30–8, pizza, pasta, subs,desserts. ■ *Other services:* bank with ATM and medical center, (434) 299-5951.

**West** 6.0 miles to **Glasgow, Va. [P.O. ZIP 24555: M–F 8:30-11:30, 12:30–4:30, Sa 8–11; (540) 258-2852].** ■ *Lodging and Restaurant:* Tired Feet Café Restaurant & Motel, (540) 258-2039, 853 Rockbridge Rd., $49.95D, pet $10, short-term resupply, hiker box, restaurant M–Sa 7–8, Su 8–8. ■ *Groceries:* Glasgow Grocery Express, open 6–11:30, has Coleman fuel by the ounce, denatured alcohol, and Heet. ■ *Restaurant:*

AJ's Produce, (540) 258-2012, <ajsproduceanddeli@yahoo. com>, M–Sa 8–6, deli, burgers; Tired Feet Café (above); Bernice's Place, 406 Pocahontas St., specializing in soul food, L/D. ■ *Internet access:* library, (540) 258-2509, M–W 10–5:30, Th 11:30–7, Sa 10–1. ■ *Other services:* Dollar General, coin laundry, bank with ATM. ■ *Shuttles:* Mary Ann Williams, (540) 463-2068, between Big Island and Waynesboro; Ken Wallace, (800) 918-6612, (434) 609-2704, between Black Horse Gap and Tye River (May–Oct), sometimes farther.

**Johns Hollow Shelter** (1961)—Sleeps 6. Privy. Water source is a spring to the left of the shelter or a stream to right 25 yards from the shelter.

**Bluff Mountain**—Site of a monument to four-year-old Ottie Cline Powell. In the fall of 1890, Ottie went into the woods to gather firewood for his schoolhouse and never returned. His body was found five months later on top of this mountain. Some NBATC members erected a permanent gravestone for his final resting place, seven miles from the monument.

**Punchbowl Shelter** (1961)—Sleeps 6. Privy. Some believe this shelter is haunted by the ghost of Little Ottie. Tentsites nearby if the shelter is full, which it often is. Water source is a spring by a tree next to the pond drainage in front and to the left of the shelter. An alternative water source is a spring in the ravine north 0.4 mile, shortly after crossing the BRP.

**Brown Mountain Creek Valley**—Community of freed slaves lived here from the Civil War until about 1918; remains of cabins and interpretive signs tell of life in the valley then. ATC-involved archaeological studies are underway.

**Brown Mountain Creek Shelter** (1961)—Sleeps 6. Privy. Water source is a spring in front of, and uphill from, the shelter. In dry conditions, get water from Brown Mountain Creek, crossed on the side trail to the shelter.

**U.S. 60**—West 9.3 miles to **Buena Vista [P.O. ZIP 24416: M–F 8:30–4:30, Sa. 9–11; (540) 261-8959].** ■ *Lodging:* Buena Vista Motel, (540) 261-2138, $40-$48; Budget Inn, (540) 261-2156, $44.95 one bed, $59.95 two beds, $5EAP, $5 pet fee (allowed in smoking rooms only), laundry, Subway restaurant in motel, WiFi, continental B on weekends, possible shuttle to and from the Trail. ■ *Camping:* Glen Maury Campground, (540) 261-7321, tentsites with shower, $20 + 9% tax per tent, $2 shower without stay, pool $2 for guests. ■ *Groceries:* Food Lion (long-term resupply). ■ *Restaurants:* Todd's Barbeque and several fast-food options. ■ *Shuttles:* Aubrey Taylor, (540) 261-6998; Rockbridge Taxi Service, (540) 261-7733, provides local shuttles, $2 per mile, farther distances with advance notice. ■ *Other services:* coin laundry, banks with ATM, hardware store, doctor, dentist, pharmacy, and veterinarian. ■ *Other attractions:* The annual Maury River Fiddlers Convention, popular with hikers, will be held at Glen Maury Park, the third weekend (Th, F, Sa) in Jun; Bluegrass Festival, the 4th weekend (Th, F, Sa) in Sep.

**West** 15 miles to **Lexington [P.O. ZIP 24450: M–F 8:30–5, Sa 9–12; (540) 463-6449]**. A large town with groceries, motels, doctors, vets. *Outfitter:* Walkabout Outfitter, (540) 464-HIKE, 15 W. Washington St., M–Sa 10–5, owned by Kirk Miller (Flying Monkey '99), full-service outfitter, white gas by ounce, MSR canisters.

**Cow Camp Gap Shelter** (1986)—Sleeps 8. Privy. Water source is on blue-blazed trail to the left of the shelter; if you have crossed a small stream, you missed the spring.

**Cold Mountain**—Bald Knob, south of Cold Mountain, isn't a bald, but Cold Mountain and Tar Jacket Ridge are. A mowing project was undertaken by NBATC and the Forest Service to preserve the open views and habitat for northern cottontail rabbits, various raptors, turkey, and grouse. A 1994 law created the Mt. Pleasant National Scenic Area, including Cold Mountain and areas east.

**Seeley–Woodworth Shelter** (1984)—Sleeps 8. Privy. Continue 0.1 mile farther on blue-blaze to a piped spring.

**Porters Field**—West to a spring and campsite 300 feet down the second of two dirt roads.

**Fish Hatchery Road**—This "road" is a gated, one-lane dirt road with no traffic.

**West** 1.5 miles to the fish hatchery, 0.7 mile farther to **Montebello, Va. [P.O. ZIP 24464: M–F 8–4:30, Sa 9–12; (540) 377-9218]**, on Va. 56. Turn left, and reach town in 0.3 mile, with post office, grocery store, and campground. ■ *Lodging:* Montebello Camping and Fishing (long-term resupply), (540) 377-2650, special thru-hiker-rate tentsites with shower $10S, $3EAP, furnished efficiency cabin $45–$115, shower only (without stay) $3.50/pay at store first, denatured alcohol, propane fuel, laundry; Dutch Haus B&B, owners Earl and Lois Arnold, (800) 341-9777, $30PP, free L to thru-hikers May–Jun (SOBOs, call ahead), D extra, fuel by the ounce, credit cards accepted, laundry, shuttle, Internet access, holds mail drops sent to 655 Fork Mountain Ln., Montebello, VA 24464, call from top of Fish Hatchery Road for pick-up at bottom gate.

**Crabtree Farm Road**—**West** 0.5 mile to campsite and spring; 2 miles farther on the Crabtree Falls Trail to Crabtree Falls, one of the highest cascades in the East.

**The Priest Shelter** (1960)—Sleeps 8. Privy. Named for the massif dominating the area, this shelter is near a busy access for backpackers and is often full. Water source is a spring to the left of the shelter.

**Va. 56/Tye River—West** 4 miles to *Camping:* Crabtree Falls Campground (short-term resupply), (540) 377-2066, <www.crabtreefallscampground.com>, <cfcg@ceva.net>. The 0.5-mile blue-blazed Crabtree Falls Trail leads to Va. 56, then east 0.5 mile to the campground. The campground offers tentsites with shower $22D, cabins $55D w/tax; M–Th 9–6, F–Sa 9–10, Su 9–2, no charge for shower without stay. Must show current *Thru-Hikers' Companion* to get quoted rate, if prearranged. Campground accepts packages for guests mailed to 11039 Crabtree Falls Hwy., Tyro, VA 22976; packages accepted are limited to shoebox size.

---

**Tidewater Appalachian Trail Club**—TATC maintains the 10.5 miles between the Tye River and Reeds Gap. Correspondence should be sent to P.O. Box 8246, Norfolk, VA 23503; <president@tidewateratc.org>; <www.tidewateratc.org>.

---

**Mau-Har Trail**—Traversing an area rich in waterfalls and good swimming holes, this steep, 3-mile blue-blaze connects with the A.T. at Maupin Field Shelter. It's shorter, but harder, than the white-blazed route.

**Harpers Creek Shelter** (1960)—Sleeps 6. Privy. Designated low-impact tentsites, which campers are requested to use. Water source is Harpers Creek, in front of the shelter. In extreme droughts, go upstream, and find water in the spring-fed ponds.

**Maupin Field Shelter** (1960)—Sleeps 6. Privy. Designated low-impact tentsites, which campers are requested to use. The Mau-Har Trail begins behind the shelter and rejoins the A.T. 3 miles south. Water source is a dependable spring behind the shelter.

**Fire Road to Blue Ridge Parkway**— From Maupin Field Shelter, turn left on fire road (just north of shelter), 1.5 miles to BRP. **South** on BRP 0.5 mile and turn right on Rt. 814, entrance driveway, 200 yards to *Lodging:* Royal Oaks Cabins, (800) 410-0627, (540) 943-7625, <www.vacabins.com>, <royaloak@ntelos.net>. Run by Keith, Sharon, and Kris Smith. Cabins only (sleep 2–12), no camping; M–Th $105–$245, F–Su $135–$365 per night; deli (short-term resupply).
    **South** on BRP 1.3 miles to *Hostel:* Rusty's Hard Time Hollow—Rusty Nesbitt's gravel driveway with gray pipe gate is on the left at BRP mile 16.7. Open 365/24/7. Section-hikers, thru-hikers, long-distance cyclists, and weekenders are wel-

come (no groups). Since 1982, Rusty has hosted more than 12,000 hikers, cyclists, white-blazers, yellow-blazers, and blue-blazers. The signs along the road are for your entertainment. The Holler is a primitive, 19-acre, back-to-basics, Appalachian mountain farm and includes bunkhouses, springhouse, out-house, rainwater shower. No tenting allowed during peak season. Limited stay; exceptions for medical conditions. No dogs. Trips to nearby Sherando Lake for swimming. Rides back to the Trail. Keep in mind that the Hollow is Rusty's home. Minimum $20 donation per person per night up front. Unlimited soft drinks and snacks included. No alcohol or il-legal drugs allowed. Mail drops not accepted.

**Old Dominion Appalachian Trail Club**— ODATC maintains the 19.1 miles between Reeds Gap and Rockfish Gap. Corre-spondence should be sent to P.O. Box 25283, Richmond, VA 23260; <trailguymike@aol.com>; <www.odatc.org>.

**Humpback Rocks**—The Trail circumvents the rocks, but, if you are seeking a bouldering opportunity, they may still be reached by a short, blue-blazed side trail.

**Paul C. Wolfe Shelter** (1991)—Sleeps 10. Privy. Built by ODATC and the Konnarock Crew, this shelter has windows and a porch cooking area. Tentsites available. Water source is Mill Creek, located 50 yards in front of the shelter.

**Paul Wolfe Shelter to Rockfish Gap**—The Trail passes through an old settlement, including home sites, terraced gardens, and a cemetery, all reputedly haunted.

*"Climb the mountains and get their good tidings. Nature's peace will flow into you as sunshine flows into trees. The winds will blow their freshness into you, and the storms their energy, while cares will drop off like autumn's leaves."*
          —JOHN MUIR

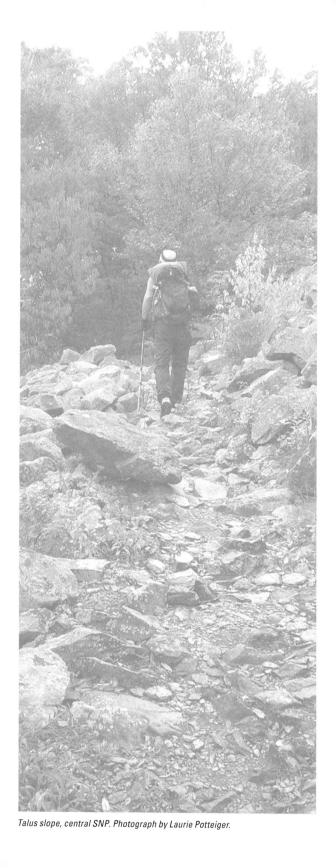

*Talus slope, central SNP. Photograph by Laurie Potteiger.*

# Virginia—Part 3
## (Shenandoah National Park)

| Miles from Katahdin | Features | Services | Elev. | Miles from Springer |
|---|---|---|---|---|
| 1,325.7 | U.S. 250, I-64, Rockfish Gap **Waynesboro, VA 22980** | R, G, L, M (W–1m L; 4.5m PO, H, C, G, L, M, O, D, V, cl, sh, f, @) | 1,902 | 850.5 |
| 1,325.6 | I-64 overpass | R | 1,902 | 850.6 |
| 1,325.4 | Skyline Drive mp 105.2 | R | 1,902 | 850.8 |
| 1,324.9 | SNP kiosk for camping permits self-registration; park entrance station | Kiosk on trail (W–0.2m R) | 2,200 | 851.3 |
| 1,322.0 | Skyline Drive mp 102.1; McCormick Gap | R | 3,450 | 854.2 |
| 1,320.7 | Bear Den Mtn | | 2,885 | 855.5 |
| 1,320.2 | Skyline Drive mp 99.5; Beagle Gap | R | 2,550 | 856.0 |
| 1,318.7 | **Calf Mtn Shelter** *12.3mS; 13.5mN* | W–0.3m S, w | 2,700 | 857.5 |
| 1,318.1 | Spring | w | 2,200 | 858.1 |
| 1,317.7 | Skyline Drive mp 96.9; SNP southern boundary; Jarman Gap | R | 2,250 | 858.5 |
| 1,317.5 | Spring | w | 2,150 | 858.7 |
| 1,315.9 | Skyline Drive mp 95.3; Sawmill Run Overlook | R | 2,200 | 860.3 |
| 1,314.3 | Skyline Drive mp 94.1; Turk Gap | R | 2,600 | 861.9 |
| 1,312.3 | Skyline Drive mp 92.4 | R | 3,100 | 863.9 |
| 1,308.2 | Skyline Drive mp 88.9 | R | 2,350 | 868.0 |
| 1,306.4 | Skyline Drive mp 87.4; Blackrock Gap | R | 2,321 | 869.8 |
| 1,306.2 | Skyline Drive mp 87.2 | R | 2,700 | 870.0 |
| 1,305.7 | **Blackrock Hut** *13.5mS; 13.5mN* | E–0.2m S, w | 2,645 | 870.5 |
| 1,305.1 | Blackrock | | 3,100 | 871.1 |
| 1,304.1 | Skyline Drive mp 84.3 | R | 2,800 | 872.1 |
| 1,302.6 | Skyline Drive mp 82.9; Browns Gap | R | 2,600 | 873.6 |
| 1,301.7 | Skyline Drive mp 82.2 | R | 2,800 | 874.5 |
| 1,301.3 | Skyline Drive mp 81.9; Doyles River Parking Overlook | R | 2,800 | 874.9 |

| Miles from Katahdin | Features | Services | Elev. | Miles from Springer |
|---|---|---|---|---|
| 1,300.4 | Skyline Drive mp 81.1; Doyles River Cabin (locked) | R (E–0.3m w) | 2,900 | 875.8 |
| 1,298.3 | +Loft Mtn Camp-ground | W–0.2m C, G, cl, sh; 1.2m M | 3,300 | 877.9 |
| 1,297.2 | Frazier Discovery Trail to Loft Mtn Wayside | W–0.3m R, M | 2,950 | 879.0 |
| 1,296.5 | Loft Mtn | | 3,200 | 879.7 |
| 1,296.2 | Spring | W–0.1m w | 2,950 | 880.0 |
| 1,294.1 | Skyline Drive mp 77.5; Ivy Creek Overlook | R | 2,800 | 882.1 |
| 1,292.5 | **Pinefield Hut** *13.5mS; 8.4mN* | E–0.1m S, C, w | 2,430 | 883.7 |
| 1,292.3 | Skyline Drive mp 75.2; Pinefield Gap | R | 2,590 | 883.9 |
| 1,290.4 | Skyline Drive mp 73.2; Simmons Gap | R (E–0.2m w) | 2,250 | 885.8 |
| 1,287.1 | Skyline Drive mp 69.9; Powell Gap | R | 2,294 | 889.1 |
| 1,286.7 | Little Roundtop Mtn | | 2,700 | 889.5 |
| 1,285.5 | Skyline Drive mp 68.6; Smith Roach Gap | R | 2,600 | 890.7 |
| 1,284.3 | **Hightop Hut** *8.4mS; 12.6mN* | W–0.1m S; 0.2m C, w | 3,175 | 891.9 |
| 1,283.8 | Spring | w | 3,450 | 892.4 |
| 1,283.7 | Hightop Mtn | | 3,587 | 892.5 |
| 1,282.2 | Skyline Drive mp 66.7 | R | 2,650 | 894.0 |
| 1,280.9 | Skyline Drive mp 65.5; Swift Run Gap, U.S.33 **Elkton, VA 22827** | R (W–2.9m L; 3.2m C, L, G, M, cl; 7.5m PO, G, M) | 2,367 | 895.3 |
| 1,277.9 | South River Picnic Grounds | W–0.1m w | 3,200 | 898.3 |
| 1,274.5 | Pocosin Cabin (locked) | W–0.1m w | 3,150 | 901.7 |
| 1,274.4 | Spring | w | 3,100 | 901.8 |
| 1,272.6 | Skyline Drive mp 57.6; +Lewis Mtn Campground/Cabins | R (W–0.1m C, L, G, cl, sh) | 3,500 | 903.6 |
| 1,271.9 | **Bearfence Mtn Hut** *12.6mS; 11.8mN* | E–0.1m S, C, w | 3,110 | 904.3 |
| 1,269.3 | Skyline Drive mp 55.1; Bootens Gap | R | 3,243 | 906.9 |
| 1,268.4 | Hazeltop | | 3,812 | 907.8 |
| 1,266.5 | Skyline Drive mp 52.8; Milam Gap | R | 3,300 | 909.7 |
| 1,265.6 | Spring | w | 3,380 | 910.6 |

| Miles from Katahdin | Features | Services | Elev. | Miles from Springer |
|---|---|---|---|---|
| 1,264.8 | Big Meadows Wayside; Harry F. Bird, Sr., Visitor Ctr | R, w (E−0.4m G, M) | 3,390 | 911.4 |
| 1,263.9 | Big Meadows Lodge; +Big Meadows Campground | E−0.1m C, L, M, cl, sh, @; 0.9m G, M | 3,500 | 912.3 |
| 1,263.3 | David Spring | w | 3,490 | 912.9 |
| 1,262.3 | Skyline Drive mp 49.3; Fishers Gap | R | 3,050 | 913.9 |
| 1,260.4 | **Rock Spring Hut** and (locked) Cabin *11.8mS; 15.7mN* | W−0.2m S, C, w | 3,465 | 915.8 |
| 1,260.1 | Trail to Hawksbill Mtn, Byrd's Nest #2 Picnic Shelter | E−0.9m | 3,600 | 916.1 |
| 1,259.1 | Skyline Drive mp 45.6; Hawksbill Gap | R | 3,361 | 917.1 |
| 1,258.7 | Skyline Drive mp 44.4; trail to Crescent Rock Overlook | | 3,450 | 917.5 |
| 1,256.6 | Skyland Service Rd (south—horse stables) | R | 3,550 | 919.6 |
| 1,255.8 | Skyland Service Rd (north—best access to Skyland) | R (W−0.2m M, L) | 3,790 | 920.4 |
| 1,255.4 | Trail to Stony Man Summit | | 3,837 | 920.8 |
| 1,253.8 | Skyline Drive mp 38.6; Hughes River Gap; trail to Stony Man Mtn Overlook | R, w | 3,097 | 922.4 |
| 1,251.6 | Skyline Drive mp 36.7; Pinnacles Picnic Ground | R, w | 3,390 | 924.6 |
| 1,251.5 | Skyline Drive mp 36.4; Trail to Jewell Hollow Overlook | R | 3,350 | 924.7 |
| 1,250.5 | The Pinnacle | | 3,730 | 925.7 |
| 1,249.5 | Byrds Nest #3 Picnic Shelter | | 3,290 | 926.7 |
| 1,248.8 | Meadow Spring | E−0.3m w | 3,100 | 927.4 |
| 1,248.2 | Marys Rock | | 3,514 | 928.0 |
| 1,246.3 | Skyline Drive mp 31.5; Thorton Gap, U.S. 211 **Luray, VA 22835** | R (W−0.1m w; 4.6m L, M; 5.6m C, G, cl; 8m PO, L, M, G, O, D, V, cl, @) | 2,307 | 929.9 |
| 1,245.1 | **Pass Mtn Hut** *15.7mS; 13.5mN* | E−0.2m S, w | 2,690 | 931.1 |
| 1,244.3 | Pass Mtn | | 3,052 | 931.9 |
| 1,243.0 | Skyline Drive mp 28.6; Beahms Gap | R | 2,490 | 933.2 |
| 1,242.9 | Skyline Drive mp 28.5 | R | 2,490 | 933.3 |

| Miles from Katahdin | Features | Services | Elev. | Miles from Springer |
|---|---|---|---|---|
| 1,242.8 | Byrds Nest #4 Picnic Shelter | E–0.5m | 2,600 | 933.4 |
| 1,238.2 | Spring | w | 2,600 | 938.0 |
| 1,237.7 | Skyline Drive mp 23.9; Elkwallow Gap; Elkwallow Wayside | R (E–0.1m G, M) | 2,480 | 938.5 |
| 1,236.9 | Range View Cabin (locked) | E–0.1m w | 2,950 | 939.3 |
| 1,236.2 | Skyline Drive mp 21.9; Rattlesnake Point Overlook | R | 3,100 | 940.0 |
| 1,235.6 | Tuscarora Trail (southern terminus) to +Matthews Arm Campground | W–0.7m C | 3,400 | 940.6 |
| 1,235.2 | Skyline Drive mp 21.1 | R | 3,350 | 941.0 |
| 1,235.0 | Hogback Third Peak | | 3,400 | 941.2 |
| 1,234.9 | Skyline Drive mp 20.8 | R | 3,350 | 941.3 |
| 1,234.7 | Hogback Second Peak | | 3,475 | 941.5 |
| 1,234.5 | Spring | E–0.2m w | 3,250 | 941.7 |
| 1,234.4 | Hogback First Peak | | 3,390 | 941.8 |
| 1,233.8 | Skyline Drive mp 19.7; Little Hogback Overlook | R | 3,000 | 942.4 |
| 1,233.6 | Little Hogback Mtn | | 3,050 | 942.6 |
| 1,233.1 | Skyline Drive mp 18.9 | R | 2,850 | 943.1 |
| 1,232.0 | **Gravel Springs Hut** *13.5mS; 10.7mN* | E–0.2m S, C, w | 2,480 | 944.2 |
| 1,231.8 | Skyline Drive mp 17.7; Gravel Springs Gap | R | 2,666 | 944.4 |
| 1,230.7 | South Marshall Mtn | | 3,212 | 945.5 |
| 1,230.2 | Skyline Drive mp 15.9 | R | 3,050 | 946.0 |
| 1,229.5 | North Marshall Mtn | | 3,368 | 946.7 |
| 1,228.6 | Hogwallow Spring | w | 2,950 | 947.6 |
| 1,228.0 | Skyline Drive mp 14.2; Hogwallow Gap | R | 2,739 | 948.2 |
| 1,226.3 | Skyline Drive mp 12.3; Jenkins Gap | R | 2,400 | 949.9 |
| 1,225.4 | Compton Springs | w | 2,700 | 950.8 |
| 1,225.0 | Compton Peak | | 2,909 | 951.2 |
| 1,224.2 | Skyline Drive mp 10.4; Compton Gap | R | 2,550 | 952.0 |
| 1,224.0 | Indian Run Spring | E–0.3m w | 2,350 | 952.2 |
| 1,222.5 | SNP kiosk for camping permits self-registration; Compton Gap Fire Rd, Compton Gap Trail | | 2,350 | 953.7 |

| Miles from Katahdin | Features | Services | Elev. | Miles from Springer |
|---|---|---|---|---|
| 1,222.3 | SNP northern boundary, Possums Rest Overlook | | 2,300 | 953.9 |
| 1,221.5 | **Tom Floyd Wayside** *10.7mS; 8.1mN* | S (W−0.2m w) | 1,900 | 954.7 |
| 1,220.5 | Northern Virginia 4-H Swimming Pool | W−0.3m | 1,350 | 955.7 |
| 1,220.0 | Va. 602 | R | 1,150 | 956.2 |
| 1,218.6 | U.S. 522 **Front Royal, VA 22630** | R (W−3.2m G, L, M, O, cl, f, @; 4.2m PO, M, D, @) | 950 | 957.6 |

+Fee charged, mp=milepost

Shenandoah National Park, with 104 miles of well-graded Appalachian Trail, is memorable for its many vistas and abundant wildlife. Skyline Drive, which you will cross 28 times, has many waysides and concessions for resupply stops. Backcountry permits are required when camping in the park.

**U.S. 250, I-64/Rockfish Gap**—Where the A.T. crosses U.S. 250, it is **West** 200 yards to a small clustering of buildings (many of them vacant) at Rockfish Gap. Rockfish Gap Visitors Center, (540) 943-5187, is open daily 9–5 and offers an information packet on the area, created specifically for hikers, that notes all services and includes a list of people who provide free shuttles to town. If closed, packets are in box near door. ■ *Lodging:* Inn at Afton, (540) 942-5201, above and behind the visitors' center, $60–$100, B/L/D, pool, pets allowed, vehicles may be parked in lot; leave name, vehicle information, and date of return with desk staff. ■ *Groceries:* Afton Mountain Convenience (short-term resupply), open 8–8, phone.

**West** 1 mile to *Lodging:* Colony House Motel, (540) 942-4156, hiker rate $43.80 incl. tax., pets $10, pool, laundry, can shuttle back to Trail if asked and available.

**West** 4.5 miles to **Waynesboro, Va. [P.O. ZIP 22980: M–F 8:30–5, Sa 9–11; (540) 942-7320]**, a large, hiker-friendly town with most services. The office of tourism and the Waynesboro "Trail angels" are holding their Fourth Annual Hiker Fest on June 7, 2008, at Grace Evangelical Lutheran Church, 500 South Wayne Ave. Fest will include dinner, a movie, music, and much more for a nominal fee. All hikers are welcome! ■ *Hostel:* Grace Evangelical Lutheran Church, 500 South Wayne Ave., open May 19–Jun 22, closed Su nights, check-in 5–9 p.m., check-out 9 a.m, but will store packs for those staying over another night. Lounge with big-screen VCR and DVD, a/c, Internet, showers, cots, use of kitchen, snacks, and continental breakfast. Members of the congregation host a Thursday-night supper for hikers (max. 15) followed by an optional vespers service. No pets, drugs, smoking, alcohol, firearms, foul language. Maximum 15 hikers; 2-night limit. Donations accepted. ■ *Camping:* Waynesboro Family YMCA, (540) 942-5107, on South Wayne Ave., offers tentsites on a grassy area near the South River. Check-in at desk M–F 5:15 a.m.–10 p.m., Sa 8–5, Su 1–5. Although not officially a hostel, the YMCA offers showers (cost picked up by trail angel DuBose Egleston); restroom, gym, and pay phone; donations appreciated. ■ *Lodging:* Quality Inn, (540) 942-1171, new owners may not give hiker rate, $52–$75, pets in smoking rooms only $10; Tree Streets Inn B&B, (540) 949-4484, $65s/D includes B, shuttle, mail drops accepted for guests sent to 421 Walnut Ave. ■ *Groceries:* Kroger (long-term resupply). ■ *Restaurants:* Ming Garden, AYCE L/D; Gavid's Steaks; Scottos Italian; Ciros Pizza; Pizza Hut, AYCE L/D; Weasie's Kitchen, B/L/D with AYCE pancake B anytime, open M–Sa 5:30–8, Su 7–2; and many fast-food outlets. ■ *Outfitter:* Rockfish Gap Outfitters, (540) 943-1461, located on U.S. 250 on the way into town; fuel by the ounce, backpacking gear, large footwear selection, minor gear repairs, and manufacturer-warranty assistance. ■ *Internet access:* Waynesboro Public Library, M–F 9–9, Sa 9–5; Grace Lutheran Church during times of hostel operation (see above). ■ *Other services:* cobbler, coin laundry, pharmacy, banks with ATM, doctor, dentist, veterinarian, barber, massages, Western

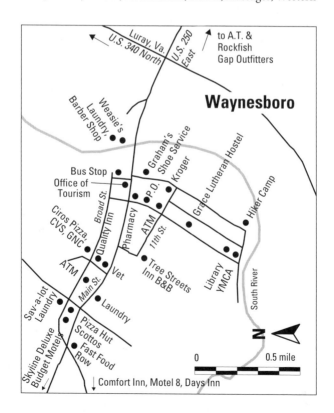

Union, and one-hour photo service. Many motels, restaurants, and groceries also are available 2 miles south of town on U.S. 340 (Rosser Ave.) at I-64.

**Potomac Appalachian Trail Club**—PATC maintains the 239.8 miles between Rockfish Gap and Pine Grove Furnace State Park in Pennsylvania. Send correspondence to PATC, 118 Park St. SE, Vienna, VA 22180; (703) 242-0693; <www.potomac appalachian.org>; <info@patc.net>.

**Shenandoah National Park**—Although the SNP presents some significant ascents and descents, long-distance hikers generally will find the Trail within the park well-graded.

*Park history*—In 1926, Congress authorized the creation of the Shenandoah and Great Smoky Mountains national parks. Unlike western parks, most of today's Shenandoah park land was privately owned; the Blue Ridge here had been dotted with communities and isolated groups of settlers since the 1750s. Areas of the mountains had long been farmed and grazed. Out-of-state corporations had exploited some areas for timber products and mineral ores. Three resorts also provided Victorian-era vacationers with cool mountain breezes and recreation. In short, the area that became Shenandoah National Park was neither pristine nor primeval.

By the 1910s, conditions were changing. A blight killing American chestnut trees, some 30–40 percent of the Appalachian forest, had destroyed not only large swaths of the forest but a way of life for many people. Those trees provided nuts that were shipped by the railroad to urban areas, providing mountain families with cash income. The chestnut tree was strong, straight, and rot-resistant, and its wood was valuable for fence posts, railroad ties, roof shingles, siding boards, and general lumber that mountain residents used and sold in the Shenandoah Valley and the Piedmont. The blight changed all that forever.

In 1927, Virginia passed laws authorizing condemnation of all privately held property within the boundary of the proposed Shenandoah National Park. More than 4,000 tracts were surveyed and evaluated, and 1,081 were ultimately purchased and given to the federal government for the park, uprooting most of the 465 families who then lived upon the land. Virginia resettled the majority of the families and evicted those who were unwilling to move. Approximately 45 elderly residents were allowed to spend the remainder of their years in their mountain homes.

In 1931, four years before Shenandoah was established, construction of Skyline Drive began. First built as a second entrance to President Herbert Hoover and First Lady Lou Henry Hoover's summer White House, Rapidan Camp, the road initially was only to go from the camp to Skyland. State leaders successfully lobbied for congressional appropriations to extend the highway north to Thornton Gap (U.S. 211), on to Front Royal, and then south to Rockfish Gap. But, until the park was established in December 1935, Skyline Drive existed only as a 100-foot right-of-way within privately held land that basically coincided with the route of the A.T. In 1933, President Franklin D. Roosevelt's CCC "boys" established camps along the route and built many of the facilities, overlooks, rock walls, and gutters seen there today. They planted hundreds of thousands of trees and shrubs, creating the landscape that draws millions of visitors to the park, and built a new route for the A.T. ATC Chair Myron Avery's acceptance of this route disruption produced an open schism between the organization's leadership and founder Benton MacKaye and his allies in New York and New England.

Today, 95 percent reforested, the park is home to wild turkey, white-tailed deer, black bears, and shelter mice. Hundreds of migrating birds and butterflies summer or stop over in this central Appalachian biome. Nearly one million visitors a year come to watch wildlife, get back to nature, view the Shenandoah Valley to the west and the foothills to the east, or visit land on which their ancestors lived. In addition to the A.T., the park includes nearly 400 miles of other trails.

*Ranger Programs*—From Memorial Day through Oct, rangers present a variety of organized hikes, programs, and participatory events highlighting the natural and human history of the park. The SNP visitors' guide, available at entrance stations and visitors centers, outlines the seasonal schedule.

*Forest Damage*—Hurricane Isabel (2003) and fires in the area before it damaged thousands of acres. Coupled with the floods of 1995 and 1996, Tropical Storm Fran in 1996, a severe ice storm in 1998 and 2006, and gypsy-moth and woolly adelgid infestations, the park has been hit hard over the past decade. Be mindful of trees and branches that have been weakened by those events and could still fall.

*Fee*—Hikers entering the park *via* the A.T. are not charged a fee; hikers entering at other trailheads in SNP may incur one. During the spring (mid-Feb to mid-Apr), the park occasionally conducts prescribed burns along the A.T. to manage vegetation. During burns, a hut may be closed up to 3 days. Check the ATC or park Web sites or ask at any NPS station for current information.

*Backcountry Permits*—While there is no charge for permits, they are required of all thru-hikers and overnight backcountry travelers. Backcountry self-registration kiosks are located on the A.T. near the north and south boundaries of SNP. If you fail to register or can't show proof of registration when rangers ask for it, they may issue a citation or fine. Permits may also be obtained at Skyline Drive entrance stations and park visitors centers when they are open. A permit can be acquired in advance by calling (540) 999-3500, M–F 8–4. Be familiar with the regulations, have your exact itinerary ready, and allow 5–7 business days for the permit to be mailed. Write to: Superintendent, ATTN: Backcountry Camping Permit, 3655 U.S. Hwy. 211 East, Luray, VA 22835. See also <www.nps.gov/shen/plan-yourvisit/cambc_regs.htm>.

*Backcountry Accommodations*—Two types of three-sided structures are near the A.T.—day-use (called "shelters") and overnight-use (called "huts"). Camping at or near the day-use shelters is prohibited. Huts are available to long-distance hikers (those having an itinerary of at least three consecutive nights) on a first-come, first-served basis. Tenting at huts is permitted in designated campsites marked with a post and a tenting symbol; all huts within the park's boundaries have campsites available. The PATC also operates several "locked cabins within the park, but those require advance reservations and other arrangements. Contact PATC for details.

*Backcountry Regulations*

- Campfires are prohibited in SNP, except at the commercial campgrounds and established fireplaces at shelters, huts, and cabins. Use a backpacking stove.

- Camping is prohibited within 10 yards of a stream or other natural water source; within 20 yards of a park trail or unpaved fire road; within 50 yards of culturally historic sites, other campers, or no-camping signs; within 100 yards of a hut, cabin, or day-use shelter (except designated sites); within 0.25 mile of a paved road, park boundary, picnic area, visitors center, or commercial facility. Several zones have been designated "noncamping areas," including Limberlost, Hawksbill Summit, Whiteoak Canyon, Old Rag summit, Big Meadows clearing, and Rapidan Camp.

- Camping is permitted almost everywhere else. New regulations encourage hikers to seek "preexisting campsites" that show signs of use and are not posted with no-camping signs. Camping at those sites is limited to two consecutive nights. If necessary, dispersed camping at undisturbed sites is permissible, but they must be left in pristine condition afterward; use such sites only one night.

- Maximum group size is 10 people.

- Food must be stored so that wildlife cannot get it—hang food from a tree branch at least ten feet from the ground and four feet away from a tree's trunk. Alternatively, overnight huts feature food-storage poles, which are to be used instead of the familiar "mouse hangers." Park-approved, bear-resistant food-storage canisters are also permissible.

- Solid human waste should be buried in accordance with Leave No Trace ethics, under 6 inches of soil, more than 200 feet from trails, water sources, or roads.

- Carry out all trash from the backcountry, and dispose of it properly.

- Glass containers are discouraged.

- Pets must be leashed at all times and are prohibited on certain trails.

*Commercial Facilities*—Campgrounds, restaurants, lodges, waysides, and small stores are normally open spring through fall and are located strategically near the A.T. and Skyline Drive. Long-distance hikers may be able to save pack weight by resupplying or taking meals at these facilities. Call the park for the precise dates and times of operation. Most operate weekends-only Apr through mid-May and daily thereafter through Oct. More details can be found at <www.visit shenandoah.com>. The campground reservation system is being revamped, and rates are subject to change.

**Calf Mountain Shelter** (1984)—Sleeps 6. Privy. Featuring two skylights, this shelter is not a part of the SNP hut system, so SNP rules don't apply here. Water source is a piped spring on the access trail to the shelter.

**Blackrock Hut** (1941)—Sleeps 6. Privy. Designated tentsites nearby. Water source is a piped spring 10 yards in front of the shelter.

**Loft Mountain Campground**—Open mid-May to late Oct. The A.T. skirts the campground, but several short side trails lead to campsites and the camp store (short-term resupply). Campsites $16, subject to change; showers $1, laundry, restroom, soda machine, and pay phone at campground entrance station. Loft Mountain Wayside and Grill serves B/L/D, short-order menu, soda machine. From the camp store, follow the paved road 1.0 mile downhill to Skyline Drive or continue north on the A.T. 0.9 mile and take the Frazier Discovery Trail 0.5 mile west (steep descent) to Skyline Drive.

**Pinefield Hut** (1940)—Sleeps 6. Privy. Designated tentsites nearby. Water source is a spring located behind the shelter 50 yards. It tends to fail during dry seasons, in which case you can get water from Ivy Creek or Loft Mountain Campground, for northbounders, and an outdoor spigot at the Simmons Gap ranger station, for southbounders.

**Simmons Gap**—Simmons Gap ranger station is down the paved road 0.2 mile east from where the A.T. crosses Skyline Drive. Water available at spigot outside buildings.

**Hightop Hut** (1939)—Sleeps 6. Privy. Designated campsites nearby. Water source is a usually reliable piped spring 0.1 mile from the shelter on a side trail. An alternative water source is a boxed spring 0.5 mile north on the Trail.

**U.S.33/Swift Run Gap/Spotswood Trail—West** from Skyline Drive to pay phone, water, backcountry self-registration station located at SNP entrance station, north of U.S. 33 bridge.

**On U.S. 33—West** 2.9 miles to *Lodging:* Country View Motel, (540) 298-0025, $38–$45, pet $5, shuttle possible back to Trail and Elkton, mail drops accepted for guests sent to 19974 Spotswood Trail, Elkton, VA 22827.

**West** 3.2 miles to *Lodging:* Elkton Motel, (540) 298-1463, $40–$50D (one bed), $52–$60D (two beds), pets allowed, CATV, refrigerator, microwave. ■ *Camping:* Swift Run Camping, (540) 298-8086, $20 campsite, laundry, pool, and snack bar. ■ *Groceries:* Bear Mountain Grocery, with a deli, daily 6–9.

**West** 7.5 miles to **Elkton, Va. [P.O. ZIP 22827: M–F 8:30–5, Sa 9–11; (540) 298-7772]**. ■ *Groceries:* Food Lion, O'Dell's Grocery (both long-term resupply). ■ *Restaurants:* several fast-food chain restaurants. ■ *Other services:* pharmacy, bank, and ATM.

**South River Parking Area**—Water, picnic benches, restrooms with sinks.

**Lewis Mountain Campground and Cabins**—(540) 999-2255. Open mid-Apr to late Oct; reservations, (800) 999-4714. The A.T. passes within sight of the campground, and several short side trails lead to campsites and the camp store. Campsites $16; cabins $71–$160; tent cabin $20 for 4; rates subject to change. Lewis Mountain Camp Store (short-term resupply), open 9–7 in summer. Showers $1, laundry, restroom, soda machine, and pay phone.

**Bearfence Mountain Hut** (1940)—Sleeps 6. Privy. Designated tentsites nearby. Located on a blue-blazed trail. Water source is a piped spring in front of the shelter; prone to fail during even moderately dry spells.

**Big Meadows Lodge, Campground, and Wayside**—The A.T. passes within sight of the campground, and short side trails lead to the lodge, which also houses a restaurant and tap room and has Internet access. ■ *Lodging:* reservations at (800) 999-4714, rooms available in main lodge, cabins, suites, and motel-type accommodations. Rates $67–$145, subject to change; reservations required. ■ *Camping:* Open early Apr thru Nov, reservations recommended. Walk-ins are possible, but the campground is often full; (800) 365-CAMP (use SHEN designator); showers $1, laundry.

■ *Restaurant:* Dining room open daily for L/D; tap room, with nightly entertainment and light fare, open daily from late afternoon to late evening. From the lodge, follow the paved entrance road 0.9 mile to Big Meadows Wayside and Grill, B/L/D, open mid-Apr–late Nov, with short-order menu.
■ *Groceries:* Wayside has a good selection (short-term resupply) and camping supplies, pay phone, and soda machine. Next door is the Harry F. Byrd, Sr., Visitors Center, which houses interpretive exhibits and videos on the history of the park and the natural history of the area.

**Rock Spring Hut** (1940, updated 1980)—former Shaver Hollow Shelter, moved and rebuilt by PATC with chestnut logs from original CCC shelters. Sleeps 8. Privy. Designated tentsites nearby. Located on 0.2-mile blue-blazed trail. Water source, down a steep trail in front of the hut, flows from beneath a rock.

**Skyland Service Road/Skyland**—Skyland was originally a 19th-century mountain summer resort owned by George Freeman Pollack, who pushed hard to evict surrounding small landholders and create a national park and then, ironically, was forced to sell and give up management of the resort when the park took over. Cross the road at the stables, and follow the A.T. north, passing a water tank on your right and the junction marked by a concrete post, which points to Skyland and dining room.
**West** 0.2 mile to *Lodging:* Skyland, (800) 999-4714, open late Mar–late Nov, cabin rooms $62–$117, motel-type accommodations and suites $85–$135, rates subject to change, reservations required for both. ■ *Restaurant:* Pollack Dining Room serves B/L/D; limited hours. Tap room, light fare, nightly entertainment.

**Pinnacles Picnic Area**—Water, restrooms, and covered area with picnic tables.

**U.S. 211/Thornton Gap/Panorama**—A short side trail, on the southern side of Thornton Gap, leads to Panorama area. Work to demolish the old Panorama Restaurant building will begin in 2008. A restroom, backcountry-camping permit station, and pay phone are located on the east side of the parking area. Entrance station is north of U.S. 211, east of where the Trail crosses Skyline Drive, with water.
**On U.S. 211**—**West** 4.6 miles to *Lodging:* Brookside Cabins, (540) 743-5698, luxury cabins $85–$195; full-menu restaurant featuring home-style foods and daily AYCE L/D buffet, weekend B buffet, open 7–8 (summer until 9). Closed mid-Dec, reopens New Year's Day.
**West** 5.6 miles to *Camping:* Yogi Bear's Jellystone Park, (540) 743-4002, <www.campwray.com>, tentsites $25–$45, cabins $45–$149, two-night minimum on weekends, camp-

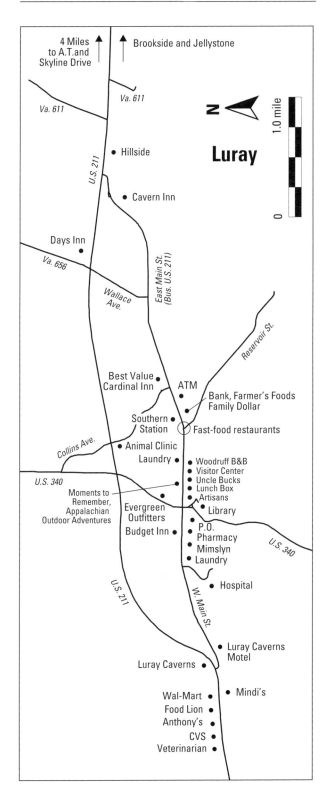

store (short-term resupply), pool, pay phone, laundry. **West** 8.0 miles to the town of **Luray, Va. [P.O. ZIP 22835: M–F 8:30–5, Sa 9–12; (540) 743-2100]**. Home of Luray Caverns. Page County Chamber of Commerce, <www.luraypage.com>, 46 E. Main St., (540) 743-3915, M–Sa 9–5, Su 12–4. ■ *Lodging:* Luray Caverns Motel, (888) 941-4531, $75–$95D, continental B, pool; Best Value Cardinal Inn, (888) 648-4633, $59 and up, no pets; Days Inn, (540) 743-4521, $59–$99D, pets $10; Woodruff Inn, (540) 743-1494, a Victorian B&B, $98D and up, includes B; The Mimslyn, (800) 296-5105, $89 and up, restaurant B/L/D; Budget Inn, (540) 743-5176, $49S and up, pets $5; Cavern Inn, (540) 743-4575, $50–$80, pets $10, pool, laundry, fridge, microwave; Hillside Motel, (540) 743-6322, $49–$75, pets $10, pool, fridge, microwave. ■ *Groceries:* Farmer's Foods, Food Lion, Wal-Mart (all long-term resupply). ■ *Restaurants:* Alexander's, B/L/D; Anthony's Pizza XII, L/D; Southern Station Diner, B/L/D; East Wok, L/D and AYCE L; Mindi's Mexican, L/D; Moment to Remember, espresso, sandwiches, desserts; Artisan's Grill, deli sandwiches and full meals; The Lunch Box, BBQ take-out or eat-in; Uncle Buck's; and several fast-food restaurants. ■ *Internet access:* Page County Library. ■ *Outfitters:* Evergreen Outfitters, (540) 843-2576, <www.evergreenoutfitters. com>, full-service outfitter, 26 N. Broad St.; Appalachian Outdoors Adventures, (540) 743-7400, (540) 742-2984, limited backpacking supplies. ■ *Other services:* veterinarian, Blue Mountain Animal Clinic, (540) 743-PETS; laundry; hospital; banks with ATM; and Page movie theater. ■ *Shuttles:* Mountain & Valley Shuttle Service, Rodney Ketterman and Jim "Skyline" Austin, Luray, Va. (540) 743-1355, (540) 671-1734, <www.mvshuttle.com>, offers shuttles between Harpers Ferry and Reeds Gap, sometimes farther. Also serves nearby airports, Amtrak, Greyhound. Other assistance includes transportation in fully insured, late-model vehicles, trail logistics, town assistance (one-day notice appreciated). Holds permit to shuttle hikers in SNP. Limited rustic camping for shuttle clients night before or upon conclusion of hike, on-site parking at base camp (A.T.-style shelter, picnic table, BBQ grill, fire pit, hot shower, flush toilet). Bobby Jenkins, (540) 743-3214, (540) 742-4714.

**Pass Mountain Hut** (1939)—Sleeps 8. Privy. Known for the "kissing trees," the shelter is located on a blue-blazed trail. Designated campsites nearby. Water source is a piped spring 15 yards behind the shelter.

**Elkwallow Wayside and Grill**—Open Apr 5–Nov 4. Visible from where the A.T. crosses Skyline Drive in Elkwallow Gap, the wayside includes a grill, gift shop, and restroom. Grill, B/L/D. Last chance in the park for northbounders to get a blackberry milkshake. Gift shop offers a limited selection of groceries and camping supplies. Pay phone and soda machine outside. Open 9–7 early Apr– early Nov.

**Mathews Arm Campground—West** 0.7 mile from the A.T., 0.3 mile south of the Hogback Parking Area *via* the Tuscarora Trail. Signs lead to nearby primitive (*i.e.*, no services) campground, open late May–late Oct, campsites $16 per night, rate subject to change. This trail junction is the southern terminus of the 260-mile Tuscarora Trail. The northern terminus is also on the A.T., south of Darlington Shelter in Pennsylvania.

**Gravel Springs Hut** (1940)—Sleeps 8. Privy. Designated tentsites nearby. Located on a blue-blazed trail. The water source is a boxed spring found on side trail near the shelter.

**Compton Gap Trail**—At the last SNP concrete post on the Trail, labeled Va. 610/Chester Gap, the A.T. will turn left. Follow the Compton Gap Trail 0.5 mile north, straight ahead to road. ■ *Shuttle:* Mike "The Grateful Greenpeace Guy" Evans (AT '95), <gratefulg@hotmail.com>, 304 Chester Gap Rd., Chester Gap, VA 22623, (540) 539-0509, is the first house on the left side of the paved road. His hostel is closed for the 2008 season, but shuttles are available if you call first.

**Southbound Registration Station**—1.0 mile south of Tom Floyd Wayside.

**Tom Floyd Wayside** (1980s)—Sleeps 6. Privy. This shelter has an overhanging front deck with storage space above, a railed deck with benches, and several designated tentsites. Outside the SNP boundary, so SNP rules don't apply here. Water source is Ginger Spring (can fail in very dry years), 0.2 mile on a blue-blazed trail to the right of the shelter.

**Northern Virginia 4-H Swimming Pool**—Blue-blazed side trail 0.9 mile north of Tom Floyd Wayside leads 0.3 mile **West** to the swimming pool. It is open to the public, including hikers, 12–6 daily (Memorial Day–Labor Day), $5 admission, swimsuits required. Snack bar and pay phone available year-round; inquire within about multiday parking availability (advance arrangements required).

*"Take nothing for granted. Not one blessed cool mountain day or one hellish, desert day, or one sweaty, stinky hiking companion. It is all a gift."*

—Cindy Ross, author and Triple Crowner

*Acadia's Waterfall, Virginia. Photograph by Laurie Potteiger.*

# Virginia—Part 4
# (Northern Virginia)

| Miles from Katahdin | Features | Services | Elev. | Miles from Springer |
|---|---|---|---|---|
| 1,218.6 | U.S. 522 **Front Royal, VA 22630** | R (W–3.2m G, L, M, O, cl, f, @; 4.2m PO, M, D, @) | 950 | 957.6 |
| 1,218.5 | Nat'l Zoological Park Research Center | | 990 | 957.7 |
| 1,215.3 | Tom Sealock Spring | w | 1,800 | 960.9 |
| 1,213.4 | **Jim and Molly Denton Shelter** *8.1mS; 5.5mN* | S, w | 1,310 | 962.8 |
| 1,212.3 | Va. 638 **Linden, VA 22642** | R (W–1m PO, G; 2.5m G, M; 7m G, L, M, O, cl, f, @) | 1,150 | 963.9 |
| 1,210.4 | Va. 55, Manassas Gap **Linden, VA 22642** | R (W–1.1m PO, G, M, L, sh, @; 2.6m G, M) | 800 | 965.8 |
| 1,207.9 | **Manassas Gap Shelter** *5.5mS; 4.6mN* | S, w | 1,655 | 968.3 |
| 1,206.1 | Trico Trail | | 1,900 | 970.1 |
| 1,203.5 | **Dick's Dome Shelter** *4.6mS; 8.6mN* | E–0.2m S, w | 1,230 | 972.7 |
| 1,202.5 | Spring | C, w | 1,850 | 973.7 |
| 1,201.3 | +Sky Meadows State Park Side Trail | E–1.7m C, S, w | 1,780 | 974.9 |
| 1,198.7 | U.S. 50, Ashby Gap | R (E–1.1m L) | 900 | 977.5 |
| 1,195.1 | **Rod Hollow Shelter** *8.6mS; 6.9mN* | W–0.2m S, w | 840 | 981.1 |
| 1,191.4 | Va. 605 | R | 1,140 | 984.8 |
| 1,190.2 | Spring | w | 1,150 | 986.0 |
| 1,188.2 | Sawmill Spring, **Sam Moore Shelter** *6.9mS; 11.2mN* | S, w | 990 | 988.0 |
| 1,185.2 | Bears Den Rocks, Bears Den Hostel | E–0.2m w, H, C, G, L, cl, sh, f, @ | 1,350 | 991.0 |
| 1,184.6 | Va. 7, Va. 679, Snickers Gap **Bluemont, VA 20135** | R (E–1.6m G; 1.7m PO) (W–0.3m M; 0.9m M; 1.0m G) | 1,000 | 991.6 |
| 1,182.4 | Spring | w | 1,083 | 993.8 |
| 1,182.1 | Va.–W.Va. State Line | | 1,140 | 994.1 |
| 1,182.0 | Crescent Rock | | 1,312 | 994.2 |
| 1,181.4 | Sand Spring | w | 1,150 | 994.8 |
| 1,181.3 | Devils Racecourse | | 1,200 | 994.9 |
| 1,178.5 | Wilson Gap | | 1,380 | 997.7 |

| Miles from Katahdin | Features | Services | Elev. | Miles from Springer |
|---|---|---|---|---|
| 1,177.3 | **Blackburn Trail Center** *11.2mS; 3.6mN* | E–0.1m C; 0.3m S, w | 1,650 | 998.9 |
| 1,174.1 | **David Lesser Memorial Shelter** *3.6mS; 16mN* | E–0.1m S; 0.4m w | 1,430 | 1,002.1 |
| 1,171.1 | Keys Gap, W.Va. 9 | R (E–0.3m G) (W–0.3m G, M, w) | 935 | 1,005.1 |

*+ Fee charged*

Higher rates of Lyme disease occur from northern Virginia into New England. Take precautions to prevent infection.

This 52-mile section follows a long, low ridge rich in American history and home to the infamous "roller-coaster" south of Snickers Gap.

**U.S. 522—West** 3.2 miles to **Front Royal, Va. [P.O. ZIP 22630: M–F 8:30–5, Sa 8:30–1; (540) 635-7983]**. The post office is 1.0 mile farther. The large town offers all major services, but they are spread out over a wide area. Except for the post office, most services are located near the U.S. 522 and Va. 55 intersection as you come into town from the A.T. Weasel Creek Outfitters is a hiker's best source for help and information in town. ■ *Lodging:* Front Royal is the gateway to Shenandoah National Park, with motel rates that vary considerably according to season; be sure to specify you are a hiker, as most have special rates. Skyline Resort Motel, (540) 635-5354, no dogs; Pioneer Motel, (540) 635-4784, pool, CATV, dogs sometimes allowed for a fee; Scottish Inns, (540) 636-6168, $54s, $59d, $5eap, dogs $5; Center City Motel, (540) 635-4050, $54s, $66d, $7eap, CATV; Super 8 Motel, (540) 636-4888, dogs $8; Quality Inn, (540) 635-3161, no dogs, CATV; Woodward House B&B, (540) 635-7010 or (800) 635-7011, no dogs, includes full B, shuttle to and from Trail, other area shuttles for a fee, no smoking in house; Blue Ridge Motel, (540) 636-7200, no dogs, free shuttle back to the Trail. ■ *Groceries:* Food Lion, Martin's, Better Thymes natural foods (all long-term resupply). ■ *Restaurants:* Victoria's, AYCE L/D; South Street Grill; Dean's Steak House; Pirate Pizza; Jalisco Mexican; Anthony's Pizza and Son's; Soul Mountain Café; Pizza Hut, AYCE; Royal Dairy, open 7–9; Villa Guissepies Italian, with N.Y. Pizza; China Jade, $6.95 AYCE L buffet; and many fast-food outlets. ■ *Outfitter:* Weasel Creek Outfitters, (540) 622-6909, closed M. Brandon, Wendy, and their team provide minor repairs, warranty work, hiker box, pack lock-up, Internet access, possible shuttles, pack fitting, all stove fuels, Coleman and alcohol by the ounce. ■ *Internet access:* Samuels Public Library and Weasel Creek Outfitters. ■ *Other services:* coin laundry, daily 7–10; banks with ATM; hospital; doctors, dentists; veterinarian; pharmacies; Stokes General; Ramsey's Hardware, (540) 635-2547, Coleman fuel and alcohol by the ounce; Royal Oak Bookstore; movie theater; Royal Taxi, (540) 635-3214; Ace Taxi, (540) 635-6100 for local and D.C. airports; flea market on Sa on U.S. 522, spring and summer.

**National Zoological Park**—Adjacent to U.S. 522 is the National Zoological Park Conservation and Research Center. On the northern side of the highway, the Trail follows along one of the center's fences. Exotic animals are sometimes visible.

**Jim and Molly Denton Shelter** (1991)—Sleeps 8. Privy. Enlarged front porch for extra sleepers. Water source is a spring on the A.T. near the solar shower (reported broken in 2007; spring reported dry).

**Va. 638—West** 1.1 mile to **Linden, Va. [P.O. ZIP 22642: M–F 8–12 & 1–5, Sa 8–12; (540) 636-9936].** A small outpost on Va. 55, Linden offers only a post office and convenience store, but it's an alternative to hitching into Front Royal to pick up a mail drop. ■ *Groceries:* Monterey Service Station (good short-term resupply), M–F 4–9, Sa 6–9, Su 6:30–9, outside pay phone, hiker-friendly.

**West** 1.5 miles to *Restaurant:* Apple House, fresh-baked pies, seasonal fruits, doughnuts, sandwiches, BBQ, buffalo(!) burgers, B, deli foods; M 7–5, Tu–Th 7–7, F–Sa 7–8, Su 7–6; credit cards accepted, ATM. ■ *Groceries:* Quarles Shell, (540) 635-1899, open 24 hrs., ATM, deli sandwiches, ice cream; good short-term resupply; pay phone outside; Apple Mountain Exxon, (540) 636-2960, large store, open 24 hrs., ATM, a must stop for hungry hikers, fresh pies, deli sandwiches, ice cream, pay phone outside.

**West** 7 miles to Front Royal on Va. 55 (see above).

**Va. 55, Manassas Gap—West** 1.1 miles into Linden (see previous entry). This is a busier road, parallel to I-66, which leads east to Washington, D.C. *Hostel:* Private cabin, sleeps up to 4, any season; $100/night, includes shower and D; Internet access, satellite TV, summer swimming pool; no dogs. Call Brandt, (304) 279-4361, for more info and pick-up at I-66 underpass/Tucker Road.

**Manassas Gap Shelter** (1940s/2002)—Sleeps 6. Privy. Food-hoist cables available. Water source is a reliable spring near the shelter on a side trail.

**Dick's Dome Shelter** (1985)—Sleeps 4. Privy. This unusually shaped shelter was built on private land by PATC member Dick George. Food-hoist cables available. Water source (which hikers should treat) is Whiskey Hollow Creek in front of the shelter. Scheduled for rebuilding.

**Sky Meadows State Park Side Trail**—Look for the resting bench at path that leads **East** 1.7 miles to the park's visitors center in Mt. Bleak Mansion, built in the 1820s. Now one of Virginia's finest parks, open daily 8–dusk. Cultural events are scheduled on summer weekends. Telephone, water fountain, and soda machine available at the visitors center. Hike-in primitive camping (12 sites) 1.25 mi from A.T. and primitive group-camping area, $12PP, on the way to the visitors center. Reservations required, (540) 592-3556 or (800) 933-7275, and campers must arrive before dusk, when the park closes.

**U.S. 50, U.S. 17/Ashby Gap—East** 0.8 mile on U.S. 50/17, then 0.3 mile south past barrier on Va. 759 to community of Paris. ■ *Lodging:* The Ashby Inn, (540) 592-3900, restaurant serves D $22–$32 and Su brunch $24; rooms $155–$275, includes B; restaurant closed M–Tu, reservations recommended.

**Rod Hollow Shelter** (1986)—Sleeps 8. Privy. Located on a blue-blazed trail. Water source is a spring or the streams just south of the shelter.

**The "Roller Coaster"**—Northbounders leaving the Rod Hollow Shelter will enter the "roller coaster," a 13.5-mile section with ten ascents and descents. Southbounders have just completed their ride. The Virginia corridor is narrow here, leaving Trail crews very little choice other than to route the path up and over each of these viewless and rocky ridges.

**Sam Moore Shelter** (1990)—Sleeps 6. Privy. Constructed of materials salvaged from the old Keys Gap Shelter. Named for maintainer Sam Moore, who gave 55 years of volunteer service to the A.T. Water source is Sawmill Spring in front of shelter or spring to left of shelter.

**Bears Den**—A stop at Bears Den Rocks provides a fine view of the Shenandoah Valley to the west. Nearby Bears Den Hostel is owned by ATC and operated by PATC; (540) 554-8708, <info@bearsdencenter.org>. Hiker Special includes bunk, shower, laundry, pizza, soda, and pint of Ben & Jerry's ice cream for $25; bunk & shower, $15; camping $8; shower only $2; laundry $3; short-term resupply; fuel by the ounce; cooking privileges; and water. Open for supplies and check-in 5–9:30 p.m. only. Hiker room is accessible all day. Free Internet and free long-distance phone in hiker room. Mail drops can be sent to Bears Den Hostel, 18393 Blue Ridge Mountain Rd., Bluemont, VA 20135.

**Va. 7, Va. 679/Snickers Gap—East** 1.7 miles to **Bluemont, Va. [P.O. ZIP 20135: M–F 8:30–12 & 1–5, Sa 8:30–12; (540) 554-4537].** Follow Va. 7 **East** 0.9 mile over Snickers Gap to the Snickersville Turnpike sign, turn right, and continue 0.8 mile to the post office on Va. 670.

**East** 1.6 mi to Bluemont General Store, open M–F 6:30–7, Sa–Su 7–7; (540) 554-2054, short-term resupply, pizza by the slice, ice cream, pies.

On Va. 679, **West** 0.3 mile to *Restaurant:* Horseshoe Curve Restaurant, (540) 554-8291, open Tu–Sa 12–11 (or later), Su 12–7. Excellent hiker portions.

**West** 0.9 mile to ■ *Restaurant:* Pine Grove Restaurant, open M–Sa 6:30–8, Su 7–1. ■ *Groceries:* **West** 1.0 mile to Village Market, (540) 554-8422, open M–Sa 7–7, Su 8–4; short-term resupply, ice cream, may give ride back to Trail if not busy.

**Blackburn Trail Center**—**East** 0.2 mile *via* either of two blue-blazed trails. This PATC facility, (540) 338-9028, is staffed during the summer months by a PATC caretaker. From the porch, on clear days, you may be able to glimpse the Washington Monument and National Cathedral in the distance to the east. The center has a free bunkhouse that sleeps 8, with a wood-burning stove, a food-storage shelter, and a picnic bench built in 2002 with ALDHA donations in memory of Edward B. Garvey. A carriage house can be used for overflow. Six tentsites and tent platforms are nearby, and a camping area with privy is 0.1 mile north of the main building on the blue-blazed trail. Water available year-round from an outside spigot, pay phone located on the porch, and solar-heated shower on front lawn. Donations appreciated. During the summer months, PATC work and hiking groups are often here. ALDHA member "Weathercarrot" has done a tremendous amount of rockwork to rebuild the stone retaining walls.

**David Lesser Shelter** (1994)—Sleeps 6. Privy. A shelter-engineering feat. Water source is a spring located 0.4 mile downhill from the shelter.

*"Every part of this soil is sacred. Every hillside, every valley, every plain and grove has been hallowed by some sad or happy event in days long vanished."*
        —CHIEF SEATTLE

# West Virginia

| Miles from Katahdin | Features | Services | Elev. | Miles from Springer |
|---|---|---|---|---|
| 1,171.1 | Keys Gap, W.Va. 9 | R (E–0.3m G) (W–0.3m G, M, w) | 935 | 1,005.1 |
| 1,167.2 | Loudoun Heights, Va.–W.Va. State Line | | 1,279 | 1,009.0 |
| 1,166.6 | W. Va. 32 (Chestnut Hill Rd) | R | 820 | 1,009.6 |
| 1,165.6 | U.S. 340, Shenandoah River Bridge (north end) | R (W–0.1m L; 1.2m C, cl, sh) (E–3.7m H, sh, cl, @) | 312 | 1,010.6 |
| 1,165.3 | ATC side trail **Harpers Ferry, WV 25425** | W–0.2m ATC, f, @; 0.4m M; 0.5m PO; 0.6m L; 0.7m O; 1.1m G, G, D, @; 1.7m C, cl, sh | 394 | 1,010.9 |
| 1,164.7 | Shenandoah Street; Harpers Ferry Nat'l Historical Park | R (W–0.1m M, O, f) | 315 | 1,011.5 |
| 1,164.6 | Potomac River, Byron Memorial Footbridge, W.Va.–Md. State Line | | 263 | 1,011.6 |

By now, at the psychological halfway point, many hikers can relate to Grandma's words. The reality has already sunk in for southbounders, who have actually seen the physical half-way point. Hikers stop at ATC headquarters to sign the register and proudly have their picture taken to be counted among the class of 2008 thru-hikers.

**W.Va. 9/Keys Gap—East** 0.3 mile to *Groceries:* Sweet Springs Country Store (short-term resupply), (504) 668-7200, M–Sa 4–11, Su 7–11, Ben & Jerry's, fountain, fried chicken, sandwiches, ATM.

**West** 0.3 mile to *Groceries:* Torlone Mini-Mart (short-term resupply), M–Th 8–9, F–Sa 8–10, Su 8–9. ■ *Restaurant:* Torlone Pizza, Pasta & Subs, (304) 725-0916, ATM and pay phone, open M–Th 11–9, F–Sa 11–10, Su 1–8.

Because of a local law-enforcement problem (not involving hikers), camping currently is prohibited from a half-mile south of Keys Gap to 1.5 miles north (the powerline cut).

**Harpers Ferry National Historical Park**—Nearly half the town of Harpers Ferry and surrounding ridges (including those south of the Shenandoah River crossing) have been a historical park since 1963, with gradual land acquisition outside the town proper. Before then, part of the town was a national monument for less than a decade. It saw extensive Civil War action, especially before the slaughter at nearby Antietam, Md., but is probably best known for the raid of John Brown, an abolitionist from Kansas who attempted to capture the federal arsenal here in 1859. The arsenal was to be the staging point for a slave uprising. A U.S. colonel named Robert E. Lee crushed the raid, and historians point to the event as a steppingstone to the war, which began 16 months after Brown was hanged for treason in nearby Charles Town. Today, the Park Service runs many interpretive exhibits in renovated buildings dating back to that era. More information on the historic town is available at ATC headquarters, (304) 535-6331, as well as the park's visitors center. The park's visitors center (west of town along U.S. 340) offers parking ($6 fee charged, up to two weeks maximum) and a free shuttle to the historic district. *Note:* Hikers parking in lot must register at the visitors center, open 8–5. Parking-lot gates open at 8, close at dusk.

**U.S. 340/Shenandoah River—East** 20 miles to Frederick, Md., with all services, including Quality Shoe Service, 319 North Market St., (301) 695-9255, for boot repair, and Trail House, an outfitter, 17 South Market St., (301) 694-8448. *Traffic can be extremely heavy at this Trailhead; mostly narrow shoulders with few safe pull-offs near the Trail junction.*

**West** 0.1 mile to *Lodging:* Comfort Inn, (304) 535-6391, $85D weekdays, $95–$150S weekends, no pets, continental B, pay phone outside, laundry $6 per load, refrigerator and microwave in room. New signs on U.S. 340 say "Appalachian Trail Visitor Center"—that's the ATC visitors center.

**West** 1.2 miles to *Camping:* Harpers Ferry KOA (short-term resupply), a family campground, (304) 535-6895, cabins $53.95 and up, tentsites M–F $33, Sa–Su $35, shower only $5, coin laundry, campstore, snack bar, pizzeria, pool, leashed pets welcome except Rottweillers, pit bulls, or Dobermans. ■ *Lodging:* Cliffside Inn, (304) 535-6302, 4328 William L. Wilson Hwy, Harpers Ferry, WV 25425, bar and grill, Su–Th $90D, $5EAP, inquire for weekend rates, microwave and refrigerator in some rooms, some rooms with Jacuzzi, WiFi with computer access for hikers, no pets allowed, coin laundry, indoor pool, FedEx and postal services available, will hold and mail out packages for guests, long-term parking for guests. ■ *Restaurant:* Surf Dining Room, B/L/D, AYCE buffet F–Sa nights, Su brunch.

**East** 3.7 miles to *Hostel:* Harpers Ferry Hostel, Keep Tryst Rd., Sandy Hook/Knoxville, Md. (see next chapter for details).

**West** 6 miles to Charles Town, W.Va., with all services, including Wal-Mart, Jefferson Urgent Care Medical Facility, and a hospital.

**West** 20 miles (U.S. 340 to W.Va. 9 before Charles Town) to Martinsburg, W.Va., with all services, including movie theaters, malls, as well as many restaurants. For bus service to those towns, see Harpers Ferry entry below.

**Harpers Ferry**

**Harpers Ferry, W.Va. [P.O. ZIP 25425: M–F 8–4, Sa 9–12: (304) 535-2479].** The post office and most services are available above the old town *via* the 0.2-mile blue-blazed trail, recently rehabilitated jointly by PATC and ATC, to ATC headquarters (see below). The A.T. itself leads through the historic district at the bottom of the hill, with museums, stores, and restaurants. Many businesses in the historic district are closed in the winter or open only on weekends then. The park is open 7 days a week year-round, but its visitors center closes Thanksgiving, Christmas, and New Year's Day. ■ *Hostel:* The Town's Inn, 179 High St., right in historic lower town, (877) 489-2447, <info@TheTownsInn.com>, beds available at $30–$50. For information on additional hostel nearby, check the first listing in Maryland. ■ *Lodging:* Hilltop House Hotel, (304) 535-2132, hiker rooms, $40S, $45D, $10EAP, pay phone; coin laundry in annex open 24/7, front desk will provide change. Several B&Bs are also located in town: Check at ATC for further information. ■ *Groceries:* 7-11 convenience store (short-term resupply), 1 mile **west** of ATC; outfitter 0.5 mile **east** of ATC (short-term resupply); supermarkets and Wal-Mart (long-term resupply) in Charles Town, 6 miles **west**. ■ *Restaurants:* King's Pizza, L/D, closed M; Hilltop House, B/L/D with occasional AYCE buffets; Country Café, B/L; Southern Smoke Barbeque and Grill; Anvil Restaurant, W–Su 11–9; Secret Six Tavern; John Brown Tea and Coffee Shop; Armory Pub, Canal House Ice Cream & Coffee. ■ *Outfitter:* The Outfitter at Harpers Ferry, 189 High St., (304) 535-2087 or (888) 535-2087, full-service outfitter (short-term resupply), open daily 10–6, Jan–Feb weekends only, <www.theoutfitteratharpersferry.com>. ■ *Internet access:* Harpers Ferry/Bolivar Library, (304) 535-2301, M, Tu, F, Sa 10–5:30, W, Th 10–8; ATC. ■ *Other services:* banks with ATM; dentist, Dr. John Mayhew, M–Th, (304) 535-2409; Caring Hands Chiropractic and Advanced Massage Therapy, Dr. Jenny Foster, a hiker (located near Middletown, Md.), (301) 371-3922, call ahead for possible pick-up (schedule permitting) at Harpers Ferry Hostel or Old South Mountain Inn; Foot and Ankle Care Office, Drs. Warren BeVards and David Grace, (304) 535-3040, W 8:30–11:30, F 1:30–4:30; bicycle sales, rental, and repair at The Outfitter's General Store, 129 Potomac St., (304) 535-2296. ■ *Bus service:* Pan Tran bus to Charles Town or Martinsburg operates M–F; limited Sa service; flag the bus across the street from the ATC office. The charge is $1.50 one-way. Bus leaves town at 6:44 a.m., 8:59 a.m., 10:29 a.m., 1:29 p.m., 3 p.m., 4:43 p.m., 7:29 p.m.; Sa 10:25 a.m., 4:25 p.m. Leaves Wal-Mart in Charles Town for Harpers Ferry at 6:30 a.m., 8:45 a.m., 10:15 a.m., 1:15 p.m., 2:45 p.m., 4:30 p.m. and 7:15 p.m.; Sa 10:10 a.m., 4:10 p.m. No dogs; packs OK unless driver believes one may be suspicious. Times are subject to change.

**Appalachian Trail Conservancy (ATC)**—Reached *via* 0.2-mile blue-blazed side trail at the top of the first hill up from the Shenandoah River and U.S. 340, west of (uphill from) the historic section of Harpers Ferry; at the corner of Washington Street and Storer College Place. ATC publications and products are for sale at the information/visitors center. Benton MacKaye's typewriter and Myron Avery's measuring wheel are on display as part of the A.T. Museum Society's first exhibit. Volunteers or staffers John Fletcher and Laurie Potteiger (Mountain Laurel of 1987) can answer your Trail questions. The office accepts donations for Coleman fuel and alcohol and holds packages sent to P.O. Box 807 or 799 Washington St., Harpers Ferry, WV 25425. If you're thru-hiking or piecing the Trail together, someone will snap your photo for the 2008 album; a register is inside, along with a scale. Volunteers are needed periodically at headquarters and almost always at the sales-distribution center 11 miles away. ATC Visitors Center, (304) 535-6331, open M–F 9–5, closed weekends and federal holidays from mid-Dec through Mar, then also open Sa–Su and holidays 9–4. Drinks for sale. Bench and picnic tables in side yard. Phone and Internet access for hikers. Ask for ATC's often-updated "Hiker's Guide to Harpers Ferry," with more details on services. Driving directions are available at <www.appalachiantrail.org>.

**Jefferson Rock**—The white blazes take you past this Harpers Ferry viewpoint that overlooks the confluence of the Potomac and Shenandoah rivers. Named in honor of Thomas Jefferson, who was inspired by the beautiful view in 1783. Several large slabs of shale originally rested naturally but not securely atop each other. "Jefferson Rock" now rests securely on a set of short pillars erected in the 1850s.

**Trains to Washington, D.C.**—Amtrak train No. 30 (Capitol Limited), (800) USA-RAIL, <www.amtrak.com>, is scheduled to depart Harpers Ferry at 11:45 a.m. ('though it is often 2 or more hours late) and to arrive at D.C.'s Union Station at 1:30 p.m. Train No. 29 leaves D.C. at 4:05 p.m., arriving in Harpers Ferry at 5:06 p.m. Coach fares are $11–$20 one way (cost may be more if coach is not available). Fares and schedule subject to change. Harpers Ferry station is not staffed. Reservations required; backpacks allowed, but not bikes. Two scheduled Maryland Rail Commuter Service (MARC) commuter trains on the Brunswick line [(800) 325-7245 outside local calling area; others call (301) 834-8360; <www.mtamaryland.com>] leave Harpers Ferry for D.C. on weekdays. They depart at 5:51 a.m. and 6:56 a.m., arriving at 7:28 a.m. and 8:30 a.m. Three trains leave D.C. for Harpers Ferry on weekdays. They depart at 4:55 p.m., 5:35 p.m., and 7:15 p.m. and arrive at 6:16 p.m., 7:09 p.m., and 8:42 p.m. Fares are $9 one way.

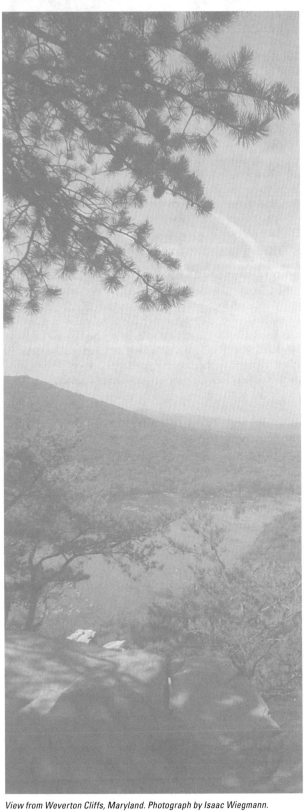
*View from Weverton Cliffs, Maryland. Photograph by Isaac Wiegmann.*

# Maryland

| Miles from Katahdin | Features | Services | Elev. | Miles from Springer |
|---|---|---|---|---|
| 1,164.6 | Potomac River, Byron Memorial Footbridge, Md.– W.Va. State Line | | 263 | 1,011.6 |
| 1,164.4 | C&O Canal Towpath (west jct) | | 290 | 1,011.8 |
| 1,163.1 | U.S. 340, Sandy Hook Bridge | R | 290 | 1,013.1 |
| 1,161.8 | C&O Canal Towpath (east jct) | | 290 | 1,014.4 |
| 1,161.7 | Keep Tryst Rd; RR tracks | R (E–2.5m L, M) (W–1.1m H, L, G, M, cl, sh, f) | 320 | 1,014.5 |
| 1,161.5 | U.S. 340 Underpass | | 400 | 1,014.7 |
| 1,161.3 | Weverton Rd | R (W–1.4m G) | 420 | 1,014.9 |
| 1,160.4 | Weverton Cliffs Trail | | 780 | 1,015.8 |
| 1,158.3 | **Ed Garvey Shelter** *16mS; 4.5mN* | E–0.1m S; 0.5m w | 1,100 | 1,017.9 |
| 1,156.3 | Brownsville Gap | | 1,140 | 1,019.9 |
| 1,154.6 | Crampton Gap, Gathland State Park, Gapland Rd (Md. 572) | R, w (W–0.4m C, G, f) | 950 | 1,021.6 |
| 1,154.2 | **Crampton Gap Shelter** *4.5mS; 5.5mN* | E–0.3m S, w | 1,000 | 1,022.0 |
| 1,151.6 | Trail to Bear Spring Cabin (locked) | W–0.5m w | 1,480 | 1,024.6 |
| 1,151.0 | White Rock Cliff | | 1,500 | 1,025.2 |
| 1,150.8 | Lamb's Knoll | | 1,600 | 1,025.4 |
| 1,149.2 | **Rocky Run Shelter** *5.5mS; 7.8mN* | W–0.2m S, C, w | 970 | 1,027.0 |
| 1,148.2 | Reno Monument Rd | R | 91,0 | 1,028.0 |
| 1,147.4 | Dahlgren Back Pack Campground | C, M, sh, w | 980 | 1,028.8 |
| 1,147.2 | Turners Gap, U.S. Alt. 40 **Boonsboro, MD 21713** | R, M (W–2.4m PO, M, D, V, cl, @; 3.8m G) | 1,000 | 1,029.0 |
| 1,145.8 | Monument Rd | R | 1,350 | 1,030.4 |
| 1,145.6 | Washington Monument Rd | R, w | 1,400 | 1,030.6 |
| 1,145.2 | Washington Monument | | 1,550 | 1,031.0 |
| 1,142.4 | Boonsboro Mtn Rd | R | 1,300 | 1,033.8 |
| 1,142.7 | Bartman Hill Trail to Greenbrier State Park | W–0.6m C, f | | 1,033.5 |

| Miles from Katahdin | Features | Services | Elev. | Miles from Springer |
|---|---|---|---|---|
| 1,142.3 | I-70 Footbridge, U.S. 40, Greenbrier State Park | R (W–0.4m M, w; 1.4m C, f) | 1,200 | 1,033.9 |
| 1,141.7 | **Pine Knob Shelter** *7.8mS; 8.3mN* | W–0.1m S, w | 1,360 | 1,034.5 |
| 1,140.1 | Trail to Annapolis Rock | W–0.2m C, w | 1,820 | 1,036.1 |
| 1,139.1 | Black Rock Cliffs | | 1,800 | 1,037.1 |
| 1,138.4 | Pogo Memorial Campsite | C, w | 1,500 | 1,037.8 |
| 1,133.7 | Md. 17, Wolfsville Rd **Smithsburg, MD 21783** | R (W–0.3m H, M, sh, cl, @; 1.8m G, D, V; 2.4m PO, G, M, D, cl, @) | 1,400 | 1,042.5 |
| 1,133.5 | **Ensign Cowall Shelter** *8.3mS; 5.2mN* | S, w | 1,430 | 1,042.7 |
| 1,132.2 | Md. 77, Foxville Rd | R | 1,450 | 1,044.0 |
| 1,130.4 | Warner Gap Rd | R, w | 1,150 | 1,045.8 |
| 1,129.6 | Md. 491, Raven Rock Hollow | R | 1,190 | 1,046.6 |
| 1,128.6 | **Devils Racecourse Shelter** *5.2mS; 9.9mN* | E–0.3m S, w | 1,480 | 1,047.6 |
| 1,126.8 | Trail to High Rock | R | 1,950 | 1,049.4 |
| 1,123.9 | Pen Mar County Park **Cascade, MD 21719** | R, w (E–1.7m PO, G, L, cl) | 1,330 | 1,052.3 |
| 1,123.7 | Mason–Dixon Line, Md.–Pa. State Line | R | 1,250 | 1,052.5 |

*Overnight camping in Maryland is allowed only at designated campsites. Please obey camping regulations in this heavily used section.*

This section boasts easy terrain, the C & O Canal towpath along the Potomac River, a free on-trail hot-water shower, Civil War history, the War Correspondents Monument, the first monument to George Washington, and the Mason-Dixon line.

**C&O Canal Towpath**—The southernmost 2.8 miles of the Trail in Maryland follow this path from which mules towed barges, between what's left of the canal on one side and the Potomac River on the other, until 1924. Stretching 185 miles from Washington, D.C., to Cumberland, Md., it was rescued from highway development by a protest hike led by Supreme Court Justice William O. Douglas, an A.T. 2,000-miler. Now, it is part of a national historical park, accessible to both hikers and bicyclists. Blazes are scarce, but the points at which the Trail enters and leaves it are hard to miss.

**Keep Tryst Road—East** 2.5 mile to Brunswick, Md., *via* U.S. 340 and Md. 478 at Knoxville exit. ■ *Lodging:* Green Country Inn, (301) 834-9151, 620 Souder Rd., B/L/D, open 24/7, rates from $69.95, pets allowed $5/day.

**West** 0.9 mile to Sandy Hook Road, turn left, 0.2 mile to *Hostel:* Harpers Ferry Hostel (Hostelling International), (301) 834-7652, <www.harpersferryhostel.org>, <mail@harpersferryhostel.org>, bunk $20PP for thru-hikers or HI members, $23PP for nonmembers, includes shower, kitchen privileges, a/c, Internet access; tenting $10PP; groups of more than 10 $6 PP. Laundry $3, nonguest shower $3, parking $6 per day. All rates subject to change. To check on availability, call 7–9 a.m. or 6–10 p.m. Possible work-for-stay on a limited basis (after each day paid); check with manager. Building closed 9 a.m.–6 p.m., check-in 6–10 p.m. Dogs allowed if camping. No alcohol. Seven-day limit per month. Closed Nov 15–Mar 14. Mail drops for hikers, send to 19123 Sandy Hook Rd., Knoxville, MD 21758-1330 (mark "Hold for A.T. Hiker" with hiker's real name). ■ *Lodging:* Hillside Motel, (301) 834-8144, with rooms beginning at $50S $55D M–Th, $65S/D F–Su, no pets. ■ *Groceries:* Hillside Station, (301) 834-5300, deli, M–F 5–8:45, Sa–Su 6–8:45. ■ *Restaurant:* Cindy Dee's, (301) 695-8181, B/L/D, Su–Th 6–10, F–Sa 6–11; fried chicken, $2.50 B specials include coffee; pay phone.

**Ed Garvey Shelter** (2001)—Sleeps 12. Privy. Two tentsites north and south of shelter. Water source is found at the end of a 0.5-mile, steep side trail in front of the shelter.

**Gathland State Park**—Located in Crampton Gap, the state-run facility has water, soda and juice vending machines, restroom, covered picnic pavilion, and telephone. No camping here. The monument to war correspondents is the only one of its kind in the country. Southbounders may want to pick up water here before heading to Ed Garvey Shelter.

**Gapland Road—West** 0.4 mile on Gapland Rd., right on Townsend Rd. to *Camping:* Maple Tree Campground, 20716 Townsend Rd., Gapland, MD 21779, (301) 432-5585, <thetreehousecamp2@aol.com>; Bill Cruz, manager; tentsite $10PP; rustic tree house $36/night, 4-hiker maximum; cottages with woodstove $50/night, 4-hiker maximum. All with picnic table, fire ring, grill. Short-term resupply; white gas, denatured alcohol, canisters; mail drops accepted; dogs okay, no extra fee.

**Crampton Gap Shelter** (1941)—Sleeps 6. Privy. Built by the CCC. Water source is an intermittent spring 0.1 mile south on the A.T. that may go dry in June. Northbounders may want to get water from faucet at Gathland State Park, 0.25 mile south on the A.T.

**Rocky Run Shelter** (1941)—Currently under renovation, plans to reopen June 2008. Privy. Tentsites can be found downhill from the shelter. Water source is a spring to the right of the shelter.

**Dahlgren Backpack Campground**—No, it's not a mirage; that really is a bathhouse with hot showers and flush toilets. Operated by the state at no charge, the bathhouse, campsites with gravel tentpads, and picnic areas are open Apr–Nov.

**U.S. 40-A/Turners Gap**—*Restaurant:* Old South Mountain Inn, (301) 371-5400, D Tu–Su, L Sa; Su brunch 10:30–2. Hikers staying at Dahlgren Campground can literally shower and shave before an elegant dining experience, then walk back to camp in minutes. (Take your pack with you.) ■ *Other services:* chiropractic and therapeutic massage, Dr. Jenny Foster, (301) 371-3922, can pick up at Old South Mountain Inn, schedule permitting.

**West** 2.4 miles to **Boonsboro, Md. [P.O. ZIP 21713: M–F 8:30–1 & 2–5, Sa 8:30–12; (301) 432-6861].** ■ *Restaurants:* Asaro's Pizza and Sub Shop; Crawford Confectionery (candy & sweets); Town Center Subs & Pizza, with pay phone; Potomac Street Creamery ice-cream shop; Mountainside Deli. ■ *Internet access:* library; Bruce Wilder's Turn the Page Bookstore Café (featuring supernovelist Nora Roberts, wife of Bruce), with A.T. books and maps. ■ *Other services:* coin laundry, bank with ATM, doctor, dentist, veterinarian, and pharmacy.

**West** 3.8 miles to *Groceries:* Cronise Market Place, Boonsboro Produce Market (both short-term resupply).

**Washington Monument State Park**—A state park built around the first monument to George Washington. The bottle-shaped structure is more modest than the big one in Washington, D.C., but impressive for small-town Marylanders in 1827. When open, the observation deck on top provides views of the surrounding countryside. South of the monument, on the A.T., are park facilities with picnic shelters, restroom, soda machine, and pay phone by the restroom near the museum. No camping permitted in the park; the campsite near the southern entrance is for youth groups with permits.

**U.S. 40/Greenbrier State Park**—North of the I-70 footbridge, the A.T. crosses U.S. 40. **West** 0.4 mile to the park entrance, across the road from *Restaurant:* Dogpatch Tavern, ATM.

**West** 1.4 miles to *Camping:* Greenbrier State Park, (301) 791-4767, open Apr–Oct, no pets allowed. Open May–Sep: visitors center, restroom, concession stand, campstore with snacks, Coleman fuel by the gallon, and swimming in Greenbrier Lake. Entrance fee $2PP weekdays, $3PP weekends and holidays, tentsites with hot showers $20. Reservations recommended on the weekends; two-night minimum.

**Pine Knob Shelter** (1939)—Sleeps 5. Privy. Shelter is located on a blue-blazed trail. Water source is a piped spring beside the shelter.

**Annapolis Rock Campsite**—13 tentsites and two privies at this popular area; caretaker on site. Tentsites are near an outstanding overlook popular with climbers. Spring location is marked.

**Pogo Memorial Campsite**—The campsite is immediately to the east of the Trail, with a spring 30 yards on a blue-blazed trail to the west.

**Md. 17/Wolfsville Road—West** 0.3 mile to *Hostel:* The Free State Hiker Hostel, owned by '06 thru-hiker Ken "Bone Pac" and Jennel Berry, (301) 824-2407, 11626 Wolfsville Road, Smithsburg, MD 21783. Open Mar 15–Nov 15; $32 includes climate-controlled bunk room, all linens, shower, laundry, high-speed Internet, phone. Credit cards accepted. Pizza and Mexican delivery available. Snacks, sodas, ice cream on site. Water available from spigot in front. No alcohol and no pets. Two-night maximum. Mail drops accepted for $2 handling fee (fee waived for overnight stay).

**West** 1.7 miles on Wolfsville Road and then left 0.1 mile on Md. 64 to a small shopping center. ■ *Groceries:* Phil & Jerry's Meats & More (short-term resupply); Dollar General Store. ■ *Other services:* veterinarian; medical clinics; pharmacy; pay phone; two banks with ATM, near shopping center.

**West** 2.4 miles *via* Wolfsville Road and Md. 77 to **Smithsburg, Md. [P.O. ZIP 21783: M–F 8:30–1 & 2–5, Sa 8:30–12; (301) 824-2828].** ■ *Groceries:* Smithsburg Market, Food Lion (both long-term resupply). ■ *Restaurants:* Vince's Pizza; South of the Border; Dixie Eatery; Subway. ■ *Internet access:* library, M–Tu 2–8, W 9–3, Th 9–6, F 2–5, Sa 9–1. ■ *Other services:* coin laundry, dentist, Rite-Aid pharmacy, and banks with ATM.

**Ensign Cowall Shelter** (1999)—Sleeps 8. Privy. Named for Ensign Phillip Cowall, who passed away in 1998. Built by the PATC and volunteers and students from Gallaudet University and its Model Secondary School for the Deaf (MSSD), located in Washington, D.C. Water source is a spring south of the shelter 0.2 mile on the A.T.

**Devils Racecourse Shelter** (1950s)—Sleeps 7. Privy. Located 70 yards down a blue-blazed trail. Water sources are a spring downhill from the A.T. and a stream in front of shelter.

**Pen Mar County Park**—Open from the first Su in May to the last Su in Oct. No camping in the park. The pavilion provides views of the countryside to the west. On weekends during the summer, bands play, with a Su-afternoon dance for seniors in the pavilion. Snack bar , outside soda machines, and museum, outside pay phone, open Sa and Su. Restroom locked in the evening. No alcohol permitted in the park.

**East** 1.7 miles to ■ *Restaurant:* CJ's Pizza, Subs, and More, (301) 241-5052, delivers to park. To reach town from the park entrance, turn left on High Rock Road to Pen-Mar Road, turn right (downhill), pass under a railroad trestle, turn right at the stop sign. CJ's is 0.3 mile farther on the left in the small community of **Cascade, Md. [P.O. ZIP 21719: M–F 8–1 & 2–5, Sa 8–12; (301) 241-3403]**. To reach the post office, continue 0.1 mile, and turn left on Ft. Ritchie Road, across from the entrance to decommissioned Ft. Ritchie. ■ *Lodging:* The Cascade Inn, 147 Eyler Ave., Cascade, MD 21719; call for rates, hiker discounts, (800) 362-9526 or (301) 241-4161, <cascadeinn@comcast.net>, shuttles available for guests. ■ *Groceries:* GT's Handimart (short-term resupply), ATM; Sanders Market (long-term resupply), open M, W–F 8:30–9, Tu and Sa 8:30–8. ■ *Other services:* Cascade Coin Laundry.

**Western Maryland Railroad**—If you think lots of picnic tables are at Pen Mar Park today, you should have been here around the turn of the 20th century, when a Lutheran picnic drew 15,000 people. The Western Maryland Railroad in 1878 opened the park, which, during its heyday, was known as the Coney Island of the Blue Ridge. Facilities included a three-story hotel that could house 400 guests and an amusement park boasting a fun house, roller coaster, and miniature railroad. The amusement park ceased operation in 1943, but remnants of the resort are visible along the A.T. south of the park.

**Mason-Dixon Line**—A marker was once on the Trail to signify the historical survey line and the Pennsylvania–Maryland state line. The marker has not been seen for several years. Incidentally, the moniker "Dixie" was not derived from Dixon. Prior to the Civil War, a Louisiana bank began printing $10 bills. In French, the word for 10 is *dix*. The bills were so widely distributed that the South soon became known as Dixie. The song "Dixie" was written by a minstrel-show musician from Ohio and was one of President Lincoln's favorite tunes.

*"The Appalachian Trail as originally conceived is not merely a footpath through the wilderness but a footpath of the wilderness."*
    —BENTON MACKAYE

# Pennsylvania

| Miles from Katahdin | Features | Services | Elev. | Miles from Springer |
|---|---|---|---|---|
| 1,123.7 | Mason–Dixon Line, Pa.–Md. State Line | R | 1,250 | 1,052.5 |
| 1,123.6 | Pen Mar Rd | R | 1,240 | 1,052.6 |
| 1,122.6 | Buena Vista Rd | R, w | 1,290 | 1,053.6 |
| 1,121.4 | Old Pa. 16 | R | 1,350 | 1,054.8 |
| 1,121.1 | Pa. 16 **Blue Ridge Summit, PA 17214; Waynesboro, PA 17268** | R (E–1.2m PO, M, D, cl, f, @) (W–2m G, M; 2.3m G; 5m PO, G, M, L, V, D, cl, f, @) | 1,200 | 1,055.1 |
| 1,120.9 | Mackie Run, Mentzer Gap Rd | R | 1,250 | 1,055.3 |
| 1,120.3 | Bailey Spring | w | 1,300 | 1,055.9 |
| 1,119.0 | **Deer Lick Shelters** *9.9mS; 2.4mN* | S (E–0.2m w) | 1,420 | 1,057.2 |
| 1,116.6 | Old Forge Park, **Antietam Shelter** *...2.4mS; 1.2mN* | R, S (w 0.2m N on A.T.) | 890 | 1,059.6 |
| 1,116.2 | Rattlesnake Run Rd | R | 900 | 1,060.0 |
| 1,115.6 | Old Forge Rd | R | 1,000 | 1,060.6 |
| 1,115.4 | **Tumbling Run Shelters** *1.2mS; 6.8mN* | S, w | 1,120 | 1,060.8 |
| 1,114.2 | Chimney Rocks | | 1,900 | 1,062.0 |
| 1,110.8 | Swamp Rd | R | 1,560 | 1,065.4 |
| 1,110.5 | Pa. 233 **South Mountain, PA 17261** | R (E–1.2m PO, M) | 1,600 | 1,065.7 |
| 1,108.8 | **Rocky Mtn Shelters** *6.8mS; 5.8mN* | E–0.2m S; 0.5m w | 1,520 | 1,067.4 |
| 1,105.8 | U.S. 30, Caledonia State Park **Fayetteville, PA 17222** | R, C, M, sh, w (W–0.3m M; 0.7m G; 3.5m PO, G, M, L, D, cl) | 960 | 1,070.4 |
| 1,103.9 | Quarry Gap Rd | R | 1,250 | 1,072.3 |
| 1,103.2 | **Quarry Gap Shelters** *5.8mS; 7.4mN* | S, w | 1,455 | 1,073.0 |
| 1,101.7 | Sandy Sod Jct | R | 1,980 | 1,074.5 |
| 1,099.1 | Middle Ridge Rd | R | 2,050 | 1,077.1 |
| 1,098.6 | Ridge Rd, Means Hollow Rd | R | 1,800 | 1,077.6 |
| 1,098.2 | Milesburn Rd, Milesburn Cabin (locked) | R, w | 1,600 | 1,078.0 |
| 1,095.8 | **Birch Run Shelter** *7.4mS; 6.2mN* | S, w | 1,795 | 1,080.4 |
| 1,094.5 | Shippensburg Rd, Big Flat Fire Tower | R | 2,040 | 1,081.7 |

| Miles from Katahdin | Features | Services | Elev. | Miles from Springer |
|---|---|---|---|---|
| 1,092.6 | Michener Cabin (locked) | E–0.3m w | 1,850 | 1,083.6 |
| 1,090.7 | Woodrow Rd | R | 1,850 | 1,085.5 |
| 1,089.6 | **Toms Run Shelters** *6.2mS; 11.1mN* | S, w | 1,300 | 1,086.6 |
| 1,086.2 | Pa. 233 | R | 900 | 1,090.0 |
| 1,085.9 | Pine Grove Furnace State Park | R, H, C, G, w, sh, cl | 850 | 1,090.3 |
| 1,084.9 | Midpoint Marker *(3.2mi N of midpoint)* | | 1,000 | 1,091.3 |
| 1,083.4 | Pole Steeple side trail | | 1,300 | 1,092.8 |
| 1,079.9 | Trail to Mtn Creek Campground | W–0.7m C, G | 1,050 | 1,096.3 |
| 1,078.7 | **James Fry (Tagg Run) Shelter** *1.1mS; 8.7mN* | E–0.2m S, w | 805 | 1,097.5 |
| 1,078.2 | Pine Grove Rd | R (W–0.4m C, M) | 750 | 1,098.0 |
| 1,077.3 | Hunters Run Rd, Pa. 34 | R (E–0.2m G, f) | 670 | 1,098.9 |
| 1,075.3 | Pa. 94 **Mt. Holly Springs, PA 17065** | R (W–2.5m PO, G, M, L, D, cl, @) | 880 | 1,100.9 |
| 1,072.5 | Whiskey Spring, Whiskey Spring Rd | R, w | 830 | 1,103.7 |
| 1,070.4 | **Alec Kennedy Shelter** *8.7mS; 18.4mN* | E–0.2m S, w | 850 | 1,105.8 |
| 1,069.5 | Center Point Knob | | 1,060 | 1,106.7 |
| 1,066.8 | Yellow Breeches Creek | R, C | 500 | 1,109.4 |
| 1,066.5 | Pa. 174, ATC Mid-Atlantic Office **Boiling Springs, PA 17007** | R, w, PO, C, sh, f (W–0.1m G, M, L; 1m G, D, M, O, V) | 500 | 1,109.7 |
| 1,064.5 | Pa. 74 | R | 580 | 1,111.7 |
| 1,062.4 | Pa. 641, Trindle Rd | R | 540 | 1,113.8 |
| 1,060.0 | Pennsylvania Turnpike | R | 495 | 1,116.2 |
| 1,058.5 | U.S. 11 Footbridge | R (E–7m O) (W–0.5m M, L, sh, cl, @; 5m G, L, M) | 490 | 1,117.7 |
| 1,057.6 | I-81 Overpass | R | 485 | 1,118.6 |
| 1,056.2 | Conodoguinet Creek Bridge, ATC Scott Farm Trail Work Center | R, w | 480 | 1,120.0 |
| 1,054.2 | Pa. 944 | R | 480 | 1,122.0 |
| 1,053.2 | Spring | w | 650 | 1,123.0 |

| Miles from Katahdin | Features | Services | Elev. | Miles from Springer |
|---|---|---|---|---|
| 1,052.3 | Tuscarora Trail (northern terminus), Darlington Trail | | 1,390 | 1,123.9 |
| 1,052.2 | **Darlington Shelter** *18.4mS; 7.3mN* | S, C, w | 1,170 | 1,124.0 |
| 1,049.9 | Pa. 850 | R | 650 | 1,126.3 |
| 1,044.9 | **Cove Mtn Shelter** *7.3mS; 8.6mN* | S, w | 1,120 | 1,131.3 |
| 1,043.0 | Hawk Rock | | 1,140 | 1,133.2 |
| 1,041.3 | U.S. 11 & 15, Pa. 274 | R (W–0.5m G; 2m L) | 385 | 1,134.9 |
| 1,040.9 | Market St **Duncannon, PA 17020** | R, PO, G, L, M, cl, f, @ | 385 | 1,135.3 |
| 1,039.8 | Pa. 849, Juniata River | R, C, sh | 380 | 1,136.4 |
| 1,039.5 | Clarks Ferry Bridge, Susquehanna River (west end) | R (W–0.1m M) | 380 | 1,136.7 |
| 1,039.0 | U.S. 22 & 322, Norfolk Southern RR | R (E–1m L; 16m G, L, M, O, D, V) | 400 | 1,137.2 |
| 1,036.3 | **Clarks Ferry Shelter** *8.6mS; 6.8mN* | S, w | 1,180 | 1,139.9 |
| 1,032.4 | Pa. 225 Footbridge | R | 1,250 | 1,143.8 |
| 1,030.4 | Table Rock | | 1,200 | 1,145.8 |
| 1,029.5 | **Peters Mtn Shelter** *6.8mS; 17.8mN* | S, w | 970 | 1,146.7 |
| 1,026.2 | Shikellimy Overlook | | 1,320 | 1,150.0 |
| 1,025.4 | Spring | w | 700 | 1,150.8 |
| 1,025.0 | Pa. 325, Clark's Valley | R, w | 550 | 1,151.2 |
| 1,022.0 | Stony Mtn; Horse-Shoe Trail | | 1,650 | 1,154.2 |
| 1,018.6 | Yellow Springs Village Site | | 1,450 | 1,157.6 |
| 1,014.3 | Cold Spring Trail | | 1,400 | 1,161.9 |
| 1,012.0 | **Rausch Gap Shelter** *17.8mS; 13.6mN* | E–0.3m S, w | 970 | 1,164.2 |
| 1,007.4 | Pa. 443, Green Point, Pa. | R (W–2.6m C, M, cl, sh) | 550 | 1,168.8 |
| 1,006.0 | Pa. 72, Swatara Gap | R (E–2.4m C, G, L, M, cl, @) | 480 | 1,170.2 |
| 1,005.6 | I-81 Underpass | R | 450 | 1,170.6 |
| 998.7 | **William Penn Shelter** *13.6mS; 4.2mN* | S, w | 1,300 | 1,177.5 |
| 996.5 | Pa. 645 | R | 1,250 | 1,179.7 |
| 994.6 | Pa. 501, **501 Shelter** *4.2mS; 15.5mN* **Pine Grove, PA 17963** | R (W–0.1m S, w; 0.5m H; 3.7m PO, G, M, L, D, V, cl, sh) (E–2m PO, V, @) | 1,460 | 1,181.6 |

| Miles from Katahdin | Features | Services | Elev. | Miles from Springer |
|---|---|---|---|---|
| 994.1 | Pilger Ruh Spring Trail | C, w | 1,450 | 1,182.1 |
| 991.5 | Round Head, Shower Steps | w | 1,500 | 1,184.7 |
| 989.0 | Hertlein Campsite | C, w | 1,200 | 1,187.2 |
| 988.9 | Shuberts Gap | | 1,200 | 1,187.3 |
| 985.6 | Fort Dietrich Snyder Marker | W–0.2m w | 1,440 | 1,190.6 |
| 985.3 | Pa. 183, Rentschler Marker | R | 1,450 | 1,190.9 |
| 984.0 | Black Swatara Spring | W–0.3m w | 1,510 | 1,192.2 |
| 980.2 | Sand Spring Trail | E–0.2m w | 1,510 | 1,196.0 |
| 979.5 | **Eagle's Nest Shelter** *15.5mS; 15mN* | W–0.3m S, w | 1,510 | 1,196.7 |
| 977.6 | Shartlesville Cross-Mtn Rd | | 1,450 | 1,198.6 |
| 974.9 | Phillip's Canyon Spring | w | 1,500 | 1,201.3 |
| 970.9 | **Port Clinton, PA 19549** | R, PO (W–0.3m S, C, L, M, sh; 6.5m H, O, D, V, cl, f) | 400 | 1,205.3 |
| 970.2 | Pa. 61 **Hamburg, PA 19526** | R (E–1m M, O, f; 5m PO, M, G, D, V, cl) | 490 | 1,206.0 |
| 967.6 | Pocahontas Spring | C, w | 1,200 | 1,208.6 |
| 965.0 | Windsor Furnace | E–0.5m C, w | 900 | 1,211.2 |
| 964.8 | **Windsor Furnace Shelter** *15mS; 9.3mN* | S, w | 880 | 1,211.4 |
| 963.2 | Pulpit Rock | | 1,582 | 1,213.0 |
| 961.4 | Trail to Blue Rocks Campground | E–1.5m S, C, G, cl, sh, f | 1,150 | 1,214.8 |
| 961.0 | The Pinnacle | | 1,615 | 1,215.2 |
| 955.7 | Hawk Mtn Rd, **Eckville Shelter** *9.3mS; 7.6mN* | E–0.2m S, w, sh | 535 | 1,220.5 |
| 949.6 | Tri-County Corner | | 1,560 | 1,226.6 |
| 948.3 | **Allentown Hiking Club Shelter** *7.6mS; 10mN* | S, w | 1,350 | 1,227.9 |
| 946.4 | Fort Franklin Rd | R | 1,350 | 1,229.8 |
| 944.2 | Pa. 309, Blue Mtn Summit | R, L, M, w | 1,360 | 1,232.0 |
| 942.4 | New Tripoli Campsite | W–0.2m C, w | 1,400 | 1,233.8 |
| 941.4 | The Cliffs, Knife Edge | | 1,525 | 1,234.8 |
| 940.7 | Bear Rocks | | 1,604 | 1,235.5 |
| 939.3 | Bake Oven Knob Rd | R | 1,450 | 1,236.9 |
| 938.9 | Bake Oven Knob | | 1,560 | 1,237.3 |

| Miles from Katahdin | Features | Services | Elev. | Miles from Springer |
|---|---|---|---|---|
| 938.3 | **Bake Oven Knob Shelter** *10mS; 6.8mN* | S, w | 1,380 | 1,237.9 |
| 935.9 | Ashfield Rd, Lehigh Furnace Gap | R (E–0.7m w) | 1,320 | 1,240.3 |
| 931.5 | **George W. Outerbridge Shelter** *6.8mS; 16.8mN* | S, w | 1,000 | 1,244.7 |
| 930.9 | Pa. 873, Lehigh Gap **Slatington, PA 18080** | R (E–2m PO, G, L, M, D, cl, sh, f, @) | 380 | 1,245.3 |
| 930.8 | Pa. 873, Lehigh River Bridge (east end) | R | 380 | 1,245.4 |
| 930.6 | Pa. 145 **Walnutport, PA 18088** | R (E–2m PO, G, M, D, V) | 380 | 1,245.6 |
| 930.6 | Pa. 248 **Palmerton, PA 18071** | R (W–2m PO, H, G, L, M, D, cl, f, @) | 380 | 1,245.6 |
| 925.6 | Little Gap, Blue Mtn Rd **Danielsville, PA 18038** | R (E–1.5m PO, G, L, M) | 1,100 | 1,250.6 |
| 920.9 | Delps Trail | E–0.25m w | 1,580 | 1,255.3 |
| 919.0 | Stempa Spring | E–0.6m w | 1,510 | 1,257.2 |
| 918.3 | Smith Gap Rd | R (W–1.0m w, sh, f) | 1,540 | 1,257.9 |
| 914.8 | **Leroy A. Smith Shelter** *16.8mS; 13.9mN* | E–0.1m S; 0.2m, 0.4m, 0.6m w | 1,410 | 1,261.4 |
| 911.2 | Hahns Lookout | | 1,450 | 1,265.0 |
| 910.2 | Pa. 33 **Wind Gap, PA 18091** | R (E–1m PO, G, L, M, D, V, cl) (W–0.1m L, w) | 980 | 1,266.0 |
| 903.2 | Wolf Rocks | | 1,550 | 1,273.0 |
| 901.6 | Pa. 191, Fox Gap | R | 1,400 | 1,274.6 |
| 901.0 | **Kirkridge Shelter** *13.9mS; 31.4mN* | S, w | 1,480 | 1,275.2 |
| 899.1 | Totts Gap | | 1,300 | 1,277.1 |
| 897.1 | Mt. Minsi | | 1,461 | 1,279.1 |
| 896.1 | Lookout Rock | | 800 | 1,280.1 |
| 895.3 | Council Rock | | 600 | 1,280.9 |
| 894.6 | Pa. 611 **Delaware Water Gap, PA 18327** | R (W–0.1m PO, H, M; 0.4m L, M, G, O, f; 5m G, M, L, O, cl) | 400 | 1,281.6 |
| 894.4 | Delaware River Bridge (west end), Pa.–N.J. State Line | | 350 | 1,281.8 |

*Camping regulations vary depending on the type of public land. Be aware of posted notices, and check maps for boundaries. Most water sources are unreliable during summer months.*

No other state has been talked about with such fear by hikers who have never been there before. Since Georgia and Maine, you've heard rumors about the Pennsylvania rocks. Now that you're here, ready to formulate your own opinion, you're probably thinking, "This isn't so bad. In fact, once I climb out of this gap, I can really get some miles on this beautiful ridge." Walking directly through four towns and being close to many more makes resupply a breeze.

**Pa. 16—East** 1.2 miles to **Blue Ridge Summit, Pa. [P.O. ZIP 17214: M–F 8–4:30, Sa 9–11:30; (717) 794-2335].** ■ *Restaurants:* Mountain Shadows, daily, B/L/D, phone; Summit Plaza, daily 7–8, B/L/D, pay phone; Unique Bar and Grill; and fast-food options. ■ *Internet access:* library, M–Th 3–8, Sa 10–4. ■ *Other services:* True Value hardware, denatured alcohol; bank with ATM; JJ's Laundromat; barber; and Blue Ridge Summit Medical Center, M, Tu, Th 8–5, W, F 8–1.

**West** 2 miles to Rouzerville, Pa., with grocery store, convenience store, bank with ATM, Red Run Grill, and Wal-Mart.

**West** 2.3 miles to *Groceries:* Food Lion (long-term resupply).

**West** 5 miles to **Waynesboro, Pa. [P.O. ZIP 17268: M–F 8:30–5, Sa 9–12; (717) 762-1513; pick-up window only, M–F 6–5, Sa 6–12:15],** with all major services. ■ *Lodging:* Burgundy Lane B&B, (717) 762-8112, phone for shuttle from Trailhead; Best Western, (717) 762-9113, $59S, $68D, $72T, $10EAP, $10 pet fee. ■ *Groceries:* Martin's (long-term resupply); 7–11 (short-term resupply). ■ *Restaurants:* Golden Corral Buffet and Grill, Pizza Hut, Dairy Queen, Domino's Pizza. ■ *Internet access:* library, M–F 9:30–8, Sa 9–4. ■ *Other services:* 24-hour coin laundry; hospital; Trudy's Taxi, (717) 762-2222; bank with ATM; Radio Shack; pharmacies; Ace Hardware, denatured alcohol; veterinarian; dentist; K-Mart; and UPS Store.

**Deer Lick Shelters** (1940s)—Two shelters, each sleeps 4. Privy. Water source is a spring 0.2 mile on a blue-blazed trail to the east of the shelter area (reported dry in Oct '07), or stream 50 feet north of shelter.

**Antietam Shelter** (1940)—Sleeps 6. Privy. Water source is 0.2 mile north on the A.T. to a springhouse with spigot by the ballfield in Old Forge Park. Southbounders should get their water before reaching the shelter.

**Tumbling Run Shelters** (1940s)—Two shelters, each sleeps 4. Privy. Located on a short, blue-blazed trail. Water source is 100 yards to the west of the shelter.

**Pa. 233—East** 1.2 miles to **South Mountain, Pa. [P.O. ZIP 17261: M–F 8–1 & 2–5, Sa 8–12; (717) 749-5833]**. *Restaurant:* Sou-Mont Hotel and Bar, a.k.a. South Mountain Bar and Restaurant (not to be confused with the Old South Mountain Inn on U.S. 40-A at Turners Gap in Maryland); (717) 749-3845, grill-type menu (no lodging), M–Sa 9 a.m.– 2 a.m., Su 11 a.m.–midnight.

**Rocky Mountain Shelters** (1989)—Two shelters, each sleeps 4. Privy. Located 0.2 mile on a steep, downhill, blue-blazed trail; for water, continue on side trail down to a road, then right 75 yards to spring.

 **U.S. 30—East** 14 miles to historic Gettysburg with many motels and most major services.
   **West** 0.3 mile to *Restaurant:* Taormina's Pizza, with ice cream, Tu–Su 11–10; pay phone.
   **West** 0.7 mile to *Groceries:* Henicle's Grocery (long-term resupply) with deli, pay phone; M–Sa 8–9, Su 8–6.
   **West** 3.5 miles to **Fayetteville, Pa. [P.O. ZIP 17222: M–F 8–4:30, Sa 8:30–12; (717) 352-2022]**. ■ *Lodging:* Rite Spot Motel, (717) 352-2144, $55S, $65D, $20 EAP, dog $15; shuttle $5 one-way, call ahead. ■ *Groceries:* convenience store (short-term resupply). ■ *Restaurants:* Flamingo Family Restaurant, Mamma's II. ■ *Other services:* doctor, pharmacy, coin laundry, barber, and ATM.

**Caledonia State Park**—(717) 352-2161, home to the Thaddeus Stevens Museum, but, more importantly for hot hikers, home to a swimming pool. The pool is visible as the A.T. enters a clearing in the park. Open only weekends from Memorial Day to mid-Jun, then daily to Labor Day; $3 admission. A snack bar with short-order grill opens at 10. Pay phone next to the pool and a second near the office. Campsites with showers; weekdays, $12 Pa. residents/$14 nonresidents; weekends, $15 Pa. residents/$17 nonresidents; shower only $2; no dogs. U.S. Sen. Stevens, an outspoken abolitionist, owned Caledonia Ironworks during the Civil War. Confederates burned the ironworks *en route* to the battle of Gettysburg. The old blacksmith shop was refurbished and now houses some artifacts.

**Quarry Gap Shelters** (1935)—Two shelters, each sleeps 4. Privy. Water source is 10 yards in front of the shelter.

**Quarry Gap Shelters to Birch Run Shelter**—Between these two shelter areas, the A.T. travels through impressive thickets of mountain laurel. Peak bloom is usually late May–early Jun.

**Birch Run Shelter** (2003)—Sleeps 8. Privy. Shelter located on the east side of the A.T. Water source is a spring 30 yards in front of the shelter.

**Toms Run Shelters** (1936)—Two shelters, each sleeps 4. Privy. Water source is a spring near old chimney.

**Pa. 233/Pine Grove Furnace State Park**—(717) 486-4920. ■ *Groceries:* Pine Grove General Store (short-term resupply), open daily 9–7 Memorial Day to Labor Day, weekends 10–6 Apr 15–Memorial Day and Sep–Oct, closed Nov 1–Apr 14. The first opportunity for northbounders to join the traditional "half-gallon club." To belong, you have to eat a half-gallon of ice cream to mark your halfway point. With relocations, the halfway point of the Trail today is now about 1.9 miles south of Pa. 233. ■ *Camping:* Nonelectric, no pets; F–Sa $12 Pa. resident, $14 nonresident; Su–Th $10 resident, $12 nonresident. Nonelectric site with pets is $2 more per night. Hot showers and flush toilets; concession stand with short-order grill, pay phone, and swimming in Laurel and Fuller lakes. An iron furnace that produced firearms used in the Revolutionary War ceased operation in the 1890s, but its remains are visible from the Trail. ■ *Hostel:* Ironmasters Mansion (Hostelling International), (717) 486-7575, south of the entrance to Pine Grove Furnace State Park. An 1827 mansion that was once a "station" on the Underground Railroad (ask to see the secret room). Hours 7:30–9:30 a.m., 5–10 p.m. Dormitory-style rooms with bunk beds, semiprivate rooms, shower, laundry, linens (sleeping bags not allowed on bunks), and kitchen privileges: $22 for HI members with membership card and for ATC, PATC, AMC members and thru-hikers; $25 for all others; shower only $4, with towel $5. Laundry facilities, wash $2, dry $2. No dogs allowed. Hiker message boards inside and out, as well as a giant outdoor chess board. The hostel holds packages sent to Ironmasters Mansion, 1212 Pine Grove Rd., Gardners, PA 17324.

**Mountain Club of Maryland**—MCM maintains the 16.4 miles from Pine Grove Furnace State Park to Center Point Knob and the 12.8 miles from the Darlington/Tuscarora Trail junction to the Susquehanna River. Correspondence should be sent to 7923 Galloping Circle, Baltimore, MD 21244; (410) 377-5625; <paulives2@aol.com>.

**Midpoint Marker**—North of the park, a wooden sign with a register marks the old midpoint of the Trail. Although the actual Trail mileage changes from year to year, the sign has remained here for several years. ALDHA member Chuck Wood, "Woodchuck" of 1985, from Norristown, built and erected the marker.

**Mountain Creek Campground—West** 0.7 mile; 349 Pine Grove Rd., Gardners, PA 17324; (717) 486-7681, <www.mtncreekcg.com>; mid-Apr–Oct, tenting $23, cabin w/o heat $45, hot showers, heated pool, camp store, camp supplies, snack shack; pets must be kept on a leash.

**James Fry Shelter at Tagg Run** (1998)—Sleeps 9. Privy (composting). Called "Tagg Run" in some sources, after the 1930s-vintage shelters it replaced. Tentsites available in the open adjacent field. Water source is 0.4 mile east of the A.T. on a blue-blazed trail; reported dry in Oct 2007.

**Pine Grove Road—West** 0.4 mile to Cherokee Family Restaurant and Campground, (717) 486-8000, B/L/D, W–Th 11–7, F–Sa 7–7, Su 7–2, comfort food; tentsites with shower $16D, $5EAP; pay phone outside.

**Pa. 34—East** 0.2 mile to the Green Mountain Store and Deli (short-term resupply), M–Sa 7–8, Su 9–6, Coleman fuel by the pint, pay phone. For southbounders, the first opportunity to join the Half-Gallon Club.

**Pa. 94—West** 2.5 miles to **Mt. Holly Springs, Pa. [P.O. ZIP 17065: M–F 8–4:30, Sa 8–12; (717) 486-3468]. ■** *Lodging:* Holly Inn and Restaurant, (717) 486-3823, call and will send car to pick up; <www.hollyinn.com>; $50S/D includes continental B and ride back to the Trail; Tu–Su L/D, Internet. ■ *Restaurants:* Deer Lodge Restaurant, B/L/D, M–Sa 8–8:30, Su 12–6 during the summer months, steaks and seafood; Laura's Family Restaurant; Sicilia Pizza and Subs. ■ *Internet access:* library. ■ *Other services:* Uni-Mart (short-term resupply), with pay phone; coin laundry; pharmacy; dentist; doctor; optometrist; and bank with ATM.

**Alec Kennedy Shelter** (1991)—Sleeps 7. Privy (composting). Built by the MCM and Tressler Wilderness School. The shelter is 0.2 mile east on a blue-blazed trail. Water source is a spring located on a side trail behind the shelter; prone to go dry during the summer. A second source is a small stream 0.5 mile south of the shelter on the A.T.

---

**Cumberland Valley Appalachian Trail Club**—CVATC maintains the 17.2 miles between Center Point Knob and the Darlington/Tuscarora Trail junction. Correspondence should be sent to P.O. Box 395, Boiling Springs, Pa. 17007; <www.geocities.com/cvatclub>; <wbohn@paonline.com>.

---

*No camping in the valley*—Between Alec Kennedy Shelter and Darlington Shelter, the Boiling Springs campsite (see next entry) is the only place where camping is allowed.

**Boiling Springs, Pa. [P.O. ZIP 17007: M–F 8–4:30, Sa 8–12; (717) 258-6668]**—Home to ATC's mid-Atlantic regional office, (717) 258-5771. Open weekdays 9–5. Staff members and volunteers can provide information on Trail conditions, weather forecasts, and water availability. Coleman fuel and denatured alcohol are available for a donation; A.T. maps and books for sale. A pay phone, picnic table, and hiker bulletin board are located on the porch. *No camping at the office.* Limited parking available at opposite end of lake in township parking lot; obtain permit from ATC office (overnight parking is only allowed with permit that you display on your dashboard). Lodging is limited in Boiling Springs, but a year-round campsite with a portable toilet in season is south of town, before the railroad tracks (toilet Memorial Day–Labor Day). The trains do run past here all night long. The water source for the campsite is a spigot behind the ATC office, next to the oil tank. ■ *Lodging:* Gelinas Manor, (717) 258-6584, $60 includes full B, no pets; Garmanhaus B&B, (717) 258-3980, Su–Th $50S, $60D, F–Sa $75S, $100S for 2 nights or camp in the back yard for $1 (no shower or bathroom privileges). Check the hiker-information board at ATC for postings of additional camping possibilities in the area.

**West** on Pa. 174—*Restaurants:* The Forge Sandwich Shop & Deli; Anile's, L/D; Boiling Springs Tavern, L/D; JC's Country Time Café, M–F 9–8, Sa 8–8, closed Su. ■ *Outfitter:* Yellow Breeches Outfitter, (717) 258-6752, limited hiker supplies, socks, clothing, rain gear, first aid, A.T. maps of Pa., bug spray, water-purification tablets. ■ *Groceries:* Karn's Store (long-term resupply), open daily 7–10; Getty Mart and Friendly Food Mart (both short-term resupply). ■ *Other services:* bank

**Boiling Springs**

0      0.3 mile

Forge Sandwich Shop & Deli
Friendly Food Mart
Forge Rd.
Karn's Foods 0.6 mile
Anile's
Tavern
Outfitters
Post Office, Bank
First St. (Pa. 174)
ATC Mid-Atlantic Regional Office
Bucher Hill Rd.
Getty
JC's Country Time Cafe
Garmanhaus B&B
Gelinas Manor B&B
Front St.
Long-term Parking
Campsite south on A.T.
Mountain Rd.
N
Pool

with ATM next to post office; doctor; dentist; veterinarian; Boiling Springs pool, (717) 258-4121, open Memorial–Labor Day, $8.50 admission, $1 hot shower, check ATC hiker bulletin board for coupons; Jumpers Shoe Service, (717) 766-3422, in nearby Mechanicsburg.

**Cumberland Valley**—Water is scarce between Boiling Springs and Darlington Shelter, as the A.T. winds along hedgerows and through Pennsylvania farmland. Thanks to an ambitious land-acquisition program, most of the Trail has been taken off roads through this heavily developed area, but it is still a hot walk on steamy summer days. Water can be obtained at one of the restaurants on U.S. 11 (see below) or at Scott Farm, which is 10.3 miles north of Boiling Springs.

**U.S. 11**—**West** 0.5 mile to various facilities spread along this busy highway. ■ *Lodging:* America's Best Inn, (717) 245-2242 or (800) 445-6715, $65D, dogs under 20 lbs. allowed, laundry; Super 8, (717) 249-7000, 10% hiker discount at check-in, $50S, $56D, call for weekend rates, free continental B, pets with manager's permission $10, laundry, pool, WiFi, accepts mail drops to 1800 Harrisburg Pike, Carlisle, PA 17013; Econolodge, (717) 249-7775, $59D, continental B, pets $10 only in smoking rooms, laundry, pool; Holiday Inn, (717) 245-2400, $110D, pets okay, laundry, pool, restaurant, WiFi; Pheasant Field B&B, (717) 258-0717, Su–Th $85D, F–Sa $105–$185D, pet-friendly room may be available, laundry, free phone, shuttle to and from Trail with stay. ■ *Restaurants:* Trailside Restaurant (limited hours), 24-hour Middlesex Diner, Bob Evans, and fast-food restaurants on the other side of I-81. The Flying J Travel Plaza has restaurant, shower $11.50 (includes refundable $5 towel deposit), laundry, store (short-term resupply).

**West**—5 miles to Carlisle, a large town with all major services.

**Conodoguinet Wetlands Project**—Volunteers from the CVATC and the ATC completed this hiker-friendly project in the fall of 2005. On the south side of the Conodoguinet Creek, across from ATC's mid-Atlantic base camp (a.k.a. the Scott Farm, next entry), the A.T. goes through an area that is prone to flooding. The old bog bridging was replaced with a 500-foot-long boardwalk. This boardwalk also provides the mobility-impaired with an accessible section of the Trail.

**Conodoguinet Creek Bridge**—An old farmhouse, known as the Scott Farm, is located next to the bridge where the Trail U-turns, passes under the bridge, and heads north. Open May–Oct, the farm has a privy, water, and a picnic table. *No camping.*

**Wolf Trail**—Water available where the A.T crosses an overgrown dirt road.

**Tuscarora Trail**—The northern terminus of the blue-blazed Tuscarora Trail, a 260-mile route to its southern terminus on the A.T. in Shenandoah National Park in Virginia. It was blazed when maintainers feared that the A.T. route would be closed by private landowners.

**Darlington Shelter** (2005)—Sleeps 8. Privy. Built by MCM to replace a 1982 shelter. Campsites available. Water source, an intermittent spring 0.2 mile on a blue-blazed trail in front of the shelter, regularly dries up early in the hiker season. It is recommended that northbounders bring water to the shelter from the Wolf Trail spring at the base of North Mountain; southbounders, from Cove Mountain.

**Cove Mountain Shelter** (2000)—Sleeps 8. Privy. Built with the help of the Timber Framers Guild using timber salvaged from a barn, some more than 100 years old. Water source is a spring 125 yards away on a steeply graded trail near the shelter.

**U.S. 11/Duncannon, Pa. [P.O. ZIP 17020: M–F 8–4:30, Sa 8–12; (717) 834-3332.** ID required for mail drops.]—The A.T. passes through the center of town, and all services are within a short walk. ■ *Camping:* Riverfront Campground (south of the Clarks Ferry Bridge), (717) 834-5252, tentsites and shower $3.50PP in designated hiker area, shuttle service, canoe and kayak rentals. ■ *Lodging:* Doyle Hotel, (717) 834-6789, one of the original Anheuser-Busch hotels, more than 100 years old, $25S, $30D, laundry, free Internet, pets allowed, shower only $5, will hold mail drops (ID required) sent to 7 North Market St., Duncannon, PA 17020, free shuttles to Mutzabaugh's, other shuttles available. On U.S. 11/15, 2 miles **north** of the truck stop, Stardust Motel, (717) 834-3191, Su–Th $40S, F–Sa $45S, $5EAP, laundry, no dogs, free shuttles to and from town. ■ *Groceries:* **West** of town 0.5 mile on Pa. 274, Mutzabaugh Market and pharmacy (long-term resupply), M–Sa 6–10, Su 7–10; Uni-Mart Convenience Store (short-term resupply), daily 5–10:30. ■ *Restaurants:* All-American Truck Plaza, B/L/D with AYCE buffet; Club Café N Cremes, B/L/D, closed Su; Doyle Hotel, L/D full menu and bar; Goodie's Café, B/L M–F, B Sa–Su; The Pub, L/D; Riviera Tavern, L/D; Sorrento's Pizza and Subs, L/D; Zeiderelli's Pizza, L/D. ■ *Outfitter:* Blue Mountain Outfitters, (717) 957-2413, <www.bluemountain-outfitters.net>, 8 miles **south** on U.S. 11 in Marysville, closed M, 10–8 T, 10–6 W–Su; fuel, water bottles, freeze-dried food, canoe and kayak rentals. ■ *Other services:* All-American Truck Plaza (short-term resupply), $8 shower, ATM; laundry; banks with ATM; Maguire Hardware with Coleman fuel, 10¢ per ounce; doctor; dentist; bank; veterinarian, Duncannon Community Library and Education Center at Duncannon Presbyterian Church, 3 N. High St., Duncannon 17020, open W 1–3, Sat 10–12, Internet, a/c, cold drinks

& snacks, hiker box, all hikers welcome; Extreme PC, (717) 834-5454, open weekdays 12–8, weekends 11 a.m.–midnight, Internet access, gaming, movie watching $3/hour or $15 all-day pass, snacks, pizza, cold drinks; Mary Parry (Trail Angel Mary), (717) 343-1317, can answer questions about services in Duncannon.

**U.S. 22 & 322**—**East** 1 mile to *Lodging:* Le Ellen Motel, (717) 921-8715, $30S, $40D, $10EAP, no pets, no phone.

**East** 16 miles to Harrisburg, Pennsylvania's capital city, with all major services, including Wildware Backcountry, (717) 564-8008, with backpacking gear and supplies.

---

**York Hiking Club**—YHC maintains the 7.1 miles from the Susquehanna River to Pa. 225. Correspondence should be sent to YHC, 2684 Forest Rd., York, PA 17402; (717) 244-6769; <president@yorkhikingclub.com>.

---

**Earl Shaffer**—Almost all hikers recognize Earl "Crazy One" Shaffer (1918–2002) from York, Pa., as the first A.T. thru-hiker. In 1948, he completed a northbound thru-hike; in 1965, he completed a southbound thru-hike, becoming the first to accomplish both northbound and southbound hikes. To celebrate the 50th anniversary in 1998 of his first hike, Earl did a northbound thru-hike at the young age of 79. ATC's first "corresponding secretary," he was active in Trail maintenance and promoting trails for the YHC and Susquehanna Appalachian Trail Club for many years.

**Clarks Ferry Shelter** (1993)—Sleeps 8. Privy. A blue-blazed trail leads 100 yards to the shelter and 100 yards farther to a reliable piped spring.

**Pa. 225**—In 2003, a pedestrian bridge was built to avoid a dangerous road-crossing; it offers a good view of Powell Creek Valley, too.

---

**Susquehanna Appalachian Trail Club**—SATC maintains the 20.4 miles from Pa. 225 to Rausch Creek. Correspondence should be sent to <hike-hbg@satc-hike.org> or SATC, P.O. Box 61001, Harrisburg, PA 17106-1001.

---

**Peters Mountain Shelter** (1994)—Sleeps 20. Privy. The little shelter that Earl Shaffer built years earlier remains nearby but may be removed in the near future for inclusion in the new A.T. Museum. Water source for shelter is down blue-blazed trail in front of shelter on north side of the mountain. The trail is a steep path of almost 300 rock steps installed by SATC and ATC's mid-Atlantic crew between 1996 and 1999.

**Clarks Ferry to Rausch Gap**—The A.T. passes near the remains of old mining villages dating back to the 1800s. Remnants of Yellow Springs Village are still visible along the Trail, and, in Rausch Gap, near where the A.T. crosses Rausch Creek, a trail leads to a small family cemetery from the 1850s. Between here and Virginia's Sinking Creek Mountain (see page 82), the Trail is in the Chesapeake Bay watershed.

**Blue Mountain Eagle Climbing Club**—BMECC maintains the 62.4 miles from Rausch Creek to Tri-County Corner and the 3 miles from Bake Oven Knob to Lehigh Furnace Gap. Correspondence can be sent to P.O. Box 14982, Reading, PA 19612; <www.bmecc.org>; <info@bmecc.org>; (610) 326-1656.

**Rausch Gap Shelter** (1972)—Sleeps 12. Privy. Built by the BMECC; no tenting. Water source is a reliable spring next to the shelter.

**Pa. 443**—**West** 2.6 miles to *Camping:* Twin Grove KOA, (717) 865-4602, <info@twingroveparkcampground. com>, $20–$45 tentsite, laundry, restaurant, ice-cream parlor, Internet, pool, pay phone, nonguest shower $5.

**Pa. 72/Swatara Gap**—**East** 2.4 miles to Lickdale, adjacent to I-81 Exit 90. ■ *Restaurants:* Bonnie Brook, Wendy's, Dairy Queen, Subway, Sbarro Italian, Subway in Exxon with short-term resupply. ■ *Lodging:* Best Western; Days Inn, pets $10, laundry, ATM, hot tub, heated indoor pool, free Internet access on hotel computer; Quality Inn, (717) 865-6600; and Red Carpet Suites. ■ *Camping:* Lickdale Campground and General Store (short-term resupply), with rotisserie chicken and pizza.

**William Penn Shelter** (1996)—Sleeps 16. Privy. With second-floor loft and windows, 0.1 mile east of the A.T., often visited by summer camping groups. Water source is 200 yards on a blue-blazed trail to the west of the A.T.

**Pa. 501**—**East** 2 miles to **Bethel, Pa. [P.O. ZIP 19507: M–F 8–12 1:15–4:30, Sa 8:30–10:30; (717) 933-8305].** ■ *Other services:* Bethel Animal Clinic, (717) 933-4916. ■ *Internet access:* Bethel Library, M–Th 10–8, F 10–5, Sa 9–4.

**West** 0.5 mile to *Hostel:* PAmoneypit, (570) 345-1119 or cell (570) 292-3350, <pamoneypit@yahoo.com>, Amy Lu Holland, $25PP includes hot shower, laundry $2, and continental B. Reservations required; call for availability. Pet-friendly; kennel on premises. Local shuttles to town for P.O., bank, pizza, grocery store, medical or dentist services. Will also shuttle to other stops along the A.T. and airports. Call for shuttle and slackpacking rates.

**West** 3.7 miles to **Pine Grove, Pa. [P.O. ZIP 17963: M–F 8:30–4:30, Sa 9–12; (570) 345-4955.** *ID required.*]. Most major services but spread out over three miles. ■ *Lodging:* Hampton Inn, (540) 345-4505; Econo Lodge, (570) 345-4099, weekdays $55S, $60D, weekends $70D, dogs $10, continental B; Comfort Inn, (570) 345-8031, $60–$109D, pets $10, includes continental B, pool; Colony Lodge, (570) 345-8095, $40–$65D, pets based on available room, $5 per pet. ■ *Groceries:* Turkey Hill Market with ATM, pay phone (short-term resupply); BG's Market (long-term resupply), daily 7–9. ■ *Restaurants:* O'Neals Pub, L/D W–Su; McDonald's; Arby's; the Original Italian Pizza Place, L/D; Do's Pizza, L/D, closed Su; Dominick's Pizza, L/D, closed M; Buddy's Log Cabin Restaurant; Burke's Dairy Bar; Sholl Family Restaurant, (570) 345-8715, B/L/D, AYCE buffets, closed M, smoke-free, return shuttle possible; Gooseberry Farms Family Restaurant, open 24/7, AYCE buffets, shower $9 with $5 towel deposit. ■ *Other services:* coin laundry, barber, bank with ATM, doctor, podiatrist, dentist, veterinarian, pharmacy, movie theater, and bus service to Harrisburg.

**501 Shelter** (1980s)—Immediately north of paved Pa. 501, go west on the blue-blaze 0.1 mile; always open, no fee. Shelter is fully enclosed, with 12 bunks, table, chairs, skylight (a potter once had her wheel underneath), privy, and solar shower. Tentsites off woods road uphill, beyond fire ring. Water available from faucet at adjacent house of BMECC caretaker, (717) 933-4327, cell (570) 681-5017, <ronh19@yahoo.com>. No smoking inside shelter; no alcoholic beverages allowed. Pets allowed (on leash only) if other shelter guests are willing to share and owner takes care of sanitary needs. Shuttles and motoring visitors park in public lot on paved 501 and walk in *via* blue-blaze.

**Eagles Nest Shelter** (1994)—Sleeps 8. Privy. Shelter is 0.3 mile from the A.T. on a blue-blazed trail. Intermittent Yeich Spring is crossed *en route* to the shelter.

**Port Clinton, Pa. [P.O. ZIP 19549: M–F 7:30–12:30 & 2–5, Sa 8–11; (610) 562-3787]**—Port Clinton allows hikers to camp free under the roof of its pavilion. The pavilion, with outhouse, is located 0.3 mile west of the A.T. on Penn Street. Water can be obtained from a spigot outside the Port Clinton Hotel. ■ *Lodging:* Port Clinton Hotel, (610) 562-3354, <www.portclinton hotel.net>, $49S, $5EAP, $10 deposit for room key and towel, shower only $5, closed M, limited rooms available, laundry, no reservations; Union House B&B, (610) 562-4076, offers bedroom, bath, and sitting room for hikers $65S, pets outside. ■ *Restaurants:* Port Clinton Hotel, L/D, closed M; 3-C's Restaurant, B/L, M–F 5–3, Sa–Su 6–2; Union House B&B, D. ■ *Other services:* The Port Clinton Peanut Shop, open Sa–Th 11–6, F–Sa 10–8, with home-made goodies and snacks, cold drinks, ATM. ■ *Bus service:* Capitol Trailways, (800) 333-8444, <www.capitoltrailways.com>, flag the bus on the road in front of Peanut Shop for connections to Pottsville, Hamburg, Reading, Harrisburg, and Philadelphia; Schuykill Transportation System, (570) 429-2701 or (800) 832-3322 in Pa., <www.go-sts. com>, service from Pottsville to Cabela's.

**West** 6.5 mile to *Hostel* and *Outfitter:* Ye Olde Backpacker, 1138 Centre Turnpike, Rt. 61, Orwigsburg, PA 17961, (570) 366-2110; Scott Russell, owner; M–Sa 9–9, Su 10–5; small hostel, sleeps 9 (no charge), with bunkbeds and microwave; indoor hot shower and soap $1.50; fuel (alcohol, canister, Esbit, Coleman by ounce); mail drops accepted and shipped UPS, photo ID required; dogs allowed if leashed and not disruptive to other hikers; pizza and Chinese delivered; free shuttle to and from Port Clinton, nominal fee for shuttles to Hamburg (see below). Shuttles for section-hikers available south to Duncannon and north to DWG.

**East** on Pa. 61 1 mile to ■ *Lodging:* Microtel Inn, <www.microtelinn.com>, (610) 562-4234, $60–$110D, continental B, pet-friendly, ATM, free long-distance phone, laundry, WiFi. ■ *Restaurants:* Cabela's Restaurant, B/L/D AYCE buffet; Wendy's; Burger King; Cracker Barrel; Poppy T's in Microtel Inn, L/D; Dunkin' Donuts–Baskin Robbins; Shell with food mart (short-term resupply), pay phone; Neopolitan Italian Eatery in RV Superstore, closed Su, subs, pizza, L/D. ■ *Outfitter:* Cabela's Superstore, <www.cabelas.com>, (610) 929-7000, M–Sa 8–9, Su 9–8, a 250,000-square-foot outfitter (nation's largest), mostly for hunting and fishing, with some A.T. publications in stock, fuel (Esbit, propane/butane, Coleman Powermax), ATM. ■ *Bus service:* M–Sa from Cabela's to Hamburg to Reading with connections to Philadelphia; (610) 921-0601, <www.bartabus.com>.

**East** on Pa. 61 3 miles to **Hamburg, Pa. [P.O. ZIP 19526; M–F 9–5, Sa 9–12; (610) 562-7812]**, with several restaurants, no lodging. Most services are located on State Street around Kings Supermarket, open daily 6–11, one block east of the town center. In town are supermarkets, laundry, pharmacy, movie theater, doctor, dentist, bakery, medical center, veterinarian, banks with ATM. ■ *Bus service:* See entry above.

**Hamburg Reservoir**—A parking area 0.3 mile **East** of the A.T. requires permits for overnight parking, available at no charge. Call the Borough of Hamburg, (610) 562-7821, for permission.

**Windsor Furnace Shelter** (1970s)—Sleeps 8. Privy. Shelter is located on a blue-blazed trail near the reservoir. Tentsites available. Water source is the creek south of the shelter. *No campfires except at shelter. No swimming in streams or reservoir.*

**Blue Rocks Campground**— **East** 1.5 miles to campground, (866) 478-5267, <www.bluerockscampground.com>, *via* a blue-blazed trail from Pulpit Rock and a yellow-blazed trail from The Pinnacle. Tentsites $25 M–F, 50% discount for thru-hikers M–Th, showers (nonguest) 25¢, swimming (nonguest) $4, laundry, pay phone. Camp store (short-term resupply), M–Th 9–7, F 9–11, Sa 8–11, Su 8–7, with Coleman fuel and limited hiker supplies. Will hold packages mailed to 341 Sousley Rd., Lenhartsville, PA 19534. Hiker-friendly.

**The Pinnacle**—A panoramic view of Pennsylvania farmland from an elevation of 1,635 feet, said to be the best view on the A.T. in the state. Below the viewpoint lies a sheer cliff and a few caves. *No camping or fires are permitted.*

**Hawk Mountain Road**—**East** 0.2 mile to Eckville Hikers Center, an enclosed bunkroom that offers space for 6. No fee. Water from a spigot at the back of the caretaker's house. Solar shower, flush toilet, and tent platforms with picnic table available. Open May–Sep.

**Hawk Mountain Sanctuary**—Atop the Kittatinny Ridge sits the Hawk Mountain Visitors Center, <www.hawkmountain.org>, accessible *via* a 2.5-mile blue-blazed trail from the A.T. Located within the visitors center are a bookstore, gift shop, and interpretive exhibits on raptors that fly by the mountain during the migratory seasons. Rosalie Edge founded the sanctuary in 1934. Prior to that time, instead of birders, hunters flocked to the mountain each fall to shoot the raptors. Several species other than raptors can be seen; 16 species of hawks, falcons, and eagles have been spotted over the mountain. Peak viewing months are Sep–Nov, with $7 entrance fee; rest of year, $5 entrance fee.

---

**Allentown Hiking Club**—AHC maintains the 10.7 miles from Tri-County Corner to Bake Oven Knob. Correspondence should be sent to P.O. Box 1542, Allentown, PA 18105; <www.allentownhikingclub.org>; <info@allentownhikingclub.org>.

---

**Allentown Hiking Club Shelter** (1997)—Sleeps 8. Privy. Tentsites available. Water source is a spring 0.2 mile downhill in front of the shelter; if dry, try spring 0.1 mile farther downhill.

**Pa. 309**—*Lodging:* Blue Mountain B&B, (570) 386-2003, <www.bluemountainsummit.com>, $95–$125 per night when available. Restaurant open Th–Sa 11–10, Su 11–8; live music all year on F 7–10, Jun–Sep Su 5–8; hiker register. Possible camping near restaurant if you ask first. Water available from outside spigot.

**Bake Oven Knob Shelter** (1940s)—Sleeps 6. No privy. One of the original Pennsylvania shelters. The first water source on the blue-blazed trail is often dry; continue 200 yards to the second, more dependable spring, although both may be intermittent.

---

**Philadelphia Trail Club**—PTC maintains the 10.3 miles from Lehigh Furnace Gap to Little Gap. Correspondence should be sent to 741 Golf Rd., Warrington, PA 18976; <pauls@deperjico.com>.

**George W. Outerbridge Shelter** (1965)—Sleeps 6. No privy. The area surrounding this shelter suffers from heavy-metal contamination from the zinc plant at Palmerton (see Superfund entry below). Water source is a piped spring north 150 yards on the A.T.

**Pa. 873/Lehigh Gap—East** 2 miles on Pa. 873 to **Slatington, Pa.** [P.O. ZIP 18080: M–F 8:30–5, Sa 8:30–12; (610) 767-2182]. ■ *Lodging:* Fine Lodging, (610) 760-0700, <finelodging@aol. com>; call ahead. Hikers are always welcome regardless of signs. Ring outside doorbell 3 times. Hiker room (may not be available in 2008) $15S, $25D, $30T, $35 for 4, 8 max; TV, microwave, a/c; other rooms are sometimes available for $32S, $35D, a/c $4, microwave $2; no dogs and no alcoholic beverages; Internet access for guests; shower without stay $4. When available, owner Ira Fine will shuttle guests to and from the A.T. and other locations. Call from the office phone at D & J Auto on Pa. 873. Will hold packages mailed to 700 Main St., Slatington, PA 18080. ■ *Restaurants:* The Shack, L/D; Mama's Pizza; Sal's Pizza; Slatington Diner B/L/D. ■ *Internet access:* Slatington Library, M, W 9–7, Tu 9–3, F 9–5, Sa 8–2. ■ *Other services:* coin laundry, bank with ATM, convenience stores, A.F. Boyer Hardware store with camp fuel and denatured alcohol, doctor, dentist, pharmacy, bowling alley, and bus service to Walnutport and Allentown.

**East** 2 miles on Pa. 145 to **Walnutport, Pa.** [P.O. ZIP 18088: M–F 8:30–5, Sa 8:30–12; (610) 767-5191]. ■ *Groceries:* Super Fresh Supermarket (long-term resupply). ■ *Restaurants:* Valley Restaurant and Pizza, $5.75 L AYCE; King Palace Chinese, $4.95 L AYCE; Great Wall Chinese; d'Sopranos Pizza; Burger King; McDonald's; Subway; Pizza Hut; ice cream. ■ *Other services:* banks with ATM, doctor, dentist, pharmacy, veterinarian, K-Mart.

**West** 2 miles on Pa. 248 or 2-mile blue-blaze to **Palmerton, Pa.** [P.O. ZIP 18071: M–F 8:30–5, Sa 8:30–12, (610) 826-2286]. *Blue-blaze directions:* **West** 1.5 miles from the gravel lot on the northwest side of the Lehigh River over the Aquashicola Creek Bridge to the back road leading to Delaware Ave. in Palmerton. ■ *Hostel:* The city tentatively allows hikers to sleep in the basement of the borough hall (may not be available in 2008), (610) 826-2505, 443 Delaware Ave., with the use of showers at no charge. Hikers should check in before 4:30; the town police (located at 401 Delaware Ave.) admit hikers after 4:30 weekdays and Sa–Su. You will need to provide an ID, name, address, Trail name, and SSN. No pets. *No alcoholic beverages or intoxicated persons are permitted. This service is in danger of being discontinued; getting "Palmerized" will not be tolerated.* ■ *Lodging:* The Palmerton Hotel, $55S, $65 efficiency unit. ■ *Groceries:* IGA, Country Harvest (both long-term resupply). ■ *Restaurants:* Bert's Steakhouse, B/L/D; The Palmerton Hotel, L/D; One Ten Tavern, L/D, closed M; Simply Something Café, B/L/D; Tony's Pizzeria; Joe's Place, deli sandwiches;

Palmerton Pizza and Restaurant; Subway; Hunan House Chinese. ■ *Internet access:* library M 10–8, T–F 10–5, Sa 9–4 (Sa Jul–Aug 9–1). ■ *Other services:* coin laundry; banks with ATM; shuttle back to the Trail, Duane Masonheimer, (610) 767-7969; Shea's Hardware and Sporting Goods, Heet, Coleman fuel, and denatured alcohol; bowling alley; pharmacy; doctor; dentist; and hospital.

**Palmerton EPA Superfund Site**—The devastation along Blue Mountain near Lehigh Gap is the result of nearly a century of zinc smelting in Palmerton. In 1980, the Environmental Protection Agency shut down the furnaces and, in 1982, put the affected area on the Superfund clean-up list. Revegetation efforts are underway, and the mountain is slowly coming back to life. A product called Ecoloam—municipal-waste sludge, fly ash, lime, fertilizer, and seeds—has been spread on the slopes. Before you curse the zinc manufacturers, consider that zinc is likely one of the metals in the grommets and eyelets on your backpack. It is used in everything from face powder to zippers. The scramble up the denuded rocks is among the most challenging on the A.T. south of New Hampshire.

---

**Appalachian Mountain Club–Delaware Valley Chapter**—AMC–Delaware Valley maintains the 15.4 miles from Little Gap to Wind Gap. Correspondence should be sent to 1180 Greenleaf Dr., Bethlehem, PA 18017; <www.amcdv.org>.

---

**Little Gap, Blue Mountain Drive**—**East** 1.5 miles to **Danielsville, Pa. [P.O. 18038: M–F 8–12, Sa 8–12; (610) 767-6822].** ■ *Lodging:* Filbert B&B, (610) 767-2559, <www.filbertbnb.com>, starting at $100D, reservations required; full, hearty, country B; will pick up and drop off hikers and possibly shuttle. ■ *Restaurant:* Blue Mountain Family Restaurant. ■ *Groceries:* Millers Market.

**Smith Gap Road**—For northbounders, it is the first road after the Stempa Spring side trail, on which it's **West** 1 mile to a water spigot at the rear of the house of Linda "Crayon Lady" and John "Mechanical Man" Stempa, (610) 381-4606; free cold shower, hiker's register, and camera for self-portraits. Pets welcome. Homemade alcohol stoves, windscreens, and methyl fuel available; shuttles to area Trailheads by arrangement; parking for a small fee.

**Leroy A. Smith Shelter** (1972)—Sleeps 8. Privy (composting). Built by the AMC–Delaware Valley Chapter, shelter is located 0.2 mile down a blue-blazed trail. Water sources can be intermittent; the first, 0.2 mile down the blue-blazed trail; a second, on a yellow-blazed trail 0.2 mile farther; a third, even farther, may be running when the first two are not.

**Batona Hiking Club**—BHC maintains the 8.6 miles from Wind Gap to Fox Gap (Pa. 191). Correspondence should be sent to BHC, 6651 Eastwood St., Philadelphia, Pa. 19149; <www.members.aol.com/Batona>; <bobleo@aol.com>.

**Pa. 33—East** 1 mile to **Wind Gap, Pa. [P.O. ZIP 18091: M–F 8:30–5, Sa 8:30–12; (610) 863-6206].** ■ *Lodging:* Travel Inn, (610) 863-4146, $50S, $60D, $5EAP, holidays and weekends higher, dogs $5, soda machine inside, shuttle back to the Trail. ■ *Groceries:* Giant Food Store located in K-Mart Plaza (long-term resupply); Turkey Hill Mini Market, Sunoco Mini Mart (both short-term resupply). ■ *Restaurants:* Tony's Pizza; Beer Stein; McDonald's; Wendy's; Burger King; Subway; Hong Kong Restaurant; diners serving B/L/D; Dunkin Donuts; Rita's Ices; other fast-food outlets. ■ *Other services:* coin laundry, K-Mart, hardware store, doctor, dentist, pharmacy, veterinarian, bank with ATM, and movie theater.

**West** 0.1 mile to *Lodging:* Gateway Motel, (610) 863-4959, $59S, $65D, $75T, nice dogs allowed $10, sodas for sale. Pete, the owner, allows hikers to fill water bottles, provides free shuttles when available.

**Wilmington Trail Club**—WTC maintains the 7.2 miles from Fox Gap to the Delaware River Bridge. Correspondence should be sent to P.O. Box 1184, Wilmington, DE 19899; <www.wilmingtontrailclub.org>.

**Kirkridge Shelter** (1948)—Sleeps 8. Privy. Shelter is on a blue-blazed trail with excellent views south. Water source is an outside tap to rear of shelter before the Kirkridge Retreat facility parking lot. Tap is secured when frost is possible.

**Pa. 611/Delaware Water Gap, Pa. [P.O. ZIP 18327: M–F 8:30–12 & 1–4:45, Sa 8:30–11:30; (570) 476-0304]**—The A.T. does not go through the center of town, but services are within a mile of where the Trail crosses Pa. 611. ■ *Hostel:* The Presbyterian Church of the Mountain Hostel, with overflow lean-to in backyard, has been overwhelmed with hikers in the past; please respect the good-will of the pastor and her parishioners. Space with shower limited to long-distance hikers—no car or van parking or support allowed. Two-night limit, donation suggested for second night. Internet for a small fee is sometimes available. ■ *Lodging:* Pocono Inn, (570) 476-0000, 101 Broad St., hiker rates $50 per room Su–Th, $75 F–Sa, accepts packages for guests; Deer Head Inn, (570) 424-2000, upscale rooms available. ■ *Restaurants:* DWG Diner, (570) 476-0132, B/L/D; Doughboy Pizza; Deer Head Inn for fine dining F–Su, pizza, and live entertainment, notably jazz; Sycamore Grille, L/D, closed Su–M, D by reservation. ■ *Groceries:* BP Mini Mart with ATM, Gulf Mini Mart (both short-term resupply); Farmer's Market with fruits, vegetables, lots of baked goods, and ice cream. ■ *Outfitters:* The Pack Shack, (570) 424-8533: backpacking gear, supplies, and a special rate for tubing the Delaware River. Owner John Greene gives thru-hikers discounts, repairs poles, sells Coleman fuel and denatured alcohol by the ounce, and holds packages mailed from manufacturers only, no regular mail drops; contact the outfitter for an address. Daily shuttle $1.75/mi for slackpacking 2 people, $5EAP; must be back by 6 p.m. Edge of the Woods Outfitters, 110 Main St. (Rt. 611), (572) 421-6681, maps, bike rentals, outerwear, activewear, footwear, national park info, all brands; will hold UPS packages for thru-hikers. ■ *Other services:* hair salon, run by Paulette, (570) 421-8218, Tu–F 10–7, Sa 10–3. ■ *Bus service:* Martz Trailways, (570) 421-4451 or (570) 421-3040, to New York, Philadelphia, and Scranton, and local service to Stroudsburg.

**West** 5 miles to East Stroudsburg and Stroudsburg, Pa., full-service towns. ■ *Outfitter:* Dunkelberger's Sports Outfitter, (570) 421-7950, with backpacking equipment, supplies, and clothing, is located at 6th and Main streets.

# New Jersey

| Miles from Katahdin | Features | Services | Elev. | Miles from Springer |
|---|---|---|---|---|
| 894.4 | Delaware River Bridge (west end), N.J.–Pa. State Line | | 350 | 1,281.8 |
| 893.4 | DWG Nat'l Rec. Area Visitors Center | R, w | 350 | 1,282.8 |
| 891.4 | Holly Springs Trail | E–0.2m w | 950 | 1,284.8 |
| 889.8 | Backpacker Campsite | C, nw | 1,300 | 1,286.4 |
| 888.5 | Sunfish Pond | | 1,382 | 1,287.7 |
| 888.4 | Spring | w | 1,400 | 1,287.8 |
| 886.7 | Herbert Hiller plaque | | 1,450 | 1,289.5 |
| 884.1 | Camp Rd; Mohican Outdoor Center | R, w (W–0.3m C, L, w, f) | 1,150 | 1,292.1 |
| 881.7 | Catfish Fire Tower | | 1,565 | 1,294.5 |
| 881.1 | Rattlesnake Spring | W–50ft w | 1,260 | 1,295.1 |
| 880.7 | Millbrook-Blairstown Rd-CR 602 | R (W–1.1m w) | 1,350 | 1,295.5 |
| 876.8 | Blue Mtn Lakes Rd | R, w (W–0.8m C, w) | 1,350 | 1,299.4 |
| 874.8 | Crater Lake | E–0.5m w | 1,360 | 1,301.4 |
| 872.0 | Rattlesnake Mtn | | 1,492 | 1,304.2 |
| 869.8 | **Brink Rd Shelter** *31.4mS; 6.9mN* | W–0.2m S, w | 1,110 | 1,306.4 |
| 866.2 | U.S. 206, Culvers Gap **Branchville, NJ 07826** | R, M (E–0.8m G; 1m M; 1.6m G, M; 2.5m G, M, L; 3.4m PO) (W–1.8m L, M) | 935 | 1,310.0 |
| 864.3 | Culver Fire Tower | | 1,550 | 1,311.9 |
| 863.2 | **Gren Anderson Shelter** *6.9mS; 5.9mN* | W–0.1m S, w | 1,320 | 1,313.0 |
| 860.8 | Sunrise Mtn | R, nw | 1,653 | 1,315.4 |
| 857.4 | **Mashipacong Shelter** *5.9mS; 3.3mN* | S, nw | 1,425 | 1,318.8 |
| 854.5 | **Rutherford Shelter** *3.3mS; 4.8mN* | E–0.4m S, w | 1,345 | 1,321.7 |
| 851.9 | N.J. 23; High Point State Park HQ | R, w (E–0.9m C, sh; 1.5m L; 2.6m G, M) (W–4.4m G, L, M) | 1,500 | 1,324.3 |
| 850.2 | **High Point Shelter** *4.8mS; 12.5mN* | E–0.1m S, w | 1,280 | 1,326.0 |
| 848.9 | County 519 | R (E–2.5m L) | 1,100 | 1,327.3 |
| 846.3 | Gemmer Rd | R | 740 | 1,329.9 |

| Miles from Katahdin | Features | Services | Elev. | Miles from Springer |
|---|---|---|---|---|
| 845.3 | Goodrich Rd | R | 610 | 1,330.9 |
| 844.9 | Trail to Jim Murray property | W–0.2m w, S, C, sh | 660 | 1,331.3 |
| 844.8 | Goldsmith Rd | R | 600 | 1,331.4 |
| 844.0 | Unionville Rd | R | 610 | 1,332.2 |
| 843.1 | Lott Rd **Unionville, NY 10988** | R (W–0.4m PO, C, G, M) | 590 | 1,333.1 |
| 842.1 | N.J. 284 | R (W–0.4m G, M, @) | 420 | 1,334.1 |
| 841.6 | Oil City Rd | R | 400 | 1,334.6 |
| 840.6 | Wallkill River | R | 410 | 1,335.6 |
| 838.3 | Lake Wallkill Rd (Liberty Corners Rd) | R, w | 440 | 1,337.9 |
| 837.8 | **Pochuck Mtn Shelter** *12.5mS; 11.7mN* | S, nw | 840 | 1,338.4 |
| 836.3 | Pochuck Mtn | | 985 | 1,339.9 |
| 835.1 | County 565 | R | 720 | 1,341.1 |
| 833.6 | County 517 **Glenwood, NJ 07418** | R (W–1.1m PO, G, L) | 440 | 1,342.6 |
| 832.9 | Pochuck Creek Footbridge | | 410 | 1,343.3 |
| 832.2 | Canal Rd | R | 410 | 1,344.0 |
| 831.3 | N.J. 94 **Vernon, NJ 07462** | R (E–1.8m L; 2.4m PO, C, H, G, L, M, V, cl, f, @; 3.5m D) (W–0.1m G) | 450 | 1,344.9 |
| 829.9 | Wawayanda Mtn | | 1,340 | 1,346.3 |
| 828.2 | Barrett Rd | R | 1,140 | 1,348.0 |
| 827.1 | Iron Mtn Rd Bridge | | 1,060 | 1,349.1 |
| 826.4 | Wawayanda Rd | R | 1,150 | 1,349.8 |
| 826.2 | **Wawayanda Shelter** *11.7mS; 12.1mN* | W–0.1m S; 0.4m w | 1,200 | 1,350.0 |
| 825.8 | Warwick Turnpike | R (E–1.9m G, M) (W–2.7m G, M) | 1,140 | 1,350.4 |
| 824.4 | Long House (Brady Rd) | R | 1,080 | 1,351.8 |
| 823.3 | Long House Creek | | 1,085 | 1,352.9 |
| 822.2 | State Line Trail; N.J.– N.Y. State Line | | 1,385 | 1,354.0 |

*Bear boxes are provided at several New Jersey shelters; please use them! Bears are extremely active in this area. One pair destroyed a hiker's tent. Never feed bears or leave food unattended. Do not bury or scatter excess food; avoid eating or preparing food in your tent. It is now estimated that the New Jersey counties where bears range have one per square mile.*

*Campfires are prohibited in New Jersey. Camping in areas other than those designated by signs also is prohibited in New Jersey.*

*Hitchhiking is illegal in New Jersey.*

New Jersey has the highest population of bears per square mile and a one-mile boardwalk. Southbounders are at the end of their deli-to-deli hike, whereas northbounders hungrily look forward to theirs. Thru-hiker legs are operating at machine level by now, which is good, because you may have to walk farther to find water.

**New York–New Jersey Trail Conference**—The NY–NJ TC maintains the 160.4 miles from Delaware Water Gap to the New York–Connecticut state line. Correspondence should be sent to NY–NJ TC, 156 Ramapo Valley Rd., Mahwah, NJ 07430; (201) 512-9348; <www.nynjtc.org>; <info@nynjtc.org>.

**Delaware Water Gap National Recreation Area**—The information center, visible from the Trail, closed due to major flooding of the Delaware River in April 2005, reopened in mid-2007. Restrooms and pay phone should be available for use. Water is available from a spigot to the left of the building. The Trail on Kittatinny Ridge runs through the NRA and state parks and forests, where regulations are different. The history of the recreation area is linked to a controversial 1960s plan to dam the Delaware, defeated by local opponents and the Trail community. Thru-hikers (defined by DWG as those who are hiking for two or more consecutive days) are permitted to camp along the Trail in the NRA with the following restrictions: one night per campsite, no more than ten persons per campsite, hiker camping allowed only within 100 feet of the A.T., no camping within 0.5 mile of an established roadway, no camping within 200 feet of another camping party, no camping from 0.5 mile south of Blue Mountain Lakes Road to a point 1 mile north of Crater Lake, no camping within 100 feet of any water source. Self-contained stoves are permitted; ground fires and charcoal stoves and grills are prohibited.

**Worthington State Forest**—Camping in Worthington State Forest is only permitted at the Backpacker Campsite 4.6 miles north of I-80 on the A.T. and at the campground on Old Mine Road within the state forest. Rangers patrol the area and issue fines for those violating camping restrictions.

**Sunfish Pond**—The southernmost glacial pond on the A.T. and one of seven protected natural areas in the state of New Jersey, the pond also has several unique man-made features and is a beauty to behold. *No camping or swimming is allowed at the pond.*

**Herbert Hiller plaque**—The 23rd A.T. 2,000-miler and a long-time Trail booster in New Jersey is memorialized on a plaque off the A.T. on Kittatinny Mountain.

**Camp Road**—**West**, on a dirt road, 0.3 mile to Mohican Outdoor Center, (908) 362-5670, operated by the Appalachian Mountain Club (AMC) as a retreat center. Thru-hikers can stay overnight for $21PP in a cabin with bunk, stove, shower, and towel. Tent-camping free to thru-hikers. Camp store with sodas, candy, and limited hiker supplies, including Coleman and denatured alcohol by the ounce. The center accepts packages sent *via* UPS to 50 Camp Mohican Rd., Blairstown, NJ 07825. Check in at the lodge, entrance on the left. Water available at the lodge or a spigot near the garage across the road.

**Rattlesnake Spring**—Located 0.6 mile north of the Catfish Fire Tower on a dirt road about 50 feet west of the A.T. Extremely dry years may cause the spring to fail.

**Millbrook–Blairstown Road, CR 602**—**West** 1.1 miles to Millbrook Village, a historical park with flush toilets and picnic area.

**Blue Mountain Lakes Road**—Camping needs to be 0.5 mile from this road in the NRA. For northbounders, the hand pump for water is on the west side of the Trail before crossing the paved road. Southbounders can get water here and, in 0.5 mile, reach several grassy areas for tenting. Those open lots were sites of former homes and cottages, acquired in the course of Trail preservation.

**West** 0.8 mile is YMCA's Camp Ken-Etiwa-Pec, a former Boy Scout camp on Long Pine Pond that offers two screened shelters to thru-hikers May–Sep. No fee, but donations accepted; outdoor pay phone.

**Crater Lake**—Located 0.5 mile east of the A.T. on a dirt road 2 miles north of Blue Mountain Lakes Road. The dirt road leads to a parking area and beach. North of the dirt road (50 yards) leading to Crater Lake is an orange-blazed trail that leads west 1.5 miles to Hemlock Pond, which offers good swimming.

**Brink Road Shelter** (1970)—Sleeps 5. Privy. Bears are especially active here. Water source is a spring 100 yards to the right of the shelter.

**U.S. 206/Culvers Gap**—*Restaurants:* Sunset Grill, open W–M, pay phone; Gyp's Tavern, located on nearby Kittatinny Lake, serves L/D (no credit cards); Joe to Go, (973) 948-2522, open daily 5–5, coffee, bagels, sandwiches.

**East** 0.8 mile to a farmer's market with fresh fruit and vegetables.

**East** 1 mile to *Restaurant:* Jumboland, B/L/D.

**East** 1.6 miles to ■ *Groceries:* Dale's Market with ATM (long-term resupply). ■ *Restaurants:* Dairy Queen; Jimmy's Pasta and Pizza; Stewarts Root Beer.

**East** 2.5 miles to ■ *Lodging:* Cobmin Ridge Motel, (973) 948-3459, $65S, $70D, EAP's not allowed; ■ *Groceries:* Yellow Cottage Deli & Bakery (short-term resupply), pay phone outside. ■ *Restaurant:* Mama Roni's Pizza/Pasta, open daily, pay phone.

**East** 3.4 miles to **Branchville, N.J. [P.O. ZIP 07826: M–F 8:30–5, Sa 8:30–1; (973) 948-3580].**

**West** 1.8 miles to *Lodging:* Forest Motel, (973) 948-5456, $50D, $5EAP, pay phone outside. ■ *Restaurant:* Rosie's Pizza, W–Su 11–9, L/D.

**Gren Anderson Shelter** (1958)—Sleeps 8. Privy. Built by the now disbanded New York section of the Green Mountain Club. Water source is a spring to the left of the shelter.

**Sunrise Mountain**—*No camping allowed at pavilion.* Nearby parking lot for day-use visitors. No water.

**Mashipacong Shelter** (1936)—Sleeps 8. Privy. High bear activity in this area. A stone shelter with wooden floor. No water is available at this shelter.

**Rutherford Shelter** (1967)—Sleeps 6. Privy. High bear activity in this area. Water source is an intermittent spring located 100 yards before the shelter on the connecting trail. Extremely dry years may cause the spring to fail.

**N.J. 23—High Point State Park Headquarters**, (973) 875-4800, on the A.T., has pay phone, indoor restroom, and outside water spigot. Rangers hold packages sent to High Point State Park, 1480 State Route 23, Sussex, NJ 07461. Offices are open year-round. Day-use area 0.9 mile to the east of the park office has a swimming area at spring-fed Lake Marcia, a concession stand, grill, and no charge to walk-ins for hot showers; available Memorial Day–Labor Day. High Point Monument, on a short side trail from A.T., marks the highest point in the state, 1,803 feet. *Camping:* Sawmill Lake Campground is located in the park; $20/night, 6 people per site.

**East** 1.5 miles to *Lodging:* High Point Country Inn; hikers may call Lee and Mike Hauck, (973) 702-1860, $69S, $79D, $10EAP, includes shuttle to/from Trail and shuttle into town for shopping, laundry service $7, soda machine, pay phone.

**East** 2.6 miles to ■ *Groceries:* Little Red Deli (short-term resupply) with ATM. ■ *Restaurants:* Parkside Pizza, Tu–Su.

**West** 4.4 miles to the town of Port Jervis, N.Y. ■ *Lodging:* Comfort Inn, (845) 856-6611, two double beds, Su–Th $99, F–Sa $119, $8EAP (ask sales manager for 10% thru-hiker discount); restaurant. ■ *Groceries:* Shop-Rite supermarket (long-term resupply). ■ *Restaurants:* Dairy Queen, McDonald's, and a pizzeria. ■ *Other services:* pharmacy; bank, ATM located at gas station next to Comfort Inn.

**High Point Shelter** (1936)—Sleeps 8. Privy. CCC-built stone shelter with wooden floor. Water sources for this shelter are two streams located on the trail to the shelter; both may fail in dry years. Potable water may be found 1.5 miles south at High Point State Park headquarters.

 **N.J. 519**—**East** 2.5 miles to *Lodging:* High Point Country Inn (see listing above).

**Trail to Jim Murray Property** (0.4 mile north of Goodrich Road)—**West** 0.2 mile to well water. For the past 11 years, Jim Murray (AT '89) has cordially allowed long-distance hikers (only) year-round use of a heated hiker cabin, with hot-water shower and privy, on his private property adjacent to the Trail; no groups. Tenting allowed. Follow the "well water" sign. This is a privately owned cabin. Be responsible, and please do not abuse this privilege.

**Lott Road**—**West** 0.4 mile to the town of **Unionville, N.Y.** **[P.O. ZIP 10988: M–F 8–12 & 1–5, Sa 8–12; (845) 726-3535]**. Lott Road is also known as Jersey Avenue. ■ *Camping:* Hikers may use Unionville Memorial Park, with water and toilet facility, to pitch a tent; fill out permission slip at Horler's General Store. A phone is located north of the post office on N.Y. 284. ■ *Groceries:* Horler's Store with ATM (long-term resupply), M–Sa 6–9, Su 7–7. ■ *Restaurants:* Backtrack Inn, open daily 12–9 (also has a hostel, $3PP, no shower); Sara's Soda Shop, B/L/D M–Tu 6–3:30, W–F 6–8, Sa–Su 7–3.

**N.J. 284**—**West** 0.4 mile to *Groceries:* End of the Line Grocery (short-term resupply), M–F 5–9, Sa 6–9, Su 6–7, with deli sandwiches, ATM, and free Internet access for thru-hiker customers.

**Pochuck Mountain Shelter** (1989)—Sleeps 6. Privy. "Pochuck" is Lenape for "out-of-the-way place." Water source is a spigot on the north side of a vacant white house at the foot of Pochuck Mountain. No camping is allowed at the house (owned by the N.J. Department of Environmental Protection). A 200-foot connecting trail located approximately 0.6 mile south (steeply downhill) from the shelter and 150 feet north of the Liberty Corners Road crossing leads to that source. Southbounders can find water at a stream south of N.Y. 565.

**N.J. 517**—West 1.1 miles to **Glenwood, N.J. [P.O. ZIP 07418: M–W,F 7:30–5, Tʜ 7:30–7, Sa 6:30–2; (973) 764-2616].** ■ *Lodging:* Apple Valley Inn and B&B, (973) 764-3735, M–Th $125–$140, F–Su $135–$150 includes full B. ■ *Groceries:* Pochuck Valley Farm Market & Deli (short-term resupply) with pay phone, outside water spigot, ATM, and restroom. Open M–F 5–6:30, Sa–Su 5–5.

**N.J. 94**—**East** 1.8 miles to *Lodging:* Appalachian Motel, (973) 764-6070, Su–Th $75D, F–Sa $89D, $10EAP.
   **East** 2.4 miles to **Vernon, N.J. [P.O. ZIP 07462: M–F 8:30–5, Sa 10–1; (973) 764-9056].** ■ *Camping:* Firehouse offers camping by the pavilion for no charge, water, and restrooms; no shower available. ■ *Hostel:* St. Thomas Episcopal Church offers space for 12. Stay limited to one night; absolutely no dogs, alcohol, or smoking permitted; Internet, laundry, shower, towels, refrigerator, microwave, and cooking in kitchen by permission; $10PP donation requested. Coleman, denatured alcohol, and butane canisters available for purchase. Hikers may have to share space with other groups, are expected to pitch in and keep the hostel clean, and must be out of the hostel by 9 a.m. on Sunday. ■ *Groceries:* A&P Supermarket (long-term resupply) and a natural-foods store. ■ *Restaurants:* Little Anthony's Pizzeria; Mixing Bowl, B/L; Lox of Bagels Deli; Mountain View Deli; Dairy Queen. ■ *Other services:* bank with ATM, dentist, coin laundry, veterinarian, pharmacy, Camera Shop, R.J. Mars Department Store, and amusement park.
   **East** 3.5 miles to *Medical:* Vernon Urgent Care, (973) 209-2260, M–F 8–8, Sa–Su 9–5.
   **West** 0.1 mile to *Groceries:* Heaven Hill Farm, fresh fruit and ice cream (short-term resupply), (973) 764-5144, M–Sa 9–8 Su 9–7, Easter to Sep. Hikers are requested to keep packs outside on left side of building.

**Wawayanda Mountain**—Near the summit, a blue-blazed side trail leads 0.1 mile to Pinwheel's Vista. The vista provides views to the west of Pochuck Mountain and High Point Monument. "Wawayanda" is Lenape for "winding waters."

**Wawayanda Shelter** (1990)—Sleeps 6. Privy. The park office is reached by going north on the A.T. 0.1 mile, then on the blue-blazed trail 0.3 mile; pay phone outside. Water source is a faucet on the maintenance building near the entrance to the fenced-in work yard.

**Warwick Turnpike**—**East** 1.9 miles to *Groceries:* Mt. Jug Deli (short-term resupply); deli, grill, ice cream, ATM. **West** 2.7 miles to a grocery store (long-term resupply) with ATM, pizzeria, bagel shop, and pharmacy.

*"Amidst the greens and blue of the forest*
*is where I belong and am at the height*
*of my contentment with life."*
     —Leonard M. Adkins, "Habitual Hiker"
     *(AT '80-'81, '82, '84, '95-'98, '07)*

# New York

| Miles from Katahdin | Features | Services | Elev. | Miles from Springer |
|---|---|---|---|---|
| 822.2 | State Line Trail; N.Y.–N.J. State Line | | 1,385 | 1,354.0 |
| 821.8 | Prospect Rock | | 1,433 | 1,354.4 |
| 819.7 | Village Vista Trail **Greenwood Lake, NY 10925** | E–0.9m PO, G, M, L | 1,180 | 1,356.5 |
| 816.3 | N.Y. 17A **Greenwood Lake, NY 10925; Bellvale, NY 10912; Warwick, NY 10990** | R (E–2m PO, G, M, L) (W–0.2m w, M; 1.6m PO, G; 4.6m PO, G, M, L, D, cl) | 1,180 | 1,359.9 |
| 815.0 | Eastern Pinnacles | | 1,294 | 1,361.2 |
| 814.5 | Cat Rocks | | 1,080 | 1,361.7 |
| 814.2 | **Wildcat Shelter** *12.1mS; 14.3mN* | S, w | 1,180 | 1,362.0 |
| 812.7 | Lakes Rd | R | 680 | 1,363.5 |
| 812.4 | Fitzgerald Falls | w | 800 | 1,363.8 |
| 810.4 | Mombasha High Pt. | | 1,280 | 1,365.8 |
| 809.2 | West Mombasha Rd | R | 980 | 1,367.0 |
| 808.3 | Buchanan Mtn | | 1,142 | 1,367.9 |
| 807.5 | East Mombasha Rd | R | 840 | 1,368.7 |
| 806.8 | Little Dam Lake | | 720 | 1,369.4 |
| 806.1 | Orange Tpk | R (E–0.5m w) | 780 | 1,370.1 |
| 805.4 | Arden Mtn, Agony Grind | | 1,180 | 1,370.8 |
| 804.3 | N.Y. 17 **Southfields, NY 10975; Arden, NY 10910** | R (E–2.1m PO, G, L, M) (W–0.7m PO; 3.7m G, L, M, cl) | 550 | 1,371.9 |
| 804.1 | NYS Thruway (I-87) | | 560 | 1,372.1 |
| 803.9 | Arden Valley Rd | R | 680 | 1,372.3 |
| 802.6 | Island Pond Outlet | w | 1,350 | 1,373.6 |
| 802.0 | Lemon Squeezer | | 1,150 | 1,374.2 |
| 801.4 | Long Path Jct | | 1,160 | 1,374.8 |
| 800.9 | Surebridge Mtn | | 1,200 | 1,375.3 |
| 799.9 | **Fingerboard Shelter** *14.3mS; 5.3mN* | S, nw | 1,300 | 1,376.3 |
| 798.8 | Arden Valley Rd | R (E–0.3m w, sh) | 1,196 | 1,377.4 |
| 796.6 | Seven Lakes Dr | R | 850 | 1,379.6 |
| 795.8 | Goshen Mtn | | 1,180 | 1,380.4 |
| 794.6 | **William Brien Memorial Shelter** *5.3mS; 3.7mN* | S, nw | 1,070 | 1,381.6 |

| Miles from Katahdin | Features | Services | Elev. | Miles from Springer |
|---|---|---|---|---|
| 793.2 | Black Mtn | | 1,160 | 1,383.0 |
| 792.5 | Palisades Interstate Pkwy | R (W–0.4m w) | 680 | 1,383.7 |
| 792.3 | Beechy Bottom Brook | w | 660 | 1,383.9 |
| 791.5 | **West Mtn Shelter** *3.7mS; 31.6mN* | E–0.4m w; 0.6m S, nw | 1,240 | 1,384.7 |
| 789.9 | Seven Lakes Dr | R | 610 | 1,386.3 |
| 788.3 | Bear Mtn | R, w | 1,305 | 1,387.9 |
| 786.5 | **Bear Mtn, NY 10911** | R, w, L, M (E–0.3m PO) | 220 | 1,389.7 |
| 785.8 | Bear Mtn Museum/Zoo | | 124 | 1,390.4 |
| 785.7 | U.S. 9W, Bear Mtn Circle **Ft. Montgomery, NY 10922** | R (W–0.7m PO, G, M, L, @) | 150 | 1,390.5 |
| 785.7 | Bear Mtn Bridge | R | 200 | 1,390.5 |
| 785.0 | N.Y. 9D | R | 230 | 1,391.2 |
| 784.5 | Camp Smith Trail to Anthony's Nose | E–0.6m | 700 | 1,391.7 |
| 783.5 | Hemlock Springs Campsite | C, w | 550 | 1,392.7 |
| 783.3 | Manitou Rd, South Mtn Pass | R | 460 | 1,392.9 |
| 779.9 | U.S. 9, N.Y. 403 **Peekskill, NY 10566** | R (E–4.5m PO, G, M, L, D, V, cl, @) (W–6.7m G, L, M, O) | 400 | 1,396.3 |
| 779.3 | Graymoor Spiritual Life Center–Franciscan Way | R, w, C, sh | 550 | 1,396.9 |
| 778.0 | Denning Hill | | 900 | 1,398.2 |
| 776.6 | Old Albany Post Rd–Chapman Rd | R | 607 | 1,399.6 |
| 774.9 | Canopus Hill Rd | R (E–1.6m G, M) | 420 | 1,401.3 |
| 773.9 | South Highland Rd | R | 570 | 1,402.3 |
| 771.2 | Dennytown Rd | R, C, w | 860 | 1,405.0 |
| 769.6 | Sunk Mine Rd | R | 800 | 1,406.6 |
| 767.5 | N.Y. 301, Canopus Lake, Clarence Fahnestock State Park | R (E–1m C, sh, w) | 920 | 1,408.7 |
| 763.3 | Shenandoah Mtn | | 1,282 | 1,412.9 |
| 762.9 | Long Hill Rd | R | 1,100 | 1,413.3 |
| 761.8 | Shenandoah Tenting Area | C, w | 900 | 1,414.4 |
| 760.5 | Hortontown Rd, **RPH Shelter** *31.6mS; 9mN* | R, S, w | 360 | 1,415.7 |

| Miles from Katahdin | Features | Services | Elev. | Miles from Springer |
|---|---|---|---|---|
| 760.2 | Taconic State Pkwy | R | 650 | 1,416.0 |
| 757.0 | Hosner Mtn Rd | R | 500 | 1,419.2 |
| 755.4 | N.Y. 52 **Stormville, NY 12582** | R (E–0.3m G, M) (W–1.9m PO, G, M) | 800 | 1,420.8 |
| 754.0 | Stormville Mtn Rd, I-84 Overpass | R | 950 | 1,422.2 |
| 751.6 | Mt. Egbert | | 1,329 | 1,424.6 |
| 751.5 | **Morgan Stewart Shelter** 9mS; 7.6mN | S, w | 1,285 | 1,424.7 |
| 750.4 | Depot Hill Rd | R | 1,230 | 1,425.8 |
| 748.5 | Old Route 55 | R | 750 | 1,427.7 |
| 748.2 | N.Y. 55 **Poughquag, NY 12570** | R (W–1.5m M; 2.1m G, M; 3.1m PO, G, M, D) | 720 | 1,428.0 |
| 747.0 | Nuclear Lake | | 750 | 1,429.2 |
| 744.2 | West Mtn | | 1,200 | 1,432.0 |
| 743.9 | **Telephone Pioneers Shelter** 7.6mS; 8.7mN | S, w | 910 | 1,432.3 |
| 743.2 | County 20, West Dover Rd, Dover Oak **Pawling, NY 12564** | R (E–w, f; 3.1m PO, C, G, M, L, O, cl, @) | 650 | 1,433.0 |
| 740.8 | N.Y. 22, Appalachian Trail RR Station, Metro North RR | R, M, C, sh, w (E–0.6m G, M) (W–2.6m G, L; 4m PO, G, L, M) | 480 | 1,435.4 |
| 740.6 | Hurds Corner Rd | R | 480 | 1,435.6 |
| 735.6 | Leather Hill Rd | R | 750 | 1,440.6 |
| 735.2 | **Wiley Shelter** 8.7mS; 4mN | S, w | 740 | 1,441.0 |
| 735.0 | Duell Hollow Rd | R | 620 | 1,441.2 |
| 734.0 | Hoyt Rd, N.Y.–Conn. State Line **Wingdale, NY 12594** | R (W–1.5m M; 3.3m PO, G, M, L, f) | 400 | 1,442.2 |

*In New York, campfires are prohibited except in designated fire rings and fireplaces at established campsites and shelters.*

*Hitchhiking is illegal in New York.*

The first miles specifically intended for the A.T. were built here through Harriman–Bear Mountain state parks in 1922–23. With many parks, roads, and a railroad station right on the Trail, many hikers are thinking, what happened to my wilderness experience? You may find this stretch to be a uniquely multicultural experience. The Trail drops to its lowest elevation point—124 feet—after, or just before, you pass through the Trailside Museum and Zoo at Bear Mountain. Hydration becomes an issue in this area. Don't pass up an opportunity for water.

**Prospect Rock**—At 1,433 feet, this is the highest point on the A.T. in New York (Bear Mountain is 1,305 feet). This and other rock faces along this ridge provide views of Greenwood Lake to the east.

**Village Vista Trail**—This blue-blazed trail leads **East** 0.9 mile to Greenwood Lake without the fast traffic of N.Y. 17A; from the vista, you can see Lion's Field below, the terminus of the trail. A water fountain on the outside of the little green building next to the softball field can be used by hikers. **Greenwood Lake, N.Y. [P.O. ZIP 10925: M–F 8–5, Sa 9–12; (845) 477-7328].** ■ *Lodging:* Breezy Point, (845) 477-8100, rates begin at $85, pay phone and ATM; Linden Motel, (845) 477-0851. ■ *Groceries:* Delicious Deli; Country Grocery; Kwik Mark; BG Bagles; and Cumberland Farms, with deli sandwiches (all short-term resupply). ■ *Restaurants:* Ashley's Pizza; Napoli Restaurant; Murphy's Tavern; Side Street Café; Sing Loong Kitchen. ■ *Other services:* one-hour photo shop; Service Star Hardware; pharmacy; Long Pond Marina, with boat rentals; and Greenwood Lake Taxi, M–Th, (845) 477-3291.

**N.Y. 17A**—Public phone. **East** 2 miles to **Greenwood Lake** (see above).

**West** 0.2 mile to Bellvale Creamery, daily 12–9, ice cream and water.

**West** 1.6 miles to **Bellvale, N.Y. [P.O. ZIP 10912: M–F 8–12 & 1–4:30, Sa 8–12; (845) 986-2880].** P.O. inside Mama's Boy Pizzeria with deli sandwiches (short-term resupply), open 7 days.

**West** 4.6 miles to the larger town of **Warwick, N.Y. [P.O. ZIP 10990: M–F 8:30–7, Sa 9–4; (845) 986-0271].** Hitchhikers have been cited leaving Warwick on 17A. ■ *Lodging:* Warwick Motel, (845) 986-4822, $76 weekdays, $86 weekends. ■ *Groceries:* ShopRite (long-term resupply) is 1.4 miles south of town on N.Y. 94. ■ *Other services:* hospital, restaurants, drug store, coin laundry, ATM, fresh fruit and ice cream at market, and hardware store.

**Wildcat Shelter** (1992)—Sleeps 8. Privy. Water source is a spring at the entrance of the side trail leading to the shelter.

**Mombasha High Point**—On a clear day, you can see the New York City skyline, including the Empire State Building.

**Sterling Forest**—Between Greenwood Lake and Arden, 6 miles of the A.T. pass through the northern portion of a 20,000-acre tract called Sterling Forest. It was the center of a decade-long struggle between a corporate private landowner and a coalition of conservation groups, state agencies in New York and New Jersey, and such organizations as the NY–NJ TC and ATC. At issue was the development of new stores, offices, golf courses, and 14,000 new homes for an estimated 35,000 people in a small area that is mostly undeveloped. All told, more than 30 environmental groups, along with foundations, individuals, states, and Congress, combined to contribute $55 million toward the 1998 purchase and protection of 14,500 acres. The last unprotected parcel was acquired in late 2006.

**N.Y. 17**—Pay phone at road crossing. **East** 2.1 miles to **Southfields, N.Y. [P.O. ZIP 10975: M–F 9–12,1–5, Sa 9–11:30; (845) 351-2628]. ■** *Lodging:* Tuxedo Motel, (845) 351-4747, $44.50S, $49.50D, $10EAP. WiFi available. ■ *Restaurant:* Take-out Chinese delivered to Tuxedo Motel, (845) 351-4428. ■ *Groceries:* Corner Deli (short-term resupply) with ATM.

**West** 0.7 mile to **Arden, N.Y. [P.O. ZIP 10910: M–Sa 10:30–11:30; (845) 351-5341].** To reach the post office, follow N.Y. 17 north to the sign that says Arden; turn right, then bear right at the fork in the road.

**West** 3.7 miles to the town of **Harriman, N.Y.,** for lodgings, groceries, restaurants, and coin laundries.

**Bear Mountain/Harriman State Parks**—Home to the first completed section of the A.T. Dry conditions and forest fires have forced the closure of the A.T. in the park for days or even weeks in the summer. In 1994, Harriman State Park instituted a policy under which, even if other trails in the park are closed, the A.T. remains open to thru-hikers.

*Major William A. Welch*—General manager of Palisades Interstate Park from 1912 to 1940, Major Welch, along with volunteers from the NY–NJ TC, was responsible for bringing together the framework for completion of the first section of Trail in Harriman and Bear Mountain state parks. The first chairman of ATC, he also is credited with designing the original A.T. marker that became "the diamond" and remains the most-recognized symbol for the Trail.

**Education Through Adventure Leadership Camp**—(845) 928-1483, 74 Baileytown Rd., Central Valley, NY 10917, located on the north shore of Upper Twin Lake; call for free pick-up (and drop-off) anywhere on A.T. in Harriman; special thru-hiker rates, cabins $12, tentsites $4, include hot showers; laundry, slackpacks, Internet, and shuttles available for a fee. Pay phones are available at junction of Route 17/Arden Valley Road and at Bear Mountain Zoo.

**Fingerboard Shelter** (1928)—Sleeps 8. No privy. A stone structure. Water is normally unavailable at the shelter; at times, a seasonal spring does flow. The closest dependable water source is the spigot at Lake Tiorati, 0.5 mile east on the blue-blazed Hurst Trail. Southbounders can get their water at Tiorati Circle, 1.1 miles north of the shelter.

**Arden Valley Road—East** 0.3 mile to Tiorati Circle, with restroom; free showers in bath house for walk-ins; open Memorial Day to Labor Day, M–F 10–5:45, Sa–Su 9–7; vending machines, ice-cream sandwiches, candy, water, and public beach on Lake Tiorati.

**William Brien Memorial Shelter** (1933)—Sleeps 8. No privy. A stone shelter built by the CCC and named in memory of the first president of the New York Ramblers. Rumored resident rattlesnake; one killed in 2007 (which could violate the Endangered Species Act in some Trail places; please don't do it.). Water source is a spring-fed well that is prone to go dry. This spring is 80 yards down a blue-blazed trail to the right of the shelter. An alternative for northbounders is to stop at Tiorati Circle, swim, cook at one of the picnic tables, and hike to the shelter for the evening. However, the shortcut back to the A.T. has been removed. Southbounders can get water at the park visitors center 0.4 mile west, on the Palisades Interstate Parkway.

**Palisades Interstate Parkway—West** 0.4 mile to park visitors center with restroom, pay phone, soda and snack machines. From here, it is a mere 34 miles to NYC on the Palisades Interstate Parkway. Hitchhiking is not allowed on this busy thoroughfare. Hikers heading to West Mountain Shelter may want to pick up water at stream north of the parkway.

**West Mountain Shelter** (1928)—Sleeps 8. No privy. Water may be available from an unreliable spring 0.4 mile down steep Timp-Torne Trail or alternately at a seasonal stream 0.2 mile before the shelter. Resident rattlesnake at this shelter (at least in past). Located 0.6 mile on the Timp–Torne Trail, this shelter provides views of the surrounding countryside and the NYC skyline.

**Bear Mountain**—At 1,305 feet, this is one of the highest points on the Trail in New York and offers views of the Hudson River Valley and the New York City skyline. In the early 1900s, the state was considering a site near the base of Bear Mountain for a prison, but Mary Averell Harriman, widow of railroad magnate Edward Harriman and primary landholder in the area, had other plans. In 1910, Mrs. Harriman agreed to donate 10,000 acres for the development of a park with the condition that the state discontinue its plans for a prison.

What was then known as Sing Sing Prison was eventually built on the Hudson River 20 miles south of the A.T., its location giving birth to the phrase, "sent up the river." No water available at the summit. Do not rely on the seasonally stocked soda vending machine. NY–NJ TC and ATC are in the middle of a major, multiyear relocation and rehabilitation project on the Trail and associated trails on the mountain, so expect to see crews on either side of the summit, and, of course, follow the white blazes.

**Bear Mountain, N.Y.**—[**P.O. ZIP 10911: M–F 8–2 (Jun 25–Sep 7), 8–10 (Sep 10–Jun 22); (845) 786-3747**]. P.O. may close early (and there's some talk of closing it altogether—call ahead). Located across the street from the park administration building on Seven Lakes Drive. Fort Montgomery (see below) may be a better option. *Lodging:* Bear Mountain Inn (on the A.T.), (845) 786-2701, <www.bearmountaininn.com>, closed for renovations in 2007; may reopen in 2008. Merry-go-round, open Sa–Su 11–5.

**Trailside Museums and Zoo**—North of the inn and south of Bear Mountain Bridge, the Bear Mountain Zoo contains many native species, including black bears, and offers a unique, and sometimes emotional, experience for thru-hikers. Within the park is also a much-photographed statue of Walt Whitman. Admission $1; A.T. hikers admitted free. The portion of the A.T. leading through the zoo to the bridge—an original section from 1923—descends to 124 feet above sea level; it's the Trail's lowest elevation between Maine and Georgia. *Dogs are not allowed in the museum/zoo section.* After 5 p.m., the gate is closed; the southern gate opens at 10:30 a.m. If you arrive when the gate is closed or are hiking with a dog, hike around on U.S. 9W, which becomes the official route for the time period/circumstances.

**Bear Mountain Circle**—West 0.7 mile to **Ft. Montgomery, N.Y.** [**P.O. ZIP 10922: M–F 8:30–5, Sa 8:30–12; (845) 446-8459**]. ■ *Lodging:* Bear Mountain Bridge Motel, (845) 446-2472, $65–$69 weekdays, higher on weekends, with shuttle back to the Trail; Holiday Inn Express, (845) 446-4277, thru-hiker rate $99 for 1 or 2 people, add $10 for third person, Internet and computer/office for guests, laundry, indoor pool, continental B; Victorian River View B&B, (845) 446-5479, $110–$160. ■ *Groceries:* M&R Grocery Store, with ATM and Mobil Mini Mart (both short-term resupply). Key Foods supermarket (long-term resupply) is two miles north in Highland Falls. ■ *Restaurants:* Trading Post Restaurant, open M–Th 3–midnight, F 3 p.m.–1 a.m., Sa noon–2 a.m., Su noon–midnight; Bagel Café with ATM, open M–F 5–3, Sa 6–2, B/L; Fox's Deli; M&R Deli. Additional services are located beyond Fort Montgomery, near the U.S. Military Academy at West Point.

**Bear Mountain Bridge**—Built at a cost of $5 million in 1923–24 by a private company run by the Harriman family. When Earl Shaffer arrived at the bridge in 1948, he had to pay a nickel to cross. Today, only vehicles must pay.

**Anthony's Nose**—Where the A.T. turns west on a dirt road, 0.5 mile north of N.Y. 9D, a turn east on this road, blazed as the Camp Smith Trail, leads 0.6 mile to the top of the mountain known as Anthony's Nose. This rock outcropping, 900 feet above the river, offers outstanding views of the Hudson River Valley. The state Office of Parks, Recreation, and Historic Preservation now owns the property; please stay on the trail. Originally, the A.T. climbed steeply to the summit but was rerouted when World War II broke out. The Nose remained closed until 1993, when the New York State Division of Military and Naval Affairs, managers of the adjacent National Guard camp, gave permission for hikers to once again walk to the summit.

**U.S. 9**—**East** 4.5 miles to **Peekskill, N.Y. [P.O. ZIP 10566: M–F 8:30–5, Sa 8–12:30; (914) 737-1340]**. If you plan to go into Peekskill, take Highland Avenue into town, rather than U.S. 9, where the two roads fork about 3 miles from the A.T. Highland Avenue leads directly to downtown. Services in town include several motels and restaurants, supermarkets, pharmacy, coin laundry, banks with ATM, shoe repair, doctor, dentist, and veterinarian. The post office is on South St., 4.5 miles from the A.T. Services are spread out over a large, bustling area, and some hikers feel it is too spread out to easily maneuver on foot. Free Internet access at the Field Library, 4 Nelson Ave., M, Tu, Th 9–9, W 11–9, F 9–5, Sa 10–2.

**West** 6.7 miles *via* Route 403 to N.Y. 9D to **Cold Spring, N.Y.** ■ *Lodging:* Countryside Motel, 3577 Route 9, Cold Spring, NY 10516, (845) 265-2090, $65S, $74D, $80 3 or 4 people, WiFi, will receive mail drops for guests; Pig Hill Inn, (845) 265-9247, $130 and up. ■ *Restaurants*: McGuires on Main, Cold Spring Pizza, Whistling Willies. ■ *Groceries:* Food Town Supermarket (long-term resupply). ■ *Outfitter:* Hudson Valley Outfitters, (845) 265-0221, <www.hudsonvalleyoutfitters.com>, 63 Main St., M–F 11–6, Sa–Su 9–6, caters to kayakers and day-hikers; clothing, boots, Leki poles and parts, MSR canisters. ■ *Shuttle:* Highland Transit Taxi, (845) 265-8294. ■ *Train:* Daily commuter service to NYC.

**Graymoor Spiritual Life Center**—Hikers are permitted to sleep at the monastery's ball-field picnic shelter, which has water, a cold-water shower during warm months, and a privy. The shelter is open all season long. *Directions:* North of U.S. 9, the A.T. climbs uphill and crosses a second paved road leading to the center. Here, northbounders should follow the blue blazes: Turn east on Franciscan Way, turn left on St. Anthony Way, and turn left on St. Joseph Drive to the ballfield. Southbounders will cross unpaved Old West Point Road onto the Graymoor driveway; continue straight on driveway, then north where the driveway forks. Pizza and deli food may be ordered for delivery to the picnic shelter.

**Canopus Hill Road**—**East** 1.6 miles to the Putnam Valley Market (short-term resupply), (845) 528-8626, with pizza, hot food from the grill, ATM, pay phone, and phone cards. Open daily 6:30–9 (closes at 7 on Su). *Directions:* east on Canopus Hill Road 0.3 mile to intersection with Canopus Hollow Road. Continue 0.1 mile south on Canopus Hollow Road, turn west on Sunset Hill Road 1.2 miles to store. Sunset Hill Road is a steep, winding road that climbs about 400 feet from Canopus Hill Road.

**Dennytown Road**—Water available from spigot on the side of the pump building. Opens third F of Apr, closes last Su of Oct. Camping area located 500 feet west on Dennytown Road, then south onto a dirt road to top of hill.

**N.Y. 301/Clarence Fahnestock State Park**—**East** 1 mile to the park's campground, (845) 225-7207. The beach area can be reached from the A.T. 2.3 miles north of N.Y. 301 *via* an unmarked downhill gully trail that begins a quarter of a mile south of the viewpoint on the A.T. at the northern end of Canopus Lake. The beach area is visible from the overlook. Campground open Apr 2–second week of Dec, tentsites $13 Su–Th, $16 F–Sa. A free tenting area provided for thru-hikers with hot showers, flush toilets, and water; inquire at the park entrance. The beach-area concession stand, (845) 225-3998, and grill (open Memorial Day–Labor Day, Su–F 9–5, Sa 9–6, grill closes one hour earlier) has grilled sandwiches, soda, ice cream, supplies, pay phone. The beach area closes Labor Day.
     **West** 7.2 miles to Cold Spring (see above).

**Shenandoah Tenting Area**—0.1 mile west. Group camping is permitted. Water is available from a hand pump.

**RPH Shelter** (1982)—Sleeps 6. Privy. Available for hikers from Apr until hunting season begins in mid-Nov; closed the remainder of the time, but the grounds are available year-round. Formerly a closed cabin, it was renovated as a three-sided shelter with a front porch to meet NPS building codes. Caretaker Joe Hrouda, (845) 221-9014, does not accept mail drops but will accept postcards and letters sent to 18 Memory Lane, Hopewell Junction, NY 12533; note your ETA. Joe stops by the shelter each day during the thru-hiker season to deliver mail and check on the shelter. Water source is the hand pump to the left of the shelter.

**N.Y. 52—East** 0.3 mile to ■ *Groceries:* Mountain Top Market Deli, (845) 221-0928, (short-term resupply), open daily 6 a.m.–8 p.m., daily specials and hot sandwiches, water for hikers on faucet at side of building, pay phone. ■ *Restaurant:* Danny's Pizzeria, open daily at 11, cheaper soda.

**West** 1.9 miles to **Stormville, N.Y. [P.O. ZIP 12582: M–F 8:30–5, Sa 8:30–12; (845) 226-2627].** ■ *Groceries:* Citgo Mini Mart (short-term resupply). ■ *Restaurant:* Stormville Pizza, M–Sa 11–9:30, Su 12–9.

**Morgan Stewart Shelter** (1984)—Sleeps 6. Privy. Water source is a well with a pump located downhill and in front of the shelter.

**N.Y. 55—** Look to the east. If a school bus is parked at the intersection, it is really a deli /hot dog stand. **West** 1.5 miles to *Restaurant:* Pleasant Ridge Pizza, pay phone, serving L/D, closed M. ■ *Other services:* Pleasant Ridge Shopping Center, pharmacy, and deli.

**West** 2.1 miles to *Groceries:* Beekman Corner's ShopRite & Cumberland Farms. ■ *Restaurant:* 7 Stars, Tailgates Grill, The Square, Luciano's Pizza Café.

**West** 3.1 miles to **Poughquag, N.Y. [P.O. ZIP 12570: M–F 8:30–5, Sa 8:30–12; (845) 724-4763],** a larger town with pharmacy, doctor, bank with ATM. ■ *Restaurants:* Great Wall Chinese Restaurant, La Contadina Pizzeria. ■ *Groceries:* convenience store with deli (short-term resupply).

**Nuclear Lake**—The site of a nuclear fuels-processing research facility until 1972. After the Park Service acquired the lands for the A.T., the buildings were razed, and the area was tested extensively and given a clean bill of health, dispelling fears that the lake was contaminated and allowing the Trail to be rerouted along the shore.

**Telephone Pioneers Shelter** (1988)—Sleeps 6. Privy. Built with the assistance of the White Plains Council of the Telephone Pioneers of America. Water source is the stream crossed by the side trail leading to the shelter. Alternative water source is 0.7 mile north at the Champion residence (see next entry).

**County 20/West Dover Road**—Ron and Holly Champion, who live in the purple house east of the Trail, have Coleman fuel for sale. Water is available from a tap at the end of their lower walk. *Please do not knock at door.*

**East** 3.1 miles to **Pawling, N.Y. [P.O. ZIP 12564: M–F 8:30–5, Sa 9–12; (845) 855-2669].** Northbound hikers might want to hike 2.4 miles more to N.Y. 22 for eaisier access to Pawling. ■ *Camping:* The town allows hikers to camp in its Edward R. Murrow Memorial Park, 1 mile from the center of town on West Main Street. The park offers lake swimming, restroom, and pay phone. No dogs permitted. Two-night maximum. ■ *Lodging:* The Pawling House Bed & Breakfast, 105 West Main St., (845) 855-3851, <innkeeper@pawlinghouse.com>, $175–$225 with breakfast; Sharadu B&B, (845) 855-1790, regularly $75, special hiker rate of $55, with continental B, no smoking or pets, call ahead for reservations or to hold packages, deli and mini-market downstairs. ■ *Groceries:* Hannaford, 2 miles south from town center on Rt. 22 (long-term resupply); CVS (short-term resupply); Latinos Mini-Market Family Quick Stop. ■ *Restaurants:* Vinny's Deli & Pasta; Chris's Deli; Mama's Pizza; Gaudino Pizzeria; Great Wall Chinese; Pawling Tavern; McKeene's Restaurant; McKinney & Doyle. ■ *Outfitters:* Pawling Cycling and Sports, (845) 855-9866, small full-service outfitter, possible shuttle service, in the Village Center at 12 West Main St.; Blue Line Sports, (845) 855-0763, miscellaneous gear, shuttles, slackpacking, 23 East Main St. ■ *Other services:* coin laundry, banks with ATM, pharmacy, and Metro-North station with train service to NYC [call (800) METRO-INFO for fare and schedule]. ■ *Internet access:* Free access at Pawling Free Library, 11 Broad St., Tu–Th 10–8, F–Sa 10–4. *Please leave packs and trekking poles outside or in the hallway.*

**Dover Oak**—Located on the north side of West Dover Road, is reportedly the largest oak tree on the A.T. Its girth four feet from the ground is more than 20 feet, 4 inches, and it is estimated to be more than 300 years old.

**N.Y. 22/Appalachian Trail Railroad Station**— **West,** within view of the Trail, a hotdog stand. *Other services:* Native Landscapes & Garden Center; owner Pete Muroski, a hiker, is very hiker-friendly. Allows camping on site (on front porch, in rain), use of restrooms, shower, kitchen, seasonal short-term employment, shuttle to village for supplies. Will hold mail drops sent to 991 Route 22, Pawling, NY 12564. Center is open daily, 7–5, year-round.

**East** 0.6 mile to *Groceries:* Tony's Deli (short-term resupply), open daily 5 a.m.–midnight.

**West** 2.6 miles to *Lodging:* Dutchess Motor Lodge, (845) 832-6400, $73, $7 laundry. ■ *Groceries:* Village Deli & Market, Ben's Store (both short-term resupply).

**West** 4 miles to the village of Wingdale (see Hoyt Road entry, below).

**Commuter Train**—On the south side of N.Y. 22, the Trail passes the A.T. station of a New York City commuter train (Metro-North). Trains leave the platform every Sa and Su at 2:41 p.m., 4:41 p.m., and 6:35 p.m. and arrive at Grand Central Terminal at 4:35 p.m., 6:35 p.m., and 8:20 p.m. Trains leave Grand Central at 7:48 a.m. and 9:50 a.m. on Sa and Su and arrive at the A.T. platform at 9:37 a.m. and 11:37 a.m. Fares are one-way $11.50 off-peak, $15.25 peak, and round-trip $23 off-peak, $30.50 peak. Weekday and additional weekend services are available to New York from stations in nearby Pawling and Wingdale.

**Wiley Shelter** (1940)—Sleeps 6. Privy. Water source is a pump 0.1 mile north of the shelter on the A.T. beyond tent platform; water should be treated.

**Hoyt Road**—**West** 1.5 miles to *Restaurant:* Buttonwood Café with bakery, serving B/L and ice cream; M, W 9–3, Th–F 9–5, Sa–Su 10–9.

**West** 3.3 miles *via* Hoyt and Webatuck roads to **Wingdale, N.Y. [P.O. ZIP 12594: M–F 8–5, Sa 8–12:30; (845) 832-6147]**. To reach Wingdale Metro-North Station, continue south on N.Y. 22 for about one mile. ■ *Lodging:* Dutchess Motor Lodge (see above). ■ *Groceries:* Wingdale Super Market with ATM and Food Market (both long-term resupply). ■ *Restaurants:* Ben's Deli; Pizza Express; Adams Diner, open 24 hours; Cousin's Pizza; Peking Kitchen; Cousin's Café, deli and ice cream. ■ *Other services:* Wingdale Hardware.

*"I think," said Christopher Robin,*

*"that we ought to eat all our provisions now,*

*so that we shant' have so much to carry."*

—A.A. MILNE

# Connecticut

| Miles from Katahdin | Features | Services | Elev. | Miles from Springer |
|---|---|---|---|---|
| 734.0 | Conn. State Line– Hoyt Rd, N.Y. **Wingdale, NY 12594** | R (W–1.5m M; 3.3m PO, G, M, L, f) | 400 | 1,442.2 |
| 733.3 | Conn.55 **Gaylordsville, CT 06755** | R (E–2.5m PO, G) | 580 | 1,442.9 |
| 732.2 | Ten Mile Hill | | 1,000 | 1,444.0 |
| 731.2 | **Ten Mile River Lean-to** *4mS; 8.4mN* | S, w | 290 | 1,445.0 |
| 731.0 | Ten Mile River | C, w | 280 | 1,445.2 |
| 730.3 | Trail to Bulls Bridge Parking Area | E–0.2m R; 0.5m G, @ | 450 | 1,445.9 |
| 729.6 | Schaghticoke Rd | R | 320 | 1,446.6 |
| 727.9 | Schaghticoke Mtn | | 1,331 | 1,448.3 |
| 726.7 | Conn.–N.Y. State Line | | 1,250 | 1,449.5 |
| 726.3 | Indian Rocks | | 1,290 | 1,449.9 |
| 725.7 | Schaghticoke Mtn Campsite | C, w | 950 | 1,450.5 |
| 723.8 | Thayer Brook | | 900 | 1,452.4 |
| 722.8 | **Mt. Algo Lean-to** *8.4mS; 7.3mN* | C, S, w | 655 | 1,453.4 |
| 722.5 | Conn. 341, Schaghti-coke Rd **Kent, CT 06757** | R (E–0.8m PO, G, M, L, O, D, f, cl, sh, @; 3.3m L) | 350 | 1,453.7 |
| 719.7 | Skiff Mtn Rd | R | 850 | 1,456.5 |
| 718.3 | State Johns Ledges | | 900 | 1,457.9 |
| 717.8 | River Rd | R | 480 | 1,458.4 |
| 715.5 | **Stewart Hollow Brook Lean-to** *7.3mS; 10mN* | C, S, w | 425 | 1,460.7 |
| 715.1 | Stony Brook Campsite | C, w | 440 | 1,461.1 |
| 713.1 | River Rd | R | 460 | 1,463.1 |
| 712.3 | Silver Hill Campsite | C, nw | 1,000 | 1,463.9 |
| 711.4 | Conn. 4 **Cornwall Bridge, CT 06754** | R (E–0.9m PO, G, L, O, V, f, @; 1.9m C, sh) | 700 | 1,464.8 |
| 711.3 | Guinea Brook | | 650 | 1,464.9 |
| 711.2 | Old Sharon Rd | R | 750 | 1,465.0 |
| 710.0 | Hatch Brook | | 880 | 1,466.2 |
| 709.3 | Pine Knob Loop Trail | E–0.9m C, sh | 1,150 | 1,466.9 |
| 708.9 | Caesar Rd, Caesar Brook Campsite | C, w | 760 | 1,467.3 |
| 706.7 | Carse Brook | w | 810 | 1,469.5 |

| Miles from Katahdin | Features | Services | Elev. | Miles from Springer |
|---|---|---|---|---|
| 706.6 | West Cornwall Rd **West Cornwall, CT 06796; Sharon, CT 06069** | R (E–2.2m PO, G, M, O) (W–4.7m PO, G, M, L, D, cl) | 800 | 1,469.6 |
| 705.5 | **Pine Swamp Brook Lean-to** *10mS; 12.8mN* | S, w | 1,075 | 1,470.7 |
| 704.6 | Sharon Mtn Rd | R | 1,150 | 1,471.6 |
| 704.3 | Mt. Easter | | 1,350 | 1,471.9 |
| 703.1 | Sharon Mtn Campsite | C, w | 1,200 | 1,473.1 |
| 700.3 | Belter's Campsite | C, w | 770 | 1,475.9 |
| 699.9 | U.S. 7, Conn. 112 | R | 520 | 1,476.3 |
| 699.3 | U.S. 7, Housatonic River Bridge | R | 500 | 1,476.9 |
| 699.2 | Mohawk Trail | E–0.2m L, M | 500 | 1,477.0 |
| 697.4 | Water Street, Hydroelectric Plant | R, w, sh (E–0.5m PO, L, C, M) | 530 | 1,478.8 |
| 697.3 | Iron Bridge, Housatonic River **Falls Village, CT 06031** | R | 510 | 1,478.9 |
| 696.7 | Housatonic River Rd, Great Falls | R | 650 | 1,479.5 |
| 696.2 | Spring | w | 750 | 1,480.0 |
| 693.9 | Prospect Mtn | | 1,475 | 1,482.3 |
| 693.2 | **Limestone Spring Lean-to** *12.8mS; 8mN* | W–0.5m C, S, w | 980 | 1,483.0 |
| 693.1 | Rand's View | | 1,250 | 1,483.1 |
| 692.3 | Billy's View | | 1,150 | 1,483.9 |
| 689.8 | U.S. 44 **Salisbury, CT 06068** | R (W–0.4m PO, G, L, M, @; 2.4m M, L, D, cl, f) | 700 | 1,486.4 |
| 689.1 | Conn. 41, Undermountain Rd **Salisbury, CT 06068** | R (W–0.8m PO, G, L, M, @; 2.8m M, L, D, cl, f) | 720 | 1,487.1 |
| 688.9 | Plateau Campsite | C, w | 800 | 1,487.3 |
| 686.4 | Lions Head | | 1,738 | 1,489.8 |
| 685.7 | **Riga Lean-to** *8mS; 1.2mN* | C, S, w | 1,610 | 1,490.5 |
| 685.1 | Ball Brook Campsite | C, w | 1,650 | 1,491.1 |
| 684.5 | Brassie Brook (south branch), **Brassie Brook Lean-to** *1.2mS; 8.8mN* | C, S, w | 1,705 | 1,491.7 |
| 684.0 | Undermountain Trail, Riga Jct | | 1,820 | 1,492.2 |

| 683.8 | Bear Mtn Rd | | 1,920 | 1,492.4 |
|---|---|---|---|---|
| 683.1 | Bear Mtn | | 2,316 | 1,493.1 |
| 682.4 | Conn.–Mass. State Line | | 1,800 | 1,493.8 |

*Campfires are prohibited on the Trail in Connecticut, and camping is permitted only at designated sites. Ridgerunners patrol the state's 52 A.T. miles and serve as caretakers at Sages Ravine campsite.*

Southbounders and northbounders pass each other regularly now, each with a determined mindset. Take a moment to hear each direction's viewpoint. For a while, you'll be following a wheelchair-accessible trail. How apropos after experiencing the hiker shuffle. Lodging becomes pricier, but hospitality abounds. Southbounders should consider the hunting seasons and the need to wear bright "blaze" orange. If hiking with a four-footed friend, keep its safety in mind, too.

**AMC–Connecticut Chapter**—The Trails Committee of the AMC–Connecticut Chapter maintains the 52.3 miles from the New York–Connecticut state line to Sages Ravine, just across the Massachusetts line. The club can be reached at (413) 528-6333; <www.ct-amc.org>.

**Conn. 55—East** 2.5 miles to **Gaylordsville, Conn. [P.O. ZIP 06755: M–F 7:30–1 & 2–5, Sa 7:30–12:30; (860) 354-9727].** *Groceries:* Gaylordsville Country Store, (860) 350-3802 (short-term resupply), M–F 6–8, Sa 6–6, Su 6–3, with deli, ATM, and pay phone.

**Ten Mile River Lean-to** (1996)—Sleeps 6. Privy. Tentsites available nearby at a campsite. Water source is a hand pump 0.2 mile north of the lean-to.

**Bulls Bridge Road—East** 0.5 mile to Country Market (short-term resupply) with fruit, Ben & Jerry's, water, ATM, and Internet access. On the way to the store, you will cross the Housatonic River on Bulls Bridge, one of a handful of covered bridges still standing in Connecticut. A bridge has spanned the river here since the mid-1700s. During the Revolutionary War, George Washington and his army used this crossing on several occasions. The current bridge dates to the early 1800s.

**Indian Rocks**—Half a mile north of the only place along the entire A.T. where the Trail (briefly) crosses an Indian reservation. Most of the land from here down to the river is claimed by the Schaghticoke tribe, recognized by the state and briefly (January 2004–May 2005) by the federal government. The tribe, actually the remnants of several tribes, played a unique communications role during the Revolutionary War by transmitting signals along the ridges between Long Island Sound in N.Y. and Stockbridge, Mass., a distance of nearly 100 miles, in about 2 hours.

**Mt. Algo Lean-to** (1986)—Sleeps 6. Privy. Water source is on blue-blaze leading to lean-to, 15 yards in front of shelter.

**Conn. 341—East** 0.8 mile to **Kent, Conn. [P.O. ZIP 06757: M–F 8–1 & 2–5, Sa 8:30–12:30; (860) 927-3435].** ■ *Lodging:* Fife 'n Drum Inn & Restaurant, (860) 927-3509, closed Tu, rooms $125D weekdays, $140D weekends, $15EAP, no dogs, call for reservations, please discard broken gear and excess trash in the dumpster next to the restaurant; Gibb House B&B, (860) 927-1754; Star Bucks Inn, (860) 927-1788, $175D-$235D plus tax, includes full B, check-in 4 p.m., check-out 11 a.m., reasonable level of personal hygiene appreciated, <frontdesk@starbuckinn.com> or <www.starbuckinn.com>. ■ *Groceries:* Davis IGA (long-term resupply); Kent Market (short-term resupply), with deli sandwiches, 6–8 daily. ■ *Restaurants:* Wasabi Japanese; Shanghai Chinese; Kent Pizza Garden, L/D, 11–10; Kent Coffee and Chocolate Co.; Stroble Baking Co., with home-made breads; Kent Pharmacy, ice cream; Paison's Italian; Panini Café, ice cream, free Sa-night concerts 7–8 Memorial Day–Labor Day. ■ *Outfitter:* Backcountry Outfitters, (860) 927-3377, <info@bcoutfitters.com>, backpacking gear and supplies, holds UPS packages shipped to 5 Bridge St., Kent, CT 06757, white gas & denatured alcohol by the ounce, open M–Sa 9–6, Su 10–4. ■ *Internet access:* Kent Memorial Library. ■ *Other services:* banks with ATM; Kent Laundromat with CATV, WiFi, free shower and storage locker area for hikers, open 6 a.m. –11 p.m., last wash at 10; doctor; dentist; pharmacy; House of Books, with guides, maps, fax, UPS and FedEx services, open daily; Kent Video & Photo, same-day film service; Eisner Limo and Taxi, (845) 877-3613, <LIMOMAN3613@aol.com>, service 24/7 to nearby hospital and all airports, Metro North stations, *etc.*, will transport well-behaved dogs.

**North** 2.5 miles *via* U.S. 7 to *Lodging:* Rosewood Meadow B&B, (860) 927-4334, shuttle provided to and from town.

**Red-pine plantation**—The pines along the "river walk" north of Kent have seen hard times due to an insect blight. Most of the trees are now dead. The Connecticut Chapter of AMC harvested some of the dying trees to build new shelters, including the one at Ten Mile River.

Kent

**Stewart Hollow Brook Lean-to** (1980s)—Sleeps 6. Privy. Water source is reliable Stony Brook, 0.4 mile north of the lean-to on the A.T.

**Silver Hill Campsite**—Campsite, with privy, swing, and pavilion sheltering two picnic tables, are what's left of the Silver Hill Shelter that burned down in 1991. No water. Water pump is broken. Northbounders can get water from stream 0.5 mile south or spring 1.1 miles south. Southbounders can get water from Guinea Brook 1.2 miles north.

**Mohawk Trail**—The former route of the A.T. starts north of Guinea Brook on the A.T., passes through Cornwall Bridge, and returns to the A.T. near Falls Village.

**Conn. 4—East** 0.9 mile to **Cornwall Bridge, Conn. [P.O. ZIP 06754: M–F 8–1 & 2–5, Sa 9–12:30; (860) 672-6710].** ■ *Lodging:* Hitching Post Motel, (860) 672-6219, $65D and up weekdays, $85D and up weekends, $15EAP, laundry service $5 and up, shuttle available depending on staffing; Housatonic Meadows Lodge B&B, (860) 672-6067, $110; Cornwall Inn & Restaurant, open year-round, (800) 786-6884, <www.cornwallinn.com>, hiker rate $125D, $150 for 4 in room with 2 queen beds; includes continental B, pool, hot tub, Internet access, restaurant and lounge open Th–Su, L/D $8–$30. ■ *Groceries:* Baird's General Store (short-term resupply), with deli, full B, ice cream, and pay phone. ■ *Outfitter:* Housatonic River Outfitters, (860) 672-1010, <www.hflyshop@aol.com>, open 7 days 9–5, limited hiker gear, canister fuel and fuel by ounce, will accept UPS and FedEx sent to 24 Kent Rd., Cornwall Bridge, CT 06754, but not responsible for packages. Shuttle available by appointment only, $20 and up depending on distance. ■ *Other services:* Housatonic Veterinary Care, (860) 672-4948. ■ *Camping:* Housatonic Meadows State Park, (860) 672-6772, 1 mile north of town on U.S. 7. Campsite $16 per night for up to 6 per site; open mid-Apr to Jan 1, water shut off Oct 15. The park may be self-service in midweek; registration information at the main cabin by the gate. Showers free but check with registration desk; pay phone; no pets, no alcoholic beverages allowed. Accessible from the A.T. *via* Pine Knob Loop Trail (see below).

**Guinea Brook**—The AMC Connecticut Chapter installed stepping stones in the brook. In heavy rain, you may want to take the bypass: Northbounders should turn east on Conn. 4 and go downhill to unpaved Old Sharon Road on the north, which rejoins the A.T. on the other side of the stream. Southbounders should turn east on the dirt road that the Trail crosses before the brook, then follow it to Conn. 4, and turn south.

**Pine Knob Loop Trail**—Housatonic Meadows State Park (see above) can be reached from the A.T. by taking the blue-blazed Pine Knob Loop Trail 0.5 mile to U.S. 7, then following the highway north for 0.4 mile. You can return to the A.T. *via* the Pine Knob Loop Trail.

**West Cornwall Road—East** 2.2 miles to **West Cornwall, Conn. [P.O. ZIP 06796: M–F 8–1 & 2–5, Sa 8:30–12; (860) 672-6791]**, site of a historical covered bridge spanning a whitewater section of the Housatonic River. ■ *Groceries:* Berkshire Country Store (short-term resupply), deli, picnic benches, M–F 7–7, Sa 8–6, Su 8–5; West Cornwall Market (short-term resupply), M–Th 6–7, F–Sa 6–8. ■ *Other services:* restaurants and gift shops. ■ *Outfitter:* Clarke Outdoors, (860) 672-6365, <www.clarkeoutdoors.com>, is located on U.S. 7 south of the village, with tube, canoe, and kayak rentals; limited outdoor gear and sportswear.

**West** 4.7 miles to **Sharon, Conn. [P.O. ZIP 06069: M–F 8–5, Sa 9:30–1:30; (860) 364-5306]**, with a supermarket, restaurant serving B/L/D, laundry, motel, bank with ATM, pharmacy, and hospital.

**Pine Swamp Brook Lean-to** (1989)—Sleeps 6. Privy. Water is available on the blue-blazed trail.

**Hang Glider View**—Occasionally still used as a hang-glider launch site, the view is toward Lime Rock Park, where Paul Newman and other celebrities have sped their cars around a classic 1.53-mile racecourse. Hikers staying at nearby Sharon Mountain Campsite on Jul 4 can stroll to the viewpoint for a huge fireworks show.

**U.S. 7/Mohawk Trail**—*Restaurant* and *Lodging:* Mountainside Café, (860) 824-7886, M–Th 6:30 a.m.–3 p.m., F 6:30–8, Sa 7–8, Su 6:30–8; cabin rental $75 (hiker rate), no restrictions on number in room; call for reservations. Not available in winter. *Directions:* At bridge over Housatonic River 0.2 mile north on U.S. 7, or stay on A.T. and take blue-blazed Mohawk Trail 0.2 mile east to U.S. 7.

**Wheelchair-accessible trail**—South of Falls Village, the A.T. hooks up with the River Trail, converted to create a handicap-accessible loop trail using part of the A.T. and an old racetrack. Also nearby is a nature trail that provides insight into the area's history. The stone ruins near the Trail were part of a pre-Civil War plan to turn the town into a giant industrial city. A stone canal would have channeled water from the Housatonic to power the village's dreams of grandeur. When crowds gathered for the opening of the canal in 1851, the walls leaked; builders had failed to place mortar between its rocks, and the project eventually died, leaving Falls Village the quiet backwater it is today.

**Water Street**—**East** 0.5 mile to **Falls Village, Conn. [P.O. ZIP 06031: M–F 8:30–1 & 2–5, Sa 8:30–12; (860) 824-7781]**. ■ *Lodging:* Falls Village Inn & Restaurant, (860) 824-4910, $105–$200D plus tax weekdays, $135–$230D plus tax weekends, $25 cot in room, $25EAP, includes voucher for hot B at local restaurant, check-in 3 p.m., check-out 11 a.m. ■ *Restaurants:* Toymakers Café, (860) 824-8168, B/L, Th–F 7–2, Sa–Su 7–4, free tentsites; Falls Village Inn and Restaurant, open W–Sa L 11:30 a.m.-2:30 p.m., D 5–10, Su brunch 11–3, D 5–8, German-American cuisine, historic inn and tavern; Pizza Restaurant; Mountainside Café (one mile south on Route 7, see Mohawk Trail entry above); Sweet William's Bakery, open M–Sa 10–3. ■ *Other services:* Liquor store has sodas and hiker snacks; Jacob's Garage has snack machines, but please remove your pack so that the dog won't be alarmed; free railroad-car exhibit, including a rebuilt caboose, offers self-serve information; information also available at the town hall; bank with ATM and pay phone.

**Hydroelectric Plant**—Cold shower and water are available outside the small, vine-covered building past the transformer. Look for silver shower head poking through ivy, with a small concrete pad below. Water faucet is below shower head.

**Iron Bridge over Housatonic**—Built by the Berlin Construction Co. of Connecticut in 1903. The same company built the iron bridge that now takes hikers over Swatara Creek in Pennsylvania.

**Picnic Area**—North of bridge along the river, opposite the power plant, are picnic tables (no water), fire pits, a privy, trash cans, and parking area.

**Great Falls Dam**—North 0.5 mile on the A.T. are the Great Falls that gave Falls Village its name. Because the power plant below draws most of the river's water, the falls appear "great" only during heavy rains or snowmelt. In 1996, Falls Village played host to a most unusual visitor from the north. A bull moose that wandered down the Trail tried to negotiate the sluiceway near the dam, but fell in. Workers from the power plant managed to rescue the bewildered beast. For a few days, it attracted throngs of villagers and day-hikers as it munched on river plants and other vegetation. The animal eventually died, but not from a broken leg, as first believed; the cause was attributed to a brain disease that affects moose.

**Limestone Spring Lean-to** (1986)—Sleeps 6. Privy is uphill to the right. Follow the stream to where a spring comes out of a small limestone cave.

**Rand's View**—The A.T. passes by this vista, which offers views of the Taconic Range from Lion's Head to Mt. Everett and Jug End. *No camping allowed.*

**U.S. 44**—West 0.4 mile to **Salisbury, Conn. [P.O. ZIP 06068: M–F 8–1 & 2–5, Sa 9–12; (860) 435-5072]**. Revolutionary War leader Ethan Allen, famous in Vermont history, studied here for a short time in preparation for entrance to Yale University (which he never attended). Allen moved to the New York area that later became Vermont. For northbounders, turn west on U.S. 44 to town. For southbounders, it is best to follow Conn. 41, Undermountain Road, 0.8 mile into town. Water is available from a fountain at town hall and also from a spigot in the cemetery on Lower Cable Road. ■ *Lodging:* White Hart Inn, (860) 435-0030, <www.whitehartinn.com>, $89 hiker rate up to 4 depending on room, pets $25, restaurant B/L/D, mail drops accepted for guests, UPS or FedEx to 15 Undermountain

Salisbury

Road, Salisbury, CT 06068, or USPS to P.O. Box 545, Salisbury, CT 06068; Maria McCabe offers rooms in her home to hikers, (860) 435-0593, $35PP, includes shower, use of living room, cooking outside, pets outside (no fee), no visitors in home, cash only, mail drops accepted for guests at 4 Grove Street, Salisbury, CT 06068; Vanessa Breton offers 3 rooms in her home, each with 2 single beds, to hikers, (860) 435-9577, $35 per person, includes shower, laundry $5, use of living room, cooking outside, pets outside (no fee), no visitors in home, cash only, mail drops accepted for guests at 7 The Lockup Road, Salisbury, CT 06068. ■ *Groceries:* LaBonne's Epicure Market, (860) 435-2559 (long-term resupply), M–Sa, open 8–7, Su until 6. ■ *Restaurants:* White Hart Inn, (860) 435-0030, B M–Sa 7–10, Su 8–10, L M–Su 11:30–3, D M–Su 5–9; The Roast Coffee House & Internet Café, (860) 435-0600, B/L, with fruit and vegetable juices, M–Sa 7–2, Su 8–12. ■ *Internet access:* Scoville Memorial Library and The Roast. ■ *Other services:* pay phone; pharmacy, M–Sa 8–6, Su 8–4; bank with ATM. When open, town hall offers restroom inside.

**West** 2.4 miles to Lakeville, Conn. ■ *Lodging:* Inn at Iron-masters, (860) 435-9844, $115S, $125D weekdays, $180 weekends, $15EAP, continental B, dogs allowed in certain rooms without fee, pool. ■ *Other services:* hardware store, pizza restaurant, laundromat 7–9, doctor, bank with ATM, and dentist.

 **Conn. 41 (Undermountain Road)—West** 0.8 mile to Salisbury (see previous entry).

**Riga Lean-to** (1960s)—Sleeps 6. Privy. The only shelter in Connecticut with a view. Trail to the shelter reported overgrown and not marked, shelter sign missing; without a map, the shelter is easy to miss. The shelter opens to the east, providing sunrise views. Tentsites are also available. Water is a spring on a blue-blazed trail to the left of the clearing at the A.T. A second source is where the trail to the lean-to crosses a small stream. Spring may not run in dry years.

**Brassie Brook Lean-to** (1980s)—Sleeps 6. Privy. A log lean-to with tentsites available. Water is available from a stream on the A.T. 50 feet north of the side trail to the lean-to.

**Bear Mountain**—At 2,316 feet, this is the highest peak in Connecticut but not the highest ground, which instead falls on the flank of nearby Mt. Frissel, the peak of which is in Massachusetts. The northbound descent into Sages Ravine is rocky and steep. In foul weather, an alternative route for northbounders is east on the Undermountain Trail for 0.8 mile, then north on the Paradise Lane Trail for 2.1 miles, reconnecting with the A.T. near Sages Ravine, a net 1.7-mile detour.

*"I am not going to advocate...the abandoning of the improved modes of travel, but I am going to brag as lustily as I can on behalf of the pedestrian, and show how all the shining angels second and accompany the man who goes afoot, while all the dark spirits are ever looking out for a chance to ride."*
—John Burroughs

# Massachusetts

| Miles from Katahdin | Features | Services | Elev. | Miles from Springer |
|---|---|---|---|---|
| 682.4 | Mass.–Conn. State Line | | 1,800 | 1,493.8 |
| 682.3 | Sages Ravine Brook Campsite | C, w | 1,360 | 1,493.9 |
| 681.7 | Sages Ravine | w | 1,340 | 1,494.5 |
| 680.4 | Laurel Ridge Campsite | C, w | 1,750 | 1,495.8 |
| 678.6 | Race Mtn | | 2,365 | 1,497.6 |
| 677.5 | Race Brook Falls Trail | E–0.4m C, w | 1,950 | 1,498.7 |
| 676.8 | Mt. Everett | R | 2,602 | 1,499.4 |
| 676.1 | Guilder Pond Picnic Area | R | 2,050 | 1,500.1 |
| 675.7 | **The Hemlocks Lean-to** *8.8mS; 0.1mN* | S, w | 1,880 | 1,500.5 |
| 675.6 | **Glen Brook Lean-to** *0.1mS; 14.3mN* | S, w | 1,885 | 1,500.6 |
| 675.0 | Elbow Trail | | 1,750 | 1,501.2 |
| 673.3 | Jug End | | 1,750 | 1,502.9 |
| 672.2 | Jug End Rd | R (E–0.1m w) | 890 | 1,504.0 |
| 671.3 | Mass. 41 **South Egremont, MA 01258** | R (W–1.2m PO, G, M, L, @) | 810 | 1,504.9 |
| 669.5 | South Egremont Rd, Shays' Rebellion Monument | R | 700 | 1,506.7 |
| 667.7 | U.S. 7 **Sheffield, MA 01257; Great Barrington, MA 01230** | R (E–3.2m PO, G, M, L; 6m C, M) (W–0.1m C, G, sh; 1.5m G; 1.8m PO, G, M, L, O, D, V, cl, f) | 700 | 1,508.5 |
| 666.8 | Housatonic River | R | 720 | 1,509.4 |
| 664.8 | Homes Rd | R | 1,150 | 1,511.4 |
| 663.4 | East Mtn | w | 1,800 | 1,512.8 |
| 661.3 | **Tom Leonard Lean-to** *14.3mS; 5.3mN* | S (E–0.2m w) | 1,540 | 1,514.9 |
| 660.2 | Lake Buel Rd | R | 1,150 | 1,516.0 |
| 659.3 | Mass. 23 **Monterey, MA 01245** | R (E–4.3m PO, G, M, @) (W–1.6m H; 2.7m M; 4m PO, G, M, L, O, D, V, cl, f) | 1,050 | 1,516.9 |
| 658.1 | Blue Hill Rd (Stony Brook Rd) | R | 1,550 | 1,518.1 |
| 657.3 | Benedict Pond | W–0.5m C, w | 1,620 | 1,518.9 |
| 656.7 | The Ledges | | 1,820 | 1,519.5 |

| Miles from Katahdin | Features | Services | Elev. | Miles from Springer |
|---|---|---|---|---|
| 656.0 | **Mt. Wilcox South Lean-to** *5.3mS; 2.1mN* | S, w | 1,720 | 1,520.2 |
| 654.2 | **Mt. Wilcox North Lean-to** *2.1mS; 14.8mN* | E–0.3m S, w | 1,950 | 1,522.0 |
| 653.6 | Beartown Mtn Rd | R, w | 1,800 | 1,522.6 |
| 650.4 | Fernside Rd | R, w | 1,200 | 1,525.8 |
| 650.1 | Shaker Campsite | C | 1,000 | 1,526.1 |
| 648.3 | Jerusalem Rd **Tyringham, MA 01264** | R, w (W– 0.6m PO, L; 0.9m C) | 930 | 1,527.9 |
| 645.3 | Webster Rd | R, w | 1,800 | 1,530.9 |
| 642.9 | Goose Pond Rd | R | 1,650 | 1,533.3 |
| 641.0 | Upper Goose Pond | | 1,500 | 1,535.2 |
| 640.2 | **Upper Goose Pond Cabin** *14.8mS; 9.3mN* | W–0.5m C, S, w | 1,483 | 1,536.0 |
| 639.0 | Mass. Turnpike (I-90) | | 1,400 | 1,537.2 |
| 638.9 | Greenwater Brook | w | 1,400 | 1,537.3 |
| 638.6 | U.S. 20 **Lee, MA 01238** | R (E–0.1m L) (W–5m PO, G, L, M, D, V, cl, f) | 1,400 | 1,537.6 |
| 637.8 | Tyne Rd | R | 1,750 | 1,538.4 |
| 637.3 | Beckett Mtn | | 2,180 | 1,538.9 |
| 635.5 | Finerty Pond | w | 1,900 | 1,540.7 |
| 633.2 | County Rd | R | 1,850 | 1,543.0 |
| 633.0 | Bald Top | | 2,040 | 1,543.2 |
| 631.4 | **October Mtn Lean-to** *9.3mS; 9mN* | S, w | 1,930 | 1,544.8 |
| 630.7 | West Branch Rd | R | 1,960 | 1,545.5 |
| 629.2 | Washington Mtn Rd, Pittsfield Rd **Becket, MA 01223** | R (E–0.1m C, w; 5m PO, D, V) | 2,000 | 1,547.0 |
| 627.2 | Stream | w | 1,950 | 1,549.0 |
| 626.0 | Blotz Rd | R | 1,850 | 1,550.2 |
| 625.3 | Warner Mtn | | 2,050 | 1,550.9 |
| 622.6 | **Kay Wood Lean-to** *9mS; 17.1mN* | E–0.2m S, w | 1,860 | 1,553.6 |
| 622.3 | Grange Hall Rd | R | 1,650 | 1,553.9 |
| 620.2 | CSX RailRd | | 1,199 | 1,556.0 |
| 619.6 | Mass. 8, Mass.9 **Dalton, MA 01226** | R, PO, G, M, L, D, cl, f, @ | 1,200 | 1,556.6 |
| 618.6 | Gulf Rd | R | 1,180 | 1,557.6 |
| 614.9 | Crystal Mtn Campsite | E–0.2m C, w | 2,100 | 1,561.3 |
| 614.5 | Gore Pond | | 2,050 | 1,561.7 |
| 612.0 | The Cobbles | | 1,850 | 1,564.2 |

| Miles from Katahdin | Features | Services | Elev. | Miles from Springer |
|---|---|---|---|---|
| 610.9 | Church St, Hoosic River **Cheshire, MA 01225** | R, PO, M, O, G, w | 950 | 1,565.3 |
| 610.8 | Hiker Kiosk | R | 970 | 1,565.4 |
| 610.3 | Mass. 8 **Adams, MA 01220** | R (E−0.8m L, cl; 2.4m O, f; 4m PO, G, L, M, D, V, cl) (W−0.2m G) | 990 | 1,565.9 |
| 609.5 | Outlook Ave | R | 1,350 | 1,566.7 |
| 606.8 | Old Adams Rd | R | 2,350 | 1,569.4 |
| 605.9 | **Mark Noepel Lean-to** *17.1mS; 7.1mN* | E−0.2m S, C, w | 2,750 | 1,570.3 |
| 605.3 | Jones Nose Trail, Saddle Ball Mtn | | 3,150 | 1,570.9 |
| 603.1 | Notch Rd; Rockwell Rd | R | 3,290 | 1,573.1 |
| 602.6 | Mt. Greylock, Bascom Lodge, Summit Rd | R closed | 3,491 | 1,573.6 |
| 599.4 | Notch Rd | R, w | 3,400 | 1,576.8 |
| 599.3 | **Wilbur Clearing Lean-to** *7.1mS; 10.4mN* | W−0.3m S, w | 2,325 | 1,576.9 |
| 597.2 | Pattison Rd | R, w | 900 | 1,579.0 |
| 596.3 | Mass. 2 **North Adams, MA 01247; Williamstown, MA 01267** | R (E−0.6m G, M, cl; 1m sh; 2.5m PO, G, L, M, D, V, cl) (W−0.4m G, L; 1.4m G, L, M; 2.6m PO, C, G, L, M, O, D, V, cl, sh, f) | 660 | 1,579.9 |
| 594.5 | Sherman Brook Campsite | w (W−0.1 m C) | 1,300 | 1,581.7 |
| 593.5 | Pine Cobble Trail | | 2,010 | 1,582.7 |
| 593.0 | Eph's Lookout | | 2,254 | 1,583.2 |
| 592.2 | Mass.−Vt. State Line, Long Trail (southern terminus) | | 2,330 | 1,584.0 |

*The state line is south of Sages Ravine, near the junction with Paradise Lane Trail. The painted state abbreviations on a tree are so faded they're almost invisible.*

From the peaks of Mt. Greylock to Mt. Everett, over hills and valleys, through towns and hamlets of the Berkshires, one is reminded of the cultural mecca of New England's famous writers, artists, and performers. Juicy, sweet blueberries abound in season near Becket. Water and mosquitoes seem to be everywhere—you've been warned!

**Sages Ravine**—Tent platforms and campsites available, staffed by ridgerunners who take turns as caretakers. No fires permitted. No fees charged. More than 100 acres of forest in the Sages Ravine area have never been cut.

---

**Berkshire Chapter of the Appalachian Mountain Club**—The A.T. Committee of the AMC–Berkshire Chapter maintains 89.5 miles from the Sages Ravine area to the Massachusetts–Vermont state line. Correspondence should be sent to Berkshire A.T. Committee, 964 South Main St., Great Barrington, MA 02130; <www.outdoors.org>; (413) 528-8003.

---

**Berkshire Bus Service**—The Berkshire Regional Transit Authority, (413) 499-2782 or (800) 292-2782, <www.berkshirerta.com>, serves the Trail towns of Great Barrington, Lee, Dalton, Cheshire, Adams, North Adams, and Williamstown. The buses run M–F 5:45 a.m.–7:20 p.m. and Sa 7:15–7; no service Su or holidays. Schedules may be posted in stores and post offices, but, to be sure, call for accurate, up-to-date information. The buses can be flagged down anywhere along Mass. 2 or 8 or U.S. 7, but there are designated bus stops. Popular trips for hikers include rides from Dalton west into Pittsfield, the region's hub with all major services, and from Cheshire south to the Berkshire Mall, with 103 shops and a 10-screen cinema. Maximum fare one way is $4.40 ($1.10 per community crossed, cash; drivers cannot make change); ask for free transfers.

**Peter Pan Bus Lines**—(888) 751-8800, <www.peterpanbus.com>. Buses run daily each way between NYC and Williamstown, Mass., stopping at towns near the A.T., including Canaan and Danbury in Connecticut and Great Barrington, Lee, Pittsfield, and Williamstown in Massachusetts. Call for schedules and rates.

**Laurel Ridge Campsite**—0.1 mile south of Bear Rock Falls, four campsites with single and double tent platforms and one group site with double tent platforms. Privy (composting). Water source is a spring off a short side trail south of campsites. *No fires permitted in this area.*

**Race Mountain**—A spectacular walk on a clear day; spooky when foggy. It's a steep drop-off to the east.

**Mt. Everett**—This mountain range is the second-highest on the A.T. in Massachusetts.

**Guilder Pond**—At 2,042 feet, the short side trail to the west leads to this highest body of water in Massachusetts. Picnic table and privy. For conservation reasons, please, no camping, swimming, or fishing.

**The Hemlocks Lean-to** (1999)—Sleeps 10. Privy (composting). Nestled in a hemlock grove, the lean-to offers a sleeping loft with overhang. Water source is on the blue-blazed access trail. If you cannot find water here, Glen Brook crosses the A.T. 50 yards north of the access trail to the lean-to.

**Glen Brook Lean-to** (1960s)—Sleeps 6. Privy. Tent platforms. Water source is a reliable stream to the left of the lean-to.

**Jug End Road—East** 0.1 mile to a reliable, piped spring, off the road to the right.

**Mass. 41—West** 0.1 mile to the Appalachian Trail Conservancy's Kellog Conservation Center (KCC) at the old April Hill farm, opened in May 2007. For the moment, it functions solely as an office for one ATC and one Appalachian Mountain Club staff member, both of whom are frequently in the field. There are no visitor or hiker services available, but the conservation work done out of this office helps ensure that beautiful and serene places like the farmland here is preserved as part of the A.T. experience forever. The property is insured for that business use only, and no public parking is allowed. Trailhead parking is available at Sheffield/Egremont Road, 1.8 Trail miles north. For more information, contact Adam Brown at (413) 528-8002 or <abrown@appalachiantrail.org>.

   **West** 1.2 miles to **South Egremont, Mass. [P.O. ZIP 01258: M–F 8:15–12 & 12:30–4, Sa 9–11:30; (413) 528-1571].** ■ *Lodging:* The Egremont Inn, (413) 528-2111, <www.egremontinn.com>, <theinn@vgernet.net>, a building dating back to 1780; $75s/D, $20EAP, B included, call for availability, free WiFi, no pets, pool, shuttle back to the Trail, mail drops accepted for guests if sent to 10 Old Sheffield Road, or P.O. Box 418, South Egremont, MA 01258; Weathervane Inn, (413) 528-9580, (800) 528-9580, <www.weathervaneinn.com>, 11-room B&B, each with private bath, full B, afternoon tea, a/c, $135–$250D, $30EAP, several rooms accommodate 3–4 people, prior arrangements for shuttle to and from Trail, outdoor pool, on-site massage services and yoga, walk to town services, packages accepted with stay and prior arrangements, no pets. ■ *Groceries:* Country Market, (413) 528-8081, with deli and lunch counter, 7 days 6–8, hiker-friendly. ■ *Restaurants:* Egremont Inn, W–Su; Mom's Country Café, with pizza and ice cream. ■ *Internet access:* library. ■ *Other services:* bank with ATM.

**Shays' Rebellion Monument**—Stone marker commemorates the last skirmish of a bloody farmers' revolt led by Revolutionary War veteran Daniel Shays against government taxes and tactics in 1787. The incident assisted Federalists in making their case for a strong central government with powers to tax and maintain a standing army.

**U.S. 7—East** 3.2 miles to **Sheffield, Mass. [P.O. ZIP 01257: M–F 9–4:30, Sa 9–12; (413) 229-8772]**. ■ *Lodging:* Race Brook Lodge, (413) 229-2916, <www.rblodge.com>, a restored 1790s barn open Su–Th $95–$150, F–Sa $125–$275, $20EAP, pets allowed in same room $15, Th–Sa D, mail drops accepted for guests at Route 41, Sheffield, MA 01257. ■ *Groceries:* Sheffield Market Place (long-term resupply), 6–9, hot foods, deli, and ice cream. ■ *Restaurant:* Village on the Green Restaurant and Pizzeria, M–F 10–9, Sa–Su 8–9. ■ *Other services:* bank, hardware store, ATM, and bus service.

**East** 6 miles to *Work for Stay:* Moon in the Pond Organic Farm, (413) 229-3092, <dom@mooninthepond.com>, 816 Barnum St., Sheffield, MA 01257. Organic meat-and-vegetable farmer Dominic Palumbo offers tentsites, an outdoor shower, and organic meals for a day or two to a week, in exchange for farm work. Transportation can be arranged to and from the Trail. Keep trying to call; not always next to the phone.

**West** 0.1 mile to the Corn Crib, (413) 528-4947, with fresh fruit, vegetables, ice cream, cold drinks, snacks, water, phone, shower, tenting, long-term parking.

**West** 1.5 miles to Guido's, with organic produce and deli.

**West** 1.8 miles to **Great Barrington, Mass. [P.O. ZIP 01230: M–F 9–4:30, Sa 9–12; (413) 528-3670]**. ■ *Lodging:* Lantern House Motel, (413) 528-2350, $55S, $65D, higher on weekends, $10EAP, call for reservations, free WiFi, continental B, one room available for pets $10 additional; Travelodge, (413) 528-2340, $55S, $65D, higher on weekends and during special events, pets allowed in some rooms for $10 fee, laundry, free WiFi but no computers available for guests, continental B, outdoor pool; Mountain View Motel, (413) 528-0250, $65S, $75D, higher on weekends, $5EAP, call for reservations, pets $20, free WiFi, some rooms with CATV, phone, refrigerator, microwave, continental B; Holiday Inn Express, (413) 528-1810, 20% discount on current rates, extended continental B, no pets, free WiFi and computers available for guests; Comfort Inn, (413) 644-3200, <www.berkshirecomfortinn.com>, 25% discount on current rates, deluxe continental B, laundry, no pets, indoor and outdoor pools, free WiFi and computers available for guests; Monument Mountain Motel, (413) 528-3272, <www.monumentmountainmotel.com>, $50S, $60D, $10EAP, higher on weekends and during special events, pets allowed $10, laundry, pool, coffee and tea when office is open, mail drops accepted for guests at U.S. 7, 247 Stockbridge Road, Great Barrington, MA 01230; The Seven Stones, <www.the-sevenstones.com>. ■ *Groceries:* Big Y Foods, open 7 days 7–9, and Price Chopper, M–Sa 6–midnight, Su 7–midnight (both long-term resupply). ■ *Restaurants:* numerous, in town center and north along U.S. 7. ■ *Other services:* K-Mart, ice-cream store, banks with ATM, hardware store, shoe repair, hospital, dentist, optician, pharmacy, veterinarian, movie theater, coin laundry, and taxi, (413) 528-0911. ■ *Bus service:* Bus tickets at Bill's Pharmacy, cash only.

**Tom Leonard Lean-to** (1970)—Sleeps 10. Privy. Located just south of Ice Gulch, a deep cleft in the landscape; the lean-to is visible from the A.T. Water source is a very cold stream 0.2 mile down a ravine to the left of the lean-to.

 **Mass. 23—East** 4.3 miles to **Monterey, Mass. [P.O. ZIP 01245: M–F 8:30–1 & 2–4:30, Sa 9–11:30; (413) 528-4670].** ■ *Groceries:* Monterey General Store (long-term resupply), with café, Internet, and pay phone; open M–Sa 7:30–6, Su 8–12.

**West** 1 mile to Lake Buel Road, turn left, first right driveway 0.6 mile uphill to *Hostel:* East Mountain Retreat Center, (413) 528-6617, <emrc@bcn.net>, $10 with shower; laundry $3; use of the library; 10 p.m. quiet curfew (no guests admitted after this hour) and prompt 8:30 a.m. checkout.

**West** 2.7 miles to *Restaurant:* Panda West L/D.

**West** 4 miles to Great Barrington (see above).

**Benedict Pond—West** 0.5 mile on a blue-blazed side trail to a sandy beach with picnic tables, pay phone, tentsites $10.

**Mt. Wilcox South Lean-to** (1930/2007)—Old lean-to sleeps 6. Privy. Built as a CCC project; approach trail was part of the original A.T. in Massachusetts. New shelter just beyond old one, completed in 2007. Water source is the spring crossed *en route* to the lean-to.

**Mt. Wilcox North Lean-to** (1930s)—Sleeps 10. Privy. Lean-to is on a 0.3-mile blue-blazed trail. Water source, the stream in front of the privy, may go dry in late summer.

**Shaker Campsite**—Tent platforms and privy available. Water is located north on the A.T.

**Tyringham Cobble**—Formed by a geological event that separated this hill from the mountain behind it, the cobble rises 400 feet above the village below. The hill and nearly 200 acres around it are owned by a conservation trust.

 **Jerusalem Road—West** 0.6 mile to **Tyringham, Mass. [P.O. ZIP 01264: M–F 9–12:30 & 4–5:30, Sa 8:30–12:30; (413) 243-1225].** May also be reached from Tyringham Main Road 1.1 mile north on A.T. Water fountain outside post office; pay phone next to library (no Internet). ■ *Lodging:* Cobble View B&B, (800) 467-4136, call for rates; no pets, no visitors; across from P.O.; drinks and snacks available.

**West** 0.9 mile to *Camping:* tenting allowed at outdoor pavilion next to the firehouse; Porta-potty.

**Jerusalem Road Spring—West** several yards to short path on left that leads to a piped spring (if you pass the first house on the right, you've gone too far).

**Upper Goose Pond Cabin**—AMC–Berkshire Chapter A.T. Committee maintains this cabin on a 0.5-mile side trail north of the pond. The cabin offers bunks, fireplace, covered porch, privy, swimming, and tent platforms. Open daily Memorial Day–Labor Day, then weekends through Columbus Day. During summer months, the resident volunteer caretaker brings water by canoe from a spring across the pond; otherwise, the pond is the water source. When the caretaker is not in residence, or when the cabin is closed for the season, hikers may camp on the porch or tent platforms. Privy behind the cabin and near tentsites. There is no fee for staying at this site; donations appreciated.

**U.S. 20**—**East** 0.1 mile to *Lodging:* Southern Comfort Lodge, (413) 243-9907, $49–$99; pets allowed, no fee; beach on Greenwater Pond; use of outside grill, canoes, kayaks, and rowboats; mail drops accepted for nonguests, no fee, 3949 Jacob's Ladder Road, Becket, MA 01223.

**West** 5 miles to **Lee, Mass. [P.O. ZIP 01238: M–F 8:30–5, Sa 9–12; (413) 243-1392],** home of the famous Tanglewood Festival at Tanglewood Performing Arts Center, an outdoor theater that hosts a series of rock, jazz, and country concerts throughout the summer. ■ *Lodging:* Best Value Inn, (413) 243-0501, Su–Th $65–$85, F–Sa $110–$195; Rodeway Inn, (413) 243-0813, Su–Th $65–$85, F–Sa $99–$185; Pilgrim Inn, (413) 243-1328, Su–Th $79–$95, F–Sa $95–$195. ■ *Groceries:* Price Chopper Supermarket (long-term resupply). ■ *Restaurants:* Joe's Diner, Athena's Pizza House, and several fast-food outlets. ■ *Other services:* Lee Coin-Op Laundromat, banks, hardware store, doctor, dentist, pharmacy, health clinic, veterinarian, and taxi.

**October Mountain Lean-to** (1980s)—Sleeps 12. Privy. Food-hoist cables available. Do not leave packs unattended. A large lean-to with porch. Water source is a stream just south of the lean-to on the A.T.

**Washington Mountain Road**—**East** 0.1 mile to the "Cookie Lady," Marilyn Wiley, (413) 623-5859, who lives on a blueberry farm on the left of Washington Mountain Road. Water spigot near the garage door is for hikers. A.T. signs are posted; please sign register on the steps. Homemade cookies are often available to munch on as you watch hummingbirds buzz her feeder; pick your own blueberries at reasonable rates during season. Camping is allowed on the property if you ask permission first. Will also hold packages and provide shuttles. Roy and Marilyn Wiley, 47 Washington Mountain Rd., Becket, MA 01223.

**East** 5 miles to **Becket, Mass. [P.O. ZIP 01223: M–F 8–4, Sa 9–11:30; (413) 623-8845],** where the A.T. is listed as a historical site in a town settled more than 300 years ago. Only available services are a doctor and veterinarian.

**Kay Wood Lean-to** (1980s)—Sleeps 10. Privy, bear box. Lean-to is named for Kay Wood, a 1972 thru-hiker. Ms. Wood is now in her 80s and continues to work as a Trail maintainer in the area. Water source is the stream in front of the lean-to.

**Dalton, Mass. [P.O. ZIP 01226: M–F 8:30–4:30, Sₐ 9–12; (413) 684-0364]**—The A.T. goes through the eastern side of town, where most services are available. Depot Street, which the A.T. follows into town from the south, offers a pharmacy and restaurants. Other services are within 0.5 mile of the A.T. ■ *Lodging:* Thomas Levardi, 83 Depot St., allows hikers to use a water spigot outside his home and provides the hospitality of his front porch and back yard for tenting (get permission first), Internet when Tom is available, no restroom or garbage facilities (so, be gracious hikers); Shamrock Village Inn, (413) 684-0860, S–Th $62S, $69D, F–Sa $90S, $99D, hiker box, well-behaved pets allowed. ■ *Groceries:* Cumberland Farms with

**Dalton**

Pizza Palace

Dalton Coin Laundry

Dalton General Store

Center Pond

Mass. 8-A & 9

Duff & Dell's Mill Tavern

Depot St.

Centennial St.

L.P. Adams

Levardi's

Cumberland Farms

Angelina's Subs

Shamrock Inn

Shamrocks Pub

Daly St.

Dalton Restaurant

Post Office

Bank

Library

Pharmacy

High St.

Town Hall

Town Garage

Mass. 8 & 9

Main Street Cemetery

Housatonic St.

Walker Brook

Park Ave.

Main St.

Crane Paper Museum

N

0          0.5 mile

ATM, Dalton General Store with deli (both short-term resupply). ■ *Restaurants:* Mill Tavern, L/D; Duff & Dell's Variety, B/L, closed Su; Pizza Palace; Angelina's Subs with veggie burgers; Dalton Restaurant, serves D daily, Th–Sa with live entertainment; Shamrocks Restaurant and Pub, L/D, closed M. ■ *Internet access:* library, 1-hour limit. ■ *Other services:* Dalton Laundry, M–F 8:30–6, Sa 8:30–4, Su 8:30–12, provides towel and wash cloth for clean-up in bathroom sink and TV while you wait; banks; L.P. Adams sells Coleman fuel; doctor; dentist; pharmacy. ■ *Bus service:* Connections to Pittsfield, with all major services and various AYCE options.

**Crystal Mountain Campsite**—0.2 mile east. Privy. Water is north on Trail.

**The Cobbles**—These outcroppings of marble overlook the Hoosic River Valley and offer views of the town of Cheshire and Mt. Greylock. The Hoosic River, which is crossed south of Cheshire, flows north and empties into the Hudson River in New York.

**Cheshire, Mass. [P.O. ZIP 01225: M–F 8:30–1 & 2–4:30, Sa 7:30–11:30; (413) 743-3184]**—The Trail skirts the center of town to the east and crosses Mass. 8 0.4 mile east of the main stoplight at Church Street. St. Mary of the Assumption Church allows hikers to get water and use the restroom, but no tenting. Church may allow hikers to stay in parish hall and use parking lot, but speak to Father David Raymond first. ■ *Groceries:* H.D. Reynolds, a general store, hiker snacks, and Coleman fuel. ■ *Restaurants:* Bass Water Grill, B/L/D, closed M; Diane's Twist, M–Su 11:30–8, mid-Apr–mid-Oct, outdoor spigot, deli sandwiches, soda, and ice cream. ■ *Other services:* bank with ATM; AT Bicycle Works & Outfitters, hiking and backpacking supplies. ■ *Bus service:* Stop across the street from the post office, connections to the Berkshire Mall and Adams, Mass.

**Hiker kiosk**—A detailed town map with hiker services marked.

**Mass. 8—East** 0.8 mile to *Lodging:* Harbour House Inn, (413) 743-8959, <www.harbourhouseinn.com>, operated by Eva and Sam Amuso, provides rooms midweek $120–$260. Rate includes B, Internet access, shuttle to the Trail; laundry available. Hiker-friendly.

**East** 2.4 miles to *Outfitter:* Berkshire Outfitters, (413) 743-5900, <www.berkshireoutfitters.com>, M–Sa 10–5, Th until 8, Su 11–4, with hiker supplies, Coleman fuel, minor equipment repairs.

**East** 4 miles to **Adams, Mass. [P.O. ZIP 01220: M–F 8:30–4:30, Sa 10–12; (413) 743-5177]**, an alternative to the smaller town of Cheshire. Adams is accessible by the Berkshire Bus Service. ■ *Lodging:* Mount Greylock Inn, (413) 743-2665, <mountgreylockinn.com>, $84–$154, includes B. ■ *Groceries:* Big Y Foods supermarket (long-term resupply). ■ *Restaurants:* Pizza Jim's, (413) 743-9161, will deliver; CJ's Pub and Daily Grind Coffee; many fast-food outlets. ■ *Other services:* Thrifty Bundle Laundromat, banks, hardware store, doctor, dentist, Brooks Drug Store, veterinarian, and Western Union.

**West** 0.2 mile to *Groceries:* Convenience store (short-term resupply), deli sandwiches, pay phone.

**Mark Noepel Lean-to & Bassett Brook Campsite** (1985)—Sleeps 10. Privy is on a 0.1-mile, blue-blazed trail. Porcupines make regular appearances at this lean-to with tent platforms. Water source is from a spring to the right of the lean-to.

**Saddle Ball Mountain**—At 3,238 feet and located at the A.T. junction with the Jones Nose Trail, Saddle Ball is the A.T.'s first 3,000-footer north of North Marshall in Shenandoah National Park.

**Mt. Greylock**—Topped by a war memorial, paved road, and Bascom Lodge (closed, see below), Greylock is Massachusetts' highest peak (3,491 feet). A stone tower, crowned by a globe lit at night, is a tribute to the state's war dead. You can climb the 89 steps to the top for views of the Green, Catskill, and Taconic mountains and surrounding towns. The mountain has inspired literary giants from Thoreau to Hawthorne. *Thunderbolt Shelter on Mt. Greylock is an emergency-only warming hut. No camping or fires on the summit.*

**Bascom Lodge**—*closed* until 2009. The road to the summit is closed for repair and repaving, with no vehicular traffic allowed to the summit. Hikers should plan accordingly, because there is no food, water, or lodging at this landmark. Hikers should *not* mail packages to the lodge or make plans to meet anyone who was thinking of driving up by car.

**Wilbur Clearing Lean-to** (1970)—Sleeps 8. Privy. Located 0.3 mile down the Money Brook Trail; very popular during the summer months. Tentsites available. Water source is an intermittent stream to the right of the lean-to.

**Mass. 2/North Adams**—BRTA hourly bus service is available on this road (see page 182). *Note: The town of North Adams extends one mile west and several miles east of the Trail; the Williamstown line is 1.4 miles west of the Trail.*

**East** 0.6 mile to ■ *Groceries:* Price Chopper Supermarket (long-term resupply), open M–Sa 6 a.m.–midnight, Su 6–10, with deli, pay phone, Western Union, ATM; West's Variety (short-term resupply). ■ *Restaurants:* Chinese Buffet, AYCE L/D; Friendly's. ■ *Other services:* Thrifty Bundle Laundromat.

**East** 1.0 mile to YMCA, shower $2.

**East** 2.5 miles to **North Adams, Mass. [P.O. ZIP 01247: M–F 8:30–4:30, Sa 10–12; (413) 664-4554]**. Large, spread-out city with most major services, including motels. ■ *Groceries:* Big Y Foods and Convenience Plus (both long-term resupply); Cumberland Farms (short-term resupply). ■ *Restaurants:* Boston Seafood Restaurant, Freight Yard Pub, other fast-food chains. ■ *Other services:* banks with ATM, hospital, shoe repair, hardware store, doctor, dentist, veterinarian, Radio Shack, and movie theater.

**West** 0.4 mile to ■ *Groceries:* Super Shop & Stop (long-term resupply), ATM, pharmacy, Western Union, bank, and pay phone. ■ *Lodging:* Redwood Motel, (413) 664-4351, $55–$149, CATV.

**West** 1.4 miles to town border with **Williamstown** and ■ *Lodging:* Chimney Mirror Motel, (413) 458-5202, $65S, $79D weekdays, $5EAP, weekends higher; Howard Johnson, (413) 458-8158, <www.howardjohnson.com>, $59–$149 rate based on season and day of week, no pets, continental B, outdoor pool, satellite TV; Maple Terrace Motel, (413) 458-9677, <www.mapleterrace.com>, $75–$148 includes B, DVD, WiFi, CATV, heated pool, picnic area, all rooms nonsmoking; Willows Motel, (413) 458-5768, <www.willowsmotel.com>, Su–Th $70–$129, F–Sa $99–$119, accepts packages for guests if notified in advance to 480 Main St., Williamstown, MA 01267. ■ *Restaurants:* Angelina's Subs, Chopsticks Asian, Colonial Pizza, Desperado's Mexican Grille, Dunkin' Donuts, Happy Star Chinese, Michael's Greek & Italian, Moonlight Diner & Grille. ■ *Groceries:* Wild Oats Whole Foods Market (long-

# Williamstown/
# North Adams

0    0.5 mile

term resupply). ■ *Other services:* Alcaro Rent-A-Car, (413) 458-1620, M–Sa; American Cab & Livery, (413) 662-2000.

**West** 2.6 miles to **Williamstown, Mass. [P.O. ZIP 01267: M–F 8:30–4:30, Sa 9–12; (413) 458-3707]**, home of Williams College. ■ *Lodging:* Williams Inn, (413) 458-9371; although $120S and $175D and up is out of the price range of most hikers, $7 gets you a towel, shower, swim, and sauna; free WiFi; parking $2/day. ■ *Restaurants:* Papa Charlie's, Helen's Place, Hot Tomatoes Pizza, Purple Pub, Red Herring Victuals, Thai Garden, Tunnel City Coffee (with extensive selection of homemade pastries), Spice Root (Indian), Water Street Grill (L buffet, M–F). ■ *Outfitter:* The Mountain Goat, (413) 458-8445, <www.themountaingoat.com>, open M–Sa 10–6 Su 12–5, with backpacking gear and supplies, Coleman fuel and denatured alcohol by the ounce, canister fuels, camping for 4 people max (2 tents, 1 dog) allowed behind the store with permission, max 2-night stay; very hiker-friendly. ■ *Other services:* banks with ATM; doctor; dentist; health clinic; pharmacy; veterinarian; movie theater; bookstore; American Cab Co., (413) 662-2000; and Bonanza Peter Pan bus line, (888) 751-8800, (800) 343-9999, <www.peterpanbus.com>.

**Sherman Brook Campsite**—Tent platforms available. A blue-blazed trail lets you bypass a boulder field north of the campsite in bad weather. Water at Pete's Spring.

*"It is better to travel well than come in first."*

—TAKOMA TEDD, MUSICIAN (AT '97, '01)

# Vermont

| Miles from Katahdin | Features | Services | Elev. | Miles from Springer |
|---|---|---|---|---|
| 592.2 | Vt.–Mass. State Line, Long Trail (southern terminus | | 2,330 | 1,584.0 |
| 591.8 | Brook | w | 2,300 | 1,584.4 |
| 589.4 | **Seth Warner Shelter** *10.4mS; 7.4mN* | W–0.2m S, C, w | 2,180 | 1,586.8 |
| 589.1 | County Rd | R | 2,290 | 1,587.1 |
| 588.0 | Ed's Spring | E–100ft w | 2,890 | 1,588.2 |
| 586.4 | Roaring Branch | w | 2,470 | 1,589.8 |
| 582.2 | **Congdon Shelter** *7.4mS; 5.9mN* | S, w | 2,060 | 1,594.0 |
| 579.7 | Harmon Hill | | 2,325 | 1,596.5 |
| 577.9 | Vt. 9 **Bennington, VT 05201** | R, w (W–5.1m PO, G, M, L, O, D, cl, f, @) | 1,360 | 1,598.3 |
| 576.3 | **Melville Nauheim Shelter** *5.9mS; 8.5mN* | E–250ft S, w | 2,330 | 1,599.9 |
| 574.7 | Hell Hollow Brook | w | 2,350 | 1,601.5 |
| 572.1 | Little Pond Lookout | | 3,060 | 1,604.1 |
| 570.3 | Glastenbury Lookout | | 2,920 | 1,605.9 |
| 567.8 | **Goddard Shelter** *8.5mS; 4.3mN* | S, w | 3,540 | 1,608.4 |
| 567.5 | Glastenbury Mtn | | 3,748 | 1,608.7 |
| 563.5 | **Kid Gore Shelter** *4.3mS; 4.6mN* | S, C, w | 2,795 | 1,612.7 |
| 560.5 | Lydia's Rest | | 3,300 | 1,615.7 |
| 559.8 | South Alder Brook | w | 2,600 | 1,616.4 |
| 558.9 | **Story Spring Shelter** *4.6mS; 10.6mN* | S, C, w | 2,810 | 1,617.3 |
| 555.3 | Stratton-Arlington Rd (Kelley Stand Rd) | R, w | 2,330 | 1,620.9 |
| 551.5 | Stratton Mtn | | 3,936 | 1,624.7 |
| 548.4 | +**Stratton Pond Shelter** *via* Stratton Pond Trail *...10.6mS; 5.4mN* | W–450ft S, w | 2,565 | 1,627.8 |
| 548.3 | Stratton Pond, North Shore Trail to +North Shore Tenting Area | w (W–0.5m C, w) | 2,555 | 1,627.9 |
| 546.4 | Winhall River | w | 2,175 | 1,629.8 |
| 543.6 | **William B. Douglas Shelter** *via* Branch Pond Trail *5.4mS; 3.6mN* | W–0.5m S, w | 2,210 | 1,632.6 |
| 542.7 | Old Rootville Rd, Prospect Rock | R (W–150ft w) | 2,150 | 1,633.5 |
| 540.6 | **Spruce Peak Shelter** *3.6mS; 5mN* | W–0.1m S, w | 2,180 | 1,635.6 |

| Miles from Katahdin | Features | Services | Elev. | Miles from Springer |
|---|---|---|---|---|
| 540.2 | Spruce Peak | W–300ft | 2,040 | 1,636.0 |
| 537.8 | Vt. 11 & 30 **Manchester Center, VT 05255** | R, w (E–2.1m L, M, cl,@; 2.5m G; 2.7m L, M, @; 3m L; 6m L; 6.3m L, D, cl, @) (W–5.5m PO, G, M, L, O, D, V, cl, f, @) | 1,800 | 1,638.4 |
| 535.8 | **Bromley Shelter** *5mS; 8.2mN* | E–0.1m S, w (N–0.1m C) | 2,560 | 1,640.4 |
| 534.8 | Bromley Mtn | | 3,260 | 1,641.4 |
| 532.3 | Mad Tom Notch, USFS 21 | R, w | 2,446 | 1,643.9 |
| 530.7 | Styles Peak | | 3,394 | 1,645.5 |
| 529.0 | Peru Peak | | 3,429 | 1,647.2 |
| 527.7 | **+Peru Peak Shelter** *8.2mS; 7.2mN* | S, w | 2,605 | 1,648.5 |
| 527.2 | Griffith Lake, +Griffith Lake Tenting Area | C, w | 2,600 | 1,649.0 |
| 527.0 | Griffith Lake | w | 2,600 | 1,649.2 |
| 525.0 | Baker Peak | | 2,850 | 1,651.2 |
| 523.0 | **Lost Pond Campsite** | W–100ft C, w | 2,150 | 1,653.2 |
| 521.5 | **Old Job Shelter** *via* Old Job Trail *7.2mS; 1.2mN* | E–1m S, w | 1,525 | 1,654.7 |
| 521.3 | **Big Branch Shelter** *1.2mS; 3mN* | S, w | 1,460 | 1,654.9 |
| 520.0 | Danby–Landgrove Rd, USFS 10, Black Branch **Danby, VT 05739** | R, w (W–3.5m PO, G, M, L, f, @; 5.5m C, sh, f) | 1,500 | 1,656.2 |
| 518.3 | **+Lula Tye Shelter** *3mS; 0.7mN* | E–100ft S, nw; N–0.4m w | 1,920 | 1,657.9 |
| 518.0 | +Little Rock Pond Tenting Area | C; N–0.1m w | 1,854 | 1,658.2 |
| 517.9 | Spring | w | 1,854 | 1,658.3 |
| 517.7 | Green Mtn Trail to Homer Stone Brook Trail | | 1,854 | 1,658.5 |
| 517.6 | **+Little Rock Pond Shelter** *0.7mS; 4.6mN* | E–100ft S, nw; S–0.3m w | 1,885 | 1,658.6 |
| 513.7 | Trail to White Rocks Cliff vista | W–0.2m | 2,400 | 1,662.5 |
| 513.2 | **Greenwall Shelter** *4.6mS; 5.3mN* | E–0.2m S, w | 2,025 | 1,663.0 |
| 511.8 | Sugar Hill Rd | R | 1,260 | 1,664.4 |
| 511.7 | Vt. 140 | R, w (W–2.8m PO, G, M, L, D, f, @) | 1,160 | 1,664.5 |

| Miles from Katahdin | Features | Services | Elev. | Miles from Springer |
|---|---|---|---|---|
| | **Wallingford, VT 05773** | | | |
| 509.6 | Bear Mtn | | 2,220 | 1,666.6 |
| 508.1 | **Minerva Hinchey Shelter** *5.3mS; 3.8mN* | E–200ft S, C, w | 1,605 | 1,668.1 |
| 505.5 | Clarendon Gorge-Mill River Suspension Bridge | w | 800 | 1,670.7 |
| 505.4 | Vt. 103 | R (W–0.5m M, V; 1m G) | 860 | 1,670.8 |
| 504.4 | **Clarendon Shelter** *3.8mS; 5.9mN* | E–0.1m S, w | 1,190 | 1,671.8 |
| 503.9 | Beacon Hill | | 1,740 | 1,672.3 |
| 503.5 | Lottery Rd | R | 1,720 | 1,672.7 |
| 501.5 | Lower Cold River Rd | R | 1,400 | 1,674.7 |
| 500.7 | Gould Brook (ford) | w | 1,480 | 1,675.5 |
| 500.0 | Upper Cold River Rd | R, w | 1,630 | 1,676.2 |
| 498.6 | **Governor Clement Shelter** *5.9mS; 4.3mN* (see text) | S, w | 1,900 | 1,677.6 |
| 494.4 | Trail to Killington Peak | E–0.2m | 3,900 | 1,681.8 |
| 494.3 | **Cooper Lodge** *4.3mS; 3mN* | S, w | 3,850 | 1,681.9 |
| 491.8 | Jungle Jct; Sherburne Pass Trail to **Pico Camp** *3mS; 2.5mN* | E–0.5m S, w | 3,510 | 1,684.4 |
| 489.9 | **Churchill Scott Shelter** *2.5mS; 3.4mN* | W–0.1m S, C, w | 2,560 | 1,686.3 |
| 488.0 | U.S. 4 **Rutland, VT 05701** | R, w (E–0.9m L, M) (W–0.9m L, cl, @; 1.5m L, M, cl, @; 11m PO, H, L, G, M, O, D, V, cl, f, @) | 1,880 | 1,688.2 |
| 487.0 | Willard Gap, Maine Junction, Long Trail, **Tucker Johnson Shelter** *3.4mS; 9.5mN* | W–0.4m S, w | 2,300 | 1,689.2 |
| 486.1 | Sherburne Pass Trail | E–0.5m L, M | 2,440 | 1,690.1 |
| 484.7 | Vt. 100, Gifford Woods State Park **Killington, VT 05751** | R, w, C, S, sh (E–0.6m PO, G, L, M) | 1,660 | 1,691.5 |
| 483.7 | Thundering Brook Rd, Kent Pond | R, L, M, @ | 1,450 | 1,692.5 |
| 482.3 | River Rd | R | 1,214 | 1,693.9 |
| 479.0 | Quimby Mtn | | 2,550 | 1,697.2 |
| 478.0 | **Stony Brook Shelter** *9.5mS; 10.2mN* | E–0.1m S, w | 1,760 | 1,698.2 |

| Miles from Katahdin | Features | Services | Elev. | Miles from Springer |
|---|---|---|---|---|
| 473.3 | Chateauguay Rd | R | 2,000 | 1,702.9 |
| 472.6 | Lakota Lake Lookout | | 2,640 | 1,703.6 |
| 470.5 | Trail to the Lookout | W–0.2m | 2,320 | 1,705.7 |
| 468.1 | **Wintturi Shelter** *10.2mS; 11.9mN* | W–0.2m S, w | 1,910 | 1,708.1 |
| 464.3 | Vt. 12, Gulf Stream Bridge **Woodstock, VT 05091** | R, w (E–4.4m PO, G, L, M, D, @) (W–0.2m G) | 882 | 1,711.9 |
| 462.8 | Woodstock Stage Rd (Bartlett Brook Rd) **South Pomfret, VT 05067** | R, w (E–1m PO, G) | 770 | 1,713.4 |
| 460.6 | South Pomfret–Pomfret Rd | R, w | 980 | 1,715.6 |
| 458.8 | Cloudland Rd | R (W–0.2m S, G) | 1,370 | 1,717.4 |
| 456.8 | Thistle Hill | | 1,950 | 1,719.4 |
| 456.5 | **Thistle Hill Shelter** *11.9mS; 9mN* | E–0.1m S, w | 1,480 | 1,719.7 |
| 455.0 | Joe Ranger Rd | R | 1,280 | 1,721.2 |
| 451.7 | Patriot Bridge, White River, Vt. 14 **West Hartford, VT 05084** | R (E–0.3m PO, C, G, M, @; 6m H, G, M, L) | 390 | 1,724.5 |
| 451.1 | Tigertown Rd, Podunk Rd | R | 540 | 1,725.1 |
| 450.3 | Podunk Brook, Podunk Rd | R, w | 860 | 1,725.9 |
| 447.7 | **Happy Hill Shelter** *9mS; 7.4mN* | E–0.1m S, w | 1,420 | 1,728.5 |
| 443.4 | U.S. 5 **Norwich, VT 05055** | R (E–0.25m PO, G, L, M, @) | 537 | 1,732.8 |
| 442.4 | Connecticut River, Vt.–N.H. State Line | R | 380 | 1,733.8 |

*+ Fee charged*

"Are you thru-hiking?" becomes a dual-trail question as the A.T. hiker will follow 105 miles of the Long Trail, America's first long-distance hiking trail. Thru-hikers of both the L.T. and A.T. will meet any given time of year. Here the mountains and wildlife get bigger. Now's a good time to review your weather-protection gear. Avoid Vermont trails in "mud season," mid-Apr to Memorial Day. Hiking there in wet, sloppy conditions leads to serious Trail erosion.

---

**Green Mountain Club**—GMC maintains the 127.9 miles from the Massachusetts–Vermont border to Vt. 12. Correspondence should be sent to GMC at 4711 Waterbury–Stowe Rd., Waterbury Center, VT 05677; (802) 244-7037; fax, (802) 244-5867; <gmc@greenmountainclub.org>.

**GMC Shelter Fees**—Fees are collected at high-use campsites to help defray the costs of field programs and shelter and Trail maintenance along the A.T. in Vermont. The fee is $5PP per night. This fee applies to anyone camping within 0.5 mile of a fee site. In addition, all hikers who pay the $5 fee in cash at one of the three southern-pond fee sites (Stratton Pond, Griffith Lake, and Little Rock Pond—see chart for details) will receive a dated receipt that they can then use for one free night at either or both of the other two fee sites. The receipt must be used within 7 days. No receipt, no free nights; no exceptions. This offer does not extend north of Maine Junction on the Long Trail. This deal only works if you pay cash; it does not apply to folks who promise to pay later.

| Fee Site | Includes (listed S to N) |
|---|---|
| Stratton Pond | Stratton Pond Shelter<br>North Shore Tenting Area |
| Griffith Lake | Peru Peak Shelter<br>Griffith Lake Tenting Area |
| Little Rock Pond | Lula Tye Shelter<br>Little Rock Pond Campsite<br>Little Rock Pond Shelter |

Caretakers are present throughout the hiking season, May–Oct, at several locations. Through conversation and example, caretakers educate hikers about Leave No Trace practices and perform Trail and shelter maintenance. Most importantly, caretakers compost sewage at high-use fee sites and a few no-fee shelter sites in southern Vermont.

A ridgerunner may be found along the Coolidge Range at the following locations, although a fee is not charged: Clarendon Shelter, Governor Clement Shelter, Cooper Lodge, Pico Camp, and Churchill Scott Shelter.

**Long Trail**—At the Vermont–Massachusetts state line, the A.T. joins the Long Trail (L.T.) for 105.2 miles, to "Maine Junction" at Willard Gap. At Maine Junction, the A.T. leads toward Maine, and the L.T. continues north, reaching the Canadian border in another 167.8 miles. Completed in 1930, the L.T. served as one inspiration for the A.T. The L.T. and A.T. are seeing increased traffic in Vermont. Please use only designated shelters and campsites, and make use of privies and wash pits to protect water quality and greatly reduce the visible and permanent impact of greater use of the Trail.

*Public transportation*—Amtrak to Rutland and White River Junction, (800) 872-7245; Greyhound Bus between Rutland and White River Junction, and national connections, (800) 231-2222; Green Mountain Express–Green Mountain Chapter of the American Red Cross community bus from Bennington to

Manchester, (802) 447-0477, M–F 8–5; Marble Valley Regional Transit community bus serves Manchester, Rutland, and Killington, (802) 773-3244; local taxi service is also available.

*Bears*—In 2005, Vermont had another campsite-bear incident. To prevent future problems and costly interventions, please hang all food from tree limbs at least 12 feet off the ground, and practice Leave No Trace camping.

**Seth Warner Shelter** (1965)—Sleeps 8. Privy. Tentsites available. Water source, a brook 150 yards to the left of the shelter, is known to fail in dry years.

**Congdon Shelter** (1967)—Sleeps 8. Privy. Tentsites available behind the shelter on the ridge. Water source is a brook in front of the shelter. If the brook is dry, follow downstream to larger Stamford Stream.

**Vt. 9—West** 5.1 miles to **Bennington, Vt. [P.O. ZIP 05201: M–F 8–5, Sa 9–2; (802) 442-2421]**. Information for the most current hiker-friendly services can be obtained at Nature's Closet at downtown intersection of U.S. 7 & 9. Note: Aug 1, 2008, BTown ChowDown for hikers at Merchants Park; free food, free beer, and music by local artists; hosted by local merchants, including Nature's Closet, Rattlesnake Café, and Madison Brewing Co. ■ *Lodging:* Samuel Safford Inne, (802) 442-5934, 722 Main St., Bennington, VT 05201; Kirkside Motor Lodge, (802) 447-7596, totally smoke-free facility; Autumn Inn, (802) 442-2866, <theautumninn.com>, $49S, $59D (sale pending, rates may go up), restaurant and laundry facilities nearby, mail drops accepted, no fee, at 924 East Main Street, Bennington, VT 05201; Knotty Pine Motel, (802) 442-5487, <kpine@knottypinemotel.com>, 130 Northside Dr. (Routes 67 and 7A), occasional shuttle back to the A.T., rates during the spring and summer $71–$75D depending on room, fall $87–$93D, $8EAP, pets accepted on limited basis, WiFi, laundry, restaurants and groceries within walking distance, pool. ■ *Groceries:* Price Chopper, Hannaford supermarkets (both long-term resupply). ■ *Restaurants:* Rattlesnake Café, open Tu–Su, L/D, Mexican fare; Izabella's B/L; Blue Benn Diner, B/L/D; South Street Café, B/L, WiFi. ■ *Outfitter:* Nature's Closet, (802) 442-0476, <www.naturescloset.net>, clothing, some backpacking supplies, denatured and white gas by the ounce, canister fuel, open M–Sa 10–6, Su 12–5, shuttles available before and after the store opens, will hold packages mailed to 400 Main St., Bennington, VT 05201. ■ *Internet access:* Bennington Free Library. ■ *Other services:* Townwide, free use of yellow bikes to ride to area businesses: must be over 18, sign release, and return bike to business from which it was originally borrowed; coin laundry; banks with ATM; hospital; movie theater; shoe repair; doctor; dentist; pharmacy; hardware store; and $1 showers available at Town

Recreation Center on Gage Street. ■ *Shuttles:* Bennington Taxi, (802) 442-9052 or -9019; Green Mountain Express, (802) 447-0477, <www.greenmtncn.org>, M–F, 7:30–5:30, call to arrange $2 shuttle to Route 9 Trailhead and, M–F, four trips daily, $2 service between Bennington and Manchester (see above under "Public transportation").

**Melville Nauheim Shelter** (1977)—Sleeps 8. Privy. Water source is a stream just north of the spur to the shelter.

**Vt. 9 to Kelly Stand Road**—Please note: *This section of the Trail is receiving heavy use and experiencing resource damage as a result. GMC encourages hikers to use the designated shelters and campsites. If you must camp between shelters, please follow Leave No Trace practices, and camp 200 feet away from the Trail and all water sources.*

**Goddard Shelter** (2005)—Sleeps 10. Privy. The shelter has a front porch with a view to the south. Please tent above the shelter, to the west of the A.T. Water source is a spring 50 yards south on the A.T. *To preserve the pristine nature of the spring, no tenting is allowed east of the trail up the mountain.*

**Glastenbury Mountain** (3,748 ft.). The original firetower was built in 1927 and renovated once in 1970 and again in 2005 by the Long Trail Patrol, USFS, and volunteers from the GMC. The nearby ridges seen from the observation deck are the Berkshires to the south, the Taconics to the west, Mt. Equinox and Stratton Mountain to the north, and Somerset Reservoir, Mt. Snow, and Haystack Mountain to the east. Remains of the old firewarden's cabin and woodstove can be seen to the west of the Trail, south of the summit. Porcupines are active in this area; take precautions with your gear.

**Kid Gore Shelter** (1971)—Sleeps 8. Privy. Ecologically fragile area. Tentsites available at the closed Caughnawaga Shelter. Water source is a brook near Caughnawaga. An unreliable spring is north of Kid Gore Shelter.

**Caughnawaga Shelter** (1931)—Tentsites only. Shelter *closed* by the GMNF in the fall of 2006 due to safety concerns over its deteriorating condition. Please do not use this shelter; instead, go to the nearby Kid Gore Shelter.

**Story Spring Shelter** (1963)—Sleeps 8. Privy. Tentsites. Water source is a spring north on the A.T. 50 yards.

**Stratton Mountain**—Although he offered a number of variations on the story about how he first thought of the A.T., many believe it was on the slopes of Stratton Mountain that Benton MacKaye first imagined a long-distance trail that would link the high peaks of the Appalachian Mountains. A firetower tops the summit and is open to hikers. A GMC summit caretaker is in the area during the day to interpret the area's cultural and natural history for hikers. No camping or fires on the summit. A side trail at the summit leads east 0.8 mile to a ski gondola at the top of Stratton Ski Area; this hut is not available for hiker use. The gondola has operated in past years, allowing hikers to ride down to Stratton Village, which has a grocery store and restaurants. Please check with the GMC summit caretaker or Stratton Mountain staff to see if the gondola is available for hiker use.

**Stratton Pond Shelter** (1999)—Sleeps 16. Privy. Overnight fee. Go 0.2 mile west *via* Stratton Pond Trail. No tenting is available at this shelter, but you may tent on platforms at the nearby North Shore Tenting Area; otherwise, within 0.5 mile of the pond, camping is permitted only at designated sites. Shelter has an open first floor, table, bunks, and an enclosed loft. Water source is Bigelow Spring at Stratton Pond about 0.1 mile down the Lye Brook Trail. *No fires at this shelter.*

**William B. Douglas Shelter** (1956)—Sleeps 10. Privy. Go 0.5 mile west *via* the Branch Pond Trail. A log shelter renovated by GMC Brattleboro Section volunteers in 2005. Water source is a spring located south of the shelter.

**Spruce Peak Shelter** (1983)—Sleeps 14. Privy. This shelter, 0.1 mile west on a spur trail, was constructed by GMC, USFS, and a work crew from the Rutland Community Correctional Center. Water source is a boxed spring 35 yards to the right of the shelter.

**Vt. 11 & 30**—**East** 2.1 miles to *Lodging:* Bromley Sun Lodge, (800) 722-2159, rooms starting at $70s/D, tavern fare, indoor pool, game room, WiFi, laundry, Rt. 11 & 30 Trailhead shuttle, and mail drops for guests only to 4216 Vt. 11, Peru, VT 05152.

**East** 2.5 miles *via* Vt. 11 to *Groceries:* Bromley Market, (802) 824-4444, short-term resupply, open M–Sa 6–6, Su 6–5, Ben & Jerry's, home-baked goodies, some hiker supplies, mail drops accepted, 3776 Vt. 11, Peru, VT 05152.

**East** 2.7 miles *via* Vt. 11 to *Lodging:* Johnny Seesaw's Lodge, (802) 824-5533, <www.johnnyseesaw.com>, $65D, restaurant B/D ($7.50 B with room), lounge, Rt. 11 & 30 Trailhead shuttle, WiFi, pets $10 based on room availability, mail drops accepted at P.O. Box 68 or 3574 Vt. 11, Peru, VT 05152.

**East** 3.0 miles *via* Vt. 30 to *Lodging:* Bromley View Inn, (877) 633-0308, <www.bromleyviewinn.com>, $85D weekends higher, includes B, call for shuttle to and from Rt. 11 & 30 Trailhead only, mail drops accepted at 522 Vermont 30, Bondville, VT 05340.

**East** 6.3 miles *via* Vt. 30/Old Town Road/Winhall Hollow Road to *Lodging:* Alpenrose Inn, (802) 297-2750, <www.alpen-

rose.com>, <alpenrose@comcast.net>, $75–$95, includes B, fee for laundry, free Internet access, D available, shuttle to/from Manchester Trailhead when available.

**West** 5.5 miles to the bustling factory-outlet town of **Manchester Center, Vt. [P.O. ZIP 05255: M–F 8:30–4:30, Sa 9–12; (802) 362-3070]**. Pick up mail at the post office on the way into town to avoid an extra walk. The Mountain Goat and EMS are good resources for hiker services in town. ■ *Lodging:* Sutton's Place, (802) 362-1165, <www.suttonsplacevermont. com>, $50s, $65D, $75T plus tax; Avalanche Motel, (802) 362-2622, $55–$85 rate depends on season, restaurant L/D, pet-friendly, WiFi, Bob's Diner next door for B; Carriage House Motel, (802) 362-1706, <www.carriagehousemotel.com>, $32.55PP, no pets, opens in May. ■ *Groceries:* Price Chopper, Shaw's supermarkets (both long-term resupply). ■ *Restaurants:* Manchester Pizza House, Sirloin Saloon, Mrs. Murphy's Doughnuts and Coffee Shop, Friendly's, Up For Breakfast, Christo's Pizza, Ben & Jerry's Scoop Shop, and several fast-food outlets. ■ *Internet access:* Mark Skinner Library, Tu–Sa; I Ship Express (below). ■ *Outfitters:* The Mountain Goat, (802) 362-5159, open M–Sa 10–6, Su 11–5, full-service outfitter, fuel

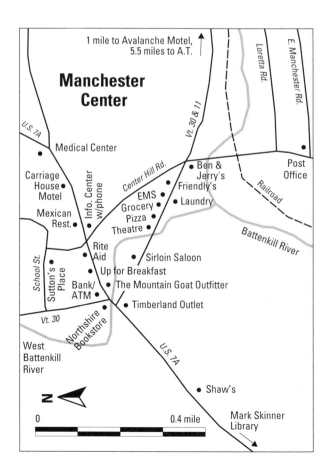

by the ounce, custom footbeds and orthotics, mail drops (USPS, UPS & FedEx) accepted at 4886 Main Street, Manchester, VT 05255; Eastern Mountain Sports (EMS), (802) 366-8082, open Su–Th 10–6, F–Sa 10–7, Coleman and alcohol fuel by the ounce, authorized Leki repair service. ■ *Other services:* coin laundry; cobbler; bank with ATM; doctor; dentist; pharmacy; veterinarian; movie theater; Manchester Taxi, (802) 362-4118 and (802) 362-0062; Green Mountain Express, (802) 447-0477, <www.greenmtncn.org>, $2 bus service between Manchester and Bennington, flag stop across from RiteAid and Shaw's; I Ship Express, 5018 Main St., (802) 362-1652, M-F 9:30–5, Sa 9:30–noon, packing and shipping services.

**Bromley Shelter** (2003)—Sleeps 12. Privy (composting). Tent platforms and campsite are north 0.1 mile. Water is a brook at the end of the spur trail.

**Bromley Mountain**—An observation tower offers a five-state view. Ski trails lead to Bromley Base Lodge area.

**Peru Peak Shelter/Griffith Lake Campsite** (1935/1980/2000)—Sleeps 10. Privy. Overnight fee. Originally built by the CCC and renovated twice. Camping permitted only at designated sites within 0.5 mile of Griffith Lake. Water source is a brook near the shelter.

**Lost Pond Campsite.** Privy. Shelter burned down in 2001, was rebuilt in 2002, burned down again in Nov 2006. Tentsites provided.

**Old Job Shelter** (1935)—Sleeps 8. Privy. Built by the CCC. Water source is in front of the shelter at Lake Brook.

**Big Branch Shelter** (1963)—Sleeps 8. Privy. This site is close to USFS 10 and receives heavy weekend use. Good soaking pools. Water source is Big Branch, located in front of the shelter.

**Danby–Landgrove Road**—*Light traffic, may be a difficult hitch.* **West** 3.5 miles to **Danby, Vt. [P.O. ZIP 05739: M–F 7:15–12 & 1:15–4, Sa 7:30–10:30; (802) 293-5105].** ■ *Lodging:* Silas Griffith Inn, (802) 293-5567, <www.SilasGriffith.com>, <stay@SilasGriffith.com>, 1891 inn owned by hiker-friendly Brian and Cathy Preble; $135 queen bed midweek, $159 weekend (higher in leaf season), B included; pool, spa, wireless DSL Internet; laundry $8/load; pet-friendly; shuttle for guests only; mail drops accepted at 178 South Main St., Danby, VT 05739; Emma's Restaurant on premises, Th–Su 9–9, will accommodate dietary restrictions and other meals by prior arrangement; off-season (Nov–Apr) lower rates and specials; participates in the <www.inntoinn.com> hiking network in Vt. ■ *Groceries:* Mt. Tabor Country Store, Nichols Store (both short-term resupply). ■ *Restaurants:* Mountain View Café,

7–3 B/L, closed Tu, cash/checks only; Emma's; White Dog Tavern, D, W–Su.

**West** 5.5 miles *via* U.S. 7 to **Campground:** Otter Creek Campground, (802) 293-5041, tentsites $16, coin showers, camp store with Coleman fuel, prepackaged deli sandwiches, small selection of food items and camping supplies; possible shuttle service for fee, call for rates. Hikers are allowed to park here for extended periods. Owners George and Alice Araskiewicz hold UPS and USPS packages addressed to the campground at U.S. 7, Danby, VT 05739.

**Lula Tye Shelter** (1962)—Sleeps 8. Privy. Overnight fee. Within 0.5 mile of Little Rock Pond, camping is permitted only at designated sites. Water source (shared with Little Rock Pond Shelter) is a spring 0.3 mile north on the A.T.

**Little Rock Pond Tenting Area**—Platforms. Privy. Overnight fee.

**Little Rock Pond Shelter** (1962)—Sleeps 8. Privy. Overnight fee. Within 0.5 mile of the pond, tenting is restricted to designated sites. Water source (shared with Lula Tye Shelter) is a spring 0.3 mile south on the A.T.

**Greenwall Shelter** (1962)—Sleeps 8. Privy 0.2 mile east on spur trail. Water source is a spring, prone to fail in dry seasons, 200 yards along a side trail behind the shelter.

**Vt. 140—West** 2.8 miles to **Wallingford, Vt. [P.O. ZIP 05773: M–F 7:45–4:45, Sa 9–12; (802) 446-2140]**, with expensive inns. ■ *Restaurants:* Mom's Restaurant, B/L, open 'til 2; Sal's Pizza, L/D, Su D only. ■ *Groceries:* The Market, Wallingford Country Store & Deli (short-term resupply), Cumberland Farms, Midway Mobil Mart. ■ *Internet access:* Gilbert Hart Library, Tu–Sa. ■ *Other services:* hardware store, ATM, dentist.

**Minerva Hinchey Shelter** (1969/2006)—Sleeps 10. Privy. Water source is a spring 50 yards south of shelter; follow "Wada" signs. Tenting area.

**Clarendon Gorge**—A suspension bridge 0.1 mile from Vt. 103 overlooks a favorite swimming hole for residents. Built in 1974, this bridge is dedicated to the memory of Robert Brugmann, who drowned while trying to cross the swollen Mill River. Swimming in the gorge is hazardous during high water. Watch for broken glass. *No camping permitted in the gorge.*

**Vt. 103—West** 0.5 mile to *Restaurant:* Whistle Stop, (802) 747-3422, 6:30-8 B/L/D. ■ *Other services:* veterinarian.

**West** 1 mile to *Groceries:* Clarendon General Store, (802)

786-0948, short-term resupply, M–Sa 7–7:30, Su 7:30–6, Ben & Jerry's, pay phone, call for mail-drop information.

**Clarendon Shelter** (1952)—Sleeps 10. Privy. Located near the old Crown Point Military Road that was built during the French and Indian Wars. Water source is a stream 25 yards from the shelter.

**Governor Clement Shelter** (1929)—Sleeps 12. Privy. Named for former Vermont Governor Percival W. Clement. *Due to its close proximity to a public road, this shelter has a long history of visits by local revellers creating serious problems with vandalism and hiker harassment. For the safety of all hikers, ATC strongly discourages any overnight use of the Gov. Clement Shelter site.* ATC and the Green Mountain Club are working toward a long-term solution for the site. GMC is working with the USFS and the town of Shrewsbury to limit inappropriate use. Move on if you encounter problems. Water source is a stream across the road and north of the shelter.

**Cooper Lodge** (1939)—Sleeps 16. Privy. This enclosed stone cabin was built by the Vermont Forest Service. Behind the shelter is a 0.2-mile side trail to Killington Peak. Water source is a spring north of shelter on A.T. Tent platforms.

**Killington Peak**—Reached by a steep 0.2-mile side trail from Cooper Lodge. At 4,235 feet, this is the highest point near the Trail in Vermont and the second-highest peak in the state. The open, rocky summit offers panoramic views, and, on a clear day, you can see the White Mountains of New Hampshire and the Adirondacks of New York. A short side trail leads from the summit to a snack bar and ski lift operated by the Killington ski resort; shops are located at the village reached by the gondola. Snack bar with pay phone opens Th–Su, 9–4, mid-Jul through Labor Day. A GMC ridgerunner patrols the Coolidge Range (including Killington and Pico) and may be available to answer natural-history and Trail questions.

**Jungle Junction–Sherburne Pass Trail**—Named after a 1938 hurricane left behind a "jungle" of blowdowns (and essentially broke the A.T. as a continuous footpath a year after it opened as such). The blue-blazed Sherburne Pass Trail (former A.T.) leads 3.1 miles north to Sherburne Pass on U.S. 4, directly to the Inn at Long Trail (opened in 1938, ironically), and continues north of the inn 0.5 mile to reconnect with the A.T.

**Pico Camp** (1959)—Sleeps 12. Privy. An enclosed shelter located 0.5 mile east on the Sherburne Pass Trail, the former A.T. Water source is 45 yards north on the Sherburne Pass Trail.

**Rutland city watershed**: The western flanks of the Coolidge Range comprise a significant portion of the city of Rutland's watershed. Fires are not permitted. Please camp only at designated sites and use facilities provided.

**Churchill Scott Shelter** (2002)—Sleeps 8. Privy (composting). Tent platform available; water on spur trail downhill behind shelter.

**U.S. 4—East** 0.9 mile uphill along a busy thoroughfare to ■ *Lodging:* The Inn at Long Trail, (802) 775-7181, open year-round except temporarily for innkeeper vacation mid-Apr to mid-Jun. The inn offers discount rooms for hikers with full B; no dogs in the lodge. McGrath's Irish Pub serves L/D. Amenities include laundry facilities, hiker box, outside water spigot, WiFi. Only accepts UPS or Fed Ex packages; send to The Inn at Long Trail, 709 Route 4, Sherburne Pass, Killington, VT 05751. Bus service daily from inn to Rutland and White River Junction. *A safer alternative to the roadwalk in heavy traffic is to cross Route 4 and continue on the A.T. north 1.9 miles to the northern terminus of the Sherburne Pass Trail, which will lead you 0.5 mile south directly to the inn.*

**West** 0.9 mile to *Lodging:* Edelweiss Motel, (802) 775-5577, on bus route, $36 and up.

**West** 1.5 miles to *Lodging:* Mendon Mountain View Resort Lodge & Restaurant, (802) 773-4311, on bus route, $25PP group rate, seven hiker rooms available, shuttle to Trail in morning and pick-up from the Trailhead if available, free Internet, WiFi, laundry services, will hold packages mailed to 78 U.S. 4, Killington, VT 05751.

**West** 11 miles to the city of **Rutland, Vt. [P.O. 05701: M–F 8–5, Sa 8–12; (802) 773-0222]**, with all major services and chain motels. ■ *Hostels:* Back Home Again Café, (802) 775-9800 or (802) 773-0160, <www.twelvetribes.com>, check-in at restaurant, closed Sa, call to reach a member to gain access, work for stay or donation, common room with kitchen facilities, separate bunk rooms for men and women, pets stay outside, located near downtown Rutland Transit Center, mail drops accepted at 23 Center Street, Rutland, VT 05701; A-Towns Place, work for stay or suggested donation $20 (bunk), $5 (tenting space), short-term resupply, shuttles to/from all A.T. and L.T. trailheads (free for guests), laundry (free for guests), Internet access, mail drops accepted at 335 Grove St., Brandon, VT 05733, (803) 465-0136, <azchipka@mac.com>. ■ *Restaurants:* Back Home Again Café, L/D, only organic food, closed Sa; Applebee's; A Crust Above; Pizza Hut; Sal's Italian Restaurant; Sirloin Saloon; Tokyo House; Kong Chow; Gill's Delicatessen. ■ *Outfitters:* Mountain Travelers Outdoor Shop, (802) 775-0814, <www.mtntravelers.com>, 147 Woodstock Ave., with backpacking equipment and supplies, fuel by the ounce, open M–S 10–6, Su 12–5; The Great Outdoors, (802) 775-9989, <www.joejonessports.com>, 219 Woodstock Ave., general sporting-goods store with backpacking equipment; Simon the Tanner, (802) 282-4016, <www.simonthetanner.com>, 21 Center Street adjacent to Back Home Again Café, M–Th 11–9, F 11–3, closed Sa, Su 12–7, footwear, clothing, fuel, backpacking items. Dick's Sporting Goods at Green Mountain Shopping Plaza and Eastern Mountain Sports at Diamond Run Mall both can be reached *via* local MVRT bus. ■ *Internet access:* Rutland Free Library. ■ *Bus service:* MVRT bus ($2 per ride) is available from Killington to Rutland; the bus can be flagged anywhere along U.S. 4. The bus travels from downtown Rutland Transit Center to Killington and back approximately once every 2 hours, leaving Rutland beginning at 7:15 a.m. until 5:15 p.m. ■ *Train service:* Amtrak provides daily train service on the Ethan Allen Express, (800) USA-RAIL, from Rutland to Albany and New York City. Call for reservations and to confirm arrival and departure times, as they are constantly changing. Amtrak service on the Vermonter is also available at White River Junction, 35 miles east. ■ *Other services:* Wal-Mart; Rutland Regional Medical Center Hospital; veterinarian; Rutland Taxi, (802) 236-3133. The Vermont Long Trail Festival will be held mid-Aug at the Vermont Fairgrounds; <www.longtrailfestivalvt.com>.

**Maine Junction–Willard Gap.** The L.T. continues north 167.8 miles to Canada, while the A.T. diverges to the east toward New Hampshire and Maine.

**Tucker-Johnson Shelter** (1969)—Sleeps 8. Privy. Located on the L.T. 0.4 mile north of Maine Junction. Water source is nearby Eagle Square Brook.

**Vt. 100**—The A.T. passes through Gifford Woods State Park, (802) 775-5354, with shelters, tentsites, and bathhouse visible from the Trail; office has ice cream and soda machines inside. ■ *Camping:* shelters $21–$23; tentsites $14–$16 up to 5 people, cabin $42 for 4 people, coin-operated showers 50¢, water spigot, pay phone, restroom located at the park. Space fills up quickly during the fall "leaf season."
**East** 0.6 mile to **Killington, Vt. [P.O. ZIP 05751: M–F 8–4:30, Sa 8–12; (802) 775-4247].** ■ *Lodging:* Sherburne-Killington Motel, (802) 773-9535, summer rates Su–Th $54s/D, F–Sa $59s/D, fall-foliage and winter rates higher, WiFi, computer available to hikers for Internet access. ■ *Groceries:* Deli at Killington Corners (short-term resupply), 6:30 a.m.–7 p.m. daily, excellent sandwiches, daily hot-meal specials, and ATM.

**Kent Pond**—on A.T. *Lodging:* Mountain Meadows Lodge, (802) 775-1010, <www.mountainmeadowslodge.com>, hikers welcome, owner is a hiker; $59 includes B, D available $10 most nights; free use of computer, dogs permitted outside; hikers not staying at the lodge can have a reasonably priced B/L/D; outdoor pool, hot tub, sauna, kayaking;

hiker box inside; mail drops to 285 Thundering Brook Rd., Killington, VT 05751.

**Thundering Falls**—This $300,000 relocation eliminates the road walk on Thundering Brook Road and River Road and adds views of Thundering Falls and the Ottauqueechee River. The new path in the woods descends through northern-hardwood forest to the base of high Thundering Falls and then passes through the open Ottauquechee River floodplain. A new wheelchair-accessible bridge built by the Green Mountain Club and financed by ATC and the National Park Service crosses the river.

**Stony Brook Shelter** (1997)—Sleeps 8. Privy. Water source is brook 100 yards north of shelter on A.T.

**Side Trail to the Lookout**—One of the few views between Killington Peak and New Hampshire. Follow side trail 0.2 mile west from A.T. to a private cabin. Use care on ladder that leads up to an observation deck. No water available. The owners permit its use *as a viewpoint* by hikers; please be responsible to ensure that this privilege continues.

**Wintturi Shelter** (1994)—Sleeps 8. Privy. Frame shelter. Water source is a spring to the right of the shelter.

 **Vt. 12**—Please respect landowners at this road crossing by not camping in woods or fields near Vt. 12.
　　**East** 4.4 miles to **Woodstock, Vt. [P.O. ZIP 05091: M–F 8:30–5, Sa 9–12; (802) 457-1323]**. Services include several motels and inns, grocery (long-term resupply), restaurants, bank with ATM, doctor, dentist, pharmacy, and movie theater open F–Su. ■ *Internet access:* library, M–Sa.
　　**West** 0.2 mile to *Groceries:* On the Edge farm stand, open daily in summer 10–6; seasonal veggies, fruit, cold drinks, ice cream.

---

**Dartmouth Outing Club**—DOC maintains the 75.3 miles from Vt. 12 to Kinsman Notch in New Hampshire. Correspondence should be sent to DOC, P.O. Box 9, Hanover, NH 03755; (603) 646-2428; <www.dartmouth.edu/student/doc>. The DOC no longer uses orange-and-black paint for blazes, although many are still visible. The DOC does continue to use orange and black on trail signs.

---

**Woodstock Stage Road (Bartlett Brook Road)**—**East** 1 mile to **South Pomfret, Vt. [P.O. ZIP 05067: M–F 8:00–1 & 2:00–4:45, Sa 8:30–11:30; (802) 457-1147]**. *Groceries:* Teago's General Store (short-term resupply), M–Sa 7–6, Su 8–4, with deli sandwiches and post office inside the store.

**Cloudland Road—West** 0.2 mile to *Groceries:* Cloudland Farm Country Market; water, cold drinks, beef jerky, ice cream. This operating farm is run by Bill and Cathy Emmons. Tenting and overnight stays may be available on a work-for-stay or donation basis. The Old Cloudland Shelter on their property is always available.

**Thistle Hill Shelter** (1995)—Sleeps 8. Privy. The Cloudland privy was moved to Thistle Hill, partly with ALDHA's help. Water source is a stream near the shelter.

**Vt.14**—*Groceries:* West Hartford General Store and snack bar, (802) 280-1713, short-term resupply, is on the A.T., full B/L, M–Sa 7–8, Su 8–2, information about nearby camping.
    **East** 0.3 mile to **West Hartford, Vt. [P.O. ZIP 05084: M–F 7:30–11:30 & 1–4:45, Sa 7:30–10:15; (802) 295-6293]**. Window at post office closes 15 minutes before lobby. *Internet access:* library.
    **East** 6 miles to White River Junction, a large town with all services. Amtrak provides daily train service on the Vermonter, (800) USA-RAIL. *Hostel:* Hotel Coolidge (Hostelling International), (802) 295-3118, (800) 622-1124, <www.hotelcoolidge.com>, <info@hotelcoolidge.com>, 39 South Main St., White River Junction, VT 05001; nonmember rates: twin bed $35s $55D, full bed $55s/D; member rates: twin bed $25s, full bed $45s $55D; private rooms available; walk to restaurants, banks, stores; on-site laundry; CATV; WiFi.

**Happy Hill Shelter** (1998)—Sleeps 8. Privy. The oldest A.T. shelter (built in 1918, before the A.T.) was torn down, then burned on-site; the debris was carried out. In 1998, a new shelter was built about 0.2 mile north of the original. ALDHA members worked on this project after the 1997 Gathering. Water source is the brook near the shelter.

**Norwich, Vt. [P.O. ZIP 05055: M–F 8:30–5, Sa 9–12; (802) 649-1608]**—**East** 0.25 mile to *Lodging:* Norwich Inn, (802) 649-1143, <www.norwichinn.com>, May–Sep $99D motel, $154–$239 inn, call for fall and winter rates; one room for those with dogs; reservations strongly recommended; WiFi; built in 1791 as a stagecoach inn, reportedly the inspiration for the "Newhart" TV show. ■ *Restaurants:* Norwich Inn, Tu–Su B/L/D, Su brunch. ■ *Groceries:* Dan & Whits (long-term resupply), open daily 7–9, a sprawling, eclectic general store; Allechante Bakery and Café, M–F 7:30–5:30, Sa 7:30–3. ■ *Internet access:* library. ■ *Other services:* bank with ATM.

# New Hampshire

| Miles from Katahdin | Features | Services | Elev. | Miles from Springer |
|---|---|---|---|---|
| 442.4 | Connecticut River, N.H.–Vt. State Line | R | 380 | 1,733.8 |
| 441.9 | N.H. 10, Dartmouth College **Hanover, NH 03755** | R, PO, C, G, M, L, O, D, V, f, @ (E–2m L, cl; 16m H, f) (W–1.5m cl; 2.5m L) | 520 | 1,734.3 |
| 441.2 | N.H. 120 | R | 490 | 1,735.0 |
| 440.4 | **Velvet Rocks Shelter** *7.4mS; 9.5mN* | S (N–0.2m w) | 1,040 | 1,735.8 |
| 439.9 | Ledyard Spring | W–0.4m w | 1,200 | 1,736.3 |
| 437.4 | Trescott Rd | R | 490 | 1,738.8 |
| 436.0 | Etna-Hanover Center Rd | R (E–0.7m G) | 880 | 1,740.2 |
| 433.5 | Three Mile Rd | R | 1,350 | 1,742.7 |
| 433.3 | Mink Brook | w | 1,320 | 1,742.9 |
| 431.7 | Moose Mtn (South Peak) | | 2,250 | 1,744.5 |
| 430.9 | **Moose Mtn Shelter** *9.5mS; 5.9mN* | S, w | 1,850 | 1,745.3 |
| 429.0 | South Fork, Hewes Brook | w | 1,100 | 1,747.2 |
| 427.7 | Goose Pond Rd | R | 920 | 1,748.5 |
| 425.7 | Holts Ledge | | 2,100 | 1,750.5 |
| 425.2 | **Trapper John Shelter** *5.9mS; 6.9mN* | W–0.2m S, C, w | 1,345 | 1,751.0 |
| 424.3 | Dartmouth Skiway, Lyme-Dorchester Rd **Lyme, NH 03768** | R (W–3.2m PO, G, M, L, ATC NE Office) | 880 | 1,751.9 |
| 422.3 | Lyme–Dorchester Rd | R, w | 850 | 1,753.9 |
| 418.6 | Smarts Mtn Tentsite | C, w | 3,200 | 1,757.6 |
| 418.5 | **Firewarden's Cabin** and Fire Tower *6.9mS; 5.6mN* | S, w | 3,220 | 1,757.7 |
| 414.6 | South Jacob's Brook | | 1,450 | 1,761.6 |
| 413.2 | **Hexacuba Shelter** *5.6mS; 7.7mN* | w (E–0.3m S) | 1,980 | 1,763.0 |
| 411.6 | Side trail to Mt. Cube (north summit) | | 2,911 | 1,764.6 |
| 408.3 | N.H. 25A **Wentworth, NH 03282** | R (E–4.8m PO, G) (W– 1.9m C, G) | 900 | 1,767.9 |
| 406.5 | Cape Moonshine Rd | R (E–1m C, sh) | 1,480 | 1,769.7 |
| 405.9 | **Ore Hill Shelter** *7.7mS; 8.6mN* | E–0.1m S, w | 1,720 | 1,770.3 |
| 403.5 | N.H. 25C **Warren, NH 03279** | R (E–4m PO, G, L, M, D, cl, @) | 1,500 | 1,772.7 |

| Miles from Katahdin | Features | Services | Elev. | Miles from Springer |
|---|---|---|---|---|
| 401.0 | Mt. Mist | | 2,200 | 1,775.2 |
| 398.5 | N.H. 25 **Glencliff, NH 03238** | R (E–0.4m PO, H, sh, cl, f) | 1,140 | 1,777.7 |
| 397.4 | **Jeffers Brook Shelter** *8.6mS; 6.8mN* | S, w | 1,350 | 1,778.8 |
| 392.8 | Mt. Moosilauke | | 4,802 | 1,783.4 |
| 390.6 | **Beaver Brook Shelter** *6.8mS; 9.1mN* | S, C, w | 3,650 | 1,785.6 |
| 389.0 | N.H. 112, Kinsman Notch **North Woodstock, NH 03262** | R (E–0.3m w; 5m PO, G, M, L, cl, f) | 1,812 | 1,787.2 |
| 384.4 | Mt. Wolf (East Peak) | | 3,478 | 1,791.8 |
| 381.5 | **Eliza Brook Shelter** *9.1mS; 4.1mN* | S, C, w | 2,500 | 1,794.7 |
| 379.0 | South Kinsman Mtn | | 4,358 | 1,797.2 |
| 378.1 | North Kinsman Mtn | | 4,293 | 1,798.1 |
| 377.5 | **+Kinsman Pond Campsite and Shelter** *4.1mS; 15.3mN* | E–0.1m C, S, w | 3,750 | 1,798.7 |
| 375.6 | +Lonesome Lake Hut | L, M, w | 2,760 | 1,800.6 |
| 372.7 | I-93, U.S. 3, Franconia Notch, Lafayette Place Campground **North Woodstock, NH 03262; Lincoln, NH 03251** | R (E–0.7m sh; 0.8m M; 5.8m, 7.3m PO, G, M, L, cl, f) (W–2.1m C, G, sh; 8m G, L, M, sh, @) | 1,450 | 1,803.5 |
| 370.1 | +Liberty Springs Tentsite | C, w | 3,800 | 1,806.1 |
| 368.0 | Little Haystack Mtn | | 4,800 | 1,808.2 |
| 367.3 | Mt. Lincoln | | 5,089 | 1,808.9 |
| 366.3 | Mt. Lafayette, +Greenleaf Hut *via* Greenleaf Trail | (W–0.2m w; 1.1m L, M, w) | 5,249 | 1,809.9 |
| 363.5 | Garfield Pond | | 3,860 | 1,812.7 |
| 362.8 | Mt. Garfield | | 4,488 | 1,813.4 |
| 362.4 | **+Garfield Ridge Campsite** *15.3mS; 6.3mN* | W–0.1m C, S, w | 3,560 | 1,813.8 |
| 359.7 | +Galehead Hut | L, M, w | 3,800 | 1,816.5 |
| 358.9 | South Twin Mtn, North Twin Spur | | 4,902 | 1,817.3 |
| 356.9 | Mt.Guyot; **+Guyot Campsite** *via* Bondcliff Trail *6.3mS; 9.7mN* | E–0.7m C, S, w | 4,560 | 1,819.3 |
| 353.9 | Zeacliff | | 4,084 | 1,822.3 |
| 352.7 | +Zealand Falls Hut | L, M, w | 2,630 | 1,823.5 |

| Miles from Katahdin | Features | Services | Elev. | Miles from Springer |
|---|---|---|---|---|
| 347.9 | +**Ethan Pond Campsite** *9.7mS; 20.5mN* | C, S, w | 2,950 | 1,828.3 |
| 345.0 | U.S. 302, Crawford Notch **Bartlett, NH 03812** | R (E–1.8m C, cl, sh; 3m C, G, sh; 10m PO) (W–1m M; 3.7m L, M, sh; 8.4m G, L, @) | 1,277 | 1,831.2 |
| 344.9 | Saco River | | 1,277 | 1,831.3 |
| 343.1 | Webster Cliffs | | 3,350 | 1,833.1 |
| 341.7 | Mt. Webster | | 3,910 | 1,834.5 |
| 340.3 | Mt. Jackson | | 4,052 | 1,835.9 |
| 338.6 | +Mizpah Spring Hut, +Nauman Tentsite | C, L, M, w | 3,800 | 1,837.6 |
| 337.8 | Mt. Pierce (Mt. Clinton) | | 4,312 | 1,838.4 |
| 336.9 | Spring | w | 4,350 | 1,839.3 |
| 335.6 | Spring | w | 4,480 | 1,840.6 |
| 335.3 | Mt. Franklin | | 5,004 | 1,840.9 |
| 333.8 | +Lakes of the Clouds Hut | L, M, w | 5,012 | 1,842.4 |
| 332.4 | Mt. Washington, Mt. Washington Auto Rd **Mt. Washington, NH 03589 (not recommended)** | R, PO, M (8m *via* Auto Road to N.H. 16) | 6,288 | 1,843.8 |
| 332.4 | Tuckerman Ravine Trail to +**Hermit Lake Shelter** and Pinkham Notch | (E–2m S; 4.2m R, G, M, L, sh, f) | 6,288 | 1,843.8 |
| 329.0 | Edmands Col | w | 5,000 | 1,847.2 |
| 328.3 | Israel Ridge Path to +**The Perch Shelter** *20.5mS; 23.4mN* | W–0.9m C, S, w | 4,313 | 1,847.9 |
| 327.7 | Thunderstorm Jct, Trail to +RMC Crag Camp Cabin; Lowe's Path to Mt. Adams & +RMC Gray Knob Cabin | W–1.1m, 1.2m C, S, w | 5,500 | 1,848.5 |
| 326.8 | +Madison Spring Hut | L, M, w | 4,800 | 1,849.4 |
| 326.8 | Valley Way Tentsite | W–0.6m C, w | 3,900 | 1,849.4 |
| 326.3 | Mt. Madison | | 5,363 | 1,849.9 |
| 323.8 | Osgood Tentsite | C, w | 2,540 | 1,852.4 |
| 323.0 | West Branch Peabody River | w | 2,300 | 1,853.2 |
| 320.9 | Lowe's Bald Spot | | 2,860 | 1,855.3 |

| Miles from Katahdin | Features | Services | Elev. | Miles from Springer |
|---|---|---|---|---|
| 319.0 | N.H. 16, Pinkham Notch, Pinkham Notch Visitor Center +Joe Dodge Lodge | R, G, M, L, sh, f (E–16m L, O; 18m G, M, L, O, D) (W–4m AMC Camp Dodge; 11m Gorham, N.H., see below) | 2,050 | 1,857.2 |
| 316.0 | Wildcat Mtn, Peak D Tower | | 3,990 | 1,860.2 |
| 314.0 | Wildcat Mtn, Peak A | | 4,380 | 1,862.2 |
| 313.1 | Carter Notch | E–0.1m L, w | 3,350 | 1,863.1 |
| | +Carter Notch Hut | | | |
| 312.4 | Spring | w | 4,700 | 1,863.8 |
| 311.9 | Carter Dome | | 4,832 | 1,864.3 |
| 310.5 | Zeta Pass | w | 3,990 | 1,865.7 |
| 309.7 | South Carter Mtn | | 4,458 | 1,866.5 |
| 308.4 | Middle Carter Mtn | | 4,600 | 1,867.8 |
| 307.8 | North Carter Mtn | | 4,539 | 1,868.4 |
| 305.9 | **+Imp Campsite** *23.4mS; 6.2mN* | W–0.2m C, S, w | 3,250 | 1,870.3 |
| 303.8 | Mt. Moriah | | 4,049 | 1,872.4 |
| 299.8 | **Rattle River Shelter** *6.2mS; 13.7mN* | S, w | 1,260 | 1,876.4 |
| 297.9 | U.S. 2 **Gorham, NH 03581** | R, w (W–1.8m H, C, cl, sh; 3.6m PO, H, G, M, L, O, cl, f, @; 8m D) | 780 | 1,878.3 |
| 297.6 | Androscoggin River | R | 750 | 1,878.6 |
| 297.4 | Hogan Rd | R | 760 | 1,878.8 |
| 296.4 | Brook | w | 1,350 | 1,879.8 |
| 294.3 | Mt Hayes, Mahoosuc Trail | | 2,555 | 1,881.9 |
| 292.1 | Cascade Mtn | | 2,631 | 1,884.1 |
| 291.0 | Trident Col Tentsite | W–0.1m C, w | 2,000 | 1,885.2 |
| 288.3 | Dream Lake | w | 2,600 | 1,887.9 |
| 286.8 | Moss Pond | w | 2,630 | 1,889.4 |
| 286.1 | **Gentian Pond Campsite** *13.7mS; 5.5mN* | C, S, w | 2,166 | 1,890.1 |
| 283.3 | Mt. Success | | 3,565 | 1,892.9 |
| 281.4 | N.H.–Maine State Line | | 2,972 | 1,894.8 |

*+ Fee charged*                *RMC = Randolph Mountain Club*

At Hanover, southbounders will have already experienced the White Mountains. Northbounders should gear up for the conditions ahead.

Although this is considered one of the most challenging states, it is also one of the most rewarding. As the trees get shorter and the views get longer, you've entered the krummholz zone, where trees are stunted with flag-like tops due to stress from the wind and cold. Boreal bogs are home to local carnivorous plant species, sundew and pitcher plants. Hardy, yet delicate alpine flowers—Labrador tea, bunchberry, mountain sandwort, and cloudberry—may be in bloom when you pass through. Spruce grouse, winter wren, dark-eyed junco, and the white-throated sparrow will greet you along the way.

Much of the Trail is above timberline, where the temperature may change very suddenly; snow is possible in any season. Snow falls on Mt. Washington during every month of the year. High winds and dense fog are common. Most shelters and campsites charge a fee.

*Many water sources in southern New Hampshire are not always reliable, including sources at, or adjacent to, shelters.*

**Hanover, N.H. [P.O. ZIP 03755: M–F 8:30–5, Sa 8:30–12, package pick-up opens at 7 a.m.; (603) 643-4544]**—Home of Dartmouth College. The A.T. passes through the center of Hanover, and most services are along the route of the Trail (see map). At the center of town and the Dartmouth Green, a blue-blazed side trail leads (Trail-west) to Robinson Hall and the office of the Dartmouth Outing Club (DOC) in Room 113, (603) 646-2428, <www.dartmouth.edu/~doc/>. DOC has student volunteers (DOCtours), Su–Th 2–6, phone, and Internet access. This is a good place to begin in town. The college does not allow nonstudents to stay in student housing. Dartmouth College security has reported problems with improper use of college facilities and buildings by hikers; hikers must not enter dormitories, offices, laundry rooms, *etc.*, without permission or try to sleep overnight in those locations, including the DOC building. The locker rooms and showers in the DOC basement are not public. Neither the college nor the DOC is responsible for hikers who leave their packs or other belongings unattended on college property. Public (on-street) consumption of alcohol is illegal in the downtown area. ■ *Camping:* Tenting is permitted in the woods just east of downtown area; follow A.T. north 0.4 mile through town to woods at the far end of soccer field. Please keep this area clean, and pack out your trash to ensure this site remains open for future hikers. ■ *Groceries:* Hanover Food Co-op (long-term resupply), bulk and natural foods; Food Stop, CVS Pharmacy/Food Shop, and Stinson's Village Store (all short-term resupply). ■ *Restaurants:* Ramunto's Pizza; Everything But Anchovies, B/L/D; Lou's Bakery & Restaurant, B/L; Thayer Hall, the Dartmouth dining hall, B/L/D; C&A Pizza; Quizno's; Subway; Ben & Jerry's Scoop Shop; Boloco; Bagel Basement; India Queen; Dirt Cowboy Café; 5 Olde Nugget Alley Restaurant;

The Canoe Club Restaurant; Murphy's on the Green. ■ *Internet access:* Howe Public Library and the DOC. ■ *Outfitters:* Hanover Outdoors, (603) 643-1263, <www.hanoveroutdoors. com>, M–Sa 9–6, Su 10–4, clothing, outdoor equipment, and flyfishing, accepts hikers' packages mailed to 17½ Lebanon St.; Zimmermann's, sells primarily North Face clothing and packs; Omer and Bob's Sport Shop; EMS, (603) 298-7716, and L.L.Bean Outlet, (603) 298-6975, both in West Lebanon—take "Orange" bus route, switch to "Red," and ask the driver to let you off at the Powerhouse Mall. ■ *Other services:* True Value Hardware, Coleman fuel, denatured alcohol; College Cleaners on Allen Street offers "wash, dry, and fold"; One Clean Place, 1.5 miles north on N.H. 10 on "Brown" bus route, has self-service laundry; bookstores; dentist; doctor; hospital; movie theater; optician; Camera Shop of Hanover; banks with ATM; pharmacy; barber shop; Hanover Veterinary Clinic, (603) 643-3313, (603) 643-4829 after hours; Hanover Hot Tubs. ■ *Bus service:* Advance Transit is a local bus service, 6 a.m. to 6 p.m., M–F only. Most routes are free; can be picked up outside the Hanover Inn; offers transportation throughout Hanover and to White River Junction, Vt. (where there is an Amtrak station), Lebanon, and West Lebanon, with all major services. Bus to West Lebanon leaves from bookstore on Main Street. Bus schedules available in the bookstore. Vermont Transit Bus, (800) 552-8737, provides service from Hanover to Boston. ■ *Long-term parking:* available for hikers in "A" lot, east of campus. Call parking operations, (603) 646-2204, for directions and to make arrangements. ■ *Shuttles:* Big Yellow Taxi, (603) 643-8294; Apex Transportation, "Stray Kat" '96 & '06, (603) 252-8294.

**East (south)**—2.0 miles to *Lodging:* Sunset Motor Inn, (603) 298-8721, on N.H. 10, on the "Orange" bus route, $65–$95, no pets, no smoking, CATV, continental B, shuttle and laundry may be available if you ask the owners; Super 8 Motel in White River Junction, Vt., (802) 295-7577, on the "Orange" bus route; Days Inn in Lebanon, N.H., (603) 448-5070, on the "Blue" bus route.

**West (north)**—2.5 miles to *Lodging:* Chieftain Motor Inn, (603) 643-2550, on the "Brown" bus route (bus stops within 0.5 mile), $75–$100, pets $35, no smoking, CATV, continental B.

**East** 16 miles to Canaan, N.H., and *Hostel:* A.T. Hillton, (603) 252-8295 (hostel/shuttle), <apexlake@hotmail.com>, 365 Choate Rd., Canaan, NH 03741, owned by "Stray Kat." Hostel open Jun 1–Sep 30 with year-round shuttle services; bunkhouse $30PP includes bed with linens, shower with towel, and round-trip shuttle; please call ahead to make arrangements for either 11:30 a.m. or 4:30 p.m. shuttle in front of DOC/Robinson Hall at Dartmouth; other Trailhead shuttles available. Amenities include TV, radio, taped movies, BBQ grill, microwave, refrigerator, meals, pizza, soft drinks, Coleman and denatured alcohol. Pets are welcome but not allowed inside. Laundry $3. Fee for additional shuttles to town for movie theaters, P.O., groceries, and health club with pool and hot tub. Limit 15 people per night with three-day limit unless there is a medical problem or injury. Mail drops accepted. Parking $3/day, $15/week, $50/month.

**Velvet Rocks Shelter** (1980s/2006)—Sleeps 6. Privy. On blue-blazed loop trail with access from the north and south. Water source is Ledyard Spring, located along the northern access trail. During dry periods, hikers may want to bring water from town.

**Etna–Hanover Center Road—East** 0.7 mile to *Groceries:* Etna General Store (limited resupply), M–Th 6–7, F–Sa 6–8, Su 8–6, snacks, sandwiches, cold drinks, stove fuels.

**Moose Mountain Shelter** (2004)—Sleeps 8. Privy. New log shelter built entirely with hand tools by DOC. Water source is on the A.T. north of the shelter—follow loop trail to end.

**Trapper John Shelter** (1990s)—Sleeps 6. Privy uses an old chair. Tentsites. Water source is a brook 15 yards to the left of the shelter.

 **Lyme–Dorchester Road**—Water and ice cream at blue house just west of trail; sign on Trail after road intersection.
    **West** 3.2 miles to **Lyme, N.H. [P.O. ZIP 03768: M–F 7:45–12 & 1:30–5:15, Sa 7:45–12; (603) 795-4421]. ■ *Lodging:*** Dowd's Country Inn B&B, (603) 795-4712; weekdays $95S, $125D; weekends $115S, $145D; $105S weekdays includes B and afternoon tea. Kennels may be available for pets. Reservations and a minimum two-night stay required for weekends (F and Sa). ■ *Other services:* Country store and deli (short-term resupply), open daily; banks with ATM; Nichols Hardware store; and pay phone. ATC's New England regional office, (603) 795-4935, upstairs in the One Lyme Common building, is across the green from the church.

**Smarts Mountain Tentsites**—Maintained by DOC; cleared area for three tents; privy; water from Mike Murphy Spring (see next entry).

**Smarts Mountain Firewarden Cabin**—Sleeps 8. Privy. The cabin, built by the N.H. Forest Service, is now maintained as shelter by DOC. Panoramic views from the abandoned firetower on Smarts Mountain summit. Water source is Mike Murphy Spring 0.2 mile north of cabin on blue-blazed Daniel Doan Trail.

**Hexacuba Shelter (1989)**—Sleeps 8. Privy (penta-style). Constructed by DOC. Tentsites. Water source is an unreliable stream at the blue-blaze junction to the shelter. Alternative source is 0.3 mile south on the A.T. at North Jacobs Brook.

 **N.H. 25A—East** 4.8 miles to **Wentworth, N.H. [P.O. ZIP 03282: M–F 7:15–1 & 3–5, Sa 7:15–12; (603) 764-9444].** *Groceries:* Shawnee's General Store (long-term resupply), (603) 764-5553, M–Th 5 a.m.–8 p.m., F 5–9, Sa 6–9, Su 7–8; outside pay phone.
    **West** 1.9 miles to *Groceries:* Mt. Cube Sugar House & Farm House, (603) 353-4814, owned and operated by the Thomson family. Fruit stand open 8:30–dusk; home-made snacks, maple products, seasonal fruits and vegetables. Hikers may

be allowed to stay in the hay barn, known as the Governor's Mansion. No cooking or open flames allowed in hay barn; Sugar House facilities available in bad weather, with permission.

**Cape Moonshine Road—East** 1 mile to *Work for stay:* Dancing Bones Village, an independent community that offers hikers tentsites, showers, and sometimes meals in exchange for light work.

**Ore Hill Shelter** (2000)—Sleeps 8. Privy (medieval-style). Water source is a spring on the path 100 yards in front of the shelter.

**N.H. 25C—East** 4 miles to **Warren, N.H. [P.O. ZIP 03279: M–F 7:30–1 & 2:30–5, Sa 8–11:30; (603) 764-5733].** ■ *Lodging:* Warren Village Inn, (603) 764-5600, 254 N.H. 25, Warren, NH 03279, $110 plus $8.80 tax, 2-night weekday stay is $99 plus tax, includes continental B. ■ *Restaurants:* Calamity Jane's, B/L/D, (603) 764-5288, open M 6 a.m.–2 p.m., Tu–F 6 a.m.–8 p.m., Sa 6–11 p.m., Su 8–7; Twig, Th–Sa 11–11 (open mic Th 8 p.m., live music F p.m.), Su 8 a.m.–9 p.m.; 8–12 AYCE brunch $8PP; M 11–9, pizza, dinner specials. ■ *Other services:* hardware store, doctor, and laundry.

**N.H. 25—East** 0.4 mile to **Glencliff, N.H. [P.O. ZIP 03238: M–F 7–10 & 2–5, Sa 7–1; (603) 989-5154],** with pay phone located on south side of white building at driveway entrance to P.O. This is a prudent mail drop for northbounders to pick up cold-weather gear before entering the high country of the White Mountains. ■ *Hostel:* The Hikers Welcome Hostel, (603) 989-0040, P.O. Box 25, 1396 N.H. Route 25, located at the base of Mt. Moosilauke, across the street from the post office; $15 hostel/bunks (includes shower); $10 tenting includes shower; hot outdoor shower $2.50; laundry, $2.50 wash, $2.50 dryer; hiker snacks, denatured alcohol and Coleman fuel by the ounce, free wireless Internet, and shuttles. Resupply, ATM, and restaurants in Warren (5 miles; see above).

**Oliverian Brook**—The brook can be a difficult ford after rain. Be careful.

**Jeffers Brook Shelter** (1970s)—Sleeps 10. Privy. Located on a spur trail. Water source is Jeffers Brook, located in front of the shelter.

**The White Mountains**—One of the most impressive sections of the A.T., the Whites offer magnificent views with miles of above-treeline travel. Extra caution should be exercised while above treeline, due to rapidly changing weather and the lack of protection from it. Carry cold-weather gear, even in the middle of summer. Winter weather, including sleet, snow, and ice, is possible on these high ridges year-round. Each year, carelessness ends in death for a few visitors to the Whites. Pay close attention at Trail intersections. The Appalachian Mountain Club (AMC) maintains many trails that cross the A.T., and the A.T. route is commonly referred to on signs and in guidebooks by the name of the local trail it follows, such as "Franconia Ridge Trail." (And, to add to the confusion, sections above treeline from Mizpah Hut to Madison Hut are often marked with yellow blazes on rock cairns, to stand out in the snow.) When above treeline, stay on the Trail. This alpine zone is home to very fragile plants. One misplaced bootstep can destroy them.

*Backcountry regulations*—Each summer, AMC serves tens of thousands of backpackers and campers at its backcountry shelters and campsites in the White Mountain National Forest. To prevent the Whites from being "loved to death," the USFS, in conjunction with AMC and the New Hampshire state parks agency, established a strict set of backcountry rules and regulations for the White Mountains. Please follow the rules. Hikers should be aware of all pertinent rules and regulations pertaining to camping in these areas and should not be surprised if they are rigorously enforced by ridgerunners and rangers. This especially applies to those who choose to camp immediately adjacent to huts, shelters, caretaker campsites, and road crossings. Hikers who ignore posted warnings may well receive hefty tickets. You will encounter forest protection areas (FPAs), where camping and fires are prohibited. The following regulations apply in those areas: no camping above treeline (where trees are less than eight feet high); no camping within 0.25 mile of huts, shelters, or tentsites except at the facility itself; no camping within 200 feet of the Trail. Groups of 6 or more should contact AMC Group Notification System, <www.outdoors.org>, (603) 466-2721 x220, so it can effectively manage all large groups that stay at AMC sites. AMC-managed sites can accommodate groups of up to 10.

**Mt. Moosilauke**—The north side of Mt. Moosilauke is slick, particularly in rain. Be careful! Sections use rebar, rock steps, and wooden blocks for footing. For northbounders, it is the first mountain above treeline. For southbounders, the meadow at the base of the southern side is the first pastureland they encounter on the A.T. From the summit, Franconia Ridge, as well as the rest of the Whites, can be seen to the northeast; the Green Mountains are visible to the west. The remnants of the 1860 Prospect House, a popular tourist spot that burned to the ground in 1942, can still be seen at the summit.

**Beaver Brook Shelter** (1980s)—Sleeps 10. Privy (composting). Completed by DOC and ALDHA members, site includes tentsites and a nice view of Franconia Ridge. Water source is Beaver Brook on the spur trail to the shelter.

**Appalachian Mountain Club**—AMC maintains the A.T. and surrounding trails between Kinsman Notch and Grafton Notch in Maine, a total of 122.2 miles; (603) 466-2721; <www.outdoors.org>.

**AMC Tentsites, Shelters, and Campsites**—"Tentsites" have designated tenting areas and platforms or pads. "Shelters" are three- or four-sided structures. "Campsites" have designated tenting areas and a shelter. See below for description of "huts," where reservations are required. Tentsites, shelters, and campsites are on a first-come, first-served basis. USFS parking fees are established throughout the Whites; be prepared to pay if you park at a Forest Service trailhead. Caretakers are in residence at the following tentsites, shelters, and campsites, where a $8 overnight fee is charged: Kinsman Pond Campsite, Liberty Spring Tentsite, Garfield Ridge Campsite, 13 Falls Tentsite, Guyot Campsite, Ethan Pond Campsite, Nauman Tentsite, Imp Campsite, and Speck Pond Campsite (Maine). A caretaker works at those sites due to the locations' popularity and the fragility of their resources. The remaining tentsites, shelters, and campsites, except those operated by the Randolph Mountain Club (see below), are available to backcountry travelers at no charge.

*Work exchange at campsites and shelters*—A work-for-stay option is possible for thru-hikers at the tentsites and shelter sites that have caretakers. This is at the discretion of the caretaker and may not always be available. A maximum of two thru-hikers per night can be accommodated in that way at each site, and each will be expected to contribute an hour of work.

**AMC Huts**—These large, enclosed lodges sleep from 36 to 90 people and are open with full service from early Jun to Sep or Oct, depending on the hut. All huts are either closed or already booked for Jun 1–3, 2008. Rates range from $71 to $94, depending on the day, AMC membership, and the hut. Lonesome Lake, Carter Notch, and Zealand Falls huts have an additional self-service season. A crew ("croo") staffs these facilities during the full-service season. An overnight stay includes bunk space, pillow, blanket, bathroom privileges (no showers), and potable water. If you plan to stay three consecutive nights, there is a package rate, available all summer. Rates for self-service seasons are significantly less ($27–$30) than full-service seasons. Each hut has trained wilderness EMT and wilderness first-responders, and the facilities' crews give natural- and cultural-history evening programs. The huts also contain excellent libraries and displays on cultural and natural history.

If you plan to pay for a stay in one of the huts, make reservations, (603) 466-2727, especially for the weekends, when bunk spaces fill quickly. Call AMC or check <www.outdoors. org> to verify the huts' opening and closing dates as well as rates. You may also be able to make a reservation by having a caretaker at one of the other huts or campsites radio ahead for you. The huts cater mainly to families and weekend hikers. AMC had wells drilled at all the huts, so you can look forward to water that meets state health standards. During the self-service season, a caretaker is at Lonesome Lake, Zealand, and Carter huts. Schedules vary from hut to hut; check individual listings for specific dates.

*Work exchange at the huts*—Thru-hikers can sometimes arrange with the croo to work off their stays at the full- or self-service huts on the A.T. Most huts can accommodate one or two working thru-hikers each night—except for Lakes of the Clouds Hut, which takes up to four thru-hikers—but availability of work is never guaranteed. This work exchange is on a first-come, first-served basis. Work varies, but you can expect to put in 1–3 hours in the morning; at times when work is not available, the full fee may be charged. Please give other thru-hikers a chance to work off their stay, and limit your use of the work-for-stay option to no more than three huts.

The AMC *Thru-Hiker's Guide to AMC-Maintained Trails & Facilities in the White Mountains & Mahoosucs* is a resource written for those who plan to stay at the fee sites (both back-country and hospitality). It is not a tool for thru-hikers who correctly follow backcountry regulations and camp through this area; see <www.outdoors.org/thru-hikers>.

**AMC Shuttle**—603-466-2727, <www.outdoors.org/lodging/ lodging-shuttle.cfm>, daily Jun 1–Sep 16, weekends only Sep 16–Oct 14; $12 AMC members, $14 nonmembers, reservations strongly recommended; walk-ons accepted on a space-available basis, see driver; drop-offs on route between scheduled stops may be arranged with driver. Stops include trailheads at Liberty Spring/A.T. on I-93, Lafayette Place Campground, Old Bridle Path, Gale River, Zealand Falls, Ammonoosuc Ravine, Highland Center at Crawford Notch, Webster Cliff/ A.T. at Rt. 302, Pinkham Notch Visitors Center, 19-Mile Brook Trail, Gorham Irving Gas Station, Valley Way/Appalachia. Check Web site for further details.

**N.H. 112/Kinsman Notch—East** 0.3 mile to Lost River Gorge, a series of streams and waterfalls owned by the Society for the Protection of New Hampshire Forests. Self-guided tour of gorge, ecology trail, and nature garden, $12, daily 9–5, from mid-May to mid-Oct, last ticket sold at 4 p.m. Phone available during business hours, with permission and a phone card.

**East** 5 miles to **North Woodstock, N.H. [P.O. ZIP 03262: M–F 8–12:30 & 1:30–5, Sa 8–12; (603) 745-8134]**, which also is accessible from Franconia Notch (below). ■ *Lodging:* Woodstock Inn, (603) 745-3951 or (800) 321-3985, shared bath $65PP, private bath $89PP, rates vary on weekends and holidays, no pets permitted, includes B, nonsmoking rooms, pool at Alpine Village, restaurant L/D; Autumn Breeze, (603) 745-8549, $68–$90, no dogs, rooms have kitchenettes; Carriage Motel, (603) 745-2416, $64–$78, game room, gas grills, picnic tables, pool, hiker box, deli, laundry, P.O. across street. ■ *Groceries:* Wayne's Market (long-term resupply), deli and excellent grinders. ■ *Restaurants:* Truants Taverne, Landmark II Family, Peg's, and Woodstock Station. ■ *Other services:* ATM, barber shop and beauty salon, Handy Wash Laundry, Fadden's General Store, ice cream, fudge shop, and Cascades town beach. ■ *Shuttles:* The Hiker Shuttle Connection, (603) 745-3140, 6 a.m.–2 a.m. year-round; from A.T. in Franconia Notch, follow Rt. 3 south to Exit 34A for shuttle pick-up.

**Eliza Brook Campsite** (1993)—Shelter sleeps 8. Privy (composting). Two hardened tent pads. Water source is Eliza Brook.

**Kinsman Pond Campsite and Shelter** (2007)—Shelter sleeps 15, replaces one built in 1966. Privy (composting). Two single and two double tent platforms. Overnight fee $8PP, caretaker on site. Water source is Kinsman Pond; treat your water.

**Lonesome Lake Hut**—This southernmost hut offers swimming in Lonesome Lake. Full service Jun 4–Oct 18. Self-service the rest of the year.

**I-93/U.S.3/Franconia Notch**—**East 0.7 mile to** *Shuttle: via* Whitehouse Brook Trail to hiker parking lot on U.S. 3 and AMC hiker shuttle stop.

    **East**—0.8 mile to Flume Visitor Center, with snack bar/restaurant, and ice cream. Open daily early May to late Oct, 9–5. ATM during business hours; pay phone 24 hours. Admission to see The Flume itself is $10.

    **East** 5.8 miles to North Woodstock (see above).

    **East** 7.3 miles to **Lincoln, N.H. [P.O. ZIP 03251: M–F 8–5, Sa 8–12; (603) 745-8133]**. *Hostel:* One Step At A Time, (603) 745-8196, 197 Pollard Rd., owned by former hiker Chet West, bunk space for 6, work for stay, barter, donation, laundry (small fee), dogs okay; central to supermarket, outfitters, restaurants, movie theater, medical center, pharmacy, bus service, and Whale's Tale Water Park.

    **West** 2.1 miles to *Camping:* Lafayette Place Campground, (603) 823-9513, with tentsites $19D, coin-operated hot showers 25¢, store (short-term resupply), Coleman fuel by the gallon. Park rangers hold packages mailed to Franconia State Park, Lafayette Place Campground, Franconia, NH 03580. Write the date you expect to arrive on the package. Open mid-May to Columbus Day. Campground is usually filled by noon.

**West** 8 miles to Franconia. ■ *Lodging:* Gale River Motel, (603) 823-5655 or (800) 255-7989, <www.galerivermotel.com>, <info@galerivermotel.com>, $90–$99 Jun–Sep, $95–$180 foliage season, $45–$95 in between and ski season, shuttle to and from Trail when available, laundry, call ahead for mail drops. ■ *Groceries:* Kelly's Supermarket (long-term supply). ■ *Internet access:* library. ■ *Other services:* pizza, restaurant, bank, ATM, Concord Trailways bus service, and AMC hiker shuttle stop at Lafayette Place Campground.

**Liberty Springs Tentsite**—Privy (composting). Seven single and three double tent platforms. Overnight fee $8PP, caretaker on site. Water source is the spring.

**Franconia Ridge**—In any kind of weather, this ridge walk will leave you awestruck. Beautiful views from the summit of Mt. Liberty can be reached from the A.T. *via* a side trail.

**Greenleaf Hut**—Visible from the summit of Mt. Lafayette, it is 1.1 miles on the Greenleaf Trail to the hut. Self-service May 9–31. Full service Jun 4–Oct 18.

**Garfield Ridge Campsite** (1970)—Shelter sleeps 12. Privy (composting). Two single and five double tent platforms. Overnight fee $8PP, caretaker on site. Water source is a spring at the junction to the campsite.

**Galehead Hut**—Rebuilt 1999–2000, with wheelchair-accessible design. Self-service May 9–31. Full service Jun 4–Oct 18.

**Guyot Campsite** (1977)—Shelter sleeps 12. Privy (composting). Four single and two double tent platforms. Located 0.7 mile east on Bondcliff Trail. Overnight fee $8PP, caretaker on site. Water source is a spring at the campsite.

**Zealand Falls Hut**—Next to beautiful falls. Full service Jun 4–Oct 18. Self-service the rest of the year.

**Ethan Pond Campsite** (1970s)—Shelter sleeps 10. Privy (composting). Three single and two double tent platforms. Metal bear box. Overnight fee $8PP, caretaker on site. Water source is the inlet brook to the pond.

**U.S. 302/Crawford Notch**—**East** 1.8 miles to ■ *Camping:* Dry River Campground, (603) 374-2272, $18D, coin laundry, and showers 25¢. ■ *Shuttle*: AMC shuttle stop at Webster Cliff/A.T. Trailhead.

**East** 3 miles to *Camping:* Crawford Notch Campground and General Store, 1138 U.S. 302, Harts Location, NH 03812, <www.crawfordnotchcamping.com>, (603) 374-2779; owners Marvin and Glenn Powell; bunkhouse (hostel) with heat and mattresses, $20PP includes coin-operated shower, towel, shuttle back to Trail, no dogs; campsites $21 each for 2 people, additional fee for up to 4 people; laundry for overnight guests only; long-term resupply; fuel by the ounce; open daily mid-May–mid-Oct.

**East** 10 miles to the small town of **Bartlett, N.H. [P.O. ZIP 03812: M–F 9–1 & 1:30–5:30, Sa 9–12; (603) 374-2351].**

**West** 1 mile to the Wiley House, with snack bar and pay phone, open daily mid-May to mid-Oct, 9–5.

**West** 3.7 miles to ■ *Lodging:* AMC's Highland Center, (603) 278-4453, <www.outdoors.org>, limited hiker supplies, AYCE B $9.75, 6:30–8:30; *a la carte* L $8–$10, 10–4; 4-course D $23, reserve seat by 6; bunk room in lodge $64PP, includes B/D; private room in lodge $109–$159PP, includes B/D; Shapleigh Bunkhouse, $30PP AMC member, $35PP nonmember, includes bunk, shower, towel, and B. Facilities generally are for overnight guests only. Mail drops accepted sent to AMC Highland Center at Crawford Notch, Route 302, Bretton Woods, NH 03575. ■ *Shuttle:* AMC shuttle stop.

**West** 8.4 miles to *Lodging:* Above the Notch Motor Inn, (603) 846-5156, <www.abovethenotch.com>, rooms with phones, bath, and TV, microwave, refrigerator, coffee/tea/condiments, WiFi, $78–$88 weekdays, $83–$93 weekends, $10EAP, will accept mail drops; no pets, no smoking. Grocery store (short-term resupply) nearby.

**Presidential Range**—The highest part of the Trail in New Hampshire, with 25 miles of ridge-walking between Crawford Notch and Pinkham Notch, most of which is above treeline (about 4,400 feet). The A.T. skirts many peaks, which can be reached by short side trails leading to, and often over, the summits.

**Mizpah Spring Hut & Nauman Tentsite**—Constructed in 1964 and 1965. Self-service May 9–31; full-service Jun 4 to Oct 18. Tentsite, five single and two double tent platforms, composting privy, metal bear box. Overnight fee $8PP. Water source for tentsite is a stream or potable water from hut (if open).

**Lakes of the Clouds Hut**—Constructed in 1915 at an elevation of 5,050 feet, this is the highest, largest, and most popular hut. Full-service Jun 4 to Sep 13, with no self-service operation. "The Dungeon," a small basement shelter, is available to hikers for $8, with access to hut restroom and the common area; it sleeps only 6, so reservations are still suggested. Call ahead from another hut or campsite. "The Dungeon" is an emergency-only shelter when the hut is closed; must not be used as a destination.

**Mt. Washington Auto Road/Mt. Washington**—The highest peak in the Northeast (6,288 feet). Since it is also accessible by the Auto Road and a cog railroad, more touristy services are here than one might expect to find. *Note: In 2007, 8 hikers were arrested for mooning said cog railroad, with newspapers around the world running the story; take heed.* The summit building is operated by the New Hampshire Division of Parks and Recreation and houses Mt. Washington Observatory, <www.mountwashington.org>; Mt. Washington Museum ($2 admission); a snack bar; a post office; and pay phones. The state park is open daily 8–8 early May–early Oct, weather permitting. A hiker room is downstairs, with a table, restroom, and a space to rest. (Absolutely no overnight stays are allowed.) Over the years, many buildings have come and gone on the summit, including a 94-bedroom hotel completed in 1873 and destroyed by fire in 1908. The summit is under cloud cover about 55 percent of the time. Average summertime high is 52 degrees, and the average wintertime high is 15 degrees. On April 12, 1934, an on-land wind speed of 231 mph was recorded, which still stands as the world's record. If you see a staff meteorologist, ask about the "Century Club." The upper plateau is home to large grassy areas, strewn with rocks but known as "lawns." These lawns hold many species of plants and animals otherwise found only on high mountain peaks and in tundra areas hundreds of miles to the north.

**Mt. Washington, N.H. [P.O. ZIP 03589: (603) 466-3347]**—The post office in the summit building is *not* recommended as a mail drop. Its hours are limited, and it caters to those who visit the summit and desire to have the distinguished Mt. Washington postmark; since there is little space for storing mail drops, they may be redirected to other New Hampshire post offices, well off the Trail.

**East** 8 miles *via* Auto Road to N.H. 16.

**Tuckerman Ravine Trail**—A steep, 4.2-mile route from Mt. Washington to Pinkham Notch. In bad weather, you may wish to use this trail to get below treeline and bypass the exposed northern loop of the Presidential Range, but this precarious route is no picnic in icy conditions.

**Hermit Lake Shelters**—At the base of the Tuckerman Ravine bowl, 2 miles downhill, with some steep rock- and boulder-scrambling from the summit; 8 lean-tos, 3 tent platforms, $10PP; pets are not permitted overnight in the shelters; caretaker year-round.

**Edmands Col**—Just down to the east in the col is a reliable spring and the site of the former Edmands Col emergency shelter. Also, look for a bronze tablet in memory of J. Rayner Edmands, who was instrumental in the construction of most of the graded paths through the northern Presidentials.

**Crag Camp/Randolph Mountain Club (RMC) Cabins and Shelters**—Randolph Mountain Club, Randolph, NH 03570. RMC maintains a network of 100 miles of hiking trails, principally on the northern slopes of Mounts Madison, Adams, and Jefferson in the Presidential Range of the White Mountain National Forest and on the Crescent Range in the town of Randolph. Its trails are maintained through the joint efforts of volunteers, two seasonal trail crews, and one Student Conservation Association crew. The RMC maintains several cabins and shelters below treeline in the Presidential Range that are often used by A.T. hikers seeking shelter from the exposed ridgeline. Crag Camp (capacity 15) and Gray Knob (capacity 15) are cabins. The Perch is a lean-to with tent platforms. Another lean-to, the Log Cabin (capacity 10), is on Lowe's Path, 1 mile below Gray Knob. All camps are available to the public on a first-come, first-served basis. If a site is full, the caretaker may ask visitors to move to another RMC facility, if space is available. Groups are limited to 10. To maintain serenity, cellular phones may not be used at any of the camps. Since it is insulated and outfitted with a woodstove for cold-months use, Gray Knob has a caretaker year-round. Although fall and winter hikers are asked to bring up a couple of hardwood sticks, only its caretaker operates Gray Knob's woodstove. In Jul and Aug, Crag Camp has a caretaker. In those months, gas stoves at both camps are available to the public; at all other times, users must bring their own stoves. The Log Cabin, located at a lower elevation than the other RMC camps, is well-suited to families with younger children and hikers making a late-in-the-day start. Year-round, the weather is far harsher and colder here than "below the notches." RMC relies on visitors to carry out their trash and help keep the cabin and woods clean. To support the caretakers' wages and maintain the camps, fees are charged on a per-night basis: Crag Camp and Gray Knob, $12; The Perch, Log Cabin, and tent platforms, $7. If the caretaker is absent, please mail fees to: Treasurer, RMC, Randolph, NH 03570.

**The Perch** (1948)—Shelter sleeps 8. Privy. Four tent platforms, $7PP fee. Water source is crossed *en route* to the shelter.

**Madison Spring Hut**—Located in a col 0.5 mile south of the summit of Mt. Madison. Full service Jun 4–Sep 13, with no self-service operation.

**Valley Way and Osgood Tentsites**—These two no-fee U.S. Forest Service tentsites, below treeline on Mt. Madison, are often used by hikers starting or finishing the traverse of the Presidential Range. Valley Way Tentsite is off the A.T., 0.6 mile west of Madison Springs Hut, with two large tent platforms and a privy. Osgood Tentsite is 3 miles north of the hut, along the A.T., and has three tentsites, privy, and spring.

**N.H. 16/Pinkham Notch**—Pinkham Notch Visitors Center; front desk, (603) 466-2721. AMC's New Hampshire headquarters, located on the A.T., offers a store with limited hiker supplies, restroom, coin-operated showers (open 24 hours), AMC shuttle stop, and Concord Trailways bus service (see below). The center holds packages sent to AMC Visitors Center, c/o Front Desk, N.H. 16, Gorham, NH 03581. ■ *Restaurant:* Cafeteria with AYCE $7.75 B, deli L (not AYCE) 9:30–4, trail L $7.75, $16 D (slightly lower for members; thru-hikers get member rates). ■ *Lodging:* Joe Dodge Lodge, (603) 466-2727, $57 includes B/D. Prices can change; contact AMC for the most current rates. ■ *Camping* is permitted in the notch, 0.25 mile from the road and 200 feet from any trail.

**East** 16 miles to Intervale, N.H. ■ *Lodging:* Cranmore Mountain Lodge, (603) 356-2044, $30–$38 includes B, shower, bed, $5 fee for bed linens, heated pool, spa, mail drops accepted at 859 Kearsage Rd., Kearsarge, NH 03847. ■ *Outfitter:* Ragged Mountain Equipment, (603) 356-3042, open daily with backpacking gear and repair service. ■ *Other services:* Peter Limmer & Sons Shop, (603) 356-5378, located on N.H. 16A, home of legendary hand-made hiking boots, will repair many brands of boots and hiking gear with priority to thru-hikers; closed Su.

**East** 18 miles to North Conway, N.H., a tourist town with most major services, including several outfitters, a supermarket, cobbler, laundry, bank, ATM, doctor, pharmacy, one-hour photo, movie theater, hotels, and restaurants.

**West** 2 miles to the Wildcat Mountain Gondola, operates daily mid-Jun to mid-Oct, 10–4:45, and offers rides to and from the A.T. on the top of Wildcat Mountain; $12 round-trip, $6 down only.

**West** 4 miles to Camp Dodge Volunteer Center, (603) 466-3301, headquarters for AMC's summer volunteer trail crew. Two hikers per night can arrange to work two hours in exchange for a space in bunkhouse, with shower, B, D, and laundry privileges. Call ahead to see if space is available, and allow the phone to ring a long time. Open mid-May to mid-Sep.

**West** 11 miles to Gorham, N.H. (see below).

**Concord Trailways Bus Service**—Provides service between Boston and Pinkham Notch, as well as Gorham, Berlin, and Conway, (800) 639-3317, <www.concordtrailways.com>. The bus leaves Pinkham Notch daily at 8:12 a.m. and arrives at Boston South Station at 12:20 p.m. The bus to Pinkham Notch leaves Boston at 5:15 p.m. and arrives at Pinkham Notch at 9:10 p.m. One-way, $31; round-trip, $58.

**Carter Notch Hut**—The northernmost hut, located on the banks of two small lakes in Carter Notch. It is the original hut, built in 1914. Full service Jun 4–Sep 13; self-service rest of year.

Gorham

**Imp Campsite** (1980s)—Shelter sleeps 16. Privy (composting). Four single and one double tent platform. Overnight fee $8PP, caretaker on site. Water source is the stream near shelter.

**Rattle River Shelter** (1980s)—Sleeps 8. Privy. Shelter built by USFS. Water source is Rattle River.

**U.S. 2—West** 1.8 miles to *Hostel:* White Birches Camping Park, owners Bob/Janet Langlands; (603) 466-2022, <www.whitebirchescampingpark.com>, <whbirch@ncia.net>; 218 State Rt. 2, Shelburne, NH 03581, May 1–end of Oct, tentsites $11s, hostel $13s per night, private cabins available, inquire. Hot showers and laundry for guests only, limited resupply, microwave, refrigerator, coin laundry, dogs welcome, local restaurants deliver, swimming pool, mail drops accepted for guests, limited shuttle to town/trailhead, Visa/MasterCard.

**West** 3.6 miles to **Gorham, N.H. [P.O. ZIP 03581: M–F 8:30–5, Sa 8–12; (603) 466-2182]**. The postmaster requests that all packages include your legal name and use bold letters/colors and that you have ID; can knock on door inside lobby to pick up mail drops after hours. ■ *Hostels:* Hikers Paradise Hostel at Colonial Fort Inn, 370 Main St., (603) 466-2732, <www.hikersparadise.com>, <paradise@ncia.net>; owners Mary Ann and Bruno Janicki offer three hostel units, $19PP, each with bath, kitchen, phone, linen, and heat; motel rooms available; pool; no pets, no mail drops; limited shuttle service to Trail-head, coin laundry, Coleman fuel and denatured alcohol; special hikers' B at motel restaurant. The Barn Hostel, (603) 466-2271, <theskilift@aol.com>, at Libby House B&B offers room in the hostel, $20PP; microwave, TV, coin laundry, shower, occasional shuttle, no pets, $5 laundry; will hold mail drops, for guests only, mailed to 55 Main Street, Gorham, NH 03581. ■ *Lodging:* Libby House B&B, (603) 466-2271, begin-ning at $70S, $85D, includes B; Royalty Inn, (603) 466-3312, $76S, $83D; Northern Peaks, (603) 466-3374, $41.04 up to 3 hikers, dogs welcome, a/c, pool; Town & Country Inn, (603) 466-3315, $50–60S, $74–84D, $6EAP, pets welcome, mail drops accepted at U.S. 2, Gorham, NH 03581. ■ *Groceries:* Shaw's and Super Wal-Mart (both long-term resupply) are located 1.5 miles north of town on N.H. 16. ■ *Restaurants:* Mr. Pizza, J's Steak and Seafood, and various fast-food opportunities. ■ *Outfitters:* Moriah Sport-Hike-Bike-Ski, (603) 466-5050, owned and run by Mike Micucci, hiker gear, Coleman fuel and alcohol by the ounce; Gorham Hardware/Sports Center, hiker gear, Coleman fuel by the ounce. ■ *Internet access:* public library, M, W, F, 10–7, Tu, Th 10–8, closed weekends, located near railroad, nominal fee. ■ *Other services:* coin laundry, bank with ATM, dentist, free concerts on the com-mon Tu evenings. ■ *Shuttles:* Arthur Jolin, (603) 466-2127, to any point north and south on the A.T.

**West** 8 miles to the small city of Berlin, N.H., and the Androscoggin Valley Hospital.

**Trident Col Tentsite**—Four tent pads. Privy (composting). Wa-ter source is an intermittent spring on a side trail.

**Gentian Pond Campsite** (1974)—Shelter sleeps 14. Privy (com-posting). Three single and one double tent platform. Water source is the inlet brook of Gentian Pond.

# Maine

| Miles from Katahdin | Features | Services | Elev. | Miles from Springer |
|---|---|---|---|---|
| 281.4 | Maine–N.H. State Line | | 2,972 | 1,894.8 |
| 280.9 | **Carlo Col Shelter and Campsite** *5.5mS; 4.7mN* | W–0.3m C, S, w | 2,945 | 1,895.3 |
| 280.5 | Mt. Carlo | | 3,565 | 1,895.7 |
| 278.7 | Goose Eye Mtn (East Peak) | | 3,790 | 1,897.5 |
| 277.5 | Goose Eye Mtn (North Peak) | | 3,675 | 1,898.7 |
| 276.5 | **Full Goose Shelter and Campsite** *4.7mS; 5.1mN* | C, S, w | 3,030 | 1,899.7 |
| 276.0 | Fulling Mill Mtn (South Peak) | | 3,395 | 1,900.2 |
| 275.0 | Mahoosuc Notch Trail Mahoosuc Notch (west end) | w | 2,400 | 1,901.2 |
| 273.9 | Mahoosuc Notch (east end) | w | 2,150 | 1,902.3 |
| 272.3 | Mahoosuc Arm | | 3,770 | 1,903.9 |
| 271.4 | +**Speck Pond Shelter and Campsite** *5.1mS; 6.9mN* | C, S, w | 3,500 | 1,904.8 |
| 270.3 | Old Speck Trail | | 3,985 | 1,905.9 |
| 267.9 | Brook | w | 2,500 | 1,908.3 |
| 266.8 | Maine 26, Grafton Notch | R (E–4.7m H, M, cl, sh, f; 12.7m C, f; 17m G, L, M, O, f; 20m H, C, cl) | 1,495 | 1,909.4 |
| 264.5 | **Baldpate Lean-to** *6.9mS; 3.5mN* | S, w | 2,645 | 1,911.7 |
| 263.7 | Baldpate Mtn (West Peak) | | 3,662 | 1,912.5 |
| 262.8 | Baldpate Mtn (East Peak), Grafton Loop Trail | | 3,810 | 1,913.4 |
| 261.0 | **Frye Notch Lean-to** *3.5mS; 10.5mN* | S, w | 2,280 | 1,915.2 |
| 257.3 | Dunn Notch and Falls | w | 1,350 | 1,918.9 |
| 256.5 | East B Hill Rd **Andover, ME 04216** | R (E–8m PO, H, G, L, M, f, cl, @; 11m H) | 1,500 | 1,919.7 |
| 254.7 | Surplus Pond | w | 2,050 | 1,921.5 |
| 251.8 | Wyman Mtn | | 2,920 | 1,924.4 |
| 250.5 | **Hall Mtn Lean-to** *10.5mS; 12.8mN* | S, w | 2,635 | 1,925.7 |
| 249.1 | Sawyer Notch, Sawyer Brook (ford) | w | 1,095 | 1,927.1 |
| 248.2 | Moody Mtn | | 2,440 | 1,928.0 |

| Miles from Katahdin | Features | Services | Elev. | Miles from Springer |
|---|---|---|---|---|
| 246.4 | South Arm Rd, Black Brook (ford) **Andover, ME 04216** | R (E–9m PO, H, G, L, M, f, @; 12m H) (W–3.5m C, G, cl) | 1,410 | 1,929.8 |
| 243.6 | Old Blue Mtn | | 3,600 | 1,932.6 |
| 240.4 | Bemis Stream Trail | | 3,350 | 1,935.8 |
| 239.4 | Bemis Range (West Peak) | | 3,580 | 1,936.8 |
| 237.7 | **Bemis Mtn Lean-to** *12.8mS; 8.3mN* | S, w | 2,790 | 1,938.5 |
| 233.9 | Bemis Stream (ford) | w | 1,495 | 1,942.3 |
| 233.1 | Maine 17 **Oquossoc, ME 04964** | R (W–11m PO, G, M, cl, f) | 2,200 | 1,943.1 |
| 231.5 | Moxie Pond | w | 2,400 | 1,944.7 |
| 229.7 | Long Pond | w | 2,330 | 1,946.5 |
| 229.4 | **Sabbath Day Pond Lean-to** *8.3mS; 11.2mN* | S, w | 2,390 | 1,946.8 |
| 224.8 | Little Swift River Pond Campsite | C, w | 2,460 | 1,951.4 |
| 222.1 | South Pond | w | 2,174 | 1,954.1 |
| 220.0 | Maine 4 **Rangeley, ME 04970** | R (W–9m PO, H, G, L, M, O, D, cl, f, @; 15m G, M, cl; 23m H) | 1,700 | 1,956.2 |
| 219.9 | Sandy River | | 1,595 | 1,956.3 |
| 218.2 | **Piazza Rock Lean-to** *11.2mS; 8.9mN* | S, C, w | 2,080 | 1,958.0 |
| 216.3 | Eddy Pond | w | 2,616 | 1,959.9 |
| 214.3 | Saddleback Mtn | | 4,120 | 1,961.9 |
| 212.7 | The Horn | | 4,040 | 1,963.5 |
| 210.7 | Saddleback Junior | | 3,655 | 1,965.5 |
| 210.3 | Stream | w | 3,200 | 1,965.9 |
| 209.3 | **Poplar Ridge Lean-to** *8.9mS; 8mN* | S, w | 2,920 | 1,966.9 |
| 206.6 | Orbeton Stream (ford) | w | 1,550 | 1,969.6 |
| 203.5 | Lone Mtn | | 3,260 | 1,972.7 |
| 202.4 | Mt. Abraham Trail | | 3,184 | 1,973.8 |
| 201.3 | **Spaulding Mtn Lean-to** *8mS; 18.6mN* | S, w | 3,140 | 1,974.9 |
| 200.5 | Spaulding Mtn | | 4,000 | 1,975.7 |
| 198.4 | Sugarloaf Mtn Trail | E–0.3m w; 0.6m to summit | 3,540 | 1,977.8 |
| 196.2 | South Branch Carrabassett River (ford) | w | 2,100 | 1,980.0 |

| Miles from Katahdin | Features | Services | Elev. | Miles from Springer |
|---|---|---|---|---|
| 196.1 | Caribou Valley Rd | R | 2,220 | 1,980.1 |
| 195.1 | Crocker Cirque | E–0.2m C, w | 2,710 | 1,981.1 |
| 194.0 | South Crocker Mtn | | 4,040 | 1,982.2 |
| 193.0 | North Crocker Mtn | | 4,228 | 1,983.2 |
| 187.8 | Maine 27 **Stratton, ME 04982** | R (E–2m G) (W–5m PO, H, G, L, M, cl, f, @; 10m H) | 1,450 | 1,988.4 |
| 187.0 | Stratton Brook Pond Rd | R | 1,250 | 1,989.2 |
| 186.8 | Stratton Brook | w | 1,230 | 1,989.4 |
| 185.9 | Cranberry Stream | C, w | 1,350 | 1,990.3 |
| 184.6 | Bigelow Range Trail, Cranberry Pond | W–0.2m w | 2,400 | 1,991.6 |
| 182.9 | Horns Pond Trail | | 3,200 | 1,993.3 |
| 182.7 | **Horns Pond Lean-tos** *18.6mS; 10.2mN* | S, w | 3,160 | 1,993.5 |
| 182.4 | Spring | w | 3,400 | 1,993.8 |
| 182.2 | South Horn | | 3,831 | 1,994.0 |
| 180.1 | Bigelow Mtn (West Peak) | | 4,145 | 1,996.1 |
| 179.8 | Bigelow Col, Avery Memorial Campsite, Fire Warden's Trail | C, w | 3,850 | 1,996.4 |
| 179.6 | Spring | w | 3,900 | 1,996.6 |
| 179.4 | Bigelow Mtn (Avery Peak) | | 4,090 | 1,996.8 |
| 177.5 | Safford Brook Trail | | 2,260 | 1,998.7 |
| 177.4 | Safford Notch | E–0.3m C, w | 2,230 | 1,998.8 |
| 174.2 | Little Bigelow Mtn (east end) | | 3,010 | 2,002.0 |
| 172.5 | **Little Bigelow Lean-to** *10.2mS; 7.3mN* | S, C, w | 1,760 | 2,003.7 |
| 171.1 | East Flagstaff Rd | R | 1,200 | 2,005.1 |
| 171.0 | Bog Brook Rd, Flagstaff Lake (inlet) | R, w | 1,150 | 2,005.2 |
| 168.7 | Long Falls Dam Rd | R | 1,225 | 2,007.5 |
| 167.0 | Roundtop Mtn | | 1,760 | 2,009.2 |
| 165.9 | West Carry Pond | w | 1,320 | 2,010.3 |
| 165.2 | **West Carry Pond Lean-to** *7.3mS; 10mN* | S, w | 1,340 | 2,011.0 |
| 164.5 | West Carry Pond | w | 1,320 | 2,011.7 |
| 162.6 | Sandy Stream, Middle Carry Pond | w | 1,229 | 2,013.6 |
| 161.1 | East Carry Pond | w | 1,237 | 2,015.1 |
| 159.4 | Logging Rd | R | 1,300 | 2,016.8 |

| Miles from Katahdin | Features | Services | Elev. | Miles from Springer |
|---|---|---|---|---|
| 158.7 | North Branch Carrying Place Stream | w | 1,200 | 2,017.5 |
| 155.2 | **Pierce Pond Lean-to** *10mS; 9.7mN* | S, w | 1,150 | 2,021.0 |
| 154.8 | Trail to Harrison's Pierce Pond Camps | R (E–0.3m L, M, w) | 1,100 | 2,021.4 |
| 151.5 | Kennebec River | w | 490 | 2,024.7 |
| 151.2 | U.S. 201 **Caratunk, ME 04925** | R (E–0.2m M; 0.3m PO; 16.5m G, L, M, cl) (W–2m C, L, M, sh, cl; 7m L, G; 25m D) | 520 | 2,025.0 |
| 148.5 | Holly Brook | w | 900 | 2,027.7 |
| 145.9 | Boise-Cascade Logging Rd | R | 1,400 | 2,030.3 |
| 145.5 | **Pleasant Pond Lean-to** *9.7mS; 9mN* | S, w | 1,320 | 2,030.7 |
| 144.2 | Pleasant Pond Mtn | | 2,470 | 2,032.0 |
| 139.3 | Moxie Pond | R, w | 970 | 2,036.9 |
| 136.5 | **Bald Mtn Brook Lean-to** *9mS; 4.1mN* | S, w | 1,280 | 2,039.7 |
| 134.5 | Moxie Bald Mtn | | 2,629 | 2,041.7 |
| 132.4 | **Moxie Bald Lean-to** *4.1mS; 8.9mN* | S, w | 1,220 | 2,043.8 |
| 130.3 | Bald Mtn Pond | w | 1,213 | 2,045.9 |
| 126.6 | W Branch Piscataquis River (ford) | w | 900 | 2,049.6 |
| 123.5 | **Horseshoe Canyon Lean-to** *8.9mS; 12mN* | S, w | 880 | 2,052.7 |
| 121.2 | E Branch Piscataquis River (ford) | w | 650 | 2,055.0 |
| 120.8 | Shirley-Blanchard Rd | R | 850 | 2,055.4 |
| 117.8 | Blue-blaze to Monson | E–0.3m R; 2m PO, G, M, L, cl, sh, f, @ | 900 | 2,058.4 |
| 114.5 | Maine 15 **Monson, ME 04464** | R (E–4m PO, G, M, L, cl, sh, f, @) (W–8m G, M, L, O, D, f, @) | 1,215 | 2,061.7 |
| 114.4 | Spectacle Pond-outlet | w | 1,163 | 2,061.8 |
| 113.3 | Bell Pond | w | 1,278 | 2,062.9 |
| 112.6 | Lily Pond | w | 1,130 | 2,063.6 |
| 111.5 | **Leeman Brook Lean-to** *12mS; 7.4mN* | S, w | 1,070 | 2,064.7 |

| Miles from Katahdin | Features | Services | Elev. | Miles from Springer |
|---|---|---|---|---|
| 110.7 | North Pond (outlet) | w (W−0.4m H, M, sh, f) | 1,000 | 2,065.5 |
| 107.9 | Little Wilson Falls | | 850 | 2,068.3 |
| 107.7 | Little Wilson Stream (ford) | w | 750 | 2,068.5 |
| 104.8 | Big Wilson Stream (ford) | w | 600 | 2,071.4 |
| 104.5 | Canadian Pacific RR | | 850 | 2,071.7 |
| 104.1 | **Wilson Valley Lean-to** *7.4mS; 4.7mN* | S, w | 1,000 | 2,072.1 |
| 100.2 | Long Pond Stream (ford) | w | 620 | 2,076.0 |
| 99.4 | **Long Pond Stream Lean-to** *4.7mS; 4.4mN* | S, w | 930 | 2,076.8 |
| 96.3 | Barren Mtn | | 2,660 | 2,079.9 |
| 95.4 | **Cloud Pond Lean-to** *4.4mS; 7.3mN* | E−0.4m S, w | 2,420 | 2,080.8 |
| 93.3 | Fourth Mtn | | 2,380 | 2,082.9 |
| 90.8 | Third Mtn, Monument Cliff | | 1,920 | 2,085.4 |
| 90.2 | West Chairback Pond Trail | w | 1,770 | 2,086.0 |
| 88.9 | Columbus Mtn | | 2,325 | 2,087.3 |
| 88.5 | **Chairback Gap Lean-to** *7.3mS; 9.9mN* | S, w | 2,000 | 2,087.7 |
| 88.0 | Chairback Mtn | | 2,180 | 2,088.2 |
| 85.8 | East Chairback Pond Trail | W−0.2m w | 1,630 | 2,090.4 |
| 84.6 | Katahdin Iron Works Logging Rd | R (E−20m C, G) | 750 | 2,091.6 |
| 84.1 | West Branch Pleasant River (ford) | w | 680 | 2,092.1 |
| 83.8 | The Hermitage | W−8m L | 695 | 2,092.4 |
| 82.8 | Gulf Hagas Trail | w | 950 | 2,093.4 |
| 82.1 | Gulf Hagas Cut-off Trail | w | 1,050 | 2,094.1 |
| 78.6 | **Carl A. Newhall Lean-to** *9.9mS; 7.2mN* | S, w | 1,840 | 2,097.6 |
| 77.7 | Gulf Hagas Mtn | | 2,683 | 2,098.5 |
| 76.8 | Sidney Tappan Campsite | C (E−0.2m w) | 2,425 | 2,099.4 |
| 76.1 | West Peak | | 3,178 | 2,100.1 |
| 74.5 | Hay Mtn | | 3,244 | 2,101.7 |
| 73.9 | White Brook Trail | | 3,125 | 2,102.3 |
| 72.8 | White Cap Mtn | | 3,650 | 2,103.4 |
| 71.4 | **Logan Brook Lean-to** *7.2mS; 3.6mN* | S, w | 2,530 | 2,104.8 |

| Miles from Katahdin | Features | Services | Elev. | Miles from Springer |
|---|---|---|---|---|
| 69.8 | W Branch Ponds Rd | R | 1,650 | 2,106.4 |
| 67.8 | **East Branch Lean-to** *3.6mS; 8.1mN* | S, w | 1,240 | 2,108.4 |
| 67.5 | East Branch Pleasant River (ford) | w | 1,200 | 2,108.7 |
| 65.9 | Mtn View Pond | w | 1,597 | 2,110.3 |
| 65.6 | Spring | w | 1,580 | 2,110.6 |
| 64.3 | Little Boardman Mtn | | 1,980 | 2,111.9 |
| 62.9 | Kokadjo-B Pond Rd | R | 1,380 | 2,113.3 |
| 62.0 | Crawford Pond | w | 1,240 | 2,114.2 |
| 59.7 | **Cooper Brook Falls Lean-to** *8.1mS; 11.4mN* | S, C, w | 910 | 2,116.5 |
| 56.0 | Jo-Mary Rd | R, w (E–6m C, G, cl, sh; 20m G) | 625 | 2,120.2 |
| 53.1 | Mud Pond (outlet) | w | 508 | 2,123.1 |
| 51.8 | Antlers Campsite | C, w | 500 | 2,124.4 |
| 50.1 | Sand Beach, Lower Jo-Mary Lake | w | 580 | 2,126.1 |
| 48.3 | **Potaywadjo Spring Lean-to** *11.4mS; 10.1mN* | S, w | 620 | 2,127.9 |
| 47.7 | Pemadumcook Lake | w | 580 | 2,128.5 |
| 46.0 | Maher Trail, Maher Tote Rd | E–1.2m G, L, M, sh, f | 580 | 2,130.2 |
| 44.0 | Nahmakanta Stream Campsite | C, w | 600 | 2,132.2 |
| 40.8 | Nahmakanta Lake | R, w | 650 | 2,135.4 |
| 38.2 | **Wadleigh Stream Lean-to** *10.1mS; 8.1mN* | S, w | 685 | 2,138.0 |
| 36.3 | Nesuntabunt Mtn | | 1,520 | 2,139.9 |
| 34.2 | Crescent Pond | w | 980 | 2,142.0 |
| 32.5 | Pollywog Stream | w | 682 | 2,143.7 |
| 30.1 | **Rainbow Stream Lean-to** *8.1mS; 11.5mN* | S, w | 1,005 | 2,146.1 |
| 28.1 | Rainbow Lake (west) | w | 1,080 | 2,148.1 |
| 26.3 | Rainbow Spring Campsite | C, w | 1,100 | 2,149.9 |
| 22.9 | Rainbow Lake (east) | w | 980 | 2,153.3 |
| 21.1 | Rainbow Ledges | | 1,517 | 2,155.1 |
| 18.6 | **Hurd Brook Lean-to** *11.5mS; 13.7mN* | S, w | 715 | 2,157.6 |
| 15.1 | Golden Rd, Abol Bridge, West Branch Penobscot River | R, w, C, G, sh (E–20m PO, G, M, L, D, cl) | 588 | 2,161.1 |
| 14.4 | Abol Stream, Baxter Park Boundary | | 620 | 2,161.8 |

| Miles from Katahdin | Features | Services | Elev. | Miles from Springer |
|---|---|---|---|---|
| 14.0 | Katahdin Stream | w | 620 | 2,162.2 |
| 11.0 | Pine Point | w | 640 | 2,165.2 |
| 8.8 | Big Niagara Falls | w | 900 | 2,167.4 |
| 7.6 | +Daicey Pond Campground | E–0.1m L, w | 1,100 | 2,168.6 |
| 5.3 | Pack Tote Rd | R | 1,080 | 2,170.9 |
| 5.2 | +Katahdin Stream Campground, **+The Birches** 13.7mS | C, w (E– 0.25m S) | 1,080 | 2,171.0 |
| 4.0 | Katahdin Stream Falls | w | 1,550 | 2,172.2 |
| 1.0 | Thoreau Spring | w | 4,620 | 2,175.2 |
| 0.0 | Katahdin (Baxter Peak) | | 5,268 | 2,176.2 |

*+ Fee charge, ~ Northbound long-distance hikers only at The Birches*

Hikers in Maine encounter approximately 281 miles of lakes, bogs, moose, loons, hand-over-hand climbs, and a 100-mile wilderness that is neither 100 miles nor truly a wilderness. It is a mystical, magical place to begin or end your A.T. journey.

**Carlo Col Shelter and Campsite** (1980s)—Shelter sleeps 8. Off trail 0.3 mile west. Privy (composting). Two single and one double tent platforms. Water source is a spring left of the lean-to.

**Full Goose Shelter and Campsite** (1978)—Shelter sleeps 8. Privy (composting). Many hikers choose to stay here before or after Mahoosuc Notch. Three single and one double tent platforms. Water source is stream behind shelter.

**Mahoosuc Notch**—Famous for ice found in deep crevices throughout the year. Many call this scramble under, around, over, and between the boulders the most difficult mile on the Trail.

**Speck Pond Shelter and Campsite** (1978)—Shelter sleeps 8. Privy (composting). Three single and three double tent platforms. Cookstoves only. Overnight fee $8PP. Speck Pond is the highest body of water in Maine. Water source is a spring on the blue-blazed trail behind the caretaker's yurt.

**Maine 26/Grafton Notch**—Difficult hitch, very light traffic. **East** 4.7 miles to *Hostel*: Mahoosuc Guide Service, 1513 Bear River Rd (Rt. 26), Newry, ME 04261, (207) 824-2073, fax (207) 824-3784, <info@mahoosuc.com>, 2 bunk rooms with shower, $35PP including towel, extra fee for bed linen, full kitchen; mail drops accepted; no dogs; fuel by the ounce (white gas, alcohol); prepared meals available with advance notice; call from Old Spec/Baldpate for shuttle from parking lot (fee); shuttles to town possible.

**East** 12.7 miles to *Camping:* Stony Brook Recreation Camping Area, (207) 824-2836 or (207) 824-2789, <www.stonybrookrec.com>, tentsite $20 for 4, $3EAP; lean-to $25 for 4; includes shuttle to Grafton Notch, shower, laundry, pool, miniature golf, rec room, and convenience store (short-term resupply) with Coleman fuel. Mail drops held if sent c/o SBRCA, 42 Powell Place, Hanover, ME 04237.

**East** 17 miles to the town of Bethel, offering most major services. ■ *Lodging:* Chapman Inn, (877) 359-1498 or (207) 824-2657, <www.chapmaninn.com>, $33 for bunk in hiker dorm with shower, B, kitchen privileges, $5 laundry, and possible shuttle back to A.T.; mail drops accepted at 2 Church St., P.O. Box 1067, Bethel, ME 04217. ■ *Restaurant:* Moose's Tale Food and Ale, Sunday River Brewery. ■ *Groceries:* Bethel IGA Food Liner (long-term resupply), Irving Mainway convenience store with Subway & Dunkin' Donuts. ■ *Outfitter:* True North Adventurewear, (207) 824-2201, M–Sa 10–6, Su 10–5, full-service backpacking outfitter, stove fuel. ■ *Camping:* Bethel Outdoor Adventure & Campground, (207) 824-4224, <www.betheloutdooradventure.com>; tentsites $16D, $3EAP; restaurant nearby, phone, mail drops accepted if sent to 121 Mayville Rd., U.S. 2, Bethel, ME 04217-4410; offers canoe services on the Androscoggin River from Shelburne, N.H., to Bethel, Maine, 18 river miles, six hours, up to $60 for 1 canoe with 2 people, includes shuttle. ■ *Other services:* bank with ATM.

**East** 20 miles to *Hostel:* Bethel Outdoor Adventure's "Snowboarding House," (800) 533-3607, members of Hostelling International USA $19PP, coin laundry, kitchen with microwave, mail drops accepted to Bethel Outdoor Adventure & Campground, address above.

---

**Maine Appalachian Trail Club**—MATC maintains the 266.8 miles from Grafton Notch to Katahdin. Correspondence should be sent to MATC, P.O. Box 283, Augusta, ME 04332-0283; <www.matc.org>.

---

**Baldpate Lean-to** (1995)—Sleeps 8. Privy. Lean-to built to replace Grafton Notch Lean-to, which was too close to a road. Water source is a spring behind the lean-to.

**Frye Notch Lean-to** (1983)—Sleeps 6. Privy. Water source is Frye Brook in front of the lean-to.

**East B Hill Road/Andover**—**East** 8 miles to **Andover, Maine** [P.O. ZIP 04216: M–F 8:30–1:30 & 2–4:45, Sa 9–12:15; (207) 392-4571]. Andover also can be reached *via* South Arm Road, 9.5 miles north on the A.T. Neither road has much traffic. ■ *Hostel:* Pine Ellis Hiking Lodge, (207) 392-4161, <www. pineellis.com>, <www.geocities.com/pineellis/pineellis. html>; owner Ilene Trainor and son-in-law David Rousselin; located near P.O. and stores; bunkroom $15PP, private room $30S, $45D, $50T, large shared room in the house $20PP (four separate beds), all include shower, kitchen privileges for all meals, separate hiker refrigerator, Internet, CATV in all rooms; living room with VCR and use of separate phone line, (207) 392-1405; hiker box; laundry $1.50 wash, $1.50 dry; pick up at Trailhead if called in advance; multiday slackpacking packages; shuttles back to Trail, nominal fee, and other shuttles by arrangement; all major credit cards accepted; will hold packages mailed to 20 Pine St., P.O. Box 12, Andover, ME 04216; very hiker-friendly. ■ *Lodging:* The Andover Road-house, (207) 392-1209, <www.andoverroadhouse.com>, 28 South Main St., Andover, ME 04216; bunkhouse $20PP, rooms $45S, $50D, includes free laundry, free long-distance phone, laundry, CATV, kitchen privileges, free shuttles to Trail; mail drops accepted; pet-friendly. ■ *Groceries:* Andover General Store, with ATM and Coleman fuel by the gallon, and Mill's Market, with deli and homemade pizza (both short-term re-supply). ■ *Internet access:* Andover Public Library, Tu–Th, Sa 1–4:30. ■ *Other services:* ice-cream shop; massage therapist Donna Gifford, call for rates and availability, (207) 392-1474 or (207) 357-5686.

**East** 11 miles to East Andover and *Lodging:* The Cabin, (207) 392-1333, <thecabin@megalink.net>, <www.thecabin inmaine.com>; owned by semiretiring Margie and Earle Towne (Honey and Bear); log cabin with bunkroom and pri-vate room. Call to see if they are home and for reservations. Alumni always welcome.

**Surplus Pond**—See and hear an abundance of wood warblers during spring and summer.

**Hall Mountain Lean-to** (1978)—Sleeps 6. Privy. Water source is a spring south of the lean-to on the A.T.

 **South Arm Road**—**East** 9 miles to Andover, Maine (see above).

**West** 3.5 miles to *Camping:* South Arm Campground, (207) 364-5155, open May 1–Oct 1; $15 per site, up to 4. Camp-store (short-term resupply); showers 25¢; coin laundry; canoe, kayak, and boat rentals. No credit cards. Packages accepted at P.O. Box 310, Andover, ME 04216.

**Bemis Mountain Lean-to** (1988)—Sleeps 8. Privy. Water source is a small spring to the left of the lean-to.

**Maine 17—West** 11 miles to **Oquossoc, Maine [P.O. ZIP 04964: M–F 8–1 & 1:30–4:15, Sa 9–12; (207) 864-3685].** ■ *Groceries:* Carry Road Country Store (short-term resupply), with deli, bakery, and Coleman fuel. ■ *Restaurants:* Gingerbread House, B/L/D with vegetarian specials and gourmet ice cream; Four Seasons Café, daily 11–11, serves Mexican and vegetarian specialties, L/D. ■ *Other services:* fruit and vegetable stand, laundromat, pay phone, and swimming area.

**Sabbath Day Pond Lean-to** (1993)—Sleeps 8. Privy. A sandy beach, 0.3 mile south on the A.T., provides an excellent swimming opportunity. Water source is Sabbath Day Pond in front of the lean-to.

**Little Swift River Pond Campsite** (1975)—Privy. Water is available from piped spring near pond.

 **Maine 4—West** 9 miles to **Rangeley, Maine [P.O. ZIP 04970: M–F 9:30–4:15, Sa 9:30–12; (207) 864-2233],** where services are spread along Maine 4. ■ *Hostel:* Gull Pond Lodge, (207) 864-5563, hosted by Bob O'Brien, offers a bunkroom $20PP, private room $30S, $50D, includes shower or tub, linens, and fuel refill; use of kitchen and grill, TV, phone, laundry, slackpacking, shuttles in and out of town and back to Trail. Packages accepted if mailed to P.O. Box 1177, Rangeley, ME 04970. ■ *Lodging:* Rangeley Inn, (800) MOMENTS or (207) 864-3341, $84–$99; Saddleback Motor Inn, (207) 864-3434, $93D, WiFi. ■ *Groceries:* IGA Supermarket (long-term resupply). ■ *Restaurants:* Parkside Main Café, L/D; Sarge's Pub & Grub, L/D and bar; Red Onion, L/D; BMC Dinner, B/L. ■ *Outfitter:* Alpine Shop, (207) 864-3741, with alcohol and Coleman fuel by the ounce. ■ *Internet access:* Rangeley Public Library. ■ *Other services:* banks with ATM; Village Scrub Board laundry; doctor; Rangeley Region Health Center, (207) 864-4397; dentist; pharmacy; bookstore; and natural-foods market off Maine 16.

   **West** 15 miles to Oquossoc (see entry above).

   **West** 23 miles *via* Route 16 to *Hostel:* The Maine Roadhouse, (207) 246-2060, will pick up hikers in Rangeley (see Stratton entry below).

**Piazza Rock Lean-to** (1993)—Sleeps 8. Privy. Constructed by MATC's team of maintainers from L.L.Bean, this lean-to and tent platforms are home to a two-seat privy and cribbage board. Water source is the stream that passes through the campsite.

**Saddleback Mountain**—One of the most spectacular abovetreeline stretches of the Trail in Maine; you may not notice the ski resort on one side. For many years, Saddleback was the controversial "missing link" in Maine during federal attempts to buy lands along the Trail to protect it from encroaching development. In late 2000, a deal was struck to sell a Trail corridor across Saddleback to the government, but it does permit future development of the resort, which was sold in 2003 to a local family that is investing heavily in lakeside facilities downslope.

**Poplar Ridge Lean-to** (1961)—Sleeps 6. Privy. This shelter uses the increasingly rare "baseball bat" design for its sleeping platform. No tentsites. Water source is the brook in front of lean-to.

**Spaulding Mountain Lean-to** (1989)—Sleeps 8. Privy. Water source is a small spring to right of lean-to.

**Sugarloaf Mountain**—A 0.6-mile side trail to the east leads to the summit of Sugarloaf and the large summit house of Sugarloaf Ski Resort, where, on clear days, panoramic views include glimpses of Katahdin and Mt. Washington. Cool spring water can be found at 0.3 mile. This side trail was the last section of the original A.T. to open, in August 1937.

**Crocker Cirque Campsite** (1975)—Privy. Numerous campsites; east on a 0.2-mile side trail, one large group platform, 2 small platforms. Water source is the spring.

**Maine 27—East** 2 miles to *Groceries:* Mountainside Grocers (long-term resupply), (207) 237-2248, at the base of Sugarloaf access road; open 8–6 May–Nov 1, 8–8 after that.
**West** 5 miles to **Stratton, Maine [P.O. ZIP 04982: M–F 9–1 & 1:30–4, Sa 9–11:30; (207) 246-6461].** ■ *Hostel:* Stratton Motel & Hostel, (207) 246-4171, <www.thestrattonmotel.com>, owned by Susan Smith; hostel $20PP includes hiker kitchen, free Internet and long-distance phone; motel rooms $40S, $50D, $10EAP; free shuttle to Trail, local shuttles available; send mail drops to P.O. Box 284, Stratton, ME 04982. ■ *Lodging:* Spill-over Motel, (207) 246-6571, $52S, $68D, pets okay with a $20 deposit and $5 charge, continental B, located before town; White Wolf Inn, (207) 246-2922, closed Tu, $30S, $35D, dogs $5, accepts packages mailed to Main St., P.O. Box 590, Stratton, ME 04982; Diamond Corner B&B, (207) 246-2082, <www.bbonline.com/me/diamondcorner>, rooms $70–$100, includes B, shuttle to Trail, accepts mail drops at 8 Rangeley Road, P.O. Box 176, Stratton, ME 04982. ■ *Groceries:* Fotter's Market (long-term resupply), with deli, Coleman fuel and denatured alcohol by the ounce, open 8–8 M–Sa, 9–5 Su; Northland Cash Supply (short-term resupply) and pizza open 5–9, hiker box, accepts packages sent to 152 Main St., Stratton, ME 04982. ■ *Restaurants:* Stratton Diner B/L/D, Th–Tu, B only on W, soft ice cream, daily specials; White Wolf Café, L/D (closed Tu, D-only W); Stratton Plaza, Tu–Sa 11–10, pizza, L/D; Mainely Yours, Tu–Sa B/L/D, Su B/L, closes Su 2 p.m. ■ *Internet access:* library. ■ *Other services:* laundry;

bank; ATM; Mt Abram Regional Health Center, (207) 265-4555, located in Kingfield. ■ *Shuttles:* Susan at Stratton Motel, (207) 246-4171.

West 10 miles *via* Route 16 to *Hostel:* The Maine Roadhouse, (207) 246-2060, <www.maineroadhouse.com>, owned by Susan Smith; bunk room $20PP, semiprivate rooms $40S, $50D, $10EAP; includes free laundry, free long-distance phone, laundry, satellite TV, hiker kitchen, and BBQ, free shuttles to Trail (Routes 4 and 27) and post office. Mail drops can be sent to 901 Rangeley Rd, Coplin Plantation, ME 04982.

**Cranberry Stream Campsite** (1995)—Privy. Stream is the water source.

**Horns Pond Lean-tos** (1997)—Two lean-tos; each sleeps 8. Privy. Located on a clear pond at which fishing is permitted. A MATC caretaker is in residence in this heavily used area. Water source is an often-dry spring on the A.T., north of the lean-tos, or Horns Pond.

**Bigelow Mountain**—Known as Maine's "Second Mountain," the Bigelow Range might look very different today had it not been for the efforts of many conservation groups, including MATC. During the 1960s and '70s, land developers had plans to turn the Bigelow Range into the "Aspen of the East," but opponents forced a state referendum on the issue. In 1976, the citizens of Maine decided, by a 3,000-vote margin, to have the state purchase the land and create a 33,000-acre wilderness preserve.

**Bigelow Col/Avery Memorial Campsite**—This deep cleft between West Peak and Avery Peak is a beautiful (although often cold) place to spend the night. You can catch the sunset or sunrise views from either peak. Avery Memorial Campsite, with tent platforms, privy, and spring, is located in the col. The spring is unreliable in dry years (2007); one maintained water site is behind the red maintenance shack, to left down unblazed trail.

**Safford Notch Campsite**—Privy. Located 0.3 mile east. Tent pads and platforms. Water source is Safford Brook, downhill from the campsite.

**Little Bigelow Lean-to** (1986)—Sleeps 8. Privy. Plenty of tentsites at this lean-to. Swimming in "the Tubs" along the side trail. Water source is a spring 50 yards in front of the lean-to.

**West Carry Pond Lean-to** (1989)—Sleeps 8. Privy. Swimming in pond. Water source is a spring house located to the left of the lean-to or West Carry Pond.

**Arnold Trail**—From West Carry to Middle Carry Pond, the A.T. follows the route of the historic Arnold Trail. In 1775, Benedict Arnold and an army of 1,150 men used this trail *en route* to Quebec, where they hoped to mount a surprise winter attack on the British. Like so many hikers, the army literally bogged down in the streams and swamps of the area, and, as a result, the remaining 650 men were so weakened by the passage that the attack was unsuccessful. Prior to Arnold's transit, the Abenaki Indians used the route as a portage around rapids on the Dead River, the waters of which now fill artificial Flagstaff Lake.

**Pierce Pond Lean-to** (1970)—Sleeps 6. Privy (moldering). Located on the east bank of Pierce Pond, with swimming, sunsets, and wildlife. Water source is the pond. A trail near here leads to Harrison's Pierce Pond Camps (see below).

**Harrison's Pierce Pond Camps** (1934)—These traditional Maine camps are on a blue-blaze across Pierce Pond Stream. Owner Tim Harrison caters primarily to vacationers and anglers; summer radio phone, (207) 672-3625; winter phone, (603) 524-0560; B $6–$8, reservations required the night before. Hiker rate for cabin, shower, and B $35S, $50D. Hikers may use phone for emergencies.

**Kennebec River Ferry**—Over the last 20 years, canoes have ferried in excess of 18,000 hikers across the Kennebec River. For the 2008 hiker season, Rivers & Trails, (207) 663-4441, <www.riversandtrails.com>, <stevelongley@midmaine.com>, once again will handle this monumental task. The ferry will operate daily, at no cost to hikers, tentatively from:

|             |                            |
| ----------- | -------------------------- |
| May 16–Jul 17 | 9–11 a.m. |
| Jul 18–Sep 30 | 9–11 a.m. and 2–4 p.m. |
| Oct 1–Oct 6 | 10 a.m.–12 noon |

The updated 2008 schedule will be posted at Pierce Pond and Pleasant Pond lean-tos. Please do not call from the Trail on your cell phone requesting "special" off-hour ferry service.

**Kennebec River**—The most formidable unbridged water-crossing on the Appalachian Trail. Ironically, the Indian word "Kennebec" means "long, quiet water." A thru-hiker drowned in 1985 trying to ford the river, and many other hikers have had close calls. Dangers include rocks, strong currents, and unpredictable water levels due to releases from the dams upstream. ATC and MATC strenuously urge hikers not to attempt to ford the river. Purists also should note that a ferry is the official "white-blaze" route, as well as the original, historical route of the A.T. across the Kennebec. This is a free service funded by ATC and MATC. Hikers need to arrive a half-hour before the ferry ceases operation. If late, be prepared to wait, and note that camping and fires are prohibited on both banks of the river. You will be required to sign a release form before crossing, wear a life jacket during the crossing, and follow the instructions of the ferry operator; please cooperate in these matters. If river conditions or weather make the crossing dangerous, the service will be discontinued until conditions improve. The ferry is for hiker and pack—the operator will not carry your pack so you can attempt to ford.

**U.S. 201**—**East** 0.3 mile on Main Street to **Caratunk, Maine** **[P.O. ZIP 04925: M–F 7:30–11:30 & 12–3:45, Sa 7:30–11:15; (207) 672-3416]**. The post office accepts credit and debit cards with limited cash back. Pay phone.

**East** 0.2 mile to *Restaurant:* Moose Crossings Takeout, W–Su 11–6, Memorial Day to Labor Day, burgers, hot and cold sandwiches, pizzas, milkshakes, ice cream, and cold drinks.

**East** 16.5 miles to the small town of Bingham, with restaurants, laundry, pharmacy, and grocery facilities. *Lodging:* Bingham Motor Inn, (866) 806-6120, <www.binghammotorinn.com>, $53S, $68D, $78T.

**West** 2 miles to *Lodging:* Northern Outdoors Resort, (800) 765-7238, lodge rooms $56.72/room (max 4 persons), cabin tents $9.63PP, tent sites $7.20PP, includes all taxes; B/L/D, shuttle service to the A.T., coin laundry, free showers, free Internet access, hot tubs; Kennebec River rafting trips (class IV) start at $69.

**West** 7 miles to Berry's General Store, (207) 663-4461, <www.theforsarea.com>.

**West** 25 miles to Jackman Regional Health Center, (207) 668-2691, 24-hour ER.

**Pleasant Pond Lean-to** (1958, renovated 1991)—Sleeps 6. Privy. Sandy beach on Pleasant Pond is 0.2 mile from the lean-to. Water source is a small brook crossed on the path to the lean-to or pond.

**Bald Mountain Brook Lean-to** (1994)—Sleeps 8. Privy. Water source is Bald Mountain Brook, in front of the lean-to.

**Moxie Bald Lean-to** (1958)—Sleeps 6. Privy. Many moose in the area. Water source is Bald Mountain Pond in front.

**West Branch of Piscataquis River**—Normally knee-deep, this ford can be dangerous during periods of heavy rain. Do not attempt to cross in high water.

**Horseshoe Canyon Lean-to** (1991)—Sleeps 8. Privy. Lean-to is located on a blue-blaze. Water source is a spring at the A.T. junction or the river in front of, and below, the lean-to.

**East Branch of the Piscataquis River**—Like its West Branch, the 50-foot-wide East Branch of the Piscataquis can be tricky fording during periods of heavy rain.

**Blue-blaze to Monson**—Northbounders have an alternative route to Monson (see below), 3.3 miles south of Maine 15, near Lake Hebron; signs will point you in the right direction. This route leads a short distance to Pleasant St., where you will go left 2 miles into town.

 **Maine 15—East** 4 miles to **Monson, Maine [P.O. ZIP 04464: M–F 7:30–11:30 & 12:30–4, Sa 7:30–11:00; (207) 997-3975].** No ATM, but post office accepts debit cards with *limited* cash back. ■ *Lodging:* Lake Shore House Lodging, Pub & Eatery, (207) 997-7069, <www.lakeshore-house.com>, <info@lake-shore-house.com>, open year-round; new owners Rebekah and Jeff Santagata have expanded their downtown business to include a restaurant and pub with outdoor seating on the shore of Lake Hebron; bunks up to four $25, private rooms $40S $60D, lakefront room with two double beds (sleep four) $80, all include shared bath, living room, dining area; kitchen closes 9 p.m.; check-in 2 p.m., check-out 11 a.m.; advance reservations appreciated; laundromat open 24 hours; coin-op shower for nonguests; mail drops for guests only to P.O. Box 215, Monson, ME 04464; use of house phone with credit card; kayaks and paddleboats free for guests; occasional work-for-

stay; Internet access (fee) for guests; shuttle, slackpack, and food-drop arrangements anywhere; Pub & Eatery hours Tu–Th 4–closing, F–Su 12–closing; Lake Shore House guests welcome at Shaw's for breakfast, $7; well-behaved dogs welcome; floating bonfire weekends. Shaw's Lodging, (207) 997-3597, P.O. Box 72, Monson, ME 04464, <www.shawslodging.com>, <info@shawslodging.com>; new owners Dawn MacPherson-Allen and Sue Stevens continue the Shaw's tradition of hospitality; open May to Oct, no credit cards; tenting $12PP, bunkhouse and bunkroom $23PP, guest rooms $32S $53.50D, semiprivate $26.75PP; advance reservations accepted; famous AYCE B $7, D Su–W $12; please sign up for meals in advance; dogs welcome in bunkhouse; nonguest showers $6; shuttles and laundry facilities available; mail drops accepted free for guests, small fee for nonguests; camp store open for 2008 season, long-term resupply and gear. ■ *Groceries:* Tim's Monson General Store (long-term resupply), debit/credit cards accepted, Coleman fuel by the ounce, alcohol-stove fuel; Friday nights, an old-fashioned bluegrass jam session fills the store with locals and hikers; be sure to sign the famous register. A.E. Robinson Mobil Mart (short-term resupply), pizzas, hiker-sized calzones, hot sandwiches. ■ *Restaurants:* Spring Creek BBQ, open Th–F 10–8 or until food runs out, Su 8–4 (food runs out at 3); work-for-food offered to thru-hikers, one hour of work for lunch, two hours for dinner. ■ *Internet access:* Monson Public Library, closed Sa–Su. ■ *Other services*: Monson Laundromat. ■ *Shuttles:* Buddy Ward, cell (207) 343-2564, home (207) 997-3792, <Buppyx4@midmaine.com>, provides shuttles in and out of the 100-Mile Wilderness, food drops, and emergency pick-ups, and will help set up slackpacking trips across the A.T. in Maine; Shaw's Lodging provides full-service shuttles throughout Maine and along A.T. between Caratunk and Baxter State Park.

**West** 8 miles to Greenville, Moosehead Lake's major tourist town and gateway to Maine's North Woods. ■ *Lodging:* Indian Hill Motel, (207) 695-2623, <indianhillmotel@gmail.com>, $68S/D, $10EAP. ■ *Groceries:* Village Food Mart and Indian Hill (both long-term resupply). ■ *Restaurants:* Kelly's Landing, AYCE B on Su; Auntie M's Family Restaurant; The Boom Chain Restaurant; Flatlanders, Rod and Reel. ■ *Outfitter:* Northwoods Outfitters, (207) 695-3288, <www.maineoutfitter.com>, daily 7–7, Internet (fee), and coffee at the Hard Drive Café inside store. ■ *Other services:* Indian Hill Trading Post, <www.indianhill.com>, (800) 675-4487; banks with ATM; Harris Drug Store, (207) 695-2921; Charles A. Dean Memorial Hospital, 24-hour ER, (207) 695-5200.

**"100-Mile Wilderness"**—Signs at each end of this section proclaim this area's remoteness and warn the unprepared hiker to stay away, but don't be intimidated. For those who don't think they can go 100 miles without resupply, supplies can be shuttled in at Jo-Mary, Kokadjo-B, and Katahdin Iron Works roads. There is a $9 fee for out-of-state residents to pass through the forest-road gates in vehicles. A local resupply provider is Kathy Preble, (207) 965-8464, <svivor@midmaine. com>, 191 Main St., Brownville, ME 04414. The White House Landing Wilderness Camp is 32.3 miles south of Abol Bridge and 73.5 miles north of Monson; it no longer accepts mail drops but does have limited short-term resupplies. Hikers should remember to bring cash for the Abol Bridge Store and Baxter State Park.

**Leeman Brook Lean-to** (1987)—Sleeps 6. Privy. Water source is the stream in front of the lean-to.

**North Pond** (outlet)—**West** 1.0 mile to *Hostel*: North Pond Haven, (207) 343-2787, hot showers, some food and beverages, transportation to town, propane stove and lights, woodstove with firewood provided, outhouse, $20 (1 or 2), $30 (3 or 4), $40 (5 or 6).

**Wilson Valley Lean-to** (1993)—Sleeps 6. Privy. Located north of Big Wilson Stream. Water source is a small spring in front of the lean-to, on the opposite side of the A.T.

**Long Pond Stream Lean-to** (1991)—Sleeps 8. Privy. Swimming in the scenic Slugundy Gorge and falls located 0.1 mile south, on a side trail 150 yards off the A.T. Water source is a small stream to the left of the lean-to.

**Cloud Pond Lean-to** (1992)—Sleeps 6. Privy 0.4 mile east. Water source is Cloud Pond, in front of the lean-to, or a spring to the north of the side trail to the lean-to.

**Chairback Gap Lean-to** (1954)—Sleeps 6. Privy. Water source, a small spring downhill and north of the lean-to 25 yards, is prone to go dry in drier years.

**Katahdin Iron Works (KIW) Road/West Branch of Pleasant River**—Just east of the A.T., on the KIW logging road, is a parking lot for Gulf Hagas.

**East** 20 miles to Maine 11 and Brownville Junction. ■ *Groceries:* The Junction General Store and Trackside Café (short-term resupply), (207) 965-8876, <www.thejunction general.com>, deli, live outdoor music on summer weekends, primitive camping available for the '08 season. ■ *Other services:* Kathy Preble provides food drops and shuttles on the Jo-Mary, Kokadjo-B, and Katahdin Iron Works roads. Contact her well in advance: (207) 965-8464, <svivor@midmaine.com>, 191 Main St., Brownville, ME 04414.

**The Hermitage**—Camping is not allowed inside this protected area, a national landmark owned by The Nature Conservancy. Look for the plaque to learn the meaning of its name. Home to magnificent old-growth white pines. ■ *Camping:* Maine North Woods campgrounds and $7 tentsites available near the Hermitage area. Maine North Woods, P.O. Box 425, Ashland, ME 04732, (207) 435-6213, <www.northmainewoods.org>, <info@northmainewoods.org>; contact it at the gatehouses; advance reservations are strongly recommended.

**West** 8 miles to *Lodging:* AMC Little Lyford Pond Camps, (603) 466-2727; $92 for bunkroom space, two-night minimum, B/L/D included.

**Gulf Hagas**—If you've got the food and the time, you may want to take this side trail. The gulf was formed by water eroding the slate walls of a narrow canyon. The result of this sculpting is a stretch of many spectacular waterfalls nestled in a chasm about 500 feet deep. If you want a taste of the gulf's scenery, Screw Auger Falls is only 0.2 mile from the A.T. on Gulf Hagas Brook. A 5.2-mile loop hike is possible using the Rim and Gulf Hagas trails. MATC stations a ridgerunner in the Gulf Hagas area, which receives a tremendous amount of day use. *No camping allowed.*

**Carl A. Newhall Lean-to** (1986)—Sleeps 6. Privy. Lean-to is north of Gulf Hagas Brook, the water source.

**Sidney Tappan Campsite**—Privy. Follow the blue-blaze 0.2 mile east to water; trail begins just north of the campsite.

**Logan Brook Lean-to** (1983)—Sleeps 6. Privy. Water source is Logan Brook behind the lean-to; cascades are farther upstream.

**East Branch Lean-to** (1996)—Sleeps 8. Privy. Water source is the East Branch of the Pleasant River, in front.

**Cooper Brook Falls Lean-to** (1956)—Sleeps 6. Full-moon privy. Tentsite on trail to lean-to. A waterfront lean-to with numerous pools and falls. Water source is Cooper Brook in front of the lean-to.

**Jo-Mary Road**—**East** 6 miles to *Camping:* Smith's Jo-Mary Lake Campground, (207) 723-8117, <www.camp-maine.com/jo-mary>, mid-May–Oct 1, campsites $18.50, campstore B/L, showers, laundry, bean-hole suppers W after Jul 4, shuttle, dogs welcome. For those wishing to resupply, Jo-Mary Road sees some traffic, thanks to the campground; 20 miles to Maine 11 and Brownville Junction.

**Antlers Campsite**—Campsites are on the edge of Lower Jo-Mary. Fort Relief privy to the west of the Trail. Water source is Jo-Mary Lake.

**Potaywadjo Spring Lean-to** (1995)—Sleeps 8. Privy. Water source is the 15-foot-wide Potaywadjo Spring, to the right of the lean-to.

**Maher Trail/Maher Tote Road/White House Landing Wilderness Camp**—**East** 1.2 miles to *Lodging:* White House Landing, (207) 745-5116. *Northbound directions:* Follow A.T. 2.8 miles north of Potaywadjo Spring Lean-to to third road north of lean-to, go east 0.2 mile on Maher Trail/Maher Tote Road to Pemadumcook Lake, follow lake shoreline south 1.0 mile to boat dock. *Southbound directions:* Follow A.T. 1.5 miles south of Nahmakanta Stream Campsite, go east 0.2 mile on Maher Trail/Maher Tote Road to Pemadumcook Lake, follow lake shoreline south 1.0 mile to boat dock. At boat dock, sound airhorn one short blast for ferry ride to camp; no ferry after dark. Owners Bill, Linda, and Ben Ware offer bunkhouse $35PP, private rooms $45PP, includes AYCE B and shower for guests only. Open year-round; L and grill menu 11–1 (try Linda's famous one-pound burger); D for all, but, if you're not staying, be packed up and ready for the boat ride immediately afterward. Ben & Jerry's, cold drinks, campstore (short-term resupply), butane/propane canister fuel, denatured alcohol, white gas, and canoes. *No* mail drops. Shuttle service may be available with advance notice, but not every day. Round-trip shuttle to Millinocket takes 3 hours. Visa and MasterCard accepted; fee may be charged.

**Nahmakanta Stream Campsite**—Privy. Water is a stream in front of the campsite.

**Wadleigh Stream Lean-to** (1981)—Sleeps 6. Privy. Located 0.5 mile north of Nahmakanta Lake, which has a sandy beach. Water source is a spring on the beach.

**Rainbow Stream Lean-to** (1971)—Sleeps 6. Privy. Home of the A.T.'s best totem pole; often crowded with hiker groups. Good tenting and hammocking above and behind the lean-to. Water source is Rainbow Stream, in front.

**Hurd Brook Lean-to** (1959)—Sleeps 6. Privy. During high water, Hurd Brook, 50 feet south of the lean-to, can be deep and swift, and the ford dangerous. Area is frequented by hunters. Water source is Hurd Brook. Southbounders might want to tank up at the spring 0.7 mile north of the lean-to.

**"Golden Road"/Abol Bridge**. ■ *Camping:* Abol Bridge Campground, open May 15–Sep 30, privately run and located along the road on the West Branch of the Penobscot River, campsites $10PP, coin-op showers for guests only, all visitors must register; Abol Pines, seasonal, tentsite or space in one of two new six-person lean-tos, $7PP out-of-state residents, reached by following the dirt road in front of the camp store east 75 yards, then right on another small road for 100 yards. ■ *Groceries:* Linda's Store at Abol Bridge (short-term resupply), subs, sandwiches, microwave foods, ice cream, A.T. souvenirs, cellular pay phone ($1 per minute for all calls, even toll-free); credit cards accepted.

**East** 20 miles to Millinocket, Maine (see page 252).

**Baxter State Park**—The northern terminus of the Appalachian Trail is Baxter Peak on Katahdin, Maine's highest mountain. Katahdin, along with the surrounding landscape, is part of a 209,501-acre wilderness sanctuary and forest preserve, Baxter State Park; <www.baxterstateparkauthority.com>. The lands were donated in perpetual trust to the people of Maine by former Governor Percival Proctor Baxter, who served from 1921 to 1924. BSP is self-supporting, in large part due to Baxter's trust funds and by his design, and is administered separately from any other agency or state park in Maine. Baxter's goal was to place preservation of natural resources as a priority over their recreational use, so some of BSP's regulations and policies are distinct from what may be encountered elsewhere along the A.T. They were created to address protection of the park's natural features and wilderness, protection of the visitor's wilderness experience, and promotion of an attitude of personal responsibility and safety. There is no other entity comparable to BSP along the Trail corridor. All visitors here are recipients of a very special gift, so please work with park authorities to honor the intent of such generosity by upholding its policies and regulations.

Most of Baxter's A.T-related rules stem from the weather. Unlike the surrounding landscape south, Katahdin is exposed to extreme weather, including high winds, and has gotten snow during every month of the year. No shelters are located above treeline (north of Katahdin Stream Campground), and all trails to the summit are completely exposed. On humid, unsettled, late-summer days, for example, it is wise to start down by 1 p.m. to avoid electrical storms.

*Dogs*—Dogs are not allowed in the park. See Millinocket and Medway entries for kennels.

*Katahdin*—The translation of the Indian word is "greatest mountain." Maine Indians considered the mountain a holy place and believed in Pamola, the deity of Katahdin, who purportedly would destroy any man who ventured too close to the mountain. The first recorded ascent of Katahdin by Euroamericans came on Aug 13, 1804, when a party led by Charles Turner, Jr., reached the summit by the same rocks-and-roots route used by the A.T.—the Hunt Trail (named after the Hunt family that had a homestead below). Since then, the mountain has captured the imagination of many, including Henry David Thoreau, who explored the area in 1846. Thoreau Spring on the Tableland bears his name, although he never made it there. From Katahdin Stream Campground, it is a 10.4-mile trip to the summit and back. The ascent packs an elevation gain of 4,000 feet into 5 miles. Backpacks may be left at the ranger station at the campground, where you can borrow a daypack and obtain information on weather conditions. The park posts "cut-off" times for beginning your climb: In Aug, you must start before 11 a.m.; in Sep, 10 a.m.; in Oct, 9 a.m. Park rules require that you sign in at the campground before your climb and sign out on your return. Don't forget to make your final, or first, register entry on the ranger station's front porch.

*Weather*—Baxter State Park posts daily weather reports during the hiking season at 7 a.m. The categories tell you what to expect for your hiking day:

- *Class I*—Recommended for hiking above treeline.

- *Class II*—Not recommended for hiking above treeline.

- *Class III*—Not recommended for hiking above treeline, with the following trails closed (specified trails will follow).

- *Class IV*—All trails closed at the trailheads. A hiker who climbs Katahdin on a Class IV day is subject to a court summons, a fine, seizure of equipment, and revocation of park privileges.

*Register*—Every hiker must register with a ranger upon entering BSP. An information kiosk is located on the A.T. 1 mile north of Abol Bridge. The 12 hikers using The Birches (see below) must sign up at the Abol Stream kiosk and also with the ranger at Katahdin Stream Campground. A MATC/Baxter Park trailrunner patrols the area to help hikers with information on the A.T. and the park.

*Reservations*—A new "rolling reservations" policy is available four months in advance of the day you wish to stay within the park. If you want Jun 3, you need to know your reservation will not be processed before Feb 3. The traditional opening day to make walk-in reservations is Jan 17. More information, and a chart outlining when reservations can be made, is at <www.baxterstateparkauthority.com>.

The overnight camping season is May 15–Oct 15 each year. After Oct 15, overnight camping is prohibited anywhere within the park. You may camp at the private Abol Bridge campground or the Maine DOC Abol Pines Campground downriver of Abol Bridge. Both charge fees. Your hike to the summit is then 15 miles one way from this area outside the park. Another option when BSP is closed for camping is to stay in Millinocket and hire a taxi or shuttle in and out of Baxter on the day of your hike. Southbounders should note that the A.T. from Katahdin Stream Campground to Baxter Peak might not be open until Jun 1. Northbounders should note that they can phone the park about openings at the campground and mail in their reservations request. Campsite reservations may be made *via* phone no sooner than 14 days before the desired date, if available, with a credit card. If you can't get camping space at one of the reservation-only camp-grounds or the 12-slot Birches (see below), a very fit and fast thru-hiker, with 2,000 miles under her (or his) belt, might try leaving from and returning to Abol Bridge *via* the Blueberry Ledges Trail, a 19.2-mile round-trip to Katahdin's summit that includes the most challenging ascent and descent on the entire A.T. It wouldn't be a very leisurely way to end your thru-hike.

*Pamphlet—Thru-Hiking in Baxter State Park*, a pamphlet, is available on request from BSP. It has a map of the A.T. and the Blueberry Ledges Trail, a wealth of information about the park, and a message from park management.

*Mail and Messages*—BSP does not accept mail or packages. Mail drops should be arranged through the Millinocket post office.

*Trail closings at Katahdin*—It is advised to plan to reach BSP by Oct 1. A.T. hikers must arrange to climb Katahdin before Oct 15; park officials emphasize that this is the cut-off date for climbing Katahdin. It also coincides with the end of the summer/fall camping season in the park. Statistics show that, in this northerly climate, chances are slim that you will be able to successfully finish your hike at Katahdin's summit after this date. Winter hiking season is Dec 1–Mar 31; you must obtain a permit from the park to climb Katahdin then, and you must have a minimum of four people in your climbing party.

In some years, access to the park road and trails up Katah-din can be closed by snowstorms for up to two weeks *before* Oct 15. On those days, the A.T. up to Baxter Peak is open only when weather permits (see above). Each day at 7 a.m., park rangers post the weather forecast and determine the "class" for trails above treeline. Class III and IV days, which involve trail closures, are common in late Sep–Oct. When the day has been classified as a Class IV, anyone hiking beyond the Trail-head at Katahdin Stream toward the summit of Katahdin is subject to a summons and fine, seizure of equipment, and permanent revocation of park privileges. If you must be rescued, assistance will be delayed until the rescuers can proceed safely; you could be found negligent and liable for all costs of search and rescue.

After Oct 15, Baxter State Park is open for day use only (sunrise to sunset) for all hiking, conditions permitting. Vehicular access to the park usually ends completely by Nov 1 or whenever conditions that pose a threat to personal safety or to the resources have locked in for the season.

*Beginning at Katahdin*—Thru-hikers beginning their trek at Katahdin should make reservations for campsites well in advance of their starting dates. During July and Aug, campsites normally are booked to maximum levels.

*Ending at Katahdin*—Northbounders who plan to have family and friends meet them at the park should reserve campsites in advance. Labor Day weekend is especially packed, with a traditional Indian festival reserving the entire Katahdin Stream Campground. If driving into the park, there is a $12 fee at the gate for out-of-state residents. Advise those who are meeting you to be waiting in line when the south gate, Togue Pond, opens at 5 a.m. between July 1 and Labor Day, and to park tightly in that limited area. When the parking lot is full, visitors will be directed to open lots and alternate trailheads by the rangers at the gatehouse. Plan ahead!

Southbounders, it is suggested you reserve a site for the nights before and after climbing Katahdin. For reservations and information, contact BSP, 64 Balsam Dr., Millinocket, ME 04462, (207) 723-5140.

*Camping in Baxter State Park*—Two 4-person lean-tos and tenting space for 4 additional people are available at a site called **The Birches**, not far from Katahdin Stream Campground. Advance reservations are not required; the fee to stay there is $9PP. At reservation campgrounds, the fee is $18 for either lean-to or tentsite and $9EAP. *Cash only inside park.*

**The Birches** is 9.8 miles from Abol Bridge *via* the A.T. or 4.4 miles from Abol Bridge *via* the Blueberry Ledges Trail. Use of the The Birches facilities is limited strictly to long-distance or thru-hikers (must be hiking, at a minimum, the "100-Mile Wilderness") *and is limited to one night.* Park authorities have posted a sign-up sheet for long-distance hikers at the information kiosk just north of Abol Bridge. If all 12 spaces are claimed for the night that you planned to stay at The Birches, you will need to stay elsewhere. Your choices include the Abol Bridge private campground; the nearby Department of Conservation Abol Pines site on the West Branch of the Penobscot (both are fee sites); standard-reservation campsites at Katahdin Stream Campground, Foster Field Group Campsite, or any other available site of your choice in the park, if they are not already full; or staying in a campground or motel near Millinocket, if available. In Jul and Aug, and on all fall weekends, it is difficult to get a site at Katahdin Stream or elsewhere in the park, because sites are often reserved months in advance. However, Labor Day–Oct 15, it is possible (although not certain) that you will find vacant sites at Katahdin Stream during the week.

*2,000-Miler Certificate Applications*—ATC has asked rangers at Katahdin Stream Campground to hand out forms to all northbounders who are about to finish the Trail, in an effort to expedite the processing of 2,000-miler certificates. See requirements on page ix.

*Reaching Baxter State Park*—No public transportation is available to and from BSP. Unless you have someone meeting you at the park, you'll need to hitch 24 miles from the Trail to Millinocket. Rides are usually easy to find, since almost everyone headed out of the park must go through Millinocket.

**Baxter State Park Road**—BSP Togue Pond Visitors Center, M–Th 7–3, F–Su 7–6; maps, guidebooks, additional information; beach, and picnic area (no camping).

    **East** 2 miles from the park's south gate to *Lodging:* Maine Timberland Company's Katahdin Forest Cabins, (877) 622-2467, log cabin on Sunday Pond, spectacular view of Katahdin, $87 per night, sleeps 6, with gas heat, stove, and privy; advance reservations necessary.

    **East** 2.6 miles to *Camping:* Penobscot Outdoor Center on Pockwockamus Pond, (207) 723-3580, tentsites, showers, sauna, hot tub, restaurant, and lounge; call for rates.

    **East** 7 miles to Golden Road junction (8 miles from here to Abol Bridge).

    **East** 8.3 miles to ■ *Groceries:* Northwoods Trading Post (short-term resupply), (207) 723-4326, open 7–9, last gas station, pay phone, and ATM before entering BSP. A.T. maps, books, trail guides, patches, and souvenirs. ■ *Lodging:* Big Moose Inn, (207) 723-8391, <www.bigmoosecabins.com>, inn room with shared bath weekday $40, weekend $44; camping $10PP; lean-to $13PP; cabins, call for rates; restaurant and bar open W–Su, B available Sa–Su, no pets.

    **East** 15.6 miles to *Camping:* Hidden Springs Campground, (888) 685-4488 or (207) 723-6337, <www.hiddenspring.com>, tentsites $10PP/night, shower without stay $3.

    **East** 17 miles from the park's south gate to **Millinocket, Maine [P.O. 04462: M–F 9–4, Sa 9–11:30; (207) 723-5921]**. BSP Headquarters, (207) 723-5140, 64 Balsam Dr., park reservations, publications, maps, and general information. ■ *Camping:* Rice Farm Campgrounds, (207) 723-8475, tentsites $10–$12PP, canvas tents $22–$28PP, showers included. ■ *Lodging:*

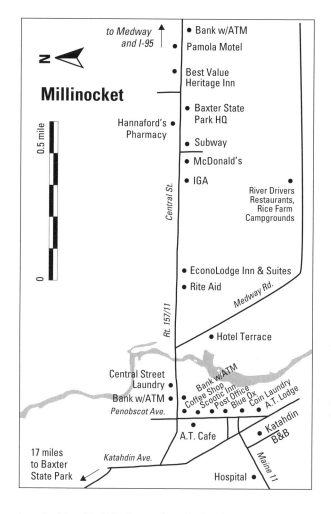

Appalachian Trail Lodge and Café, (207) 723-4321, <www.appalachiantraillodge.com>, new owners Paul (OleMan) & Jaime (NaviGator) Renaud, $25 bunkroom, $35S, $55D, furnished apartment call for rates; parking $1/day; showers for nonguests $3; WiFi, fuel, some hiking supplies; shuttles to and from bus in Medway, other shuttles by arrangements; one private room available for hikers with pets; accept mail drops at 33 Penobscot Ave., Millinocket, ME 04462; credit cards accepted for lodge at café. Econolodge Inn & Suites, (207) 723-4555, $69S, $89D, $10EAP, dogs okay, continental B, indoor pool, hot tub, restaurant/lounge on premises. Best Value Heritage Motor Inn, (207) 723-9777, $79S, $89D, $10EAP, dogs welcome $10, continental B. Katahdin B&B, (207) 723-5220, 96 Oxford St., <katahdinbandb@yahoo.com>, e-mail for reservations, hosts Mary Lou and Rodney (a Maine guide), $60–$75, laundry available, accepts mail drops; hiker supplies, hot tubs, no pets; call ahead for shuttles; no credit cards accepted. Pamola Motor Lodge, (800) 575-9746, (207) 723-9746,

<wwwpamolamotorlodge.com>, $59S, $67D, dogs okay, continental B, Internet access, outdoor pool, hot tub, lounge, laundry service; call ahead for shuttles. Hotel Terrace, (207) 723-4525, $47S, $56D, $5EAP. The Young House B&B, (207) 723-5452, <www.theyounghousebandb.com>, 193 Central Ave., $80, credit cards accepted, WiFi, accepts mail drops.

■ *Restaurants:* Appalachian Trail Café, open 5–8, owned by Paul and Jaime Renaud, home of the Sundae Summit Challenge, home-made food, free Internet access, one-of-a-kind countertop of A.T.; Hotel Terrace, B/L, AYCE only on weekends; Hang Wong at Pamola Inn, (207) 723-6084, M–Sa AYCE L; Mountain Village Company, with bakery, deli, and Internet access ($3.50 for 20 minutes); Central Street; Scootic Inn Restaurant, (207) 723-4566; Blue Ox Saloon; Neoc River Drivers Restaurant, with coffee shop, bakery, deli, and Internet access ($3.50 for 30 minutes). ■ *Other services:* Most major services are available in town, including supermarkets, coin laundries, and banks with ATM; Town Taxi, (207) 723-2000, provides service to the bus station ($12) in Medway and ($45) to Baxter State Park; Millinocket Regional Hospital, (207) 723-5161. ■ *Kennel services:* Connie McManus, (207) 723-6795, and Natalie Voisine, (207) 723-5722, will pick up at Abol Bridge and house dogs for thru-hikers. There is no bus service in Millinocket, but Cyr Bus Lines of Old Town, Maine, serves nearby Medway (see below).

**Medway**—*Lodging:* Katahdin Shadows Motel, (207) 746-5162, 10 miles east on Maine 157, <www.katahdin-shadows.com>, $49S, $54D, $10EAP; Gateway Inn, <www.medwaygateway.com>, (207) 746-3193, $55 and up, dogs welcome; Pine Grove Campground and Cottages, (207) 746-5172, <www.pinegrovecamping.com>, tentsites, fully equipped cottages, dogs welcome, free use of canoe and kayak for guests, will pick up at bus station. ■ *Outfitter:* Nicatau Outfitter, <www.mainecampingtrips.com>, (207) 746-3253 or (207) 746-3251, call ahead for shuttles or boarding pet. ■ *Bus service:* Cyr Bus Lines of Old Town, Maine, serves northern Maine; 10 miles east on Maine 757, (207) 927-2335, (207) 827-2010, or (800) 244-2335, <info@cyrbustours.com>. A bus leaves Bangor at 6:00 p.m. and arrives at Medway at 7:40 p.m.; leaves Medway at 9:30 a.m. and arrives at Bangor at 10:50 a.m.; fee $10.50 one way. ■ *Kennel services:* North Ridge Boarding Kennel, (207) 746-9537, <northridgekennels.com>, new owner Jack Misiaszek will pick up and deliver dogs (and packages), $50 each way; hours for drop-off and pick-up are 9–10 a.m. and 6–7 p.m.; $12 per day per dog. Pawprints Resort, (207) 746-3434, <www.pawprintsresort.com>, day care and boarding, pick-up/drop-off services.

**Bangor**—A city with all major services, <www.bang-orinfo.com>. For those traveling to or returning from BSP, Bangor offers a bus station and airport. The Chamber of Commerce, (207) 947-0307, can provide information as you prepare for your hike or return. For information on local transportation in the Bangor area: BAT Commuter Connection, (207) 992-4670, <www.bangormaine.gov>. ■ *Lodging:* Many motels and a mall are near the airport, including Days Inn, (207) 942-9272; Econo Lodge, (207) 945-0111; Fairfield Inn, (207) 990-0001; Howard Johnson's, (207) 947-3464; Holiday Inn, (207) 947-0101. ■ *Outfitters:* Epic Sports, (207) 941-5670, <www.epicsportsofmaine.com>, 6 Central St., M–Sa 9–8, Su 9–5; Dick's Sporting Goods, (207) 990-5932, located in the Bangor Mall. ■ *Bus service:* Concord Trailways, (800) 639-3317; Cyr Bus Lines with daily transportation to Medway, (800) 244-2335 (see above).

*"I now have new respect for the term 'within walking distance.'"*

—Welches (A.T. '00).

# Post Offices along the A.T.

Post offices are listed here in south-to-north order.

Local post office telephone numbers can be verified by calling (800) 275-8777 (ASK USPS).

Post offices printed in **bold** are located on, or within one mile of, the Trail.

| Town | ZIP Code | Hours / Phone |
|------|----------|---------------|
| Suches, GA | 30572 | M–F 7:30–11:30 & 1–4:30, Sa 7:30–11:30 (706) 747-2611 |
| Helen, GA | 30545 | M–F 8:30–5, Sa 8:30–12 (706) 878-2422 |
| Hiawassee, GA | 30546 | M–F 8:30–5, Sa 8:30–12 (706) 896-3632 |
| Franklin, NC | 28734 | M–F 8:30–5, Sa 9–12 (828) 524-3219 |
| Bryson City, NC | 28713 | M–F 8:30–5, Sa 10–12 (828) 488-3481 |
| Fontana Dam, NC | 28733 | M–F 8:30–12 & 12:30–4:30, Sa 10–12 (828) 498-2315 |
| Gatlinburg, TN | 37738 | M–F 9–5, Sa 10–12 (865) 436-3229 |
| Cherokee, NC | 28719 | M–F 9–4:30, Sa 10–11:30 (828) 497-3891 |
| **Hot Springs, NC** | **28743** | M–F 8:30–11:30 & 12:30–4, Sa 8:30–10:30 (828) 622-3242 |
| Erwin, TN | 37650 | M–F 8–5, Sa 10–12 (423) 743-9422 |
| Unicoi, TN | 37692 | M–F 8–11 & 12–4, Sa 8:30–10:30 (800) 275-8777 |
| Elk Park, NC | 28622 | M–F 7:30–12 & 1:30–4:15, Sa 7:30–11 (828) 733-5711 |
| Roan Mountain, TN | 37687 | M–F 8:15–11:30 & 12:30–4:15, Sa 8:15–11 (423) 772-3014 |
| Newland, TN | 38657 | M–F 8:30–4:30, Sa 8:30–12 (828) 733-2500 |
| Hampton, TN | 37658 | M–F 7:30–11:30 & 12:30–4:30, Sa 8–10 (423) 725-2177 |
| Shady Valley, TN | 37688 | M–F 7:30–11 & 12–3:30, Sa 8–10 (423) 739-2173 |
| **Damascus, VA** | **24236** | M–F 8:30–1 & 2–4:30, Sa 9–11 (276) 475-3411 |
| Troutdale, VA | 24378 | M–F 8–12 & 1–5, Sa 8:15–11 (276) 677-3221 |
| Sugar Grove, VA | 24375 | M–F 8–12 & 1:15–4:45, Sa 8–10:30 (276) 677-3200 |
| Marion, VA | 24354 | M–F 8:30–5, Sa 9:30–11:30 (276) 783-5051 |

| | | |
|---|---|---|
| Atkins, VA | 24311 | M–F 8:30–12:30 & 1:30–4:30, Sa 9–11 (276) 783-5551 |
| Bland, VA | 24315 | M–F 8–11:30 & 12–4, Sa 8–11 (276) 688-3751 |
| Bastian, VA | 24314 | M–F 8–12 & 12:30–4, Sa 8–10:30 (276) 688-4631 |
| **Pearisburg, VA** | **24134** | M–F 8–4, Sa 9–12 (540) 921-1100 |
| **Catawba, VA** | **24070** | M–F 7:30–12 & 1–5, Sa 8–10:30 (540) 384-6011 |
| **Daleville, VA** | **24083** | M–F 8–5, Sa 8–12 (540) 992-4422 |
| Cloverdale, VA | 24077 | M–F 8–5, Sa 9–12 (540) 992-2334 |
| Troutville, VA | 24175 | M–F 8:30–5, Sa 8:30–11:30 (540) 992-1472 |
| Buchanan, VA | 24066 | M–F 8:30–5, Sa 10–12 (540) 254-2178 |
| Big Island, VA | 24526 | M–F 8:30–12:30 & 1:30–5, Sa 8–10 (434) 299-5072 |
| Glasgow, VA | 24555 | M–F 8–4:30, Sa 8–11 (540) 258-2852 |
| Buena Vista, VA | 24416 | M–F 8:30–4:30, Sa 9–11 (540) 261-8959 |
| Lexington, VA | 24450 | M–F 8:30–5, Sa 9–12 (540) 463-6449 |
| Montebello, VA | 24464 | M–F 8–4:30, Sa 9–12 (540) 377-9218 |
| Waynesboro, VA | 22980 | M–F 8:30–5, Sa 9–11 (540) 942-7320 |
| Elkton, VA | 22827 | M–F 8:30–5, Sa 9–11 (540) 298-7772 |
| Luray, VA | 22835 | M–F 8:30–5, Sa 9–12 (540) 743-2100 |
| Front Royal, VA | 22630 | M–F 8:30–5, Sa 8:30–1 (540) 635-7983 |
| **Linden, VA** | **22642** | M–F 8–12 & 1–5, Sa 8–12 (540) 636-9936 |
| Bluemont, VA | 20135 | M–F 8:30–12 & 1–5, Sa 8:30–12 (540) 554-4537 |
| **Harpers Ferry, WV** | **25425** | M–F 8–4, Sa 9–12 (304) 535-2479 |
| Boonsboro, MD | 21713 | M–F 8:30–1 & 2–5, Sa 8:30–12 (301) 432-6861 |
| Smithsburg, MD | 21783 | M–F 8:30–1 & 2–5, Sa 8:30–12 (301) 824-2828 |
| Cascade, MD | 21719 | M–F 8–1 & 2–5, Sa 8–12 (301) 242-3403 |
| Blue Ridge Summit, PA | 17214 | M–F 8–4:30, Sa 9–11:30 (717) 794-2335 |

| Waynesboro, PA | 17268 | M–F 8:30–5, Sa 9–12<br>(717) 762-1513 |
|---|---|---|
| South Mountain, PA | 17261 | M–F 8–1 & 2–5, Sa 8–12<br>(717) 749-5833 |
| Fayetteville, PA | 17222 | M–F 8–4:30, Sa 8:30–12<br>(717) 352-2022 |
| Mt. Holly Springs, PA | 17065 | M–F 8–4:30, Sa 8–12<br>(717) 486-3468 |
| **Boiling Springs, PA** | **17007** | M–F 8–4:30, Sa 8–12<br>(717) 258-6668 |
| **Duncannon, PA** | **17020** | M–F 8–4:30, Sa 8–12<br>(717) 834-3332 |
| Bethel, PA | 19507 | M–F 8–12, 1:15–4:30,<br>Sa 8:30–10:30<br>(717) 933-8305 |
| Pine Grove, PA | 17963 | M–F 8:30–4:30, Sa 9–12<br>(570) 345-4955 |
| **Port Clinton, PA** | **19549** | M–F 7:30–12:30 & 2–5,<br>Sa 8–11<br>(610) 562-3787 |
| Hamburg, PA | 19526 | M–F 9–5, Sa 9–12<br>(610) 562-7812 |
| Slatington, PA | 18080 | M–F 8:30–5, Sa 8:30–12<br>(610) 767-2182 |
| Walnutport, PA | 18088 | M–F 8:30–5, Sa 8:30–12<br>(610) 767-5191 |
| Palmerton, PA | 18071 | M–F 8:30–5, Sa 8:30–12<br>(610) 826-2286 |
| Danielsville, PA | 18038 | M–F 8–12, Sa 8–12<br>(610) 767-6882 |
| **Wind Gap, PA** | **18091** | M–F 8:30–5, Sa 8:30–12<br>(610) 863-6206 |
| **Delaware Water Gap, PA** | **18327** | M–F 8:30–12 & 1–4:45,<br>Sa 8:30–11:30<br>(570) 476-0304 |
| Branchville, NJ | 07826 | M–F 8:30-5, Sa 8:30–1<br>(973) 948-3580 |
| **Unionville, NY** | **10988** | M–F 8–12 & 1–5, Sa 8–12<br>(845) 726-3535 |
| Glenwood, NJ | 07418 | M,T,W,F 7:30–7, Th 7:30–7,<br>Sa 6:30–2<br>(973) 764-2616 |
| Vernon, NJ | 07462 | M–F 8:30–5, Sa 10–1<br>(973) 764-9056 |
| Greenwood Lake, NY | 10925 | M–F 8–5, Sa 9–12<br>(845) 477-7328 |
| Bellvale, NY | 10912 | M–F 8–12 & 1–4:30, Sa 8–12<br>(845) 986-2880 |
| Warwick, NY | 10990 | M–F 8:30–7, Sa 9–4<br>(845) 986-0271 |
| Southfields, NY | 10975 | M–F 9–12, 1–5, Sa 9–11:30<br>(845) 351-2628 |
| **Arden, NY** | **10910** | M–Sa 10:30–11:30<br>(845) 351-5341 |
| **Bear Mountain, NY** | **10911** | Sep 10–Jun 22, M–F 8–10;<br>June 25–Sep 7, M–F 8–2<br>(845) 786-3747 (call for hours) |

| | | |
|---|---|---|
| **Ft. Montgomery, NY** | **10922** | M–F 8:30–5, Sa 8:30–12<br>(845) 446-8459 |
| Peekskill, NY | 10566 | M–F 8:30–5, Sa 8–12:30<br>(914) 737-1340 |
| Stormville, NY | 12582 | M–F 8:30–5, Sa 8:30–12<br>(845) 226-2627 |
| Poughquag, NY | 12570 | M–F 8:30–5, Sa 8:30–12<br>(845) 724-4763 |
| Pawling, NY | 12564 | M–F 8:30–5, Sa 9–12<br>(845) 855-2669 |
| Wingdale, NY | 12594 | M–F 8–5, Sa 8–12:30<br>(845) 832-6147 |
| Gaylordsville, CT | 06755 | M–F 7:30–1 & 2–5,<br>Sa 7:30–12:30<br>(860) 354-9727 |
| **Kent, CT** | **06757** | M–F 8–1 & 2–5,<br>Sa 8:30–12:30<br>(860) 927-3435 |
| **Cornwall Bridge, CT** | **06754** | M–F 8–1 & 2–5, Sa 9–12:30<br>(860) 672-6710 |
| West Cornwall | 06796 | M–F 8–1 & 2–5, Sa 8:30–12<br>(860) 672-6791 |
| Sharon, CT | 06069 | M–F 8–5, Sa 9:30–1:30<br>(860) 364-5306 |
| **Falls Village, CT** | **06031** | M–F 8:30–1 & 2–5,<br>Sa 8:30–12<br>(860) 824-7781 |
| **Salisbury, CT** | **06068** | M–F 8–1 & 2–5, Sa 9–12<br>(860) 435-5072 |
| South Egremont, MA | 01258 | M–F 8:15–12 & 12:30–4,<br>Sa 9–11:30<br>(413) 528-1571 |
| Sheffield, MA | 01257 | M–F 9–4:30, Sa 9–12<br>(413) 229-8772 |
| Great Barrington, MA | 01230 | M–F 9–4:30, Sa 9–12<br>(413) 528-3670 |
| Monterey, MA | 01245 | M–F 8:30–1 & 2–4:30,<br>Sa 9–11:30<br>(413) 528–4670 |
| **Tyringham, MA** | **01264** | M–F 9–12:30 & 4–5:30,<br>Sa 8:30–12:30<br>(413) 243-1225 |
| Lee, MA | 01238 | M–F 8:30–5, Sa 9–12<br>(413) 243-1392 |
| Becket, MA | 01223 | M–F 9–4, Sa 9–11:30<br>(413) 623-8845 |
| **Dalton, MA** | **01226** | M–F 8:30–4:30, Sa 9–12<br>(413) 684-0364 |
| **Cheshire, MA** | **01225** | M–F 8:30–1 & 2–4:30,<br>Sa 7:30–11:30<br>(413) 743-3184 |
| Adams, MA | 01220 | M–F 8:30–4:30, Sa 10–12<br>(413) 743-5177 |
| North Adams, MA | 01247 | M–F 8:30–4:30, Sa 10–12<br>(413) 664-4554 |
| Williamstown, MA | 01267 | M–F 8:30–4:30, Sa 9–12<br>(413) 458-3707 |

| Bennington, VT | 05201 | M–F 8–5, Sa 9–12<br>(802) 442-2421 |
| Manchester Center, VT | 05255 | M–F 8:30–4:30, Sa 9–12<br>(802) 362-3070 |
| Danby, VT | 05739 | M–F 7:15–12 & 1:15–4,<br>Sa 7:30–10:30<br>(802) 293-5105 |
| Wallingford, VT | 05773 | M–F 7:45–4:45, Sa 9–12<br>(802) 446-2140 |
| Rutland, VT | 05701 | M–F 8–5, Sa 8–12<br>(802) 773-0222 |
| **Killington, VT** | **05751** | M–F 8:00–4:30, Sa 8:00–12<br>(802) 775-4247 |
| Woodstock, VT | 05091 | M–F 8:30–5, Sa 9–12<br>(802) 457-1323 |
| **South Pomfret, VT** | **05067** | M–F 8–1 & 2–4:45,<br>Sa 8:30–11:30<br>(802) 457-1147 |
| **West Hartford, VT** | **05084** | M–F 7:30–11:30 & 1–4:45,<br>Sa 7:30–10:15<br>(802) 295-6293 |
| **Norwich, VT** | **05055** | M–F 8:30–5, Sa 9–12<br>(802) 649-1608 |
| **Hanover, NH** | **03755** | M–F 8:30–5, Sa 8:30–12,<br>pkg pick-up open 7 a.m.<br>(603) 643-4544 |
| Lyme, NH | 03768 | M–F 7:45–12 & 1:30–5:15,<br>Sa 7:45–12<br>(603) 795-4421 |
| Wentworth, NH | 03282 | M–F 7:15–1 & 3–5,<br>Sa 7:15–12<br>(603) 764-9444 |
| Warren, NH | 03279 | M–F 7:30–1 & 2:30–5,<br>Sa 8–11:30<br>(603) 764-5733 |
| **Glencliff, NH** | **03238** | M–F 7–10 & 2–5, Sa 7–1<br>(603) 989-5154 |
| North Woodstock, NH | 03262 | M–F 8–12:30 & 1:30–5,<br>Sa 8–12<br>(603) 745-8134 |
| Lincoln, NH | 03251 | M–F 8–5, Sa 8–12<br>(603) 745-8133 |
| Bartlett, NH | 03812 | M–F 9–1 & 1:30–5:30,<br>Sa 9–12<br>(603) 374-2351 |
| **Mt. Washington, NH** | **03589** | Not recommended for mail drop<br>(603) 466-3347 |
| Gorham, NH | 03581 | M–F 8:30–5, Sa 8–12<br>(603) 466-2182 |
| Andover, ME | 04216 | M–F 8:30–1:30 & 2–4:45,<br>Sa 9–12:15<br>(207) 392-4571 |
| Oquossoc, ME | 04964 | M–F 8–1 & 1:30–4:15,<br>Sa 9–12<br>(207) 864-3685 |
| Rangeley, ME | 04970 | M–F 9:30–4:15, Sa 9:30–12<br>(207) 864-2233 |

| Stratton, ME | 04982 | M–F 9:00–1 & 1:30–4,<br>Sa 9–11:30<br>(207) 246-6461 |
| **Caratunk, ME** | **04925** | M–F 7:30–11:30 & 12–3:45,<br>Sa 7:30–11:15<br>(207) 672-3416 |
| Monson, ME | 04464 | M–F 7:30–11:30 & 12:30–4,<br>Sa 7:30–11<br>(207) 997-3975 |
| Millinocket, ME | 04462 | M–F 9–4, Sa 9–11:30<br>(207) 723-5921 |

## Mail Drops

Many thru-hikers use "mail drops" to send themselves supplies. The *Companion* lists U.S. Postal Service (USPS) offices and also establishments that accept packages from shippers such as UPS and FedEx. Mail drops can be sent to both types of locations, but it is important to address them differently. Post offices accept only mail; a post office will not accept a FedEx or UPS package. Only post offices will accept packages addressed to a "General Delivery" address. USPS will forward unopened first-class and "priority" items at no additional fee. **UPS and FedEx packages cannot be sent to "General Delivery"**—you must provide a physical address other than a post office, such as a street number, and (for FedEx) a telephone number for those shipments. Please assist the businesses and post offices by practicing the following labeling instructions:

> Your Name
> c/o the business ( *General Delivery* if a post office)
> City/State/ZIP Code
> *Please Hold for Thru-hiker or Section-Hiker*
> (and estimated date of arrival)

At the post office, be prepared to show a photo ID when you pick up your package. Postmasters are one of a thru-hiker's best friends on the Trail. Help them help you and other hikers by following the labeling instructions above for all your mail. Send a postcard if you leave the Trail for any reason, to let the post office know what to do with your package.

To ensure that your food parcels don't pick up any "unwanted visitors" before you arrive, we suggest that hikers double-bag and securely seal all parcels.

# Hostels, Camping & Showers

The first thing that comes to a hiker's one-track mind when she/he hits town is FOOD and lots of it, followed by a good hot shower and affordable accommodations. In the pursuit of just food, shower, and laundry, some hikers want to minimize the town experience and return to the Trail as soon as possible, usually the same day. This list provides low-cost options and will help you to keep the grunge at bay. Campgrounds were chosen for their proximity to the Trail, and consideration was given if they allowed nonguest showers, while keeping in mind travel by foot. There are many other campgrounds listed in the *Companion* that are best reached by car or require a longer walk.

Establishments printed in **bold** are located on or within one mile of the Trail.
NA=not available
n/c= no charge
S = shelter; H = hostel; C = camping; L = lodging

| State | Location; Establishment | Guest Fee | Nonguest Shower-only fee |
|-------|-------------------------|-----------|--------------------------|
| Ga. | **Amicalola Falls State Park** | S n/c | n/c |
| Ga. | Suches; A.T. Hiker Hostel | H $15 | |
| Ga. | **Neels Gap**; Walasi-Yi Center | H $15 | $3.50 |
| Ga. | Hiawassee; Blueberry Patch | H donation | |
| Ga. | Hiawassee; Cloud9 | H $20 C $10/$15 | |
| Ga. | Hiawassee; Hiawassee Inn | H $13 | $3 |
| N.C. | Rock Gap; Standing Indian Campground | C $14 | $2 |
| N.C. | **Wesser; Nantahala Outdoor Center** | H $15 | $3 |
| N.C. | **Fontana Dam Visitors Center** | | n/c |
| Tenn. | **Green Corner Rd**; Standing Bear Farm | H $20/$15 | |
| N.C. | **Hot Springs**; The Sunnybank Inn | L $15 | |
| N.C. | **Hot Springs**; Creekside Inn | C $5 | |
| N.C. | **Hot Springs** Resort & Spa and Campground | L $50-72 C $5pp | $2 |
| Tenn. | **Greeneville**; Hemlock Hollow | L $36 Bunk $18 C $12 | $2.50 |
| Tenn. | Erwin; Cherokee Adventures | C $5 | $2 |
| Tenn. | Erwin; Nolichucky Hostel and Outfitters | H $15 C $8 | $3 |
| Tenn. | **Greasy Creek Gap**; Greasy Creek Friendly | H $8/$12 C $5 | $3 |
| Tenn. | **U.S. 19E**; Mountain Harbour B&B | C $8 Bunk $15 | $3 |
| Tenn. | **Roan Mtn**; Abby's Place | H $5 | $3 |
| Tenn. | **Dennis Cove**; Laurel Fork Lodge | Bunk $6 | $2 |

| Tenn. | **Dennis Cove**; Kincora Hostel | H $4 donation | |
| Va. | **Damascus**; The Place | H $4 donation | |
| Va. | **Damascus**; Dave's Place, MRO | H $10 S/D | $3 |
| Va. | **USFS Hurricane Campground** | C $14 | $2 |
| Va. | Va. 16; Troutdale Baptist Church | H donation | n/c |
| Va. | **Partnership Shelter** | | n/c |
| Va. | **Groseclose**; Village Truckstop | | $5 |
| Va. | **Va. 606**; Trent's Grocery Store | C $6 | $3 |
| Va. | **Sugar Run Rd**; Woodshole Hostel | H donation | |
| Va. | Pearisburg; Holy Family Church Hostel | H donation | |
| Va. | **Pearisburg**; Rendevous Motel | | $8 |
| Va. | **U.S. 11**; Day Stop Inn Travel Centers of America | | $9 |
| Va. | **U.S. 11**; Pilot Truck Stop | | $9 |
| Va. | Va. 614; Middle Creek Campground | C $26/4 | $5 |
| Va. | Buena Vista; Glen Maury Campground | C $20 | $2 |
| Va. | Montebello; Montebello Camping and Fishing | C $10D | $3.50 |
| Va. | Tye River; Crabtree Falls Campground | C $22D | n/c |
| Va. | Lyndhurst; Rusty's Hard Time Hollow | H $20 donation | |
| Va. | Waynesboro; Grace Evangelical Lutheran Church | H donation | n/c |
| Va. | Waynesboro; Waynesboro YMCA | C donation | n/c |
| Va. | **SNP**; Loft Mountain Campground | C $16 | $1 |
| Va. | **SNP**; Lewis Mountain Campground | C $16 | $1 |
| Va. | **SNP**; Big Meadows Campground | C $19 | $1 |
| Va. | **Bears Den Hostel** | H $25/$13 C $8 | $2 |
| Va. | **Blackburn Trail Center** | H, C donations | NA |
| W.Va. | Harpers Ferry; KOA | C $33/$35 | $5 |
| Md. | Keep Tryst Road; **Harpers Ferry Hostel** | H $20/$23 C $10 | $3 |
| Md. | **Dahlgren Backpack Campground** | | n/c |
| Md. | **Md. 17/ Wolfsville Rd**; The Free State Hiker Hostel | H $32 | |
| Pa. | **Caledonia State Park** | C $12/$14 weekday; $15/$17 weekend | $2 |
| Pa. | **Pa. 233**; Pine Grove Furnace State Park, Ironmasters Mansion | H $22/$25 C $12 | $4 |
| Pa. | **Pine Grove Road**; Cherokee Family Restaurant & Campground | C $16 | |
| Pa. | **Boiling Springs**; Boiling Springs Pool; hot shower | C n/c | |
| Pa. | **U.S. 11, Carlisle**; Flyin J Travel Plaza | | $11.50 |
| Pa. | **Duncannon**; Doyle Hotel | L $25S | $5 |
| Pa. | **Duncannon**; All-American Truck Stop | | $8 |

| Pa. | **Duncannon**; Riverfront Campground | C $3.50 | |
|---|---|---|---|
| Pa. | Blue Rocks Campground | C $11 | 25¢ |
| Pa. | **Pa. 501**; PAmoneypit Hostel | H $25 | |
| Pa. | **Hawk Mountain Road**; Eckville Hikers Center; solar shower | L,C n/c | n/c |
| Pa. | Slatington; Fine Lodging | L $15 | $4 |
| Pa. | Palmerton; Borough Hall | L n/c | n/c |
| Pa. | **DWG; Presbyterian Church of the Mountain Hostel** | H $3 donation | |
| N.J. | **Mohican Outdoor Center** | L $21 C n/c | |
| N.J. | **High Point State Park** day-use area | | n/c |
| N.J. | **Sawmill Lake Campground** | C $20 | |
| N.J. | Vernon; St. Thomas Episcopal Church | H $10 donation | |
| N.Y. | **Harriman State Park**; ETA Leadership Camp | L $12 C $4 | |
| N.Y. | **Arden Valley Rd**; Tiorati Circle | | n/c |
| N.Y. | **Graymoor Spiritual Life Center** | C | n/c |
| N.Y. | N.Y. 301; Clarence Fahnestock State Park | C $13/$16 | n/c |
| Conn. | Pine Loop Trail; Housatonic Meadows State Park | C $16 | n/c |
| Conn. | **Falls Village Hydroelectric Plant**; cold water | | n/c |
| Mass. | **Sages Ravine** | C n/c | |
| Mass. | **U.S. 7**; Corn Crib | C | n/c |
| Mass. | East Mountain Retreat | H $10 | |
| Mass. | Mass. 2; North Adams YMCA | | $2 |
| Mass. | Williamstown; Williams Inn | | $6 |
| Vt. | Rutland; Back Home Again Café | H donation | |
| Vt. | Rutland; A-Towns Place | H donation | |
| Vt. | **Vt. 100**; Gifford Woods State Park | S $21 C $14 | 50¢ |
| N.H. | **Cape Moonshine Rd** | C work for stay | |
| N.H. | **Glencliff**; Hikers Welcome Hostel | H $15 C $10 | $2.50 |
| N.H. | I-93, U.S. 3, Franconia Notch; Lafayette Place Campground | C $19D | 25¢ |
| N.H. | U.S. 302, Crawford Notch; Dry River Campground | C $18D | Coin-operated |
| N.H. | U.S. 302, Crawford Notch; Crawford Notch Campground | C $20/4 | $2 |
| N.H. | U.S. 302, Crawford Notch; AMC Highland Center | H $35 | |
| N.H. | **N.H. 16**; Pinkham Notch Visitor Center | C $11 | $1 |
| N.H. | U.S. 2, Shelburne; White Birches Camping Park | H $13 C $11 | .25/ $3.25 |
| N.H. | Gorham; The Barn | H $20 | |
| N.H. | Gorham; Hikers Paradise Hostel at Colonial Fort Inn | H $19 | |

| | | | |
|---|---|---|---|
| Maine | Maine 26, Grafton Notch; Bethel Outdoor Adventure's 'Snowboarding House" | H $19 | |
| Maine | East Andover; Pine Ellis Lodging | Bunk $15 | |
| Maine | East Andover; Andover Road House | Bunk $20 | |
| Maine | Andover; South Arm Campground | C $15/4 | 25¢ |
| Maine | Rangeley; Maine Roadhouse | Bunk $20 | |
| Maine | Rangeley; Gull Pond Lodge | Bunk $20 | |
| Maine | Stratton; The Stratton Motel & Hostel | H $20 | |
| Maine | U.S. 201; Northern Outdoors Resort | C $9.63/ $7.20 L $56.72/4 | n/c |
| Maine | Monson; Lake Shore House | L $25 | Coin-op |
| Maine | Monson; Shaw's | L $23 | $6 |
| Maine | North Pond Outlet West | H $20 | |
| Maine | White House Landing | H $35 | |
| Maine | **Golden Road**; Abol Bridge Campground | C $10 | |
| Maine | **Golden Road**; Abol Pines | C $7 | NA |

# Equipment Manufacturers & Distributors

Most manufacturers and distributors stand behind their products. Companies will often replace or repair equipment while you are on the Trail. Usually, it is best to deal directly with the manufacturer rather than going through an outfitter along the Trail (except where noted below). A few telephone calls can save lost time and prevent a lot of headaches.

| | |
|---|---|
| Adventurelite | (570) 573-0209, www.adventurelight.com |
| Arc 'Teryx | (866) 458-BIRD, www.arcteryx.com |
| Asolo | (603) 448-8827, ext. 105, www.asolo.com |
| Backcountry Gear | (800) 953-5499, www.backcountrygear.com |
| Campmor | (800) 525-4784, www.campmor.com |
| Camelbak | (800) 767-8725, www.camelbak.com |
| Cascade Designs | (800) 531-9531, www.cascadedesigns.com |
| Cedar Tree Industry | (276) 780-2354, www.thepacka.com |
| Columbia | (800) 547-8066, (503) 985-4000 www.columbia.com |
| Dana Design | (888) 357-3262, www.danadesign.com |
| Danner Shoe Manufacturing | (800) 345-0430, (877) 432-6637 www.danner.com |
| Eagle Creek | (800) 874-9925, www.eaglecreek.com |
| Eastern Mountain Sports | (888) 463-6367, www.ems.com |
| Eureka/Johnson Worldwide, Inc | (888) 6EUREKA www.eurekacampingctr.com |
| Ex Officio | (800) 644-7303, www.exofficio.com |
| Feathered Friends | (206) 292-6292, www.featheredfriends.com |
| Frogg Toggs | (800) 349-1835, www.froggtoggs.com |
| General Ecology/ First Need Filter | (800) 441-8166 www.generalecology.com |
| Golite | (888) 546-5483, www.golite.com |
| Gossamer Gear | (512) 374-0133, (760) 720-0500 www.gossamergear.com |
| Granite Gear | (218) 834-6157, www.granitegear.com |
| Gregory Mountain Products | (800) 477-3420, www.gregorypacks.com |
| Hi-Tec Sports, USA | (209) 545-1111, (949) 786-4336 www.hi-tec.com |
| Jacks 'R' Better Quilts | (757) 643-8908, www.jacksrbetter.com |
| JanSport | (510) 614-4000, www.jansport.com |
| Kelty Pack, Inc. | (800) 423-2320, www.kelty.com |
| Leki | (800) 255-9982, ext 10, www.leki.com |
| Peter Limmer & Sons, Inc. | (603) 694-2668, www.limmerboot.com |
| L.L.Bean | (800) 441-5713, www.llbean.com |
| Lowe Alpine Systems | (877) 888-8533, www.loweapline.com |
| Marmot | (888) 357-3262, www.marmot.com |

| Merrell | (888) 637-7001, www.merrell.com |
| Mont-bell | (877) MONTBELL, www.montbell.com |
| Montrail | (206) 621-9303, www.montrail.com |
| Mountain Hardwear | (800) 953-8398, www.mountainhardwear.com |
| Mountain Safety Research | (800) 531-9531, www.msrcorp.com |
| Mountainsmith | (800) 426-4075, ext. 133<br>www.mountainsmith.com |
| The North Face | (866) 715-3223, prompt 7<br>www.thenorthface.com |
| Osprey | (970) 564-5900 (Mountain Time)<br>cs@ospreypacks.com |
| Outdoor Research | (888) 467-4327 (Pacific Time)<br>www.outdoorresearch.com |
| Patagonia | (800) 638-6464, www.patagonia.com |
| Peak 1/Coleman | (800) 835-3278, www.coleman.com |
| Photon | (877) 584-6898, www.photonlight.com |
| Primus | (888) 546-226, (360) 786-9559<br>www.primus.stoves.com |
| Princeton Tec | (541) 386-8751, (609) 298-9331<br>www.princetontec.com |
| PUR /Katadyn | (800) 755-6701, www.katadyn.com |
| REI | (800) 426-4840, www.rei.com |
| Royal Robbins | (800) 587-9044, www.royalrobbins.com |
| Salomon | (800) 654-2668, www.salomonsports.com |
| Sierra Designs | (800) 369-3949 (Pacific Time)<br>www.sierradesigns.com |
| Six Moon Designs | (503) 430-2303, www.sixmoondesigns.com |
| Slumberjack | (800) 233-6283, www.slumberjack.com |
| Speer Hammocks | (828) 724-4444<br>www.edspeerhammocks.com |
| Suunto | (800) 543-9124, www.suunto.com |
| Tarptent by Henry Shires | (650) 587-1548, www.tarptent.com |
| Tecnica | (800) 258-3897, ext. 2, www.tecnicausa.com |
| Teva/Deckers Corporation | (800) FOR-TEVA, www.teva.com |
| The Underwear Guys | (570) 573-0209<br>www.theunderwearguys.com |
| ULA-Equipment | (435) 753-5191, www.ula-equipment.com |
| Vasque | (800) 224-4453, www.vasque.com<br>(check with local retailer first) |
| Western Mountaineering | (408) 287-8944<br>www.westernmountaineering.com |
| ZZManufacturing (Zipztove) | (800) 594-9046, www.zzstove.com |